IN AND AROUND

STAMBOUL.

BY

MRS. EDMUND HORNBY.

"The European with the Asian shore
  Sprinkled with palaces: the ocean stream,
Here and there studded with a seventy-four,
  Sophia's cupola with golden gleam;
The cypress groves; Olympus high and hoar
  The twelve isles, and more than I could dream,
Far less describe, present the very view
Which charmed the charming Mary Montagu.'

BYRON

PHILADELPHIA:
JAMES CHALLEN & SON,
LINDSAY & BLAKISTON,
NO. 25 SOUTH SIXTH STREET.

CONTENTS.

LETTER I.

PAGE

Voyage to Calais.—Journey to Paris.—Arrival.—Soldiers.—Festivities.—Journey to Marseilles.—Valley of the Rhone.—The Alps.—Avignon.—Embark.—Scene on Board.—Sisters of Charity.—An Evening on Board 15

LETTER II.

A Night at Sea.—Party of Nuns.—Fellow-Passengers.—Corsica.—Music on Board 22

LETTER III.

Arrival at Malta.—Sunday Morning.—Ramble through Malta.—Feast and Church of St. John.—Harbor of Valetta.—Return on Board.—"The Isles of Greece."—Capes Matapan and St. Angelo 30

LETTER IV.

Syra.—A Greek Hostelry.—Pirates.—Evening.—Smyrna.—The Bazaars.—Ramble through the City.—The Church.—The Slave-Market.—The Bashi-Bazouks.—Gallipoli.—The Dardanelles.—Approach to Constantinople.—The Bosphorus.—Landing 39

LETTER V.

PAGE

Pera.—English and French Officers.—News of the War.—Therapia.—Shores of the Bosphorus.—Fall of Sebastopol.—Public Rejoicings.—Sisters of Charity.—Illuminations. 49

LETTER VI.

Therapia.—Its pleasant Climate.—Fleet at Anchor.—Beicos Bay.—Depth and Clearness of the Waters of the Bosphorus.—Phosphorescent Illumination at Night.—Sad Incidents of the War.—Wounded and Sick Officers arrive from Balaklava.—Their Conversations.—The Attack of the Redan 55

LETTER VII.

Pleasant Mornings at Therapia.—Greek Fishermen and Feluccas.—Sea-Birds, and Legend of the "Ames Damnées."—Many-colored Fish of the Bosphorus.—Terraced Gardens.—Ships returning from the Crimea.—The Camp at Buyukdere 59

LETTER VIII.

Valley of the Sweet Waters.—Picturesque Groups of Turkish Women.—The Sultan's Daughter.—Turkish Belles and Babies.—Turkish Carriages.—Arabas and Telekis.—Vendors of different Wares in the Valley.—Boiled Indian Corn.—Musicians.—Anatolian Shepherd.—English Sailors.—"Bono Johnny."—The Young Pasha.—The Valley at Sunset 65

LETTER IX.

News from Home.—Invalids from Scutari and the Crimea.—Chat about the War.—Sardinian and French Officers.—The Commissariat.—Scenery of the Crimea.—Ramble through the Sultan's Valley.—Ancient Plane-Trees and Fountain.—Dinner on Board the "Elba."—Buyukdere at Night . 75

LETTER X.

PAGE

Hospital at Therapia.—Its Garden and Burial-Place.—Grave of Captain Lyons.—White Cross erected in Memory of those who fell in the Crimea 82

LETTER XI.

Beauty of the Bosphorus.—Fishing-Village on the Asian Shore.—Turkish Cemetery and Graves of the Janissaries. —Ruins of the Castle of Anatolia.—Turkish Soldiers . . 88

LETTER XII.

Village of Kadikoi.—Sea of Marmora.—Landing at Pera.—Stamboul.—Its Silent Streets.—Behind the Lattice.—The Sultan.—His Kind and Merciful Disposition.—Desolateness of Constantinople.—Variable Climate.—The Turkish Loan.—Cholera at Yenekion 93

LETTER XIII.

Palace of the Sultan at Begler Bay.—The Bosphorus after the Attack on Sebastopol. — Difficulty of Transacting Business with a Turkish Ministry.—Wretched State of Turkish Affairs.—Caiquejees, their Dress and Appearance.—"Bono" and "no Bono."—A Proposed Kiosk at Orta-kioy 104

LETTER XIV.

Removal to Orta-kioy.—Voyage.—Rough Sea.—Arrival.—Difficulties.—Armenian Neighbors.—Fire-Guns at Night. —Roll of Drums and Discharge of Musketry at the Sultan's Palace at Daybreak 111

LETTER XV.

PAGE

Orta-kioy.—Servants.—Armenian Ladies.—Workwomen.—Villagers.—House and Gardens.—Armenian Cooking.—Village of Bebec.—Fruit and Food.—High Prices.—Pera.—State of Crime 119

LETTER XVI.

Winter on the Bosphorus.—Our Armenian Neighbors.—Questions and Answers.—Turkish Regulation of Time.—The Winter Theatre in the Crimea.—Zouave Modistes . 130

LETTER XVII.

Death of Mrs. Willoughby Moore.—Funeral of a French Soldier.—Our Turkish "Allies."—Turkish Venality.—Pashas.—Their Luxury and Dishonesty.—The Cadi.—Turkish Character 136

LETTER XVIII.

Our Greek Cook.—Calliope's Despondency.—Troubles in the Kitchen.—Approach of Winter.—The Sultan's Visit to the Mosque.—A Maltese Dog 147

LETTER XIX.

Christmas-day at Constantinople.—Beauty of the Bosphorus.—Crowd of Vessels.—Mysseri's Hotel.—Tales of the Crimea.—The Greek Christmas.—Christmas Dinner at the Embassy.—Miss Nightingale.—Christmas Games . . . 152

LETTER XX.

Greek Servants.—Calliope's Scheme.—Kneeling to the Saints.—Lying Propensities.—Domestic Life.—Greek and Turkish Character 165

LETTER XXI.

PAGE

New-Year's Eve.—Housekeeping.—Discussing Prices.—A Greek Laundress.—New Year's Morning.—Seclusion of the Turkish Women.—The Cemetery.—The Persian Embassador.—Ball at the Embassy 170

LETTER XXII.

Eastern Civilization.—The Reforming Sultan.—The Levantine Population, their Ignorance and Pretension.—Early Flirtations.—Large Families.—A Levantine Young Lady 181

LETTER XXIII.

New-Year's Day.—Costumes.—Greek Women.—Revels.—Visit to an Armenian Family.—Vassili.—Interview with a Bashi-Bazouk.—Villagers.—Turkish Children . . . 188

LETTER XXIV.

Winter Life on the Bosphorus.—Armenian Bishop.—Bill of Fare.—The Piano-forte.—Cures for Neuralgia.—Wrecks from the Black Sea.—Poor Jews 199

LETTER XXV.

Going to a Ball.—The Teleki.—Journey to Pera.—Monuments.—Administration.—Dolma Batche.—Bad Roads.—Cemetery at Pera.—Cypresses.—Soldiers.—Illuminations.—Ball at the Embassy.—The Sultan.—Chief of the Eunuchs.—A Bear at the Ball.—Espinu's Enthusiasm . . 206

LETTER XXVI.

The Sultan's Dinner.—Turkish Hospitality.—The Embassy Balls.—The Sultan.—Assassinations.—The Weather . . 227

LETTER XXVII.

PAGE

The French Embassador's Ball.—Dinner Party.—The Sultan's Visit.—French and English Belles.—Pashas at the Ball.—A Fire.—A Russian Prisoner 231

LETTER XXVIII

Shepherds.—Flocks.—The Greek Lent.—News from the Crimea.—Turkish Cemetery.—The Village of Orta-kioy. —An Armenian Burial.—Funeral of a Child 236

LETTER XXIX.

Visit to the Harem of Riza Pasha.—News from England.—Ladies of Stamboul.—Chief of the Eunuchs.—Interior of the Harem.—Dresses of the Ladies.—Circassian Beauty. —Dresses.—Hospitality in the Harem 245

LETTER XXX.

The Franks.—Arrival of Spring.—Ladies' Dresses.—Changeable Climate.—Omar Pasha and the Relief of Kars.—Knavery of the Pashas.—The Greek Easter.—Festival-days at Constantinople.—Change for a Sovereign.—A Lonely House.—A Storm 266

LETTER XXXI.

Wintry Weather.—News of the Peace.—The Rejoicings.—A Visitor from the Crimea.—Crimean Amusements.—Letters from Home 275

LETTER XXXII.

Excursion to Princes' Islands.—Scenery of the Bosphorus. —Prinkipo.—Visit to a Convent.—The Ancient Chapel.—Curiosities.—Carvings and Pictures.—Beauty of the Island.—Return in the Dark.—A Night on Board 279

LETTER XXXIII.

PAGE

Shores of the Bosphorus.—Tomb of Barbarossa.—Antiquities.—Dress.—"Apple-Blossom."—Sympathy in Misfortune.—Schooling.—Greek Names 287

LETTER XXXIV.

Tea-Party.—Visit of a Turkish Gentleman.—Morals in Turkey.—Pashas.—The Sultan.—Fashion of Learning Music.—Troubles of a Music-Master in the Harem.—Flowers.—Jasmine-sticks.—Pipes.—A Village Burnt 293

LETTER XXXV.

Excursion to the Crimea.—Wild Dogs.—Fleas.—Invasion of Rats and Mice.—Encounter with a Spider.—Gardening. 302

LETTER XXXVI.

Return from the Crimea.—Commencement of the Fast of Ramazan.—Protestant Church.—Return of the Army.—The Peace 308

LETTER XXXVII.

Start for the Crimea.—The Bosphorus.—A Swell on the Black Sea.—Pleasures of the Voyage.—Harbor of Balak lava.—Changes accomplished 311

LETTER XXXVIII.

Landing at Balaklava.—Colonel Hardinge.—Russian Gover nor's House.—A Prisoner of War.—Heights of Balaklava.—Miss Nightingale's Hospital.—"The Sisters."—Flowers.—Souvenir of the Governor 317

LETTER XXXIX.

Balaklava.—The Camp.—The Battle-field.—Visit to the Malakoff and the Redan.—Botanizing.—Baidar.—Return from the Crimea 324

LETTER XL.

PAGE

Visit to a Turkish Harem.—The Garden.—The Children.—Scenes in the Garden 335

LETTER XLI.

Fast of Ramazan.—Turkish Nationality.—The Sheik-Zadi.—End of the Fast.—Preparations.—Illumination of the Mosques.—Kara-Goz, the Turkish "Punch."—Firemen . 343

LETTER XLII.

Celebration of the Queen's Birth-day.—The *Fête-Dieu.*—Illuminations.—"The Night of Destiny."—The Sultan's Visit to the Mosque of Tophana.—Night of Prayer.—Prince Murad 352

LETTER XLIII.

A Sail on the Bosphorus.—The "Belle Poule."—Strawberry-Gardens.—Last Day of Ramazan 358

LETTER XLIV.

End of Ramazan.—Illuminations.—Night.—Palaces on the Bosphorus.—Feast of Bairam.—Torchlight Procession of the Sultan.—Ceremony in the Mosque of Tophana . . . 361

LETTER XLV.

A Stroll.—The Bosphorus.—Turkish Arsenal.—Suburbs of Constantinople.—Poverty in the East.—Kiosks.—Storks.—Turkish and Greek Dresses.—Scenes on the River.—The Sweet Waters.—Scenes on Shore.—The Sultan's Kiosk.—The Sultana and her Daughter.—Evening Scene.—Return from the Sweet Waters 366

LETTER XLVI.

PAGE

Thunder-storm.—Return of Troops.—The Commission . . 386

LETTER XLVII.

Education of Turkish Women.—Rearing of Children.—Want of Instruction.—Books.—Thoughts of Home.—The Climate.—Relics from the Crimea 389

LETTER XLVIII.

The Princes' Islands.—The "Edith Belina."—Signor Giacomo.—Church on the Island 395

LETTER XLIX.

The Sultan's Banquet.—Turkish Artificers.—Thunder storm.—Long Days.—Vassili's Misbehavior.—Domestic Changes 398

LETTER L.

Order of the Medjidi.—The Sultan's Dinner-Party.—The Palace.—Thunder-storm.—"Commissary Joe."—Visitors from the Crimea 402

LETTER LI.

Convent of Jesu Christo.—Fishing Excursion.—Bathing-house.—Early Rising.—Island of Halki 409

LETTER LII.

Erection of a Church in Prinkipo.—Monastery of Halki.—Greek Churches.—A Greek Wedding.—Bishops.—The Patriarch.—Avenue of Cypresses Illuminated.—Return Home 414

LETTER LIII.

PAGE

Excursion to Ismid.—Mountain Scenery.—Islands.—Fishing Villages.—Rambles on Shore.—Vegetation.—Island Scenery.—Insects and Fishes.—Return to Prinkipo . . 428

LETTER LIV.

Therapia.—Greek Village.—Roman Reservoirs.—Service on Board Ship 444

LETTER LV.

Climate and Scenery.—Paradise of the Greeks.—Boating Excursions.—The Monastery of St. George.—The Old Gardener.—His Summer Residence.—"The Magyar."—Armenian and Greek Ladies.—Greek Homage to Beauty.—Burning a Caique.—Fishing by Night 447

LETTER LVI.

Excursion to Maltapè.—Greek Women and Turkish Cafanée.—Marble Fountain.—An Ancient Tree.—The Mosque.—The Imaum.—Village School.—Turkish Women.—Curious Lamp 459

LETTER LVII.

Old Churches and Monasteries.—Ancient Manuscript.—Tomb of St. George.—A Picture of St. George and the Dragon.—Donkey Processions.—A Greek Beauty.—The Superior of the Monastery.—Curious Paintings.—A Legend.—Lunatics.—Tree-frogs 468

LETTER LVIII.

The Lunatic and the Priest's Donkey.—Appeal to St. Demetrius.—The Lunatic sent Home 482

LETTER LIX.

PAGE

Visit from a Turkish Lady.—Her Taste for Music.—Her Nubian Slave.—Exhibition of an English Gentleman.—Gratification afforded by the Spectacle 485

LETTER LX.

Boatmen's Songs.—Greek Singing.—Specimen 489

LETTER LXI.

Severity of Winter.—Life in a Kiosk.—The Golden Horn frozen over.—Wolves and Foxes.—Their Murderous Incursions.—Scarcity of Food and Fuel.—High Prices.—English and Greek Servants.—Death of Redshid Pasha . 495

IN AND AROUND STAMBOUL.

LETTER I.

VOYAGE TO CALAIS—JOURNEY TO PARIS—ARRIVAL—SOLDIERS—FESTIVITIES—JOURNEY TO MARSEILLES—VALLEY OF THE RHONE—THE ALPS—AVIGNON—EMBARK—SCENE ON BOARD—SISTERS OF CHARITY—AN EVENING ON BOARD.

Paris, August 24th, 1855.

My dear Mother:

We left London about half-past seven on Friday evening, and arrived at Dover at eleven. There, in the Basin, lay, with its huge red and white lights, the steamer which was to take us to Calais. It seemed to me an effort to plant myself on its deck, to be taken so far from Edith and you all. *Ma che sarà, sarà;* and it is as well to do it with a stout and thankful heart.

In a few minutes we were upon the broad sea. It was a lovely starlight night, with just breeze enough to make the waves look beautiful. Almost all the ladies went down immediately into their cabins; but I seemed spell bound to the deck, thinking over our long and uncertain journey, and saying to myself over and over again: "Farewell, England! God bless you, my dearest Edith!" whom I thought of as comfortably asleep at home.

The steamer went at a rapid rate, and soon the lights of Dover sank like a wreath of pale stars into the broad track of bright foam stretching far behind us. Still, to my comfort, the two brilliant ones on the cliff showed plainly, and still I could say that I saw England. Soon, however, Edmund pointed out the green lamps of Calais harbor; and in less time than we were in the "Fairy," on the last sail we took together, we found ourselves across the Channel. The tide was low, so we signalled for boats, and had some time to wait. While walking up and down the deck, I could distinctly see the sea-lights of Dover, and thought how ridiculous it is, in these days of steam, to fret oneself about distance. Presently boats dashed up, manned by fine strong fellows; and a different language was very striking to one's ear. It seems so extraordinary that so pleasant a two hours on a starlight sea, and with England positively in view, can bring you to so different a people.

We had a delightful run on shore, the men singing cheerily as they raced with the other boats. We soon gained the Pier, where the ladies were politely handed out by the gravest of mustachioed Frenchmen, lantern in hand, wrapped in an immense cloak, and looking as if the fate of the whole world depended upon himself.

After showing passports, etc., we adjourned to the station, where we were fortunate enough to meet Captain Wright, one of the Queen's Foreign Service Messengers. He had lived for some time at Constantinople, and, as we sipped our coffee together, gave us some very plesant chat about it.

At three o'clock in the morning we started for Paris. Our talk soon became rather drowsy, and I was so tired, and the carriage so deliciously comfortable, that when I awoke from a most refreshing sleep, dawn was peeping under the blinds.

Presently I looked out upon the corn standing in rich sheaves—a splendid harvest. Soon the country-people began to appear; their pretty dresses and the gay trappings of their horses, making the cornfields quite a picture. Then the sun burst out over many villages and towns, and we felt like poor tired owls in the bright daylight on arriving at Paris.

Nothing can exceed the splendor and gayety of the place at this moment. The flags and triumphal arches of the Queen's visit still remain; the people are flocking in crowds to the "Exposition;" splendid bodies of troops marching hither and thither through the streets, and bands playing in every direction. Temples in the Champs Elysées are illuminated every evening, and filled with musicians. Every thing to amuse and delight the people. We have just passed General Canrobert, mounted on a white charger, and surrounded by a brilliant staff, returning from escorting the Queen to St. Cloud. He was much cheered, and bowed good-naturedly to all.

We arrived at Marseilles on the evening of the 29th of August. We had been charmed throughout the whole day's journey with the wonderful beauty of the Valley of the Rhone. There you have every thing to delight the eye at once: vineyards, mountains, valleys, meadows, gardens, old castles and towers, savage heath-land, and the loveliest cultivation glowing with purple grapes, melons, peaches, and Indian corn; the happiest and most picturesque-looking peasantry in the world; and the glorious river, with its little islands of snow-white mountain sand, winding brightly through all.

Then the Alps at sunset, shining in their snow, far above the drifting rose-colored clouds which hung on the dark pine woods—nestling, as it were, here and there in their vast solitudes. It is impossible to describe one's feelings of awe and delight on first beholding them.

We dined at Avignon. The heat of the day had been intense; and with exclamations of joy the thirsty, tired passengers of a long train rushed into the station dining-room. A long table was spread in a large cool room, with sweet garden-flowers peeping in at each open window; the most delicious peaches and grapes, figs and melons, in baskets trimmed with leaves and roses, all down the table. I thought that even Petrarch, ever so much in love, must have one day eaten such as these with some complacency.

Excellent soup, fish, partridges, and other delicacies were served us in the promptest manner; and, refreshed and merry, we rushed to our steaming monster again, and left Avignon with grateful hearts.

It soon became dusk, and was quite dark long before the train arrived at Marseilles; but by an occasional glimpse, I thought the coast looked very fine. In the carriage with us was a good-looking young Frenchman, "got up" in the most exquisite style, who had traveled from Marseilles and back again, just for the chance of getting a peep at the Queen of England in the streets of Paris!

We rested comfortably for the night in an excellent hotel at Marseilles; and after breakfast the next morning, with many kind adieus and many a wish of *Bon voyage* from our host and fellow-travelers, we started in a little open carriage (with a merry ring of bells to the horses' collars) for the ship. The harbor is enormous, and crowded with ships of all nations. Our guide quickly discovered the "Simois," a fine screw-steamer, lying alongside, with her steam up. The crowd was very great; sailors, soldiers, and a motley collection of many nations it seemed, bustling about with a tremendous amount of noise and shouting in various languages.

The heat was intense, the dust extremely painful, and I looked through forests of masts, with longing eyes, at the sea.

It was a scene of the greatest confusion on deck. Troops bound for the Crimea were being hurried to the fore-part of the vessel. The hold was open, its vast recesses half filled with huge packages addressed to Miss Nightingale at Scutari, and to the army in the East generally. Immense quantities of baggage were being added every moment; horses were being stalled on deck; and people making hasty farewells. However, all was finished at last; and, as the ship steamed slowly out of harbor, we sat down to the breakfast, and took a survey of our fellow-passengers. The heat was still so overpowering that we were soon glad to get on deck again. The first group that struck us there was a party of Sisters of Charity, three young and two elderly ones. The steamer was going at a rapid rate, and the fine, many-colored cliffs of France already becoming indistinct. When they could be seen no longer, the poor young nuns, leaning against the side of the vessel, covered their faces and cried bitterly. Their Superiors (who wore massive golden crucifixes round their necks) consoled them most kindly, and kept frequently saying, "Courage, my children!"

The fore-part of the vessel was crowded with French soldiers,—mostly fine, sturdy-looking young fellows: few, I should think, much above twenty.

Many of them seemed greatly depressed; but it was really quite a lesson to see how cheerfully they put up with every discomfort, and how kind and obliging they seemed to one another—and this we noticed throughout the voyage.

We enjoyed our first evening's walk on deck extremely. Who can describe the lovely blue of the Mediterranean? The sunset had been very fine, and as there is but little or no twilight, the innumerable stars seemed to gleam out suddenly in the clear gray light, mingling sea and sky. Not a sail was to be seen, and we were running before a fresh gale.

As the night grew darker, we watched, by the side of the vessel, the beautiful star-shaped phosphorescent lights, flying fast through the foam with the prettiest effect possible. These "glow-worms of the sea," as they are sometimes called, abound on fine calm nights. We thought of you all in England as the ship sped on in this lovely sea.

The bells, fore and aft, striking the hour, sounded very sweetly, and the deck began to get quiet.

The poor Crimean soldiers were making up their

rough beds for the night, for the dew began to fall heavily. The nuns crept softly and sorrowfully below, poor things!

Every one seemed tired and weary with the heat and bustle of the day. Edmund stayed to smoke a cigar; while I, disregarding the charms of tea without milk, and fresh-gathered lemons, was soon disposed of comfortably in my berth, not feeling certain in my own mind, as I drew its tiny white curtains, whether it was really true that we were lying down to sleep on the fair but treacherous waters of the Mediterranean; and *really true*, moreover, that we were on our way to the far-famed city of the East—Constantinople.

LETTER II.

A NIGHT AT SEA—PARTY OF NUNS—FELLOW-PASSENGERS—CORSICA—MUSIC ON BOARD.

My dear Mother:

I slept well on our first night on board the "Simois," only waking now and then to hear the good ship working steadily and bravely on. At sea, in the dark hours of night, one thinks of the many lives resting entirely on the vigilance and skill of those who watch and work that complicated machinery.

We were early on deck. No one could be much disposed to laziness in fine weather on this most lovely Mediterranean—its blue waves and glittering white spray dancing in the morning sun. The poor soldiers, looking pale and cold from the night air and heavy dew to which they had been exposed, were packing up their trifle of bedding, and marching off to breakfast. The nuns were sitting in their old place by the side of the vessel; the elder ones reading their books of devotion, as calm and serene as usual—the younger ones watching the bright waves, and looking a little less wretched than on the evening before.

I thought at first that they must be going to the Crimea, and wondered at their great depression, with so much usefulness before them; but when I heard what was their dreary destination, I was no longer surprised. Two were being sent to a small French settlement in Algiers, almost in the Desert; and in all human probability would never see France or their friends again. They had left the most beautiful part of the Valley of the Rhone; and there was a crowd, we were told, at the little village-station to say adieu, with many tears on both sides. How often we have thought of these poor nuns, and wondered how they got on among the savage Algerines whom they are sent to convert!

At breakfast we began to see and know a little more of our fellow-passengers. (I write these details, thinking that it may amuse you for half an hour to read a rough sketch of a voyage eastward). There was a French lady and her daughter going to join "papa" at Scutari; Mr. Moore, Queen's Messenger, who, curiously enough, had traveled the same way twenty-five years ago with my father, and lived with him for a month at Constantinople; Mr. Newall, an engineer, going out to lay down an electric telegraph from Varna to Therapia (which they say is greatly needed during the war); his brother-in-law, Mr. Bell, bound on the same route, for amusement and sketching; and Herr S——, who traveled for some months every autumn, saw every thing, and made friends with every one worth knowing; an extremely handsome young Greek, returning to Athens from England, who spoke to every one in their own language with the marvelous fluency of his race; and a most melancholy French officer, in command of the troops on board, who spoke to no one,—makes up the list of the first-class passengers; and we thought ourselves most fortunate, not only to meet with agreeable people, but also with so *few* of them, as the mail-boats are usually crowded since the war began. The weather too was glorious; such a delicious breeze, such a blue sea and sparkling foam, such a sky! We had a nice awning on deck, which fluttered merrily in the wind. The soldiers below seemed to enjoy basking in the sun. White sails gleamed here and there around us, and it seemed as if we must be making a royal voyage of pleasure in some enchanted sea,—it is so very beautiful, this many-colored Mediterranean.

So here we are to spend one morning, we little herd of first-class passengers.

The nuns (second-class) are seated on some bales on the quarter-deck below. The youngest is crying bitterly again, and rests her poor head on the breast of one of the elder "sisters." There is a great difference in the look of the two "Superiors." One of them has a fine face, but exactly as if carved out of stone,—bloodless, almost immovable. It is easy to see that *she* has done with this world's affections. She is mild and serene, and does not strain her eyes with anguish toward France,—they look calmly everywhere, but generally on her book.

The other Superior is a dear, motherly-looking woman, comely still and rather stout. She must have been very pretty. A color still lingers on her cheek; and there are tears in her soft-brown eyes, which *could* sparkle very merrily. It is on *her* breast that the poor young nuns lean so despondingly. I point out to Edmund (who is chatting to Herr S—— about their favorite Germany) the group of second-class passengers below; they also have an awning, and are enjoying, each after his own fashion, the delicious, breezy day. The lieutenant of the troops is there—a very amiable-looking, fine young fellow. On his knee is perched a little boy of seven, in scarlet trousers and large white pinafore. His mother is a delicate, sad-looking little lady. They are going to join her husband in the Crimea; and the young lieutenant takes quite chivalrous care of his friend's wife and child. We watch him patiently trying to teach the spoiled little boy to read; but he soon escapes, and darts off to the nuns; and a kindly acquaintance begins between the two parties from that moment, in which even the most desponding nun joins at last. Of our party above, the French lady is knitting. I have given up my book to Mademoiselle Lucie, who discusses it with one of her wide trousers twisted round one of the legs of her camp-stool, and one of her long plaits of hair round the other. Mr. Bell is trying to get a sketch of a distant yacht, but it bounds away too quickly. The handsome young Greek is deep in a novel, the breeze playing riotously in his dark hair. The melancholy French officer, after fondly patting his poor sick chargers stalled on deck, has again disappeared. Mr. Newall is looking through his glass at a distant ship, which is sailing dreamily away into the blue sky.

The bells, fore and aft, chime an hour past noon. The sun is very hot, and the breeze fallen so much that scarcely a breath stirs the awning as the vessel works onward. Every now and then a heated blast comes up from the boilers, which catches your breath and gives you a sickening idea of the "Inferno." I at last disappear for a siesta, and pass through the deck cabin: there reposes, full length on the morocco cushions, the tired Queen's Messenger; his book has fallen down; he looks pale—and patient. What a life it has been during the war! A young soldier brought me a glass of cool lemonade: he was still suffering from two very severe wounds received at the Alma, but preferred doing what he could on board the "Simois" to remaining in the hospital at Scutari. He was only eighteen, he told us, and had been out since the commencement of the war. Such a pretty, gentle boy! We quite grew to like him, and his patient, quiet ways. *He* certainly did not seem to be made of the stuff to kill. What a horrible necessity is war!

The ceaseless beat of a screw, and the noise of many feet overhead, are not very great incentives to sleep on a sultry sofa; while the sun positively blisters the paint. I try to read "Evangeline," but it is too dreadful even to think of the cool, shady forests of Acadia in that scorching heat! If *I* suffer in one of the best cabins, what must it be for the poor soldiers on deck! Two of them have their wives with them,—very quiet, patient women. I often see them washing their own gowns or their husbands' shirts as well as they can, after dark. *These* are going uncomplainingly to suffering—perhaps to death.

Presently Mr. Bell called to us, and we heard the word "Corsica." "To pass Corsica, and asleep!" we exclaimed, and rushed on deck. Yes, there, rising abruptly out of the dark blue waters, were the stern-looking rocks of Corsica, upon which every eye was fixed, even to the timid ones of the nuns.

Very solitary and grand, it looks a fitting birthplace for its hero. Not a sail was near, and, from the ship no sign of man or human habitation, only, as I said, the many-colored rocks, rising sternly and abruptly out of the sea; over these two large birds were soaring, which Mr. Bell tried to convince me were eagles, but I could not help confessing they were too small to claim that honorable name.

And now, on our left, appeared the violet-tinted mountains of Sardinia, coasted by rocks of every shade, from dazzling white to deepest green; throwing as deep a shadow on the clear water beneath them. The wild "white horses" rushed in to be tamed and still among these lovely shadows, except here and there against some particularly sharp point where you saw their snowy crests furiously raging up the rugged regardless rock. I shall never forget the extraordinary beauty of the Mediterranean *summer coloring* of sea and sky and rocks; with the *violet mist* of mountains and islands in the distance, and the beautiful white sea-birds slowly flying by. On went our good ship through the dark blue waters: it still seemed a royal trip of pleasure on an enchanted sea. Far up in the distant mountains of Sicily we sometimes saw a white Italian villa glittering in the sunshine, and wondered who lived in that beautiful and solitary place. Now and then, in a creek or sheltered nook, appeared a small village with its wreathing smoke (perhaps of myrtle-wood,) and vineyards and gardens, which we made out with our glasses.

We frequently passed in the distance the pretty sailing-boats of the Mediterranean, with their white sails set, and darting along the coast, the very things of life and liberty. Small birds often perched on the rigging of our vessel, and after resting and pluming their little wings, flew away again.

Every one enjoyed the deck beyond measure when night came around again with its refreshing breezes. Again the foam made by the vessel glittered like myriads of golden phantom-stars flying past us. The stars above were almost as numerous, but looked down calm and large through the lofty ropes of the ship.

In these latitudes the Milky Way is much more distinctly visible than in England, and the southern constellations are wonderfully beautiful. Mr. Newall gave me several pleasant lessons in astronomy on these quiet evenings,—but the heavy dew soon drove prudent people below. Sometimes we passed a soldier fast asleep as we went down, and I placed lightly on his folded arms a fine peach, or bunch of grapes, which no doubt surprised him when he awoke. But it was often too sultry to think of going early to one's berth, so Mademoiselle Lucie and I had recourse to the pianoforte in the ladies' cabin. How delighted the soldiers and sailors were with our songs! Edmund came in laughing, to bid us look up at the crowd of sunburnt faces hanging over the open skylight of the saloon.

What a motley group it was! When we played dance music, one of the soldiers accompanied us admirably well with his castanets. The conclusion of each performance was followed by a peal of applause from our laughing friends in the saloon. Then came "La Suisse au bord du Lac," which elicited loud murmurs of delight from the Frenchmen, especially at the chorus of "Oh, ma patrie!" And lastly they were brought to the highest state of enthusiasm by "Partant pour la Syrie."

So usually ended our evening. Nothing remained but quiet thoughts of you all at home, and to confide ourselves through the dark hours of night to One who watches over all, both on sea and land.

LETTER III.

ARRIVAL AT MALTA—SUNDAY MORNING—RAMBLE THROUGH MALTA—FEAST AND CHURCH OF ST. JOHN—HARBOR OF VALETTA—RETURN ON BOARD—"THE ISLES OF GREECE"—CAPES MATAPAN AND ST. ANGELO.

Malta, Sunday.

My dear Mother·

At six o'clock in the morning I was startled from a sound sleep by a tremendous noise. "It is only the anchor dropping," said a drowsy voice from the opposite berth. "*Land!* Where are we then?"—"At Malta."

I climbed upon the sofa, and looked through a port-hole. The sea was dancing in huge blue waves, and the morning could not be more bright and splendid. The quiet of the vessel at anchor was very pleasant after the ceaseless noise of the engines, which had been sounding in one's ears night and day for so long. Even the poor cocks and hens on board began to crow and cackle with satisfaction at the change. Our ship was thronged with gayly-painted Maltese boats, laden with grapes and melons, which the soldiers on deck were eagerly buying, and pulling up in small wooden buckets tied to a stout rope. The sea heaved and danced in a most inconvenient way for these commercial transactions; and the confusion of French tongues above, and of loud and voluble Italian below, was most amusing to listen to.

I could not help laughing at the advantage which the soldiers had in a dispute as to the price of fruit which had been already hauled up. The sea was so rough that the expostulating Maltese could hardly keep their legs in the boats, and their customers above had only to threaten to let go the rope to put an end to the altercation at once. However, they behaved very well, and the storm soon quietly settled down to a friendly push off and nod of adieu. The Maltese have become comparatively rich since the war broke out; selling all their wares, from melons to gold and silver crosses, and lace and cameo brooches to little white lion-dogs, at a very high price to eager customers.

It was Sunday morning when we arrived at Malta. By seven o'clock I was sitting on deck. The bells of many churches were ringing to prayers. They sounded very sweetly over the sea; and the nuns, standing in their old place, looking over the side of the vessel, seemed especially to delight in listening to them. Perhaps it reminded them of old days in the Valley of the Rhone, where bells are ever sounding so musically through the gardens and vineyards of the villages.

We were anchored in the smaller harbor of Malta, appropriated entirely to the French during the war. It was crowded with ships of all sizes. It is such a terrible place for glare, that I have but a confused notion of long rows of white stone buildings rising suddenly out of the sea; a sentinel pacing up and down on a narrow white causeway before me; and a shriveled fig-tree, powdered with white dust, and looking very hot, growing against the hot white walls. However, I managed to make out a few scorched olive-trees on the hard-baked hills above.

Our breakfast-table was covered with Maltese produce: magnificent peaches and green figs (which spoke of shady gardens *somewhere*); delicious red mullet; and many-colored, gaping cockles, for those who liked them. Then jumping into a pink and yellow boat, with a beak at each end, we rowed to see the town and the great harbor of Valetta.

Mrs. Austin had kindly given us two letters to friends of hers; but they were in the *hold*, under a mass of baggage, with our books for the voyage, *life-preservers*, and other things which we wanted every moment. What a pity that it is not more generally known that travelers are seldom allowed more than one small portmanteau or carpet-bag in their cabin!

But to return to our ramble at Malta. We landed on a white stone quay, and toiled up a long flight of hot white stone steps, lined with beggars, sailor-boys, and waifs and strays of all nations. Then we followed our guide into a narrow, crowded street, where groups of black-eyed women and children were huddled together by their open doors, basking in the sun, and looking curiously at the strangers. Men, with baskets of melons, were noisily pushing along the broken and dirty pavement; and boys with beautiful flowers pressed you to buy, in strange, harsh-sounding Italian. The children seem to flourish wonderfully, basking in their picturesque rags at the door, disputing the sunniest piece of dirt with numerous kittens and curs of low degree.

Almost every house had its bird-cages. The Maltese are famous for their breed of canaries. We soon arrived at some of the principal streets,—very steep hills of narrow white houses, with carved and irregular Italian balconies filled with flowers and shrubs. We met many ladies hastening to church, all dressed in rich black silk, with a mantilla, just like a black silk petticoat gathered into a band, and held prettily over the head. It falls over the shoulders very gracefully; and eyes as black as night sparkle beneath it most effectively. I must say that an air of coquettish devotion (if I may use the expression) strikes one at Malta, as much in the ladies as in the rich-robed, sleek-looking priests, who pace the streets with an appearance of great satisfaction.

It was the feast of St. John, and we went to the service in the church of that name, built by the Knights of Malta. All the rare old tapestry illustrative of the life of our Saviour was exposed to public view. We were struck with the singular brilliancy of its colors (particularly the fine ultramarine blue) after the lapse of so many ages.

The floor of the church is a rich mosaic, each compartment being the monument of a knight. One might well spend hours here; but when we entered, Mass was being sung, and we were too much impressed with its solemnity to search even for Caravaggio's fine picture. There were no "family seats," no "respectable pews," with luxuriously-stuffed cushions and rows of gilt-leaved books, in this grand old church. Only many rows of rough wooden chairs by the arched columns on either side, where all either knelt, or sat and listened, as they liked,—from the graceful Maltese lady in her rich sweeping silks, to the wildest-looking sailor, with his bare feet and patched jacket. There were many who seemed wanderers and outcasts upon the face of the earth—so wild-looking as to have lost almost all trace of humanity.

There were many lonely, desolate-looking people—many friendless wanderers from many lands. To us all it was a most impressive service; gathered on shore again as we were, safe from the sea, in this most interesting and beautiful church.

I was particularly struck with one Maltese sailor, whose matted hair and beard, and bronzed bare feet, stood out in strong relief from one of the columns, at the foot of which he knelt with two young boys as savage and neglected-looking as himself. He prayed and crossed himself with the greatest intensity, only turning round once to make his ragged boys kneel too. It was very touching to see his rough but earnest teaching. Two little beggar-girls, weather-beaten and thin, entered alone, and sat down fearlessly on the marble steps close to the richly-robed priests.

Many in this strange assembly groaned audibly, and tears poured down many a sunburnt face. It is impossible not to be struck with the outward devotion of Southern people. The porch of the church was crowded with beggars; dogs waiting for their masters; and sellers of fruit and flowers, who had put down their baskets to pray and cross themselves most devoutly for a few minutes within sound of the organ, and then to go laughing and shouting on their way.

We greatly enjoyed our row back to the "Simois." The grand harbor of Valetta is a very fine sight just now, crowded as it is with ships of war. Gayly-painted boats, rowed by swarthy Maltese, dart about in all directions. The boatmen's boys seemed to me the most saucy and independent little fellows in the world. We saw many of these black-eyed, curly-headed young brigands rocking about in the most unconcerned manner in that turbulent sea,—a shout for every passer-by, always ready, and a merry indifference as to whether their oars were in the water or out of it. Some of them were fishing off the rocks. The water, of wonderful clearness here, reflects the dark green and purple sea-weed growing on them in the most beautiful manner.

Malta, with its steep white rocks and fortifications all round, and cannon bristling in every direction, certainly gives one an imposing idea of the home of the Knights of St. John in their palmy days. The heat and glare is certainly terrible. If it were not for the sea-breeze, one would be soon scorched up like an olive-leaf. How I pitied the poor "coalers," toiling up the sides of our great steam transports!

It is a curious thing to see a boat-load of twenty or thirty of these men leaving a ship. They are so black from coal-dust that you cannot distinguish features, and they look more like a crew of evil spirits than any thing else, dancing on the bright blue waves.

We found some new passengers on our return to the ship. A Greek lady and her daughter, both singularly handsome; the mother wearing rich plaits of hair bound round a scarlet fez; the daughter, alas! although cast in the most exquisite mould of classic Greek beauty of face and form, dressed in the last French fashion. One seemed perfectly to remember having seen her in rarely draped white marble in some hall or studio, or on some friend's mantel-piece.

Our deck-passengers were a wild-looking young

Maltese and his wife, going to Constantinople to sell their canaries, of which they had seventy-five in a large wicker cage. These hardy travelers brought nothing more for their many days' journey than a few melons, and several loaves of coarse brown bread. It was charming to have the bright, merry little canaries on board. Mademoiselle Lucie and I used to take them cool grapes to peck at, and the lame young soldier constantly brought them fresh water. Their dark mistress, with her heavy gold earrings and matted black hair, was generally stretched fast asleep upon one of her bundles; her bare brown legs appearing equally indifferent to the regards of the sun or of the numerous passers-by.

We did not sit long at dinner to-day, for it was a magnificent sunset, and we all wished to see Malta rapidly disappearing in the golden light, which was a beautiful sight. The young Greek lady was a great addition to our evening walk on deck. She was a most charming coquette, quite of the modern school, notwithstanding the antique cast of her beauty, and had all her admirers' names, written by themselves, with couplets expressing the completest devotion, upon each of the large folds of her fan. She laughed like a merry child when I asked her how many more would be added before she left the ship. Pretty graceful A——! she was most like a spoiled child after all, and even the nuns soon learned to smile on her.

The day after leaving Malta we were among "the Isles of Greece." The weather was still most lovely; the sea a deep, deep blue. Mr. Bell took sketches in water-colors all day long. Even the melancholy French officer was charmed; the nuns put down their books, and the soldiers clustered to the sides of the vessel. Herr S—— read enthusiastically, in broken English, Byron's fine stanzas:

"The isles of Greece! the isles of Greece!
Where burning Sappho loved and sung,
Where grew the arts of war and peace,
Where Delos rose, and Phœbus sprung!
Eternal summer gilds them yet;
But all except their sun is yet!'

The great truth and force of Byron's descriptions strike one very much on visiting places described by him.

Mr. Bell made an excellent sketch of Cape Matapan and its many-colored rocks. Our grave, black-bearded Maltese pilot told us that it was very well to laugh while passing it in fair weather, but that a stiff breeze would make it quite a different thing. In the olden time, learned Herr S—— informed us, Greek sailors used to hang up a votive tablet to the deities after having made this stormy headland in safety.

At Cape St. Angelo we made out plainly, by the help of our glasses, a rude hut, on a steep and barren slope of rock, on which one would think that a goat could hardly climb with safety. Here another learned person of our party mentioned the temple of Apollo, which Lady M. W. Montague had informed him, in her charming way, had once stood on those very rocks; but here *now* resides a hermit, who often hoists a little petitioning flag to ships passing by, hoping that they may take pity on his most solitary condition, and put off a boat with a present of biscuit, etc. etc. He did not do so to us, however; and we all declared that he must have caught a glimpse

4

of our fair Greek's fine eyes, which he, as a respectable and consistent recluse, could not be expected to brave. People are not always as merry as we were in passing Capes Matapan and St. Angelo.

But the pleasantest as well as the most sorrowful days must have an end; and when we arrived and cast anchor at Syra, the Greek ladies were to leave us. We parted, with many hopes of meeting again in England. The sea was very rough, and it was with great difficulty that they got into the little Greek boat dancing below. Sad to say, just as Mr. A—— was mustering up courage to make an impressive as well as a tender adieu, a cruel signal was given to let go the rope, and a remorseless wave tore the little bark away as the first sentence was trembling on his lips.

LETTER IV.

SYRA — A GREEK HOSTELRY — PIRATES — EVENING — SMYRNA — THE BAZAARS—RAMBLE THROUGH THE CITY—THE CHURCH—THE SLAVE-MARKET — THE BASHI-BAZOUKS — GALLIPOLI — THE DARDANELLES — APPROACH TO CONSTANTINOPLE—THE BOSPHORUS—LANDING.

Constantinople, September 8th, 1855.

My dear Mother:

Syra, as seen from the sea, seemed to be little more than a barren pile of rocks, with a few olive-gardens and fig-trees scattered here and there. Mr. Bell made an excellent sketch of its beautiful harbor of St. Geoge, with the hills of Tino and Myconi.

The town is built upon steep-piled rocks. A ruined castle, of evidently great antiquity and once formidable strength, crowns the topmost ridge, and beneath it houses cluster thickly on each side down to the water's edge, where their many bright colors and Eastern irregularity of outline are beautifully reflected in the dark blue waves.

Our ship was, as usual, surrounded with Greek boat-loads of fruit and vegetables. An old Greek, with a fine white beard which would have graced Nestor himself, particularly struck me. He was selling the little purple wild pigeon, for which Syra is noted, to our *maître d'hôtel;* while a brigand-looking young fellow at his side was recommending his baskets of shell-fish with an eloquence worthy of a Grecian orator. There is certainly much grace and beauty still lingering among the Greeks, if nothing more.

Herr S—— and Mr. Bell returned to the ship after a ramble of some hours, having climbed to the very summit of Syra. They declared themselves to be amply repaid for the excessive heat and fatigue by the lovely view which they had obtained of islands studding the sea like a constellation of stars in the sky, which produces a most beautiful effect, backed by the undulating outlines of the surrounding mountains. I am told that none of these islands are beautiful in themselves, being merely groups of barren rocks, with a patch of cultivation here and there.

No breakfast could be got by our hungry friends at Syra. The Greek master of a miserable pile of wood, called an inn, coolly informed them, in bad Italian, that *he had breakfasted long ago!*

"Do you mean to say, then, that we cannot even get a cup of coffee?" said the indignant artist.

"I don't think you can," replied the "host," pulling on his slipper with a yawn.

After leaving Syra, we came in sight of rocks and mountains wilder-looking than ever, with most piratical, half castle, half houselike dwellings, perched every here and there, mostly about their almost inaccessible summits. Even in these days it is not safe for merchant-vessels to pass this place unprotected; and the mails do not disdain to carry a few muskets and cutlasses in case of a visit from Greek pirates, whose mysterious-looking craft are constantly seen lurking about the rocks, or dashing at a rapid rate along the coast.

You would greatly admire the picturesque Greek boats, or rather feluccas. Their prow is shaped like the breast of a huge bird, the long neck elaborately carved and ornamented. One constantly thinks or the vessels in which Jason set sail in search of the Golden Fleece.

Still the evenings were most beautiful, a fresh gale usually springing up after sunset; and as the stars came suddenly out, it was charming to watch sea and sky mingle in a soft violet shade, with a faint outline of the mountains all around us. I used to love to listen then to the nuns' quiet talk, and sometimes to the pretty French airs whistled by the soldiers, poor fellows! as they paced the deck.

We arrived early in the morning at Smyrna, landed, and had a long ramble. The bay is very fine, and on the summit of the hills above are the ruins of a fine old castle. The first thing we met in the narrow streets was a long train of camels, and were charmed with the jingle of their bells, as they brought in heavy loads of grapes and figs from the country. The team was led by a brisk, dapper-looking little donkey, gayly caparisoned, who picked his way carefully over the wretched pavement, which reminds one, by-the-bye, more of a stable-yard in ruins (if you can fancy that) than any thing else. The Turks seemed very much astonished, to say the least of it, to see me walking along at such a rate with a party of men.

Then we strolled into the bazaars—such a striking scene! Vailed Turkish ladies,—some on foot, attended by black slaves; others in a kind of Cinderella's pumpkin carriage, and carrying fans of peacocks' feathers in their hands; noisy Greeks in richly-embroidered vests, with silver-mounted yataghans in scarfs round their waists; stately old Turks, smoking quietly in their little shops, with their yellow slippers by their side; grave-looking Armenians; hideous Nubian slaves; camel-drivers; hungry-looking dogs; strings of heavily-laden donkeys; coffee-bearers; fruit-sellers; sellers of lemonade and sherbet, tinkling their glasses as they pass rapidly along; Greek boys, rushing by with little pieces of lighted charcoal for the smokers; English and French soldiers and sailors; nondescripts of all nations bustling along through a *kennel*, about six feet wide, roofed over with canvas and old vines. It is a sight which, when seen for the first time, seems the most extraordinary one imaginable.

Passing under an ancient gateway of the town soon after, our dragoman told us, with great gravity, that had we but arrived the day before, we should have had the satisfaction of seeing the head of a brigand nailed to one of the beams, which had been exposed there for some time. We should have been much better pleased to have explored the many remains of antiquity which are still to be seen behind the town—fragments of the ancient city and Acropolis, and famous temple of Cybele.

We spent some time in the church—one of the Seven Churches of Asia Minor. It is decorated in the usual gaudy style of the Greeks: frightful pictures of saints with silver hands and "glories;" plenty of artificial flowers twined round huge waxen tapers, and innumerable glass chandeliers with trumpery colored pendents. It was sad to see so ancient and interesting a church so much disfigured.

We then looked at the fine white-marble fountain of the town, where groups of tired camels and their picturesque-looking drivers had stopped to rest. Here, for the first time, we heard a muezzin call out to prayer from a neighboring lofty minaret.

Passing onward through the narrow streets, our guide conducted us under a low, dark archway. This led into a sort of yard, with rickety wooden buildings all around, and this was the Slave Market. Such a sad, humiliating sight! There were only about a dozen blacks to sell, mostly women; and several had little children or babies in their arms. I thought they looked cheerful, and very much at home with their Turkish master, with the exception of one poor creature who sat aloof from the rest, the image of sullen despair. I gave her a peach which I had in my basket, and a little piece of money. She took hold of my hand and said something which I could not understand. Poor soul, my heart could only ache for her.

Another woman called me "dama Inglese," and pointed to her baby imploringly. This quite knocked me up, for it was a pretty, soft-eyed little thing, and looked very delicate; so we gave them a few pieces of money and made a precipitate retreat: for it was too dreadful,and we were glad to get back to the ship.

We found two heavily chained Bashi-Bazouks on deck, who were being sent back to Constantinople, where they had committed some horrid murder. They were frightfully savage-looking fellows, black Arabs, and by no means a pleasing addition to our freight. There was no more music after these wretched prisoners came on board.

We stopped once more at Gallipoli: the same picturesque-looking place from the sea as Syra, but miserable within, as only an Eastern town can be. There a detachment of French soldiers came on board *en route* for the Crimea, officered by a remarkably fine handsome young man. Two brother officers, who came to see him off, shook hands most warmly, and then they kissed each other on each rough cheek, saying, with great emotion, "Adieu, mon cher ami!" —this terrible Crimea!

We also take in many Greek, and several Turkish deck passengers at Gallipoli, with their bedding of quilts, antique-shaped earthen water-jars, and baskets of bread and melons for the journey. The poor Turkish women look very uncomfortable in their white vails and loose cumbrous cloaks. They are herded up in one corner, from which they do not move, but look like frightened sheep. The men spread their prayer-carpets and began to pray the moment they had settled themselves and their bundles; kneeling and prostrating themselves until their foreheads touched the deck.

A pretty Turkish child, wrapped in a little fur jacket, slept soundly beside one of the women, who kept spreading the corner of her red quilt very tenderly over it. Here at Gallipoli we parted with the nuns, who stepped quietly into a small boat, with their few boxes. Every one crowded round to give them the warmest adieu and best wishes. We often thought of them after they were gone, as you may suppose.

Sad to say, we were all fast asleep as, in the early morning, we swept past Mount Ida, and Sestos, and Abydos, which I was so anxious to see. However, we were wide awake to admire the white castles of the Dardanelles, and now thoroughly comprehended the vast importance of this part of the world to a man of genius and ambition like the Emperor Nicholas. It is a fine sight, steaming up the Dardanelles. We passed some great ships-of-war, French and English, every sail set to a fair wind, and crowded with troops. The Turks call the town of the Dardanelles, *Channahalis.* It is the ancient Dardanus, where the great treaty was signed between Sylla and Mithridates, (you see I learn what I can in my travels), and another, in modern times, between the Turks and English, in 1809.

The tomb of Hecuba is pointed out on the hills above the town; and across here it is said that Xerxes threw his bridge of boats. Every spot of land in this part of the world is of classic and historical celebrity.

All about the hills we now saw the white tents of the Bashi-Bazouk encampment, commanded by General Beatson. I am told that every thing at the Dardanelles strikes the traveler as most primitive. There you see the patient ox at the plow, the women grinding corn, or spinning at a rude wheel, or drawing water at the ancient wells, just as represented in the old Scripture days.

Our last evening at sea was fine, but the sun went down red and angry looking. The fires of the charcoal-burners on the mountains produced a magnificent effect as the darkness came on. Many of them extended over several acres of the steep and rugged sides, casting a red and lurid glare on the sky, as if vast cities were on fire at a distance.

At night a tremendous gale arose. The ship rocked and swayed so, that people with difficulty prevented themselves from being flung out of their berths. The

Sea of Marmora is as famous for sudden and violent tempests as the Black Sea.

We were all thankful when morning came. I dressed as well as I could, and managing to tumble on deck, held firmly by a rope, and watched the enormous waves, and huge masses of dark clouds rushing by. The ship presented a scene of great confusion; the poor soldiers had been unable to keep up their awning; Turks, Maltese, and Greeks, wet to the skin, and shivering with cold and terror. I pitied especially the poor Turkish women, whose drenched vails clung closely to their pale faces.

We arrived at Constantinople several hours later than we ought to have done, owing to the roughness of the weather; but as we approached the Golden Horn the clouds were breaking up as after an April storm, the wind gradually dropped, and so, as it were between smiles and tears, clouds and brightness, the beautiful city—the old Byzantium and once Christian capital, rival of Rome herself—with its domes and minarets and cypress-groves and white palaces, burst upon our charmed sight. The shores of Europe and Asia seemed to unite in forming a vast bay, in the middle of which rises from the dark-blue waves a city more beautiful and picturesque than words can describe. "A fine government might here guide or rule the world," is one of your first thoughts.

Long we stood delighted upon the deck, first turning our eyes upon distant Mount Olympus, whose summit glittered with snow; then upon the shadowy islands of the Propontis; then upon the sparkling Bosphorus, gay with innumerable caiques; then upon the crowds of stately ships of all nations; then upon the dark cypress-groves and white hospital of Scutari, where poor Miss Nightingale lay sick; then upon "beautiful Stamboul," with its crowning mosque of Santa Sophia and lofty minarets. But all this *must* be seen in sunshine to be believed in, and *then* you will think it a dream.

Numerous caiques and other boats crowded round our vessel here. Presently a French officer, wearing several orders, stepped on board. What a happy meeting it seemed with his wife and little daughter! Lucie clung to her father's arm with touching pride and delight. We bade adieu and congratulated at the same time.

Alas for the Bashi-Bazouks! — the wretched prisoners, who looked the image of sullen, hardened despair. Once or twice I thought they were going to throw themselves into the Bosphorus.

At last all was prepared for us to land, before the disembarkation of the troops. Crowds of caiquejees, kept at bay by a soldier on duty at the ladder, were disputing in loud Greek for the passengers. Mr. Newall was kind enough to offer us a place in the "Elba's" boat, which had been sent to meet him. So the English sailors dashed through the whole swarm, and soon set us on shore at Galata, the landing-place of Pera. It was difficult to get in through the crowds of caiques; but the boatmen of the Bosphorus, both Greeks and Turks, fine men as they are, pretty soon make way for a crew of English sailors.

At last we were on shore, among most wretched, dilapidated wooden-houses, on a filthy, broken, crowded pavement, amidst a motley group of Greeks and

Turks, soldiers and sailors, fruit-sellers and money-changers.

A few vailed black women were squatted on the edge of the bridge of boats, over which countless crowds were passing and repassing, and which reminded me of the bridge in the Vision of Mirza.

We soon found a couple of *hamals* (Turkish porters), whose backs were bowed almost to a crescent by constantly carrying heavy loads, and after a rapid walk up the steep and narrow streets, after being jostled by strings of donkeys, after having narrowly escaped being trampled on by caparisoned horses, treading on dead rats, melon-rinds, and cats—confused, enchanted with the *without*, disgusted beyond measure at the *within*—we arrived, tired and almost breathless, at Mysseri's Hotel. They have given me such a delightful room, with four large windows looking down the Golden Horn, and on the distant mountains.

LETTER V.

PERA—ENGLISH AND FRENCH OFFICERS—NEWS OF THE WAR—THERAPIA—SHORES OF THE BOSPHORUS—FALL OF SEBASTOPOL—PUBLIC REJOICINGS—SISTERS OF CHARITY—ILLUMINATIONS.

Pera, September 10th, 1855.

My dear Mr. Hornby:

You will be glad to hear that we arrived here safe and well on Saturday, after a most delightful passage, with exception of the last night, when it blew a gale in the Sea of Marmora, with the wind dead against us, which retarded our arrival by several hours.

We have suffered a good deal from heat on board ship, and now find these large and lofty rooms deliciously pleasant and cool. I sit quite enchanted at my window, which looks all down the Golden Horn, where English and French men-of-war, and a vast number of transports, lie at anchor in all their surly grandeur; while caiques and Greek boats with snow-white sails, flit about to and fro, like birds on the water. I saw the sun set on all this, on the first evening of my arrival. Such a glorious sight! the mountains in the distance mingling with the purple clouds.

It is a very striking scene at the *table-d'hôte* here. One can scarcely see to the end of the table. Almost all the guests are English and French officers, either in uniform, or in odd and semi-eastern costume—long beards and sunburnt faces. The din of so many voices is almost as confusing, I should think, as the roar of cannon at Sebastopol; but by degrees I began to pick up a few sentences here and there, which amused me very much.

"Come and try a day or two *over there*," says one handsome boy-officer to another. "I can give you a plank and some capital clean straw in my tent, within a quarter of an hour of the Redan. You won't mind a shell now and then."

Then I heard another recounting—"Doubled up for six weeks, like a ball, with cramp—my tent like a mud-pond—dreadful pain!" "Where's his Highness?" says another, further up the table. "His Highness disappeared the other day," was the reply, with a burst of laughter: "he went to take his turn in the trenches, and has never been seen since." (His Highness is evidently a nickname for some one very much laughed at.)

"Beastly shell!" drawled a tremendously tall, affected Rifle; "spoiled the best dinner we had had for a long time, and killed that very amusing fellow ——, who sat next to me. It was par-ti-cu-larly awkward; for the tent fell down upon us, and we were obliged to crawl out!"——"I felt quite out-of-sorts when it was all over—missed my arm so confoundedly (it was still in a sling), and got no dinner, for poor —— had asked me to dine with him in the morning, and he was killed half an hour before."

You may easily imagine how it startles one at first to hear all the horrible incidents of war spoken of after this fashion. I am the only lady here at present; and as there are no private sitting-rooms, I have to return to my bedroom immediately after dinner, which is very dreary. There is nothing to do here in an evening for strangers. The streets are dark and dangerous.

drunken soldiers and sailors tumbling over the wretched pavement, and noisy Greeks singing and shouting aloud.

The watchmen, with their iron-shod staves, make a strange clinking noise as they strike them against the stones. The only *English* sound is from the distant ships' bells, which is pleasant enough to me. Mysseri is Eothen's dragoman, whom he speaks of so highly. He is married to an Englishwoman, a most kind and excellent person, to whom everybody flies in all the numerous difficulties which strangers meet with here. The hotel is crowded, not even a sofa to be got; the large hall is almost filled with the baggage of officers coming and going, and constantly resounds with the clinking of spurs and the clank of swords upon the stone pavement.

It seems indeed a strange war-gathering here. Every one is anxious for news from Sebastopol; and even the sick and wounded, angry and impatient at being away from the scene of action, and from the tremendous attack which it is expected will soon take place. Numbers of English and French ships, crowded with troops, are constantly going up to Balaklava.

Poor fellows! they are always to be seen clustering thickly against the side of the vessel, seemingly delighted with the novel and splendid scene through which they are passing. What a relief it will be to one's mind when this dreadful place is taken!

Adieu, with kindest love to you all! We are perfectly well, notwithstanding the heat of the days, and the extreme chilliness of the nights; but still seem in *Dreamland.*

Therapia, Sunday, Sept. 16th, 1855.

We have been obliged to fly the heat and confusion of Pera, and find this place very delightful, with cool breezes constantly coming down from the Black Sea. The Bosphorous is certainly wondrously beautiful: the shore, on each side, is one unbroken but irregular line of white palaces with terraced gardens, mosques, and minarets, reflected in the clear blue water. The hills above are covered with cypress-trees, pretty kiosks, gardens, and wooded slopes.

I have as yet but little to tell you about the country, as Edmund has been very much engaged, and I have not ventured upon any expedition alone. However, I must first return to the three last days of our stay at Pera.

The news of the taking of Sebastopol, which has no doubt reached you by this time, was received with great delight by all here, excepting the Greeks, who were greatly enraged and disappointed. The Emperor of Russia being the head of the Greek Church, they looked forward to the success of the Russian cause as their own; and hating their masters the Turks, would have loved to see them, and their friends the Allies, humiliated.

The Bosphorous on Monday morning presented a gay and beautiful spectacle. All the ships-of-war and crowds of merchant-vessels of all nations were decked with flags, and many large and splendid ones floated from the principal balconies. The roar of guns from the different vessels was tremendous, enough to startle the echoes of Olympus, whose snows glittered brightly above the clouds of smoke.

Kind Mrs. Mysseri took me to the terrace on the

top of her house, where I had a splendid view of immense extent, almost too dazzling to be agreeable. I had a pleasant peep into the Swedish embassador's shady garden. On the other side of the hotel is what was once the Russian embassy, *now* a French hospital. Several poor wounded officers were wheeled in their chairs into the balcony to rejoice with the rest. Two or three of them threw their caps into the air in their joy, which they had not strength to pick up again. I took a great interest in watching these windows all the time I was at Pera, and seeing the good Sisters of Charity, so busy, and seemingly so kind to all. When they had a little time to spare, one or two would come out and walk up and down in an open gallery just opposite my windows. Sometimes they talked quietly and gravely together, but generally seemed to prefer reading for a few minutes.

But to return to the rejoicings of Monday. The firing began again at eight in the evening; and as far as noise and the rattle of windows went, gave us a good idea of a bombardment. All the ships on the Bosphorus, and round the Seraglio Point, and in the harbor, were illuminated, far as the eye could reach. Some of the French men-of-war burned colored lights. It was a beautiful sight. Pera and Stamboul glittered with lamps: palace and minaret illuminated, not after our fashion, but more like pale clusters of stars, shining here and there in the deep gray light and over the shifting ripples of the sea.

Presently, bands of Turkish "music" paraded the streets; and a more barbarous noise no red Indians could ever perpetrate. Edmund and I sallied forth into the streets, for, as we thought, it was a sight not to be seen again. We bought a little white paper lantern, lighted our taper, and joined the motley crowd.

Banners hung, waving in the night breeze, from almost every balcony of the principal narrow street; and every window was filled with lamps, just as we put flowers into boxes, all along the sill. It was a most curious, fitful light, and the numbers of picturesque costumes and savage faces singularly striking. Here and there—at the French, Sardinian, and Swedish Ministers', the Turkish guard-house, and at the numerous *cafanées*—it was quite a blaze of light; and in these places admiring crowds had so congregated, that we were scarcely able to get on. Presently a band of French soldiers, passing to relieve guard somewhere, cleared the way; and putting ourselves into the channel which they had made, we stumbled over dirt and broken pavement until we gladly found ourselves at Mysseri's door again, close by which the miserable-looking Turkish guard was turning out for the night.

LETTER VI.

THERAPIA—ITS PLEASANT CLIMATE—FLEET AT ANCHOR IN BEICOS BAY—DEPTH AND CLEARNESS OF THE WATERS OF THE BOSPHORUS—PHOSPHORESCENT ILLUMINATION AT NIGHT—SAD INCIDENTS OF THE WAR—WOUNDED AND SICK OFFICERS ARRIVE FROM BALAKLAVA—THEIR CONVERSATIONS ON THE ATTACK OF THE REDAN.

Therapia, September 30th, 1855.

My dear Julia:

We find this a very delightful place. Last week it was stormy; and we hear the wind very much, as the hotel projects into the Bosphorus, and northern gales rush down from the Black Sea with tremendous force. A large fleet is lying at anchor at Beicos Bay, just opposite our windows. The lights at the mast-heads look so curious at night, with the dark mountainous ridge of Asian hills frowning grimly just behind them. A few English vessels are moored close to the little causeway of our hotel, and one can hear the "All's well" of the watch, and the bells chiming the quarters. In the daytime it is by no means an uncommon thing to see a bowsprit peeping in at your window, the water is so deep close in shore. They tell me that you can see down to the depth of thirty feet on calm days; and it is charming to watch the different sorts of silvery and many-tinted fish swimming about, sword-fish darting along, and immense porpoises gambolling and romping with the bright, foamy waves further out. At night, every ripple, every stroke of the oar, is a phosphoric flash of light; and the track of a caique on the soft gray, shadowy water, is as like a fairy phantom as any thing which you can well conceive. For the last few nights it has been moonlight, so that we could see quite over to the Asian shore, and the white marble palace of the Pasha of Egypt there. The large stars look down so calm and clear upon this beautiful bay, on the dark hills around, and on the fine ships reposing, as it were, here and there, that it is difficult indeed to leave the window.

In this place one hears so much that is sad, and sees so much suffering in many ways, that, notwithstanding the numbers that are cheerful and gay, the mind becomes painfully impressed with all that is and has been so distressing in this war. My room was occupied only a few days ago by poor Mrs. ——, whose husband was killed at the attack on the Redan. She was afterward brought down here on her way back to England, and has cried for hours (Madame Patela, our hostess, tells me) in the very arm-chair in which I am now sitting. What increased the poignancy of her grief was, that after having endured agonies of suspense during the attack, she was assured by a friend that her husband had escaped unhurt; and, in the midst of her joy and thankfulness, he was carried up mortally wounded and insensible. Several wounded and sick officers have arrived here from Balaklava. Three or four of them are well enough to sit with the rest of the travelers on the divan in the public sitting-room. Now and then they talked of scenes in the camp before Sebastopol, and of incidents of the late assault; but, generally speaking, poor fellows, they seem quite wearied with so much misery and suffering, and turn with the greatest relief and pleasure to a chat about the peaceful scenes of England and home. I shall have many sad as well as merry stories to tell you when we meet, if I can but remember all I hear.

Colonel ——— has just come in from Sebastopol, well and strong, and full of news and conversation. Sometimes I pause to listen, and then, being anxious not to miss this Mail, go on writing again, with my head somewhat confused by a description of military movements, and sad, indignant comments on terrible mistakes and fatal mismanagement, on which point unfortunately all agree. Captain ——— (wounded in the head at the attack on the Redan,) is just saying that the English had no business there, and shudders as he speaks of the numbers who fell around him. He and several others are of opinion that we needed only to have supported the French as they entered the Malakoff. The French had easy work compared with ours. They had brought their earthworks within a few feet of the tower; ours were at least two hundred and eighty from the Redan; and in charging up that space, our poor fellows were mowed down by grape and canister.

The Malakoff once taken, the Redan must have fallen, as the guns of the former commanded it; so it would appear that all these English troops were thrown away, except for the slight diversion they made in favor of the French, which was really carrying courtesy to our allies rather far. Captain ——— also says that our men were much spoiled for a desperate assault by the long and harassing time in the trenches, and by a habit which they had necessarily contracted there of "sniping," as they called it; which is ducking down the head and shoulders to avoid shot and shell.

Many say that the same men ought never to have been brought up for an attack who had been repulsed and dispirited before. But I must not venture on any more recollections of military conversations, lest I make mistakes in getting out of my province so far, only I thought these particulars would interest you; and I believe that I have reported them very correctly, especially considering the crowd about me, all talking of this terrible day, so dearly won.

LETTER VII.

PLEASANT MORNINGS AT THERAPIA—GREEK FISHERMEN AND FELUCCAS—SEA-BIRDS, AND LEGEND OF THE "AMES DAMNEES"—MANY COLORED FISH OF THE BOSPHORUS—TERRACED GARDENS—SHIPS RETURNING FROM THE CRIMEA—THE CAMP AT BUYUKDERE.

Therapia, September 30th, 1855.

My dear Mr. Hornby:

You, who are so fond of early walks, would enjoy this sunny Therapia of a morning. Nothing can be more bright and sparkling; and it is so pleasant to be awakened by the splash of oars just under your window, and then to watch the gayly-dressed Greek fishermen hauling nets into their caiques, quite silvered with fish; or ancient-looking feluccas, with their picturesque crews and white sails set, dashing over the merry waves with boat-loads of wood for Stamboul.

Numberless sea-gulls and sea-swallows fly about the Bosphorus; but the most remarkable are a small, dark-gray gull, with wings lined with a silvery white. These are said by the boatmen to be the souls of the guilty wives drowned in its waters. They are for ever flying rapidly up and down, in parties of twenty or thirty, and night or day are never seen to rest. I cannot write the Turkish name, but the French have well translated it "âmes damnées." Poor "lost souls." As the punishment of drowning in the Bosphorus is now almost abolished, I suppose there will soon be no more, unless indeed no period of release is granted them for their punishment on earth—no final rest for their poor tired wings! If so, a thousand years hence the traveler may see the same swift silver shadow flit over the water which startles me to-day.

We had a very delightful walk this morning to Buyukdere. The quay at Therapia, along the shore, is so irregular and narrow, that when the Bosphorus suddenly lashes itself into a fury, as it often does, one can scarcely escape a dash of its waves.

The morning was calm and beautiful; the tints of many-colored seaweed reflected from far below. An old Turk was seated on a large stone, quietly fishing. He constantly pulled up fish of the brightest colors, which in different lights were certainly green, red, and blue. One recognized them immediately as the fish of the enchanted pond in the "Arabian Nights." I would not have put them into the frying-pan for more than four hundred pieces of gold. The wall would certainly have opened, and the Egyptian maiden have appeared, with her myrtle wand and mysterious beauty; and these things startle quiet Englishwomen. I would not therefore let Edmund enter into a negotiation to buy them; and we strolled slowly on, with the pleasant sound of waves on one side, and of whispered voices on the other—for the Greek and Armenian women are never tired of watching the English people as they pass by their shady windows and terraces.

There are some charming houses here. The first large one from our hotel is that of M. Baltazzi, a rich Greek banker. Through the trellis-arches of the walled garden we caught a tantalizing glimpse of the loveliest Eastern flowers in their fullest beauty—

three terraces, one above another; the walls clothed with luxuriant creepers, and the hills of Therapia behind.

The French embassador's is a very fine old house, once belonging to Prince Ypsilanti. Its vast white stone hall and fountain, with windows almost darkened with shady plants and flowers, look deliciously cool and pleasant to the passer-by.

The English Embassy is more shut in, the entrance being quite shaded with luxuriant myrtles and other shrubs; but the windows and terraced gardens face the Bosphorus, and command a lovely view. Further on is a small Turkish battery and guard-house, and close by a tiny mosque and fountain, near which we sat down to watch some English ships slowly steaming down from the Crimea. The decks were crowded with troops (sick and wounded going to Scutari or home), and in the fore-part of the vessels we could easily make out the gray coats of Russian prisoners. All the poor fellows seemed to be admiring the beautiful shores of the Bosphorus; and well they might, after the rugged, savage coasts of the Black Sea.

What a fine sight it is to see ships thus passing the ruined castles of Asia, and beneath the Giant's Mountain! The barren hills and rocks of the European shore gradually soften as they approach the beautiful Bay of Buyukdere, which must seem the loveliest harbor that ever a weary ship furled sail in. Many come down broken and torn from the furious tempests of the Black Sea, to cast anchor in the deep blue water, mirrored with the row of white palaces which fringe the shore, and with the cypress-trees and vineyards, and kiosks of the hills above.

6

Every scene is a picture in itself: we thought so this morning at each turn of the winding seaside path; whether looking on the gleaming Bosphorus with its mountain-girt entrance, ships sailing into the beautiful haven, and caiques flitting about among the white sea-birds; or on the many-colored cliffs on our left, tangled with brier and wild-flowers; or on the hills covered with heather and arbutus, on which Bulgarian shepherds were tending their flocks of goats and sheep.

Presently we came to the gate of a vineyard, and entering it made signs to a poor, dejected-looking Croat, lying under an old fig-tree, that we were both tired and thirsty. So he pointed to his piece of matting, which, with an earthen water-jar, seemed to be all his household possessions, and went to gather grapes, which he soon brought back to us in the coolest vine-leaves. A Greek boy was strolling about the vineyard; he spoke Italian pretty well, and entered into a friendly conversation with us; asked many intelligent questions about the war, and said he was most anxious to enter into the service of the English, who were "bravi genti." He gave me a handful of walnuts, nicely washed, and placing his hand on his heart, with the air of a prince, hoped that we might enjoy our luncheon; then, smiling, he shut the garden-gate and joined his companions. What native grace there is among the peasantry here!

Our rest in the shade, and the grapes, were both delicious; and our friend the Croat seemed to have gained an equal amount of satisfaction by the few piastres which we offered in exchange. He seemed so very poor and lonely. This vineyard had been robbed by some soldiers of the Turkish Contingent two nights before, and one of the Croat gardeners was murdered in attempting to drive them off; at least, so we were told at Therapia.

On approaching the camp at Buyukdere, we were struck by a magnificent group of plane-trees, by the side of the Bosphorus. The soldiers had put seats round one or two of them; a Greek cafeejee had set up his stall near, and a motley group were regaling themselves with coffee and the everlasting pipe under the wide-spreading boughs. The trees are called the "Seven Brothers;" and tradition says that Godfrey de Bouillon encamped beneath them in the time of the Crusades. His generalship would be rather surprised now, could he see English officers trying to drill the Sultan's miserable, dispirited-looking men into something like soldiers, to fight in a common cause. Major Johnson was so kind as to show us over the camp, a curious scene enough.

The valley was filled with white tents; and double rows of oxen, and refractory-looking mules, were tethered all around. Numerous wild dogs were prowling about the camp-fires, round which squatted some hideous black Arabs, who were cooking in large iron pots. One could not easily conceive more wild and ferocious-looking creatures than were gathered together here, as camp-followers.

The Turkish soldiers were thin, dejected, and debased-looking, to my eyes. I could just believe in their *endurance* behind earthworks, or stone walls, and that is all. An English sergeant said to me, with an expression of profound contempt, "They'll hang back, ma'am, as sure as fate, and let all their officers be killed, if ever they try to lead them to a charge." However, who can wonder at the degraded state of the poor Turkish soldiers, on learning their miserable, hopeless condition,—ill-paid, ill-fed, and cheated at every turn by their own officers?

Perhaps the men of the Contingent, honestly and kindly treated as they are, may improve. They are now expecting to be sent to Kertch; and the officers have plenty of hard work before them, if nothing else. I was in hopes that we might have heard of prospects of peace, after the fall of Sebastopol; here nothing is seen but active preparations for war. The cavalry are to winter at Scutari. Everybody is mad for *news*, both here and at Constantinople. It seems strange that we should be longing for what is authentic from England. Officers grumble about their friends in the Crimea not writing, and then again excuse them by saying, "Well, I suppose they are so busy."

LETTER VIII.

VALLEY OF THE SWEET WATERS—PICTURESQUE GROUPS OF TURKISH WOMEN—THE SULTAN'S DAUGHTER—TURKISH BELLES AND BABIES—TURKISH CARRIAGES—ARABAS AND TELEKIS—VENDORS OF DIFFERENT WARES IN THE VALLEY—BOILED INDIAN CORN—MUSICIANS—ANATOLIAN SHEPHERD—ENGLISH SAILORS—"BONO JOHNNY"—THE YOUNG PASHA—THE VALLEY AT SUNSET.

Therapia, October 26th, 1855.

My dear Julia:

On Friday we went in a caique to the Valley of the Sweet Waters of Asia"—the Turkish Hyde Park. It is a charming spot, shut in by ranges of hills on three sides, with the Bosphorus glittering before it, and a fine view of the opposite castles of Europe, with their ivy-covered walls and towers. We landed on a kind of terrace, beyond which was a very large white marble fountain, looking, as all fountains do here, like a square-built temple, ornamented with inscriptions in colored and golden letters. A stream of water fell from each side into a deep tank, out of which some poor Turkish women were filling their little earthen water-jars. Further on, under the shade of some magnificent plane-trees, sat the women of a higher class, on cushions which their slaves had brought from the caiques.

Nothing, in point of coloring and grouping, could be more strikingly beautiful than these clusters of women by the trees and fountain. Imagine five or six in a row; their jet-black eyes shining through their white vails, under which you can see the gloom of jewels which confine their hair (often dressed, by-the-bye, very much *à la Eugénie*). Your first impres sion is, that they look just like a bed of splendid flowers. The lady at the top of the row of cushions, and evidently the chief wife, is dressed in a feridjee cloak of the palest pink, edged with black velvet or silver; her face and neck all snow-white gauze, under which gleams a silver wreath or sprigs of jewels: for the *yashmak* in these days is so transparent as rather to add to the beauty of the wearer than to hide it. She generally carries a large fan of peacocks' feathers, both sides of the fan alike. The next is arrayed in the palest straw-color, shot with white; then perhaps follows an emerald-green, edged with gold; and by her side a lovely violet. The white yashmak contrasts prettily with all these colors. The feridjees of the slaves are often of a bright yellow or scarlet, edged with black, which, with the few dressed in darkest brown and green, harmonize perfectly with the light and delicate colors.

The Turkish women have certainly wonderful art in blending colors. In fact I hardly know how my eyes will bear a return to England. Here the water, the sky, the houses, the dresses, the boats are so gay and beautiful—the cypress-trees and the valleys so rich and green.

The Valley of the Sweet Waters takes its name from a small stream which winds through it and falls into the Bosphorus just above the fountain I mentioned. The water of this stream is highly prized for its purity, but, owing to the heavy rains of a day or two before, it was now rather muddy. So I braved the anger of the nymph of the spring by refusing to taste of its tiny waves, but invoked of her health and beauty for the poor Turkish women—for it is their only possession—and gave up my place to a vailed lady who was trying to drink without showing her face, which seemed to be a difficult process. We then walked through the valley, and watched the beautiful effect of light and shade upon the surrounding hills, crowned with cypress and other trees, and with here and there a pretty kiosk and garden. There are no roads here; so by a lane that would shame the roughest in Ireland, came the Sultan's married daughter—married to Aali Ghalib Pasha, the son of Reschid Pasha. Edmund helped Lady Robinson *into some brambles* on the steep bank; I was already safely wedged in the roots of an old fig-tree, and thus we quietly awaited the passage of the Asiatic beauties.

First came three or four men on horseback, in handsomely braided uniforms, and fezzes of course. Then two mounted negroes (more frightful specimens of that race I never saw) armed with long swords; then the carriage, a very droll imitation of an English one, most grotesquely ornamented; the harness covered with silver, and the reins red. Two grooms, in ugly, badly-fitting uniforms of blue and silver, guiding the horses, which were gray, and of matchless beauty and gentleness. The coachman was a droll-looking make-up, of English clothes (much too small for him) and Turkish fez and fat. I heard that this equipage is considered a wonderful display of elegance and civilization, and it was evidently greatly admired. We could not see much of the lady (who is said to be very lovely), the negroes keeping close to the windows, as they splashed up the mud all over their uniforms; besides which her yashmak was thickly folded. I could only see plainly her beautiful fan of snow-white feathers, the handle glittering with emeralds.

The lady on the opposite seat (there were three in the carriage) was more thinly vailed, very young, and very pretty. I saw her face plainly, and her feridjee being a *little* off her shoulders, I threw an envious glance on a violet-colored velvet jacket embroidered with gold, and fastened at the throat with a large jeweled clasp, which gleamed through the gauzy vail. As to beauty of mere dress and ease of attitude, nothing that I have seen in life or in pictures can give the slightest idea of the wonderful grace, the extreme delicacy, and bird-of-paradiselike uselessness of the Turkish belle. Women of rank look like hot-house flowers, and are really *cultivated* to the highest perfection of physical beauty, having no other employment but to make their skins as snow-white and their eyebrows as jet-black as possible. When young their skin is literally as white as their vails, with the faintest tinge of pink on the cheek, like that in the inside of a shell, which blends exquisitely with the tender apple-leaf green, and soft-violet colors, of which they are so fond.

The reverse of the picture is, that after the first bloom of youth is passed, the skin becomes yellow and sickly-looking, and you long to give the yashmak a pull and admit a fresh breeze to brighten up the fine features.

A belle, and a beauty too, the Turkish woman *must* be; for nothing can be more wretched than to see the poor things attempting to walk, or to make herself at all useful. She shuffles along the ground exactly like an embarrassed paroquette, looking as if her loose garments must inevitably flutter off at the next step. The drapery which falls so gracefully and easily about her in a carriage, or while reclining on cushions, seems untidy and awkward when she is moving about. In fact, if she is not a beauty, and is not the property of a rich man, she is the most miserable-looking creature in creation. It is the drollest thing in the world to see a poor Turkish woman rolling along with her baby; just preventing it from falling into the gutter, her loose yellow slipper from falling off at every step, her yashmak from showing too much of her face, her feridjee from flying away, and her open-worked stockings (which are generally full of holes if she has any) from getting splashed in the terrible filth of the roads, or rather dirty alleys.

The babies are wonderful little bundles of fat, uncomfortableness, and finery. They hardly seem like babies at all, generally having an old look, with very white faces and very black eyes. They are to us also an unnatural sort of babies, dressed in jacket and trowsers. They eat cucumbers and chestnuts, and are "nursed" at the same time. They wear richly jeweled fezzes and ragged shoes, and are altogether wonderful little illustrations of Eastern inconsistency and incompleteness, finery and untidiness.

The most curious-looking equipages at the Sweet Waters are the arabas, a huge kind of wagon, made of dark oak, rudely carved and ornamented, and drawn by two white oxen, caparisoned in the most fantastic manner. The collars, four or five feet high, are covered with scarlet tassels, and long crimson cords run from the collar to the tail of the animals, which they hold up most becomingly in a kind of festoon. Round the neck of each ox is a string of blue or many-colored beads, as a charm against the evil-eye; and the forehead and each cheek of the gentle animals is slightly tinged with red paint. A handsome canopy of scarlet cloth, (sometimes even of velvet), embroidered with gold and trimmed with gold fringe, protects the vailed ladies, children, and black slaves inside from the sun. The large cushions of the araba are often made of the same rich materials; so I leave you to imagine what a mixture of magnificence and extreme rudeness is to be seen here.

The bright fans and parasols beneath the awning of this strange equipage flutter gayly in the breeze; and thus a charming picture of Eastern out-door life does this valley present on a day of golden sunshine, with the dark blue Bosphorus on one side, and the beautiful hills of Asia on the other.

But here comes a teleki tumbling along full of ladies; and Edmund excites some surprise among its vailed occupants, by removing, with the help of a stout stick, a large stone over which the carriage of the sultan's daughter, numerous arabas, and many a pedestrian had stumbled, (and no doubt for months before), just at the entrance of the valley, notwithstanding the crowd of Turkish servants and sturdy negroes standing about. A teleki is very like the Cinderella's pumpkin-carriage of children's story-books; only I don't believe that any one could wear glass slippers in them now; for they are perfectly innocent of springs, and jolt frightfully over the wretched roads. There is seldom any place for the driver, this functionary holding the reins at full length, and running by the side of the horses. He is generally splashed all over with mud, or covered with dust, but has plenty of embroidery on his coat.

Scattered about the valley are vendors of different wares, and it is most amusing to watch them. Here is a venerable Turk of the old school, with a stately turban and silvery beard, selling sweatmeats with the air of a prince. There an Egyptian, with potteries from Egypt, consisting of little vases and water-bottles, in which we invested a few piastres. There is a wood fire, over which a Greek, in gay costume, has slung an immense iron pot, in which heads of Indian corn are gently stewing. The poorer Turkish women, strolling about on foot, stop to buy. I thought I should like to taste one; and a good-natured negress, a miracle of hideousness, with a grin meant to be fascinating, gave me the iron hook (which she had just secured), to fish one out for myself, which seemed to be considered the rare thing. However, I did not at all appreciate the dainty, and soon contrived to throw it away unseen. Here is a Greek stand of toys, windmills, Jacks-in-the-box, and eccentric-looking birds and beasts in gorgeous array. The Greek, who is a handsome young fellow, calls out: "Buy, Johnny, buy!" to the English passers-by, and looks very proud of his knowledge of the language. I thought how pleased Edith would be with all this.

Now we come to a band of "musicians" seated on the turf, and making, to *our* ears, the most atrocious noise that ever set a human being's teeth on edge. A groaning tambourine, a drum, and a little three-stringed instrument of torture, something like a guitar with some flutes as high and shrill as the screeching of a kite, form the combination of horrible sounds to which the men, in a nasal twang, scream some legend or tale, at the top of their voice, just as long as any one remains to listen. We were there, in the valley, for three hours, and on leaving, the Sultan's daughter was listening still, the slaves seated on the turf, drinking coffee and stretching themselves quite at their ease. Now we meet the Austrian embassador and his staff, who have been looking with surprise and interest at a most savage-looking Dervish, dressed as an Anatolian shepherd, and who, attired in black sheepskins, and leaning on a knotty club, which Jack might have taken from the giants, surveyed the passing scene from beneath an old fig-tree on the bank, his wild eyes half hidden with hair, as matted and as dark as his beard. Now we pass three or four French officers in full regimentals, looking at the ladies in the coolest and most persevering manner possible; utterly regardless of the fierce looks of some of the armed negroes, who mutter "Giaour" between their teeth, and roll the whites of their eyes. Edmund is now struck by a band of Greek women with wreaths on their heads, but an unfortunate attempt in the rest of their dress to look like Frenchwomen, which does not suit them at all.

Yonder is a coffee-stall, and two English sailors with tiny China cups in their huge fingers, trying to drink sugarless coffee as if they liked it, and conversing fluently with the grave, dark-eyed Turk, by the aid of "Bono" and "Johnny" and plenty of broad, eloquent smiles. By the way, the Turks call the English, male and female, "Johnny," and the French "Disdonc;" all commercial transactions being carried on in the most marvelous manner, often by the sole aid of these two words.

And now unvailed, because she is only about twelve years old, attended by two negresses and an armed Turk, comes a Pasha's daughter. The dress and trousers are of a thick kind of gauze, of a pale salmon-color, and sprigged with silver. A green velvet cap, beautifully embroidered, covers her head, and her hair hangs down her back in numerous plaits, the ends of which are frizzed out very roughly. Her shoes are of embroidered yellow leather, with peaks turning up in front, and she seems very proud of her gay-colored French parasol. This little belle shuffles languidly along, sometimes speaking a few words to her attendants, who seem to adore her.

Here is a teleki, drawn up under the shade of a large walnut-tree at the end of the valley. The horses are taken out, and fighting with a party of mules tethered by the hedge; but nobody takes any notice of them, and the drivers are asleep, or smoking quietly at a distance on the grass.

Inside this teleki are four Turks, smoking long chibouques (which project out of the door-window), as placidly as if it were the only business or delight in life. A languid wave of the hand brings another party of "musicians," who forthwith squat down between the hedge and the wheels, and begin their horrid noise. A Pasha's son rides listlessly up on his little Mytelene pony, to listen to them. I was particularly struck with this young gentleman, as a specimen of "Young Turkey." He wore a jacket and trousers (after the English shape) of fine scarlet cloth, the jacket so splendidly embroidered with gold as to be quite resplendent in the sun. Over his shoulder a golden baldric; his sword-sheath was of black and gold, the hilt shining with gems; his fez a plain dark crimson one, with the usual purple tassel. A huge slave stood beside the pony, which was splendidly caparisoned and very dirty, and the little Pasha leaned languidly on his shoulder, as if it was too great an exertion for him to listen to the "music" sitting upright in his saddle. Presently he seemed to intimate that he had heard enough; so the slave led his pony to an araba, at the side of which he dismounted, his mimic golden sword dangling about his little feet as he languidly threw himself into the laps of the ladies, who overwhelmed him with caresses. Such are the rich here—enervated from their earliest youth.

"How I should enjoy whipping that boy!" exclaimed an English gentleman of our party. Perhaps he coveted the sweets, we said, with which the young Pasha was now being regaled.

And now, my dear Julia, I think I have given you as good a rough and hurried sketch of a Turkish out-door scene as I can well do in a letter. At any rate you can depend upon its accuracy. The evening sun was resting upon it in full brilliancy, and all the Eastern gorgeousness of purple and gold, as we walked back to the crowds of caiques in waiting. Our eyes lingered long on the splendid groups still seated by the fountain, and under the trees just tinged with the first shades of autumn. It was a beautiful sight.

LETTER IX.

NEWS FROM HOME—INVALIDS FROM SCUTARI AND THE CRIMEA—CHAT ABOUT THE WAR—SARDINIAN AND FRENCH OFFICERS—THE COMMISSARIAT—SCENERY OF THE CRIMEA—RAMBLE THROUGH THE SULTAN'S VALLEY—ANCIENT PLANE-TREES AND FOUNTAIN—DINNER ON BOARD THE "ELBA"—BUYUKDERE AT NIGHT.

Therapia, November 8th, 1855.

My dear Mother:

On Tuesday last we had the great pleasure of receiving a packet of letters from England. The mail-boat had been detained at the Dardanelles, owing to some accident to her screw, and we had been anxiously expecting news from home. Edmund happened to be out when our letters were sent in from the Embassy, and he found me reading my share in high glee. Presently we came to the books and parcel of newspapers, for which we return many thanks. The papers, especially, are a great treat; and here we are just like girls and boys at school sharing all the news and books which come from home. Each floor in these Greek and Turkish houses forms a very large apartment (*salaamlik*). The upper end is all windows, with divans, or low broad sofas underneath them; so that you recline quite at your ease, and see all that is passing on the Bosphorus. On each side of this room are the different private apartments, at least bedrooms; for the hotel is so crowded just now, that a private sitting-room is quite out of the question—except for one lady who is alone here, waiting for her husband's return from Sebastopol. So when we have any papers, or any pleasant books, we put our contribution also on the table of this public room; and there is always some one grateful for a little news from England, some one sent down sick from the Crimea, or just escaped from the hospital at Scutari, and glad of a pleasant hour's reading. If you want to write here, you must resolutely shut yourself up in your own bedroom; for it is impossible to close your ears to tales of war by sea and land, to hairbreadth escapes, to every thing, in short, that is amusing, frightful, horrible. I am out a great deal, but occasionally listen with much interest to the conversation of the salaamlik.

Several invalids have arrived. Many who have borne up bravely through all kinds of privation and suffering during the siège, have totally knocked up since the taking of Sebastopol.

Poor Mr. Petre, of the 6th Dragoon Guards, is lying on the divan as helpless as a child, from the effects of fever. I often sit with him of a morning, and it seems to cheer him up to talk about getting back to England and his friends, and seeing his favorite horses and dogs once more. He cannot dine at the *table-d'hôte* of course, and always looks for a very ripe peach, or bunch of grapes, from me on my return. Sometimes I leave the table earlier, and take my coffee with him, for the evening seems his saddest time. A young officer, who was among the first in, and almost the first cut down at the assault on the Redan, has been here. He was severely wounded and very ill when he first came, but seems one of those blest with a "wonderful constitution;" for he has recovered rapidly, and is already off to England. He is missed here very much, especially by the invalids for he was full of spirits and fun. His description of the great storm in the Crimea, when all the tents were blown down, rivaled that of the "Times" correspondent. His sketch of a dandy trying to bale the muddy water out of his cherished tent with a *tin mug*, all his fine things swimming about, and two impudent stray geese in the midst, rejoicing at the increasing floods, made even the gravest of us almost die of laughing. In fact, I often wish for a short-hand writer here, for a great deal of the conversation which we hear on "our divan" would be well worth remembering, grave, gay, and political; but of course every thing relating to the war predominates. There are five Sardinian officers staying here, remarkable gentlemanly, well-informed men, and a few French. All the French officers whom we have seen give one the idea of real soldiers—soldiers in earnest, and the right men in the right place; but generally they are by no means as polished as our English officers.

We dined on board an English steamer the other day, and after dinner I walked up and down the deck with the captain. He is a rather bluff, but kind-hearted man, and told me that, much as he had been knocked about in a long service, the most miserable part of his life was when our army first landed in the Crimea. He was then in command of the ——, and said, what every one knows, that finer and braver fellows were never seen than those he had on board. For some absurd reason, or for no reason at all, they were not allowed to take their tents on shore, although it could have been done with the greatest ease. A tremendous rain came on in the evening—"such a soaking cold rain," said the captain, "as *you* never saw or felt." Our poor men, as every one knows, 'slept' out in it all, *after having just left a crowded and hot ship.* The wood and sticks which they were able to collect, were of course as wet as the shore itself. So they passed the night. In the morning hundreds of sick men were sent on board different vessels—to die. Captain —— told me that he buried from his ship ninety men in thirty hours. The chaplain could do no more than hurry from one service to another; and three or four poor fellows at a time were plunged over the ship's side. However, I dare say you have read all this in the papers, and it is too terrible a subject to dwell upon. The French not only had their tents put up for the night, but their bedding, means for getting hot water and a comforting cup of coffee before going to sleep. They said that on such a night, even with that, it was bad enough. But I must stop my pen, as usual. If I were to write you all I hear of cruel mismanagement, it would fill a volume—not a letter. Our traveling friends, Mr. Newall and Mr. Bell, returned from the Crimea on Saturday last, and came to see us directly the "Elba" cast anchor in the Bosphorus. They have been extremely interested in all they have seen.

After finishing the telegraph to Eupatoria, which nearly frightened the Turks out of their wits, as they firmly believed it to be a work of the Evil One, they explored Sebastopol, or rather its ruins, and then rambled forty miles inland. They are quite charmed with the beautiful valleys of Baidar and Alucca, and have made some capital sketches. I do hope to go up there before our return to England, and to see the vast *steppes* and fine ranges of that part of the world. This morning the "Elba's" boat took us over to the Asiatic shore, and we had a delightful walk through the celebrated "Sultan's Valley." Just at the entrance of the ruined kiosk the French have built some wooden barrack-sheds, and numbers of soldiers were lying on the grass, or *washing*, up to their knees, in the waters of a little stream.

Further up in the valley are a number of ancient and magnificent plane-trees. I stepped twenty-five long paces round two or three of them, so you may fancy their huge girth. Several of them are hollow, and the soldiers have contrived cosy little dwelling-places of these "giant boles." One of them was comfortably lined with pieces of matting; several little brackets were put up within reach, for the tin mug and pipe; and above all the name of the tenant was carved in fanciful letters deep in the rugged bark, MORIER, 1855.

This valley reminds one of the Happy Valley of Rasselas,—just its mountainous hills all around, just its delicious shade, and tinkling streams. In the centre of it is a large white marble fountain, adorned with inscriptions from the Koran (which it is always provoking not to be able to read;) and beneath the plane-trees shading it, several Turks were resting themselves. They had been loading the Seraskier's horses with water from this famous spring, and the whole party seemed averse to leave so cool and charming a spot.

At a little distance, at the foot of a hill, sat a Turkish shepherd, calmly regarding alternately his sleeping flock of sheep and goats, and the party of "Giaours, walking briskly in the sultry heat of the day, a proceeding which I dare say he considered as indicative of insanity. However, we returned to the good ship "Elba" with excellent appetites.

An immense bunch of mistletoe hung in the cabin, which grew but a few days before on an ancient tree in the Crimea, but is now destined for the Christmas *fête* of Mr. Newall's children in England. After dinner the toast in champagne was "Home, and may we all meet there again!" Just then, I don't know how it was, one of the officers of the ship mentioned, that below, in his coffin, lay the body of poor Colonel Maule, who was killed in the Crimea. So terribly do gay and painful scenes mingle here just now! It gave me quite a shock, and I was glad to retreat on deck.

Buyukdere is indeed a lovely sight at night, with the lights of the ship lying in the bay, and afar off, twinkling in kiosks high on the dark hills, and fringing the ripples on the shore. "Would you not fancy this was a Paradise?" said I to a sailor-friend of mine, who was quietly leaning over the ship's side. "Yes, ma'am, so long as you didn't land," was the reply. I passed the cook's cabin; that functionary and his man were "washing-up," but he came out to say good evening to me. I asked him how he liked the Crimea, and then said how much we had enjoyed the English dinner. "As to the plum-pudding," I said, "coming in on fire too, and with a piece of mistletoe (Crimean though it was) stuck in it, I could really have almost fancied myself in England again. Mr. Cook (a great rough fellow, with a beard up to his eyes) was quite touched at my praise of his dinner, although he declared it was not what he *could* have made it with "more properer things." "But to hear an English lady say she has enjoyed a pudding of my making, pleases *me* more than any thing has since the 'Elba' came to these heathenish parts," he exclaimed. I was very much amused at this.

The gentlemen soon left the cabin, and we walked on the upper deck in the clearest moonlight. The Bosphorus looked lovely, with the faint shadow of hills reflected all around it, and myriads of stars looking down from the clear gray sky. The captain was kind enough to fix his telescope, that I might admire Jupiter and his rings, and some curious spots in the moon, which have lately been unusually visible. Then in this pleasant stillness, only broken occasionally by the sound of oars or of a ship's bell, the captain told me "all about" his wife and little children at home, and I told him "all about" Edith; and so we poor wanderers in a strange land cheer each other up.

We had a delightful row home. The ship's boat, with the rest of the company, were rash enough to race with our fine caiquejees, and were of course ignominiously beaten.

LETTER X.

HOSPITAL AT THERAPIA—ITS GARDEN AND BURIAL-PLACE—GRAVE OF CAPTAIN LYONS—WHITE CROSS ERECTED IN MEMORY OF THOSE WHO FELL IN THE CRIMEA.

Therapia, November 10th, 1855.

My dear Mr. Hornby:

In my last budget I had not space to tell you of a very interesting visit which the Rev. Mr. Evelyn and I made to the hospital here. It was once a summer palace, and has been given by the Sultan for the use of the sick and wounded English. A little kiosk in the garden, shaded with orange and lemon trees, is devoted to the surgeons. A clergyman and his wife were at the head of it when we first arrived at Therapia. They had been for some months in the Crimea, and came down here greatly shattered, I was told, with all they had gone through. Mrs. M—— especially was a mere shadow, and suffered severely from low fever, and the shock which her nerves had sustained. Even to her friend, Lady Robinson, she could never speak of the horrors and sufferings which she had witnessed. An officer told me that she had been left one night, after an action, in a kind of ruined outhouse, with about thirty wounded men, whom the surgeons had been obliged to leave, in order to attend to others. She had but a small quantity of brandy, and knew that, weakened by loss of blood, the only chance of life which the poor fellows had, was being kept up until the return of the surgeons in the morning. All night this brave lady worked hard by the light of a single rushlight. Many died around her, but she kept on undauntedly, and *saved twelve.* Those she could not save doubtless died blessing her. I could never look upon this quiet, pale couple without the greatest emotion.

They both got better at Therapia, but were always at work, and greatly improved the hospital arrangements. I was told that Mrs. M.—— wished to return to the Crimea, but that her husband would not allow her, shattered in health and spirits as she was; and they have since started for England. They left with several poor soldiers, who could never speak of their untiring goodness without tears. The first day I visited the hospital there were many lying there very badly wounded, and neither noticing nor speaking to any one; only you saw by the sad, pale face, as each lay in his little bed in the great room (once a part of a luxurious harem), how much they had suffered. Others, who were better, looked up with pleasure at English faces. One or two wished me "Good morning," but I could not utter a word for the first few minutes, and stood at one of the windows wiping my eyes. Nothing could look cleaner and neater than the rows of little beds. Beside each of them was a small table, covered with a white cloth, on which stood a Bible and a Prayer-book, the medicine-glass, and perhaps the watch, and some other little treasure belonging to the patient. One poor soldier had walked across from another room to see a comrade, on whose bed he sat, asking many a kind question, and bidding the pale, haggard face cheer up, though looking but little better himself. On the next bed to these, sat two mere shadows of men, feebly playing at dominoes, which they told me with delight were a present from her majesty, and then showed me a backgammon-board, draughts, and some amusing and instructive books, which the Queen ("God bless her!" said the poor grateful fellows) had sent out to amuse her wounded soldiers at Therapia. It was really quite touching to see their thankfulness for all that was done for them, and how well they bore their sufferings, so far from home and kindred.

We went afterward to walk in the garden, a large and formal one, its long straight walks ornamented with rows of fine orange and lemon trees in full bearing. On sunny benches here and there were seated the convalescents, enjoying the fresh air. A few were strolling quietly up and down, reading together with great interest, an old and tattered English newspaper. From the formal part of the garden you soon wander into a wildly beautiful shrubbery, which reaches up to the hills of Therapia. This is really a lovely spot, and, what is rare in this country, the deep shade preserves the ferns and wild-flowers in freshest beauty. We walked with delight through a fine avenue of trees which reminded me of that in the garden of Boccaccio, the blue sky peeping through the interlaced branches above, and the sun just touching, here and there, leaves already tinged with the first gold of autumn. One of these fine avenues extends half way up the hills, another crossing it, and forming a charming forest picture. Gathering some pretty specimens of ferns and wild-flowers, we came suddenly to a little valley enclosed with a low mud wall. Round it were ranged, in rows, about a hundred graves, each of which contains the bodies of many men, who have died of wounds in the hospital, or been brought down from the Crimea. They are all nameless, these long rows of clay; but in the centre of the valley, erected on three white stone steps, stands a plain white cross, on which is inscribed, "I am the Resurrection and the Life;" and beneath this, "To the memory of those buried here, who fell in the Crimea; erected by their countrywomen at Therapia." Alone, at the upper end of this sad place, stands a solitary gray stone; on it is inscribed, "Captain Lyons. Her Majesty's ship Miranda."

Silently Mr. Evelyn and I sat down at the foot of an old tree. I believe that just then neither of us could have spoken a word. We had broken in, as it were, so suddenly upon the mournful resting-place, in a strange land, of our countrymen. How they had been prayed for! How many bitter tears were still shed for them in England! Could the dead speak, how many tender messages would they not send home from that harem-garden now by us, whose hearts ache over their lonely graves for them, and for those especially whom they have left behind! Mr. Evelyn told me of a friend and namesake of his, who was killed by the bursting of a shell, just before the assault —a noble and promising young man, beloved by all. His father used to say, after he had left home, "My friend and companion, as well as my son, is gone." Mr. Evelyn said that the most painful task of his life was to write to this poor father, and convey to him his son's last message.

However, I must tell you no more sad stories. We have heard enough to fill a volume, and to make the hardest heart ache. Young ladies, struck with the glitter of regimental dress, and the pleasantness of hearing the band play in the Park on a fine summer's day, would quite alter their opinion of the pomp and glory of war, were they only to see one-tenth part of its horror, and misery, and sorrow.

Mr. Evelyn hopes soon to return to his labors in the Crimea, which, however, we trust he will not attempt just yet, for he has been very near losing his life from fever, brought on by exposure and over-exertion, and has still a terrible cough, which even the fine air of Therapia does not cure. Besides attending to the sick and dying, he has had an evening-school for the soldiers of his Division, and writes all the letters of those not able to do it for themselves.

The night before the assault, he and another cnaplain administered the Sacrament to about fifty officers, at their own request. He said that the scene was a most impressive one—in a large tent, lighted by a few candles stuck on bayonets. It is remarkable that, of the number gathered together on that momentous evening, almost all fell. But the evening was now drawing to a close, and with a long, lingering look round this little Valley of the Dead, we took our departure.

On reaching the end of the avenue, we found the garden-door of the hospital-palace locked. After knocking again and again, and beginning to despair of making ourselves heard (for the invalids must have left the garden long before this time,) we heard footsteps rapidly coming along one of the long gravel walks. I peeped through the keyhole of the huge and ponderous lock, and saw the Turkish gardener hurrying toward us. This good news I communicated to my friend, who, delicate as he was from recent illness, was already beginning to feel chilled by the evening air in this deep shade of trees. Unfortunately he too looked through the keyhole just as the Turkish gardener, bent on reconnoitring who was making the loud knocking, did the same. Pity it was not my ruddy face that met his view, for a single glance at Mr. Evelyn's pale and worn one seemed to be enough. He sped away as if the shades of all the poor "Giaours" lying in the valley were after him. Seriously speaking, I have no doubt that he really mistook Mr. Evelyn for a good-looking shade—but still shade unmistakably; and I dare say that nothing could have induced him to return, for the Turks are a singularly superstitious people. We could not help laughing at this very awkward dilemma; however, nothing remained but to make the best of it. Twilight only lasts a few minutes here, and the tall shadows of the trees were rapidly mingling into darkness. So we again crossed the valley, and gaining the upper avenue, found another way home over the hills, descending through the village to our hotel by the Bosphorus.

LETTER XI.

BEAUTY OF THE BOSPHORUS—FISHING-VILLAGE ON THE ASIAN SHORE—TURKISH CEMETERY AND GRAVES OF THE JANISSARIES—RUINS OF THE CASTLE OF ANATOLIA—TURKISH SOLDIERS.

Therapia, November 15th, 1855.

My dear Julia:

The Bosphorus is certainly one of those beauties formed to turn all the heads in the world. She smiles, and nothing on earth can be more radiantly bright and sparkling; she is angry, and dashes along with a wild, untamable, yet graceful fury—the hills around grow dark and sorrowful, and the tall cypress-trees wave their heads in stately submission to her stormy humor.

Some people think her most beautiful then, but others are enchanted with her quiet, dreamy moods, when she murmurs gently on the shore, and takes delight in picturing fairy-white palaces, and shady rose and orange-gardens, and fragrant branches waving in the scented wind. Or in the stiller nights, when she flashes back every touch with a gleam of gold, and sparkles with golden stars as she moves along in the pale gray light.

But you may tire of my attempt at description—you never would of beholding the reality. Yesterday we took caique at Buyukdere, and crossed over to the Asiatic shore. I got some charming specimens for my collection of wild-flowers, and a beautiful bouquet of arbutus, laden with the richest berries. The arbutus grows wild on the hills and cliffs here, almost down to the sea-shore, and also many fine shrubs which would grace a garden. The Bosphorus was very rough, or we had planned rowing up the mouth of the Black Sea; as it was, we landed with some difficulty at a little village beneath the ancient Castle of Anatolia. It was a most picturesque-looking place, and evidently a fishing-village. Numbers of gayly-painted caiques were drawn up on the shore, and from the lofty boughs of a group of enormous lime-trees, hung fishing-nets of great length and almost snowy-whiteness. Numbers of broken-down wooden houses were clustered within the shade of the vast boughs. A few Turkish fishermen were seated on some large stones mending their nets, and many were resting before the door of a little *cafanée*, sipping coffee, and smoking with their usual sedateness. Here, in the Asiatic villages, the people are more picturesque-looking than at Constantinople, and generally retain the beard, and many-colored turban, which suits the Eastern face so well. They are also much more shy of strangers. Even at Stamboul, little children will sometimes give you a friendly smile, or even call you "Bono Johnny;" but in Asia the little things generally dart a glance of hatred or fear, and mutter "Giaour" as they fly away from you. Their mothers too show great dislike of your noticing them, fearing the "evil eye" of Europeans.

Bnt I am wandering from the ruins of the great Anatolian castle, which we came to see. It is built on the top of the mountainous range of hills overlooking the Black Sea; so you may fancy what a climb it was in the fierce heat of the day. When half-way up, we stopped in a beautiful but ruined cemetery, and sat down to rest by an ancient fountain. Some Turkish women were sitting there, but they hastily adjusted their vails, and retreated at our approach among the old and knotted cypress-trees. Higher up, through the dark funereal boughs, was the most lovely view that could be conceived of the blue winding Bosphorus, the hills and shipping of Therapia, and the great valley of Buyukdere. Some ancient graves of the Janissaries stood here, with huge and unmutilated turbaned stones. Sultan Mahmoud's vengeance had not found them out in this sequestered place, and they still slept quietly on the spot which I dare say they had chosen in their days of greatness, with only a few timid sheep straying here and there to share possession with them.*

At last we reached the fine ruins of the castle, and wished you could have seen from the tower the view of the wild rocky coast of the Black Sea, the opposite European shore and its ruined forts, the Giant's Mountain, and all the softer, wooded beauty of the Bosphorus below. It was indeed a lovely sight, and well worth the sultry walk. The tower and walls and bastions of this castle are covered with the thickest and most beautiful ivy. On the lower walls wild vine and fig-leaves of the ruined garden mingle with its dark foliage. A very pretty species of mountain-ash grows abundantly here, with large bunches of the most brilliant scarlet berries, which are shaded, almost transparent, and as fine as coral. A small patch of

* After the massacre of the Janissaries, Sultan Mahmoud ordered all the turbans on their headstones to be struck off. The headless stones are to be seen in almost all the cemeteries.

ground within the inner wall was strewn with melons and a few dried-up vegetables, evidently for the use of three or four miserable, wild-looking Turkish soldiers, who leaned over the ruined battlements of the tower, watching the flight of a couple of eagles wheeling slowly round and round, high in air. We managed to make one of these poor "sentries" understand a few words of Italian. We were "great English captains," he said, and hastened to offer one of his best melons. He afterward looked with great curiosity at our glasses, so I fixed mine for him, and pointed to the distant eagle. He was positively frightened, cried out something to his companions, and could not be induced to look again, evidently thinking it something "uncanny." These poor soldiers, and a kind of shepherd gardener, whose starved-looking flock were grazing on the adjoining hill, live in a rude kind of hut, erected inside of the castle-keep, a most dreary abode, only lighted by a crumbling entrance in the wall. Looking up far into darkness, one could only discover a gleam of light here and there. They said that immense numbers of bats and owls flew about at night. Only fancy the desolateness of these poor fellows' lives! A few piastres cheered them up wonderfully. It is said that the arms of Byzantium are still to be seen on this castle, but we were not fortunate enough to find them out. All I saw over one of the doorways was a large Genoese cross. In ancient times here stood the famous Temple of the Twelve Gods,—at least so says the learned "Murray," in whom every English traveler is bound to confide.

We had a delightful row back to Buyukdere, and again the good ship "Elba" hospitably received us.

A colonel of the Turkish Contingent had joined the party, whose chat about the camp was extremely entertaining. In these two or three stormy nights, many of the tents in the valley of Buyukdere have been flooded. The colonel seems to regret this the more on account of a Turkish hen, a prisoner-of-war, who lived under a kind of rude straw sofa in his tent, and seemed so amiably inclined to him that he always knew where to find a new-laid egg for his breakfast every morning. His cook is a wild Wallachian woman, who rides astride full speed through the camp; and he was in great spirits at having made the acquaintance of a poor Bim-Bashee (equal in rank to a major in our service) of one of the regiments, who was happy to mend or patch for a "consideration."

Poor Colonel —— showed me his only remaining *yellow* cambric handkerchief, which had acquired this very unenviable tinge from having been washed by a Turkish soldier in a small hole cut in the clay hillside of the camp. He has now got an Arab servant, a perfectly wild but intelligent creature, whom he is endeavoring to teach cooking and washing, two most valuable accomplishments here.

You would have been amused to see with what intense interest our new acquaintance listened to my instructions on the important subject of "how to make a pudding." After all, there must be a great deal of fun in camp life to those who enjoy the dignity of helping themselves. "The wise man's best servant and assistant is himself," struck me very much, even as a child, on reading the "Fortunes of Nigel."

LETTER XII

VILLAGE OF KADIKOI—SEA OF MARMORA—LANDING AT PERA—STAMBOUL—ITS SILENT STREETS—BEHIND THE LATTICE—THE SULTAN—HIS KIND AND MERCIFUL DISPOSITION—DESOLATENESS OF CONSTANTINOPLE—VARIABLE CLIMATE—THE TURKISH LOAN—CHOLERA AT YENEKION.

Therapia, November 10th, 1855.

My dearest Mother:

We returned last evening from a visit to a village called Kadikoi. It is beyond Scutari, just where the Bosphorus becomes very wide and loses itself in the Sea of Marmora. This is the point where you sit in your caique as it bounds over the waves, quite lost in wonder at the extraordinary beauty, the dreamlike loveliness of the place, of which nothing but actual beholding can give you the faintest idea. Perhaps in a dream I may see again, when in England, this very place, where the Bosphorus and the whole Propontis meet; I may again feel the delightful undulation of the caique on the dark-blue water—again see beautiful Stamboul, with its snow-white minarets and dark cypresses rising as it were from the waves—ships of all nations floating by—Princess' Islands and shadowy Mount Olympus like gray clouds in the distance; on the other side, seeming to rise out of the sea too, Pera and the tower of Galata, and the dark-green funereal trees of the great burial-ground.

The "Maiden's Tower" stands on a rock in the sea, off the steep cliffs of Scutari. You must either see this place, or *dream* it after a dose of opium or lotus-eating. No pen, no artist can paint it.

But what an awakening it is to land at Pera! Such a motley crowd, such a jostling, such a confusion of tongues and of cries, such dirt, it is utterly impossible to conceive.

This is, as you know, the "Frank" quarter, thronged with people of many nations. If you land at Stamboul, you find the landing-place crowded with caiques and Greek boats, and hundreds of people hurrying up the narrow street leading to the bazaars—*hamals*, or porters, laden with huge bales of wool and other merchandise. But turn right or left out of this busy path, and you find yourself as it were in a city of the dead—closed lattices, and not a sound to disturb the profound silence of the steep and narrow streets, across which sometimes trails a neglected trellised vine. After a long ramble one day, Mr. Bell and I sat down on an ancient fountain-stone in this silent region. Opposite to us, on the right, was a vacant space caused by a fire, over which fig-trees and creeping plants grew in uninterrupted wildness and luxuriance. Exactly opposite to the poor weary travelers was a dark-red and closely-latticed wooden house, most picturesquely decayed-looking. Presently a vailed black slave came out, and carefully closing the door, gave a suspicious glance at the "Giaours," and shuffled mysteriously out of sight. A little red-and-white kitten had evidently wished to come into the street with her; but when it saw us, it started back as if in fear of the "infidels." All the time we sat there, we saw one of its little golden eyes peeping at us through a hole in the old iron-bound door. We were very tired, so there we sat a long time, saying what a curious, silent, drowsy, and picturesque place it was, when we saw a little square bit of the trellis-work lattice quietly open, and a pair of black eyes looked down upon us through the thick white folds of a yashmak. We did not speak, and sat just as children do, scarcely daring to breathe, when a strange bird hops by which they are anxious not to scare away. The black eyes evidently scanned us both from head to foot; but presently a turbaned head crossed the lattice, and they suddenly disappeared. Mr. Turk now opened the lattice a little wider, and seemed so well pleased with his view, that Mr. Bell at length broke silence by suggesting that it would be rather awkward, alone as we were, if he were to come down and insist upon buying me at once. Mr. Bell and I are famous for making each other laugh, and here was an end of our gravity at once. The black eyes again returned to the lattice, but we could see by its wreaths of white smoke that *My lord* was close by. It seemed to us that this silent pantomime meant: "If you look at *her*, I *will* look at *him*;" for the black eyes now fixed themselves on the good-looking and susceptible Mr. Bell in the most determined and tender manner; so that out of regard to his peace of mind, I thought it better to rise from the old stone and go on our way, which we did.

Both of us, however, being rather flattered with such evident and novel admiration, we consulted together as to the expediency of waving an adieu—I to the turban, he to the black eyes and yashmak. But we were alone in the very heart of silent Stamboul, and not able to speak a word of the language; so I advised Mr. Bell to keep his head comfortably on his shoulders, and to depart with no other demonstration to the lovely black eyes than a sorrowful look. This he agreed to, provided that I did the same; to which I consented, after some disputation as to the "difference" in the way of danger. And we climbed on through another silent street, where only a blind woman sat on the door-step to a small cemetery, where a few blue and gilt turbaned stones could be seen through the thick shade of cypress and flowers, surrounded by a rusty iron railing, trellised for birds. The next turn brought us to a coffee and sherbet shop, and we made signs of being thirsty. The drowsy Turks smoke their chibouques, and look at you so quietly from their divans. I greatly enjoyed that first walk in Stamboul. One is always reminded of the Arabian Nights. By-the-bye, when we write to ask you to send out the winter clothing, etc., will you send me a copy of that book? It ought to be read *here*. Please not to forget. I will tell you how to send the parcel.

Tell Edie that I was so much amused that day at Stamboul by a parrot, just like ours at home. She was hanging in a gaudily-painted cage, inside a Turkish sweetmeat shop. As I passed by I said, "Poor Poll!" for she looked very dull, and heedless of the vailed women and Turkish children passing in and out. You can hardly imagine the delight of the poor bird at the sound of my voice. She screamed, and danced about her cage, like a mad thing, trying to fly to me all the time. I could only suppose that she had been *brought up* English, and was charmed by the sound of the language of her early sailor-days, before being sold at Constantinople and consigned to silent

Stamboul,—not a cheerful place for a parrot, I should think!

We came home by the Mosque of St. Sophia, and by the outer garden of the Seraglio, where we again rested, and a Turkish gardener gave me some flowers and a handful of fine walnuts. This ground is to the Seraglio, what Birdcage Walk is to Buckingham Palace: I mean only in its nearness, for the ground is hilly and the walls fortified. It would be a beautiful place to walk about in, for the cypress and other trees are very fine, and the view charming all down by Scutari; but you constantly regret the untidy and uncared-for exterior of all palaces and mosques here, except the entrances by the Bosphorus. These are beautiful quays, with vases of flowers, and inner marble courts, fountains, and gardens shining through the trellised arches of the walls, all in the most perfect order, as I am told the interior of the houses are. I am promised introductions to one or two great Turkish hareems; then I shall be able to tell you much.

Dr. Zohrab, who is the Sultan's physician, said, at dinner yesterday, that he hoped to be able to take me to the marriage of the Sultan's daughter, which will be a most magnificent sight, but is not to take place just yet. Dr. Zohrab is much attached to the Sultan, and indignant at the slanders which those opposed to his wish for civilization and improvement (he declares) invent. The Sultan is, he says, slightly paralyzed from extreme debility and ill-health, and this his enemies pretend to attribute to intemperance. He is very accessible to his subjects, and would be to people of any nation, if his intriguing ministers did not do all in their power to prevent it. All agree in speaking of his merciful disposition; he has never yet been induced to sign a death-warrant. You see that I can but write to you all at home what I hear from the most credible sources; it is most difficult in this country to come at the truth. However, as far as regards the sultan, I should really think he is a good but a weak man, who cannot do what he would, for fear of his thieving and fanatical ministers. His chief delight is his new palace at Dolma Batche. Mrs. Sanderson tells me that the palace at Bahjoh is just like those in the Arabian Nights, the most beautiful you can conceive. Dr. Zohrab says that he is too good for a Sultan, and is "almost an angel." Madame —— is one of the many who decidedly affirm that he is a drunkard; but she is a Greek, and a would-be *diplomate*, and Dr. Zohrab is a fine, rough, independent, but good and affectionate man, who would, I am sure, defend neither prince nor peasant if he thought them wrong. From the Bosphorus this palace looks very lovely. By the way, many of the Sultanas at the palace of Tscheran are being taught to read, and several are proud of being able to spell over the "Thousand-and-one Nights." Poor things! what a useful education to give them! However, it is a step. They are also taught music and dancing, and all practise on different instruments in the same hall at the same time. A lady who heard it in passing the palace told me what an awful noise it was.

We hear a great deal of what is going on both in Turkish and European affairs here from ——. As you may imagine, it is a great comfort to be really intimate with so clever, good, and kind-hearted a person in a country like this, which, in spite of the great beauty of the scenery, is desolate enough to live in. After the novelty has passed off, there is a sense of extreme dreariness here. Like the beauty of the day when the chilly nights come on, so vanish all your thoughts of trying to be content, directly your day's work or your day's expedition is over, and you heartily hate the place and long to be at home. Then the climate is so changeable, that a sense of its danger must always create a sort of melancholy, and aversion to remain a day longer than is positively necessary. In the morning, or even in the afternoon, when you start on a short journey, the brightest sunshine and the freshest breeze make you exclaim, "What *can* be finer or healthier than this?" A change in the wind, or a few minutes after sunset, sends you shivering home with every symptom of a sore-throat, and pains in every limb. You put your hand up to your forehead and find a few drops of cold water quietly trickling down. However, these symptoms are more felt on first arriving. We are now not nearly so sensitive to changes of temperature as we were, and better understand to manage our clothing, always carrying cloaks when frying in the sun, that they may be ready for the cold of three hours after. The weather has been oppressively close and hot these three weeks; but last night we heard the wind come roaring down from the Black Sea; violent rain followed, and *it is* winter this morning. Edmund had to go to Ortakioy, and it looked so threatening that I made him promise to stay all night, and am glad to have done so, for it is now just about the time he will have arrived at his friend's house, and the storm is frightful—the Bosphorus like a raging sea, the waves dashing right over the stone pathway against the houses. Not a caique could venture out. I have just been watching a man-of-war's boat with sixteen rowers and a sail, trying to reach the shore, which they have done with great difficulty. A part of the French fleet is anchored just off here, and also several Sardinian vessels. I was going down to Kandelij to-day, but think it more prudent to remain at home. The Sardinian Commodore here, Signor di Negri, kindly offered to bring me up his little steamer, rather than that I should be disappointed; but the wind increases every moment, and for mere pleasure, one would not brave what, they say, the Bosphorus *can* do.

I told you what gentlemanly, well-informed men the Sardinian officers are. This Signor di Negri is a delightful acquaintance. I now speak Italian with fluency, holding long conversations, and find it of great use, especially amongst the Greeks, most of whom understand it sufficiently to get you what you want. It is wonderful to see how completely the Greeks put us to shame with respect to languages; they speak several foreign ones as a matter of course, while we generally think so much of it.

I am very glad, as it happens, that we are not to winter at Pera. The streets are so crowded that it is easy enough even to murder in the confusion of dusk, with no lights and a broken-up pavement. A French officer was stabbed coming out of the Opera-house three or four nights ago; another was knocked on the head and robbed of his watch, about six in the evening, in the streets of Pera. Both these unfortunate men died on the spot, and the murderers have not been discovered. The French are very angry, and insist on having guards of their own in all the streets, as the Turks will not be at the trouble of doing so. A band of Greek robbers, disguised as English sailors, and who speak English perfectly well, are known to infest Pera, and to have perpetrated many outrages and robberies. It is confidently said that the Turkish authorities know who they are very well, and could take them if they liked. However, the French are *now* bent on taking active measures; but it is as yet not safe to venture out at Pera after dark, unless armed and escorted. I am thankful that Edmund is not compelled to run the risk. I feel now so glad to be with him. I often think that, if he were alone, he might naturally be tempted to go to the Opera, bad as it is, and so run the double danger of assassins and night air. As it is, we are always in by sunset, and after a quiet chat with our present fellow-prisoners, Lady Robinson and Signor di Negri, or reading an hour after dinner, we go to our own room and talk of Edie and you all in England till bedtime. The hotel here is now nearly empty; there remain only the two I just mentioned, a lady, who is soon leaving for Scutari to join her husband, and Mr. Gisborne, who has been here since we first arrived—our long-standing, long-suffering colleague. Mr. Gisborne is on his way to Egypt (if he ever finishes his business here,) to get permission to establish a telegraph. But he is in despair with the Turks. What you could do in five hours in any other place, you may think yourself fortunate to get done here in five months.

I left off writing here yesterday, as Edmund had ridden back from Orta-kioy and was thoroughly soaked. Dry clothes and a cup of tea soon put him all right again, and in an hour he went in to dinner. Several travelers came in, terribly knocked about by the storm on the Black Sea and the Bosphorus, and we felt grateful enough to be safely housed. I suppose none of the French officers just arrived in Beicos Bay could get on shore, for we saw none of them at dinner.

Just as we had finished our second course, the dining-room door opened to admit an English officer, whose dripping cloak was taken by the waiters, and who sat down to the table, with great satisfaction, after having warmed his hands at the stove. The entrance of a Crimean hero at dinner-time would not be quietly taken as a matter of course in England as it is here. A few days ago a fine-looking French officer sat opposite to us at table. I was the only lady present, so he rose and most politely asked permission to wear his cap, as he was suffering from a severe cold. We thought he looked very melancholy, and Edmund talked to him. His only brother had died the day before of cholera at Yenekion. They had both fought in the Crimea together. He tried to bear it manfully, but it seemed as much as he could do, poor fellow! The Sardinians had the cholera amongst them at Yenekion; unfortunately, four or five were brought down from the Crimea, and care was not taken to keep them apart; it spread into the village and many died. We were walking there when these poor fellows were carried from their ship.

Of course no one went near Yenekion who could help it, when these cases of cholera were heard of. Even the caiquejees, in rowing up the Bosphorus, kept at a respectful distance. They say that the village is quite healthy now, and these wintry storms will keep all well. It is only amongst crowds that the cholera ever seems to break out, and the thing you most wonder at in seeing the hivelike clusters of houses where the poor live, is that they can live or breathe at all. Even in the streets of these villages you feel stifled; and the people throw dead animals into the Bosphorus, which, in calm and hot weather, smell dreadfully under the very doors and windows. I am sorry to say that the English, French, and even Sardinians, show them a bad example in this respect, for they throw overboard from the transports any animal which dies on board; and the quantity of these, from the great number of transports of the various commissariats, is considerable.

The beautiful walk by the seashore to Buyukdere was completely spoiled to us by this disgusting practice. At one time there were three or four dead horses, two cows, and several sheep, washing backward and forward on the shore. These were all from the English transports. Now that the Contingent is gone, we can take a pleasant morning's walk, and nothing can be more lovely. I hope by this time Mr. Bell has shown you some of his sketches, which are excellent, although no one can paint the Bosphorus. We are going to send home, on some safe opportunity, a few photograps of this place, which are about as good as a photograph of a beautiful face without its bright coloring.

LETTER XIII.

PALACE OF THE SULTAN AT BEGLER BAY—THE BOSPHORUS AFTER THE ATTACK ON SEBASTOPOL—DIFFICULTY OF TRANSACTING BUSINESS WITH A TURKISH MINISTRY—WRETCHED STATE OF TURKISH AFFAIRS—CAIQUEJEES, THEIR DRESS AND APPEARANCE—"BONO" AND "NO BONO"—A PROPOSED KIOSK AT ORTA-KIOY.

My dear Mother:

I have just returned from the opposite Asian shore, where I have again been exploring the palace built by the Viceroy of Egypt, and presented by him to the Sultan. It is unfinished and deserted, and will most probably be allowed to fall to the ground, after vast sums of money have evidently been lavished upon it. The doors were wide open, and a number of sheep and goats either gamboling about or dozing in the spacious hall. Many of the rooms are truly magnificent, with fine colored marble floors; but the painting, or rather daubing, of the walls and ceilings is the most tawdry and barbarous that can be conceived. The view on all sides is enchanting, and on all sides different; you turn from the lofty plane-trees of the Sultan's Valley and the wild hills of Asia, to a sea view of great extent. It was a fine sight here just after the attack on Sebastopol; the Bosphorus was literally crowded with ships; one day we counted, slowly steaming up, fifteen immense transports, French and English. To-day it was a south wind, and the full white sails of several ships had a most beautiful effect, slowly and majestically moving up between the dark green shores, the sky brilliantly tinted with rose color, and the water of its usual lovely blue.

Lady Robinson is as much charmed with this place as I am, and we take many pleasant excursions together. Edmund is getting anxious and dispirited at the very great difficulties he has to encounter with the Turkish ministry, and can seldom join us now; indeed it is impossible to conceive their corrupt, degraded, and shameful way of proceeding, unless actually before your eyes every day. It is harassing and heartless work, especially to an active-minded man, sitting day after day on a divan, smoking an immense chibouque, and dragging out a few words of business in a dreamy kind of way at intervals of about half an hour. The worst part is, that he and his colleague, after weeks of anxiety, feel that they have as yet gained nothing, and have only been *finessed* with. What must not Lord Stratford have borne in all the years he has been here! However, the Commission are fully resolved to be firm, and to do their best to prevent the money of the loan being spent on diamond necklaces or new slaves; although it is certainly said here that long before the arrival of the gold, certain members of the Turkish ministry had obtained advances from their Saraffs at high interest, in anticipation of their share of the plunder. A Greek banker, supposed to be one of the lenders, himself told us so, besides one or two other persons.

Every thing here is in the most deplorable state; the Sultan is deeply in debt, even at the bazaars, for the dress and jewels of his numerous seraglio, yet he still persists in spending vast sums in building new palaces and making presents. The public buildings, once revered mosques and fountains, are wretchedly dilapidated and neglected-looking; the soldiers, meagre, dejected, miserably clothed, and worse armed. Edmund heard at the Porte the other day that Omar Pasha had written to the Seraskier (Minister of War), bitterly complaining that for many months his troops had received no pay, and were beginning to get dispirited and doubtful of his promises, which was most unfortunate just at a moment when their services might be required. On investigation it was discovered that the general had written twice before, that a large sum of money had been remitted which he had never received, and that the receipt, apparently in his handwriting, had been forged.

This must have been done by some one placed very near him it is said, but no inquiry has been made as to the guilty person. Major Fellowes was saying, the other day, that English officers ought to be appointed to pay the Turkish soldiers, as it is notorious that for months the poor fellows are cheated in the most daring manner by Turkish officers high in command. The Turkish soldier is in general profoundly ignorant, with no idea of reckoning; if the paymaster gives him five shillings instead of five pounds, he takes them silently—only he becomes in time dispirited. Their commissariat also cheat them in the most heartless and disgraceful manner; but, though done in the broad face of day, these things are unnoticed here. All officials being corrupt, a man who robs by hundreds or even thousands, is not likely to place any check upon the crowds of paltry pilferers below him. To shame, a Turkish ministry is perfectly indifferent; and from all one hears, the restoration of Mehemet Ali is a new proof of this. What he must be, to be distinguished for vice and cruelty here, it is difficult for an English mind to conceive. Although the Sultan's brother-in-law, he is but just recalled from banishment, and reinstated in his post of Capitan Pasha, or Lord High Admiral. He was once a slave and a butcher-boy. Sultan Mahmoud happened to see and take a fancy to him, and gave him an appointment in the palace.

One thing which strikes you here is the vast superiority of the poor over the rich. The poor are really the aristocracy of the country, both physically and morally. For his dignified bearing and manners, a poor man might be an emperor: he is honest, laborious, and most abstemious. A year or two of "place" under this disgraceful system, and the curious turns of fortune here, enervate and degrade him in body and mind. There seems no honest work for honest men to do, except to rear a few grapes and melons, to row a caique, or bear heavy burdens on their backs. The whole system is one of bribery and corruption, and a "place" can only be kept by doing as others do. The most amusing thing is that the Turks boast of the fine code of laws, which they certainly possess, and which is about of as much use to the wretched people as the Queen's jewels in the Tower are to our village belles on May-day.

Colonel Hinde, who is well acquainted with all classes here, was saying the other day that the respectable people were the caiquejees, the hamals, and the banditti, who are usually those that have been driven "to the mountains" by some act of cruelty and oppression. Of the latter I cannot give an opinion, not having yet had the pleasure of making the acquaintance of any of them. The caiquejees are the most magnificent men in the world, sunburnt of a fine bronze color. Their summer dress is a wide-sleeved jacket and trousers of white Broussa gauze (something between a thick gauze and muslin), which contrasts well with the scarlet fez and its large purple silk tassel. Here and there are seen one or two of the old school, with turban and fine long beard, which adds greatly to the nobility and picturesqueness of their appearance.

There is one particularly grand-looking old man, whom I often notice at Tophana. He wears a green turban, showing him to be a descendant of the Prophet, and has a silvery beard, which makes it difficult not to bow to him as to some ancient hero. He certainly might be Sultan Amurath, or Murad of the "great soul, patient of labors," moving about silently amongst his people again.

I cannot discover that the caiquejees have any songs peculiar to themselves, like those of Venetian gondoliers, or the Neapolitan fishermen. Their voices in speaking, especially those of the Turks, are very rich and sonorous; but, to our ears, all voices, in this country in singing are far from melodious. I often hear them chanting in a minor key, but it is harsh, monotonous, and grating.

The caiquejees seem to be generally quiet, peaceable men; but when they *do* quarrel before our windows, their torrent of anger is something marvelous. Resting on their oars, a few yards apart, they pour forth an avalanche of wrath with the most inconceivable rapidity and violence; the long sentences seeming to have no resting-places, where you could throw in the tenth part of a comma, or even take breath. The storm usually subsides, just as those on the Bosphorus itself, as suddenly as it came on, and each gentleman rows majestically on his way, looking calm and unruffled as usual. Although so strong and muscular, a crust of brown bread, and a melon or bunch of grapes, is their usual summer repast, with an occasional dish of pilauf—*i. e.*, rice boiled with a few tomatoes to color it, and mixed with scraps of meat.

Some of them, especially the Greeks, speak a little Italian or French; but signs, "bono," or "no bono," (nobody condescends to say "b*u*ono"), and "Johnny," does every thing here since the war began. I heard one of them say to an English officer the other day, "Coom Johnny!" in a most persuasive manner, and "Johnny" threw himself discontentedly into the painted and gilt caique, calling it a "confounded egg-shell," and not seeming at all happy in the arrangement of his long legs and great sword.

This is our last week at Therapia. The steamers cannot always run in the winter; a caique would be impossible in stormy weather; and, as there are no roads, it would be much too far for Edmund to ride night and morning to his "chambers" at Stamboul. So we have taken a pretty little kiosk, half-way up the hill of Orta-kioy, a village about seven miles from Constantinople; and I shall soon be launched into all the difficulties of English housekeeping in the East. We have bought Colonel Pitt's kit and pack-saddle; a few tables and chairs, a kettle, saucepans, plates, etc., from Pera, of an intelligent little German there; nice mattresses and pretty quilts from the bazaar at Stamboul; Turkish coffee-cups in their tiny stands; chibouques with amber mouthpieces; a nargileh, and a little brasier for charcoal. This, with a divan, and a lovely view of the Bosphorus, will be indeed charming—a kind of perpetual pic-nic. General Beatson's little daughters have given me their three pretty canaries, which have been camping it at the Dardanelles with them all the summer, and are exceedingly tame. I told you that the general, with a glittering staff of Bashi-Bazouks, has been staying here; and how sorry I was when Mrs. Beatson and her charming little girls left for Malta. They were so kind and gentle indoors, that one could scarcely believe them to be the same children who rode the most fiery Arab horses over the Osmanli camp, to the surprise and admiration of their father's wild troops, who positively adored them.

Although there are many discomforts in living this kind of camp life at an hotel, I shall be sorry to leave Therapia—gay, beautiful, sparkling Therapia—for a half-burnt-down Turkish village. Lord and Lady Stratford de Redcliffe are very kind to us; and there are several English people here whom we know, and our Sardinian commodore, and good Doctor Zohrab, and Madame Baltazzi's beautiful garden, in which I often stroll with her, and the walk to Buyukdere, with the white tents and little red flags looking down on one from the hills, reminding one of pleasant days at Chobham, and "church" on Sunday mornings at the hospital with the poor invalid soldiers. How much more there always seems to be to leave in a place, just as you are going!

LETTER XIV.

REMOVAL TO ORTA-KIOY—VOYAGE—ROUGH SEA—ARRIVAL—DIFFICULTIES—ARMENIAN NEIGHBORS—FIRE-GUNS AT NIGHT—ROLL OF DRUMS AND DISCHARGE OF MUSKETRY AT THE SULTAN'S PALACE AT DAYBREAK.

Orta-kioy, November 24th, 1855.

My dear Mother:

I must tell you something of our grand "move" from Therapia. We paid our visits of adieu, and then packed up, with stout but misgiving hearts, agreeing that whatever might happen to us, nothing could be so bad as the noise, and terrible expense of the hotels in this time of war, especially for a continuance.

Unfortunately, on the morning we were to start, Edmund had an unforeseen appointment at Stamboul; so I must start alone, we thought; for "our Commodore," Signor di Negri, who had kindly offered to put me in his beautiful little steamer, baggage and all, was obliged to go cruising about in the Black Sea, to look for a vessel from Balaklava, which, it was reported, had gone down in the late storm, with all the Sardinian invalids on board, who were returning home. This, I regret to say, has turned out to be too true. Poor Signor di Negri is sadly grieved about his fellow-officers and countrymen.

It was a very stormy morning. I said good-by to Lady Robinson, who was starting for England with her invalid son. He came down sick from the Crimea after the taking of Sebastopol, when all the previous anxiety and excitement was over, and many broke down. He had slept in the trenches the night before the attack, fearing that from weakness caused by fever, he should be unable to return when his time came round again, and giving his cloak to a poor wounded soldier, had a relapse himself, in consequence of exposure to the chilly night-air. He has suffered very much here, and certainly needed his mother's devoted nursing. This morning he was lying on the sofa, dressed, the first time for weeks, in regimentals, which hung loosely upon him, and trying to recover from the fatigue of getting up, before the caique should come to put them on board ship for England, and the home which they were so anxious to reach, after much suffering and anxiety. We were glad, and yet so sorry, to see them off.

The Bosphorus was rough, and it looked so stormy that I felt a little anxious about my voyage to Orta-kioy, short as it was. Hovever, Edmund found me a kind and efficient escort; so we started,—Edmund mounted on Turk, and bound for Stamboul; M—— and I in a two-oared caique; our luggage, including the much-prized "kit," in Signor Patela's Maltese boat, manned by two sturdy Greeks, and the white sail set. The canaries, being Bashi-Bazouks, and accustomed to move about, seemed to enjoy the fun; but, tell Edith, my poor little Turkish goldfinch fluttered, and spoiled his gay wings sadly.

We got on very well for some distance, the wind being in our favor; but the Bosphorus was angry indeed, and in one of the strong currents, "snap" went an oar. I was glad enough not to be alone. M——

was very angry that the men had not the usual spare one; and when it was too late, we noticed the leaky and crazy state of the caique. The weather looked still more threatening, and as Therapia was yet in sight, M—— ordered the boatmen to turn back; but the wind had increased so much, that it would have been difficult, even with the two pairs of oars, to have rowed against that and the current too. So nothing remained but to follow the dancing white sail of the little Maltese boat, now far before us, and to pull on toward Orta-kioy. M—— assured me that he was a first-rate swimmer; and in case of our being upset, I fixed upon a nice strong piece of his coat, on which we agreed that I should hold fast and quietly while he swam ashore. He swims in the Bosphorus every morning, and knows its rapid and treacherous currents well; but it was not fated on this day that we should dance on the waves together. However, we got wet enough notwithstanding cloaks; for two dark clouds, tired of hanging over the cypresses of Kandelji, threw themselves precipitately from the Asian hills into the Bosphorus. In western language, there was a tremendous shower.

Our caique was half filled, and ourselves completely drenched. You must know that we had an umbrella, and that, sitting at the bottom of the boat, as one does here, we ought not to have got so wet, about the shoulders at least; but M—— is in love, quite hopelessly, and quite "in secret." Whether the rain made him more desponding or not, I do not know. It is very hard, but, wet or dry, people always make me their *confidante* in these matters. M—— wrapped me kindly in his cloak, then, pulling it so as to let all the water in, and sighing like Romeo himself, began to tell me his sad story, to which I listened with an interest not even interrupted by a wave dashing the spray into our faces now and then, or a little stream of water pouring into my shoe. But at one part of the relation of his outraged feelings, I visibly shuddered, and my pity filled his handsome Greek eyes with tears. He was holding the umbrella on one side—infatuated youth!—and a threadlike stream of ice-cold water was trickling down the back of my neck. In another quarter of an hour, the story and the shower-bath were both over, and we landed in brilliant susnhine, on the little wooden quay of Orta-kioy, where, among caiquejees mopping and drying their caiques, and a few Turks, with rich-colored turbans, quietly mending their nets, or fishing with a line twined round the hand, stood our kind friend, Mr. Barker, who had come to greet and welcome me, thinking I might be alone. We stopped a moment to admire the beautiful snow-white mosque, with two minarets, which the sultan has just built here; and then, through the filthiest village I had yet seen, looking still more desolate from having been half burnt down about a year ago, and not yet rebuilt; the bakers still selling their bread under dripping and ragged tents, and the wild dogs snapping and shivering in the ruins of the houses, we toiled up the hill.

For a moment my spirits fell, and I thought to myself: "How long will it be our fate to live in this wretched place?" However, when we arrived at the pretty little house, shut-in in a nice garden, it did not seem so bad. Mr. Barker and I went in, while M—— kindly saw that the Maltese boat gave up its load in safety to the hamals, who were soon seen toiling up the hill with the cherished "kit," etc., on their backs, our canaries, portmanteaus, and the goldfinch.

The Greek maid, Calliope, had arrived, all smiles and chatter. She was recommended to us by a Greek lady of our acquaintance, who declares that the sister, Diamanti, now living with her, is also a "treasure." I did not much like the look of her, although she certainly improves a little on acquaintance.

After changing what I could of my wet garments, I took a survey of what had arrived from Pera. First of all, no provisions; not one thing of the list I had made a week ago; no tables, no chairs, no linen, no cook. It was "supposed," smilingly, by Calliope, that that functionary had been offered higher wages, and had gone to the Crimea, where he had been before with a French general. Calliope was worse than useless, and said that she would not go into that miserable-looking Turkish village alone for the world. She is from Smyrna.

I was in great distress at the thought of Edmund coming home after a hard day's work, and finding nothing ready. Our bedding was the only thing that had arrived, and Mr. Barker kindly sallied forth to look for an Armenian Jew of the village, who professed a little carpentering. When he was gone, in stalked, up the stairs, into the salaamlik where I was, slipshod and in single file, the Armenian lady next door, to whom the house belongs, two daughters, and three sons, who each saluted me after the Eastern fashion, touching the lips and forehead: which means, metaphorically, "I gather up dirt, I eat it, and cast it on my head, in sign of submission and respect to you."

I motioned with my hand to the divan, upon which, with many bows and much ceremony, they at last seated themselves all in a row. I don't know whether they spoke Turkish or Armenian, and it signified little to me, who could not understand one single word of either.

It was certainly a trial of patience, with so much to do, to sit quietly and courteously to be stared at from head to foot, to have one's mantle, dress, and collar both felt and examined; and observations made thereon, both *vivâ voce* and translated in dumb-show to the three poor mutes, who nodded and grunted in a must distressing manner. I think I told you that three of the poor lady's children are dumb. I never felt more perplexed and uncomfortable in my life, and was glad when Mr. Barker came back; with no Jew however (for he had forgotten that it was Saturday), but much better still, he had brought his daughter, who speaks both English and Greek perfectly well. She was greatly concerned at my helpless condition; for Mistress Calliope had now put on a smart jacket, and twisted a gay Greek handkerchief round her thick plaits of hair, and was quietly seated on the divan, answering all the questions of the Armenian ladies about us. Kind Miss Barker soon gave her a hint that such behavior would never do with English people, and she presently condescended to stroll away. But still there was no one even to help me do a single thing; worst of all, nothing to eat when dinner-time came, and a dripping, ruined village beneath our windows, which looked as if a mouse might easily starve there.

At last, to my great joy, I saw Mr. Grace's man-servant coming up the hill, sent most kindly by his master to us from Kandelij. He had got a basket, "in case our provisions should not have arrived," containing wine, coffee, nice rolls, and several other things for luncheon. But still more welcome were his intelligent, working face, and his three languages.

First of all he dispatched the Armenians, told Calliope that she had better prevent me from lifting things about myself, than sit chattering there, helped me to unpack the kit and portmanteaus, lighted the kitchen charcoal-stoves, and then sallied forth into the village. To look into the basket on his return from that heap of ruins was "*pro-di-gi-ous.*" First of all, a dish of fine red mullet, then an excellent fowl, a tiny leg of mutton, weighing about three pounds and a half, some delicious vegetables, grapes, and pomegranates, and a bunch of sweet autumn flowers.

When Edmund came home, he found an excellent little dinner (at which our good genius and the now smiling Calliope waited), and the salaamlik quite gay. We had borrowed a good-sized table from the Armenian lady, and a smaller one, on which stood the flowers in a Turkish vase, and the little "Bashi-Bazouks" singing merrily. I had a camp-stool to myself, and Edmund sat like a Turk on the divan. We afterward had some coffee in one of the tin mugs of our beloved kit, and then made up as good a kind of gipsy encampment as we could for the night, on the divans of the different rooms. Calliope melted into tears at the departure of our excellent Greek ally, who, when he had done all he could for us returned in his caique to Kandelij.

At night, just as I was going to sleep, the windows shook with the heavy report of a cannon. My first thought was of Russian ships having passed the entrance of the Bosphorus; but I soon recollected the fire-guns of which I had heard. The heavy crash of seven of them, at regular intervals of a few seconds, broke on the quiet night; and then the peculiar wailing cry of the watchmen, in different parts of the village, announcing fire, and the striking of their staves on the stones close by our door, effectually banished sleep for some time. Before dawn the Armenian watchmen chanted to prayers at the doors of the latticed house opposite, and of those above us. It is a peculiar, wailing chant in the minor, and strikes one as intensely melancholy at first; one of them begins, I am told: "Prayer is better than sleep." Then, just as darkness is fading into the pale, gray light of daybreak, the discharge of musketry and the roll of drums is plainly heard from the Sultan's palace at Teheran, followed by some lively Turkish airs with drums and fifes. This announces that the "Commander of the Faithful" is rising to prayers; and soon the powerful chant of the Muezzin is heard, pealing up the valley from the minarets below. You can scarcely imagine how strange it seems to be surrounded by such unfamiliar sounds, especially in the night time.

LETTER XV.

ORTA-KIOY—SERVANTS—ARMENIAN LADIES—WORKWOMEN—VILLAGERS—HOUSE AND GARDENS—ARMENIAN COOKING—VILLAGE OF BEBEC—FRUIT AND FOOD—HIGH PRICES—PERA—STATE OF CRIME.

Orta-kioy, November 24th, 1855.

My dear Mother:

I must now tell you about our second day here. Edmund rode early into Pera, promising to inquire as to the fate of our missing goods and chattels; and after he was gone, I tried to inspire Calliope with a wish to make our really pretty little house look a degree less wretched. Fortunately she speaks Italian indifferently well.

After finishing unpacking, I went into the dining-room, to look for something left there the night before. Neglected and dusty, in a corner, stood a dingy grand-pianoforte, bought in the old Armenian lady's prosperous days, as she afterward told me. I opened it, and found with great delight that it was not yet quite tuneless. I had sung about half my cantata, when, from the perfect silence and emptiness of the house, it seemed as if I had exorcised a host of strange beings; for, flourishing a pair of huge iron pincers in one hand and some strange-looking instrument in the other, with the wildest and most discordant gruntings and gestures you can conceive, in rushed Simione, one of the dumb and elfish-looking Armenians. What he wanted of course I could not at all imagine—whether he asked leave to cut off my head (I was certainly not like a white cat), or to pull out all my teeth. However, I thought it best to seem agreeable, and out of the room my visitor rushed, nodding violently, and grunting as perseveringly as usual. Presently he returned with a Turk, carrying a basket of tools, who saluted me, and spoke some very magnificent, but to me perfectly unintelligible, sentences in Turkish.

Was ever poor creature so perplexed as I! Calliope had entirely disappeared. Well, up-stairs these worthies went, I thinking it as well to follow. Off they threw all the things on my poor camp-bed. It was merely to make a little piece of ironwork secure, which had been broken the night before, in putting up. This was a great relief to my feelings, and I could not help laughing at the absurd position in which ignorance of a language places one.

While the Armenian was grunting in his strange way and making signs to the Turk, who was getting angry at my not taking *his* side of the question on being appealed to, in walked again the Armenian lady and her daughter. They had with them a villainous-looking Jew, in a large turban and tattered Eastern garments, about whom they began making extraordinary signs and grimaces.

I shall certainly go distracted here, thought I. At last I comprehended that this gentleman offered his services to clean our windows, and, holding up my fingers, I made out the number of piastres he *asked*, and, from the old lady, how many to *give*, which was quite a different thing. He cleaned two panes but imperfectly, and then slipped away without asking for any thing. I suppose he was vexed at not obtaining double the proper price. I was almost out of patience with the Armenian ladies, who again seated themselves on the divan, and again seemed to find the greatest satisfaction in looking at me. I made signs that I would search for Calliope to interpret, and crossed the little garden into the kitchen.

There was an old Armenian woman of the village, who had taken up her quarters until the cook should arrive. She was dressed in very picturesque rags, and had thick plaits of hair bound round her fez. I was rash enough to attempt showing her by signs how the "Inglesi" liked chops cut, etc. All I got for my pains was a patronizing smile, and "Bono Johnny—bono!" with a fat hand stroking down my back as if I had been her cat. I could not stand this; and, after inquiring for Calliope, and getting for answer a shake of the head, decamped with the utmost precipitation.

Presently the young lady returned, and informed me that feeling it dull (*troppo tristo*), she had been to pay a visit to Mrs. Barker's maid, Espina, who was delighted to see her; then entering into a lively conversation with the Armenian ladies, she took them into my room, and showed them my English dresses, dressing-case, etc. At last, to my great relief, they departed, with many salaams; and I am happy to say, that it is as Miss Barker assured me it would be—"that when they had thoroughly stared at me, and seen all the English things, even to the reels of cotton, which I possessed, their curiosity would subside, and my torments be over." So I took courage again, and began to hope that in time I might get a little peace.

These last two days have made a difference in the

appearance of our little kiosk. Three hamals came toiling up the hill the other morning, and to my great satisfaction battered at the ponderous knocker of our garden-door. They had at last brought up a caique-load of furniture from Pera. Nobody thinks of asking why things are delayed here, so we took them in, and were thankful. Our salaamlik really looks very pretty.

Edmund bought me a piece of chintz and plenty of white muslin, at the bazaar at Stamboul, and I at last shamed Calliope by setting resolutely at work to cover the divans and hem the curtains. The village women here seem to be perfectly uneducated, and there was no such thing as a workwoman at Orta-kioy. Perhaps, after waiting for weeks, we might have secured the services of a French upholsterer from Pera, at a great expense; but you at once see that the only plan is to help yourself in every way as much as possible, unless you have a complete staff of your own, which all large families, whether Turkish, Greek, Armenian, or European, have. It is difficult to get good servants here. The *educated* ones are very clever, and ask high wages, especially during the war. The mass, as I have said, are perfectly ignorant, and almost useless to civilized people. However, their lives and ways are so utterly different from ours, that it always seems rather absurd to me to hear the English complain of them. Give them their pilauf, their old divan, a little sunshine under a ragged vine in summer, and a brass pan full of charcoal in winter, and *voilà tout.* All articles of clothing are bought ready-made, and made by men, in the bazaars; the national shirt, of Broussa gauze admits of and requires but little washing; consequently workwomen and washerwomen are not indigenous to the soil, although no doubt the increasing taste for dressing in the European fashion, among the higher class of Greeks and Armenians, will soon make them so. The people of the villages seem very hopeless and helpless, and care to do nothing. Certainly their wants are but few, but how they live is a marvel; for you see them silently sitting in a moldy shop, in which there is nothing to sell.

As I told you, the lower part of this village has been burnt down, and many of the people are still living, with their children, alternately scorched by the sun and drenched by wind and rain, in wretched tents among the ruins, where they may remain for months and years, or until they are all carried off by some epidemic, for nobody cares for them here. Across these moldering ruins, where the dogs howl most horridly at night, and melancholy-looking Jews and Armenians stalk by day, we have a lovely peep of the Bosphorus, its shores fringed with palaces.

The two beautiful white minarets of the Sultan's mosque are illuminated to-night, and look very pretty, wreathed with lamps round the little balustrade, on which the Muezzins appear three times a day to call the Faithful to prayer. They shine on beauty and splendor enough on one side, and on poverty, dirt, and ruin on the other. This place certainly makes one's heart ache.

Simione, the dumb Armenian, has been very busy in the garden to-day, moving his orange and lemon trees, tree-geraniums, jasmines, and acacias, into the little conservatory for the winter. I am delighted to say that he has allowed me to choose as many as I please, to be considered mine; so I have lined the salaamlik, and the little room beyond (which has a charming view of Scutari), with trees, six or seven feet high, and bearing both fruit and flowers. Our floors are covered with matting from Alexandria, and here and there a Turkish rug or two is thrown down by the divan. My muslin curtains and blinds shut out as much as possible of the ruins, and only let in, by some of our numerous windows, the opposite hills of Asia, and the blue water, and the minarets. So I wish you could see how pretty our rooms are, with embroidered cloths from Stamboul over our deal tables, the vase of beautiful Eastern flowers, and Edmund's amber-mouthed chibouques. Our stock of books is very small, and, except for an occasional chance of borrowing one, there are none to be got here, so pray send me a few, should an opportunity offer—not forgetting the Arabian Nights, and Mr. Meredith's Eastern Tales, which I hear are very charming. We now get the "Spectator" every week with our letters; and news from England and from home, make a very happy evening. In the midst of so much that is pleasant however, I must admit that we are half-starved. The cook whom we had engaged has really started off to the Crimea, where they are getting eight pounds a month, and the old Armenian woman makes us positively sick. Yesterday she mashed up some lamb in fat, and we were only able to shake out a few small pieces with a fork, just as dogs do a hot bit with their noses. She evidently thought this dish a triumph, and asked inquiringly and tenderly, "Bono Johnny?" I was sorry to be obliged to reply most decidedly and with a gesture of disgust, "No bono." If we were only near the bazaars, we might at least feed upon pilauf and cabeb. If Red-jacket (whose Armenian name is unpronounceable) would only let me alone, I might manage to cook something myself; there is a beautiful frying-pan with a folding handle in our kit; but to stand an incessant torrent of Greek while hanging over a charcoal-stove, to be called "Bono Johnny," and to be patted on the back, is more than my philosophy can well put up with. However, we have heard of a very good cook, who is leaving an officer at Scutari, and whom we hope to secure.

Here the men-servants go out to buy every morning. Mrs. Barker kindly allows her man to do so for me, and he gives a written account of the number of piastres spent. Strangers of course are very easily cheated, but old inhabitants know pretty well what the price of things should be, and the buyers cannot make much by their morning's work, although it is said they almost invariably do a little. Meat is now about eight piastres the "oke," *i. e.* two pounds and a half English weight; tea, as in England; coffee, very cheap. The Turkish bread is made of leaven, and to my taste extremely nasty. It is made up into various shapes; sometimes into huge loaves, or flat, like pancakes, or in wreaths, and scattered over with a kind of caraway-seed, when it is called *semeet.*

We have heard of an American missionary baker at the village of Bebec, near here, and some day I shall take a caique and go in search of him; especially as Bebec is one of the most picturesque villages on the Bosphorus. Vegetables and fruit are very cheap, and, even in this miserable village, the stalls in the narrow and filthy "street" are prettily laid out in a morning. Here too, in large baskets, one sees the fish of the Bosphorus in singular variety:—red mullet, sword-fish, turbot, soles, beautiful little mackerel; and the shining, many-colored "enchanted fish," of which I have told you before, besides several others. Snails, of a light brown color, are very much eaten here by the Greeks, and huge baskets of them are sold every morning. Sometimes one sees an unfortunate tortoise carried along by a wisp of straw or grass. He is to be made soup of on a Greek fast-day, and has been found fast asleep in a vineyard. The melon-stalls are usually the most crowded, and immense piles of every shape and color are quickly sold. Brown bread, melons, and grapes, seem to be the principal food of the poor; coffee, yahoort (a kind of sour milk), lemonade, and sherbet, are sold in every corner of the street for them. The buying every thing prepared in public, no doubt makes the Eastern women so helpless, and so little domestic. One sees even the caiquejees and hamals eating their pilauf, and sipping their coffee at the cafanées, or smoking on comfortable divans inside, or on benches by the door. In fact, it is quite "club life" for the men, and a neglected, idle and useless one for the poor women—at least, according to our notions. But I must say adieu, for my fingers are very cold and stiff, and there is no such thing as a fireplace in the house. Calliope brought me a pan of charcoal just now, but it made my head ache, and I was obliged to send it away. Here the natives luxuriate round a *mangale*, *i. e.* a square table with a rail round the bottom, on which to place the feet: under the table is placed a pan of charcoal, and spread over all, a thick Turkish quilt. Those accustomed to the fumes of charcoal think a *mangale* very pleasant. I sat by one the other day, and soon felt very ill indeed.

The moment a storm comes on here now, it is winter at once. Last week the weather was sultry, and a slight shock of earthquake was felt at Broussa, Pera, and even Therapia. The wind changed suddenly to the north; and I now look despairingly at our little stove, which lies in the room before me, without much hope of ever getting it put up. We bought a large caique-load of wood yesterday: it is frightfully dear since the war. Nothing seems to be *restored* here; everybody cuts, and nobody plants, about Constantinople, which makes the hills so bare of any thing but cypress, except in the gardens of the Pasha. Great quantities of wood are brought down from the shores of the Black Sea, in those ancient-looking Greek feluccas which I told you of. All our acquaintances here tell us that we shall never be able to stand the sharp winter winds in a kiosk with thin wooden walls; but that remains to be seen. Any thing to me would be better than being shut up in the crowds, dirt, and noise of Pera. Besides which the rent of the filthiest houses is something enormous. All the cavalry are coming down; an "Opera" is opened, and they say it will be very gay. We do not hear much about the war now: nothing more is to be done until next year. Those in the Crimea are preparing to pass the winter as comfortably and as warmly as they can, and the sick and wounded are being sent home as expeditiously as possible. We saw the Duke of Newcastle the other day at Lord Stratford's; he is very earnestly collecting all possible information about the war and its conduct.

Pera is in a dreadful state of confusion. Ruffians and outcasts of all kinds have increased a hundredfold since the war began. There are no police or guards of any kind, and murders and all sorts of outrages are perpetrated in the crowded streets even by day, and still more in the utter darkness and confusion of the nights. You will see in the papers, no doubt, an account of a fight which took place a day or two ago between some French and Tunisian soldiers, in which one or two were killed and several wounded. The French instantly marched two regiments into Stamboul, without waiting to ask leave of the Turkish government. Every one thinks them in the right; if the Turks will not prevent murder, the Allies must. Soldiers, missed from their barracks at night, are constantly found stabbed in the morning, in the cemeteries and other places where they have been surprised and waylaid. Another French officer was stabbed on the Bridge of Boats yesterday, and it is feared that his wound will prove mortal. An English clergyman, walking quietly along, was also wounded in the arm, but it appears that, happily, the dagger missed its aim.

These crimes of revenge, it is said, are perpetrated by the Sciote Greeks, who, since the massacre of Scio, of course entertain great feelings of hatred and animosity toward the Turks, and are indignant at the Allies for helping them in their present struggle with the Russians. The band of Greek "sailors" who have committed so many enormities, still roam at large, and scarcely a day passes without a new outrage being heard of. Yesterday morning the shop of a poor Turk at Galata was observed to be shut up after the usual hour; it had been ransacked in the night, and its master cruelly murdered. Mr. Grace, a merchant here, was going to dine at Mysseri's with some friends an evening or two ago; at about seven he entered his counting-house, where he had made arrangements to dress, his country-house being at a distance. The place had only been left by his people an hour before, yet, in broad daylight, he found every thing gone that could be easily carried off, without the slightest alarm having been made, or the slightest possible clue given.

Many of the members of this formidable band of Greeks speak, I am told, English and French perfectly well. No effort is made to capture them; indeed it is well known that the Turkish (so-called) guards, wherever they may be, are so miserably paid and so completely demoralized, that each thief shares with them a certain amount of his plunder, consequently the last thing the robbers think of is being taken by the "authorities."

I always hear the clatter of my husband's horse's hoofs on his return of an evening, with a sensation of relief, especially knowing how highly incensed several Turkish dignitaries are with both himself and his colleague for their endeavors to prevent the Loan from falling into their hands.

Last night the Muezzins had long called to evening prayer before his return, and I began to feel rather nervous and lonely, watching the lengthening shadows, and then the lights in the valley, and listening to unfamiliar Greek, as Calliope sat whispering with the Armenian woman by the garden-door.

LETTER XVI.

WINTER ON THE BOSPHORUS—OUR ARMENIAN NEIGHBORS—QUESTIONS AND ANSWERS—TURKISH REGULATION OF TIME—THE WINTER THEATRE IN THE CRIMEA—ZOUAVE MODISTES.

Orta-kioy, November 28th, 1855.

My dear Mr. Hornby:

Now that our household arrangements are completed—and we are as well settled for the winter as is possible in this barbarous country—I shall find more time to write you letters, which you will read by your comfortable fireside in England.

After the beauty of scenery, and pleasantness of out-door life here in summer-time is over, the approach of winter scares one; just as it would a merry picnic party, all clad in spring garments, on our hills, could it peep in unexpectedly on them. Certain it is, that we never truly value what we have until it is lost to us. In a comfortable house, in a pretty drawing-room in England, one sometimes feels dull, wearied with every-day life, and longing for more stirring incident; but when the novelty of a strange Eastern country is once over—when your head is tired, and when your heart wants something to dwell on with pleasure—when your feet are cold and the tips of your fingers blue, because you cannot choose between being made sick with a pan of charcoal, or being half suffocated by a badly-contrived stove—when you cannot move in the streets for rivers of filth, and the beautiful Bosphorus is too rough to venture out on it in your egg-shell caique—when you can't make up your mind to have every bone shaken out of its proper place in a teleki (which jolteth and crasheth cruelly and remorselessly along at the rate of two miles an hour,)—when you cast a glance at your three books on the table, read three times over, and feel with despair that there is no probability of getting others for many a long day—when there blows a north wind from the Black Sea, driving wrecks down before your windows, and flakes of snow through the thin wooden boards of your kiosk—when the pilauf is waiting and nobody returns to dinner, and you think of nightly murders and robberies in the dark streets of Pera—*then* you look back with a perfect rapture of regret on blazing fire-places, safe roads, and lighted streets, protected at least from robbers. When you recollect that every sound we hear is strange, every custom we note different—when we are charmed to find that even a foreign tongue like Italian is, though imperfectly understood—when you remember that the Turks look upon our religion and manners with the greatest repugnance—you will not be surprised at the delight with which we receive letters, or the slightest token of a home, which shines to us out here like a distant Paradise.

Seeing the frightful political and social state of Eastern countries must make the coldest person in the world feel patriotic, and grateful too, for the comforts and the safety which we so carelessly enjoy in England. The human race has certainly a great aptitude for taking all good as a matter of course. The old Armenian lady next door often pays me a visit, and I fancy that our stay here quite cheers her dull and melancholy life. A widow in this country is pretty certain to be stripped of almost every thing, and this poor lady has a sad story to tell of houses and money taken from herself and children by the Turks under various pretenses. One of her dumb sons was sent to Italy in the days of their prosperity. He is exceedingly intelligent, writes Italian fluently, and with his assistance and interpretation my conversations with his mother and sisters are carried on.

I often wish you were present at these visits, which are really very amusing. The old lady, who is even now charming, and who must have been of the most regular and serene order of Armenian beauty, comes softly into my little drawing-room, two of her daughters following, and "Antonio" in the rear, pencil in hand, as interpreter. I rise, and we all bow, touching our lips and foreheads, with our fingers, after the manner of Eastern salutation. Then I motion them to take a seat on the divan, which the mother does, wrapping her large fur jacket around her, as she reclines in a comfortable corner. The young girls will not presume to sit with us, but timidly place themselves on the edges of stiff, uncomfortable American chairs. Antonio, after many persuasive signs, consents to take my camp-stool at a respectful distance; and I, from my little table, hand him a slip of paper, on which is written, in Italian, that I am very happy to see them, etc., etc. Antonio reads, bows, and then in dumb-show translates this with the utmost rapidity to his mother, who as rapidly replies to him. In another second I am told, in cramped and curious characters, that they all salute me, and thank me, and hope that I am happy and contented, etc. After this we gradually fall into more general conversation, and then the two pencils work away fast and furious. A large sheet of paper with the questions and answers is quite a curious document—questions about England, and London particularly, seeming without end. However, almost every thing is difficult for them to believe in; and yet I see that they trust me very much. Our excellent government—our schools and hospitals—our roads and paved and lighted streets—our shops where the *real* price is asked, and you are not obliged to spend the whole day bargaining for a shawl or gown—our just "Cadis" (magistrates,) who would *really* refuse five pounds as a bribe from a notorious ruffian to let him off, or two pounds for obligingly torturing an innocent person—are things almost above their comprehension.

However, I must say that my account of cabs at sixpence a mile was the *bouquet* (as they call the last and finest firework) of wonders which I showered upon them about England. Wonderingly the dark-eyed girl Dhudu looks at her mother, who raises her hands in her quiet and subdued astonishment. Oscu stops trilling her colomboyo, and signs to her brother, who writes for her: "If I were in your England, I might be well once more." Poor Oscu, I am afraid, is in a decline. I never beheld any human being so pale, and there is something peculiarly interesting about her. Her features are perfectly regular, her eyes large, soft, and deeply fringed with the blackest lashes, her head small and beautifully shaped; and her hair hanging down her shoulders in the marvelously long and thick plaits which one occasionally sees in this part of the world. She has been ill for three or four years. The Armenian doctor cannot find out what her complaint is; but, to ease his conscience by trying something, he frequently bleeds the poor pale thing in the foot.

Winter has regularly set in here. The rain is pouring down in torrents, and a rapid stream rushes from the hills through the middle of the steep road by the side of our house. When he cannot ride, Edmund, in high boots and water-proof poncho, gets down to the Pera steamer, which stops at the little wooden pier of the village, about nine in the morning. But as the Turks reckon time, and set their clocks and watches by the sun, of course the time of its arrival is always varying more or less; and, if not careful in your calculations from morning to morning, you either have to wait, or have the pleasure of seeing the dripping standard of the Crescent and Cross rapidly disappearing toward Stamboul.

We hear occasionally from the Crimea, and are excessively diverted by stories and scenes in camp life from some homeward-bound or "on leave" acquaintance. The military theatre there has been a source of great amusement, although the heroine was sometimes obliged to hurry the last scene a little in order to take her place in the trenches, and occasionally showed symptoms of nervousness in her attempts to keep her beard out of sight. I am told that the Zouaves are very expert at making up petticoats, caps, and other feminine garments, out of the most "novel materials." Of course a sailor danced a hornpipe between the acts, and of course a sailor sang "Wapping Old Stairs" with great applause, the Duke of Newcastle and many noted personages being present. The enemy's shells were rather troublesome in the early days of these performances, but altogether, the "Royal Theatre" was a most successful affair, and is still talked of with delight. I believe that another is proposed for this winter; but I shall hear all Crimean news when Mr. Evelyn returns, which we hope will be soon, for he is not yet strong enough to brave such severe weather "up in the front."

LETTER XVII.

DEATH OF MRS. WILLOUGHBY MOORE—FUNERAL OF A FRENCH SOLDIER—OUR TURKISH "ALLIES"—TURKISH VENALITY—PASHAS—THEIR LUXURY AND DISHONESTY—THE CADI—TURKISH CHARACTER.

Orta-kioy, December 3d, 1855.

My dear Mr. Hornby:

We saw Herbert Siborn yesterday, quite recovered, I am glad to tell you, from his late severe attack of fever. His men and horses had very uncomfortable quarters assigned them on their first arriving at Scutari; and fever was the consequence of his over-exertion and constant exposure to the sun. If he remains at Scutari, we hope he will be able to spend Christmas-day with us, as he did at Weybridge last year. Little did we imagine then that we should meet together here in the course of a few months. We can plainly see Scutari from our windows. You will be sorry to hear that poor Mrs. Willoughby Moore died there of dysentery last week, of course most deeply regretted by those whose sufferings she has relieved, and for whom she thought and labored night and day. Kind Lady Stratford was with her to the last, doing all she could. Day after day, in the stormiest weather, we have seen the embassador's caique beating its way over to the hospital at Scutari, as it did also, I am told, before Mrs. Moore went there, and when Lady Stratford was anxious that the sick and wounded soldiers should be better cared for. Poor Mrs. Moore was a woman of many sorrows.

Her husband, Colonel Moore, perished in a burning ship rather than leave his men; she had lost her only child and was left quite alone in the world, and then felt that the only thing which could make her endure life cheerfully, was to lessen the miseries of others. She said to a friend of mine just before she was taken ill, that had she been told some time ago that she could ever have felt as happy as she was at the hospital at Scutari, she could not have believed it. Her sufferings during her illness were very severe, but borne with the greatest fortitude and resignation. Many a poor fellow whom she has nursed and comforted, followed her to the grave. It was quite a day of mourning at Scutari.

Talking of funerals, Edmund stopped to take off his cap the other day, and to stand for a few minutes as the only mourner, by the grave of a poor French soldier, who was being buried at a roadside cemetery near Pera, no one attending but a priest, who hurried off after a short prayer, leaving the two Greek bearers to fling the poor fellow into strange earth, far from his country and friends. One sees many sad sights here, as well as novel ones, and it is very dispiriting to discover what a people these really are, after all they have cost us. As to gratitude, they detest us all the more for the humiliation of obligation. It is all very fine to talk of "alliance" in the newspapers or at public dinners, champagne in hand, and with the Crescent and Cross twining affectionately round the English standard and the Lilies of France. Depend upon it, that only from the most dire necessity will they ever tolerate our interference, and that East and West are not so far divided, as are our tastes, habits, and every natural tendency. However, there is a great deal of wisdom and refinement, after all, in their quiet lives, and there is no reason in the world why we should wish them to imitate us except in our *morale.* A Pasha dreams away life very pleasantly in his white marble palace, and shady gardens, and gently gliding caique. These are better than dinner-parties and balls, which some people call "civilization."

It is the means of getting these things—the worse than brigand way of going about it—which is so frightful here; indeed, it is difficult to express the painful impression made on the mind in this beautiful country on seeing its wretched state, and the open infamy of its rulers. It is notorious that most of the provincial judges live on the banks of the Bosphorus, expending in every luxury their monthly salaries of so many piastres. They sell or let their places to the highest bidder—often to some ignorant clerk or assistant in their own office, who may have saved a little money, and who extorts a living, by extra imposts or taxes on the unhappy people over whom he places himself as a tyrant, not to be dislodged until he can return, heavily laden with spoil, to Stamboul. A gentleman who has resided for many years in different parts of Asia Minor, and who takes the greatest interest in the fine and oppressed people of the country, tells me that he has known these men enter a village without a few piastres to pay for the hire of their two or three baggage-mules, and at the end of three or four years, leave it for a palace at Constantinople.

A short time ago a Pasha here murdered his wife under circumstances of the greatest atrocity. As she happened to be a Pasha's daughter, he was, singular to say, tried for the crime, and sentenced to the bagnio, or prison, and was actually sent there. However, a sentence of punishment to a Pasha who is rich is but a matter of form, and the individual to whom I allude is now generally supposed to be enjoying himself in one or other of the Greek islands.

It is seldom now that a Pasha of any rank loses his head, except it be through the successful intrigue of some reigning favorite; and then he is only murdered in his turn, with the same duplicity which he had practiced before, in getting rid of his equals in power. No Pasha is ever punished for murdering or robbing those in his power: that is considered as a matter of course. But the criminal I have mentioned, having murdered his wife instead of one of his slaves, was nominally sentenced to the bagnio, but really sent to "rule" and "govern" in the Greek island to which I have alluded —a fashionable way here of reproving Pashas who are not careful to manage their little affairs with more secrecy and address.

Mehemet Ali, the Capitan-Pasha, was originally a shop-boy at one of the bazaars; and many of the most "famous" pashas, from time immemorial, have risen from the same low station, or have been bought in the slave-market. Pleasing their masters, has advanced them step by step. Bearing false-witness with unblushing effrontery in some case of unjust seizure or frightful oppression, or in some daring intrigue on the part of their master to supplant a favorite, is a sure and certain road to favor and preferment. What we call education, talent, genius, is not marketable stuff here. Fanaticism, false-witness, calm cruelty, and above all, consummate falsehood and deceit, under a smiling, bland exterior, are the things requisite to make a Turkish favorite; these essentials to success are leading traits in the Eastern character. I heard a gentleman say, the other evening, that he really believed there were two honest men in Constantinople, *i. e.*, Kihisli Pasha, the Seraskier, or Minister of War, and Halill Pasha. Yet it is said that Halill Pasha made two millions of money during his ministry, which was not a long one.

It is scarcely difficult, when you see more closely into the state of things here, to account for the disgraceful lives of the pashas and ministers, more particularly of those who have risen from the lowest ranks of the people. Just fancy a man once a shoemaker, afterward a police-officer, made an admiral because he was a favorite; and this was the case with the late Achmet Papudgi, who, at the height of his power, could neither read nor write.

What is to be expected of men who have been brought up in poverty, oppression, and ignorance, with every bad example before their eyes in the rich men close to their own miserable hovels? While poor and oppressed, he is honest, because he has neither power to steal nor to do harm; but the moment the slightest temptation presents itself to lift him out of his misery, all those negative, so-called "good qualities" of the Turk vanish into thin air. The Cadi, or the Pasha who had noticed him, wants perhaps a false witness or two to rob a poor widow or orphans of all that is left them, or to strip a farmer or merchant of his entire possessions. The hitherto "honest" (because poor) Turk thinks he may just as well relieve his wretched poverty by a thing so common as perjury, as starve on, with a very good chance besides of being bastinadoed to death on a false charge, falsely maintained too, for having refused the "honorable" commands of his Pasha. Once get a post here, however, by favoritism and an "obliging disposition," and the road to luxury, the Turk's only ambition, is fast and easy enough. The Minister of Police, for instance, receives a large sum for subordinates. These he pays so miserably, scarcely giving them enough to sustain life, that they are well known to receive so many piastres a day from each thief; so that nothing is ever further from their thoughts than to dislodge any criminals. Of course there are a few exceptions, but the chief occupants of the prisons here are either innocent persons, who have been stripped of all they possess, or those who have fallen under the displeasure of some Pasha or other.

You ask: "How is the justice of this country administered?" My dear Mr. Hornby, I believe from all the questions which I have asked of those who know Turkey well, who have lived in it for years, and who are honorable and truthful men, that I am not in the slightest degree leading you toward an exaggerated idea of the miseries of this unhappy country, when I reply simply that there is none. Bribery and false testimony reign here supreme. The luxury of the Pashas, the summer palaces (which contrast with the hovels in which they toiled for daily brown-bread but a few years before), the caparisoned and jeweled horses, the numerous slaves and ruffian retainers, are supported by imposts and depredations of all kinds. The middle class of people have almost entirely disappeared. The "Government" have pretty well succeeded in killing the goose for its golden eggs; there will soon be nothing left to plunder. I am assured by a merchant here that twenty years ago there were many beautiful home manufactures, constantly worn by the people, which have now quite disappeared. When a Pasha found a manufactory in his district, which was flourishing, he so taxed and robbed the unhappy proprietor, who was already subject to heavy government imposts, that he was soon obliged to fly with his family, or to starve in the ruins. Or else a false charge was brought against him, and he died of the bastinado in prison, while the Pasha seized his house and goods for a fine, impossible for him to pay. So most of the lucrative manufactures have been lost to the country, and the Government, being prevented by treaties with foreign powers from increasing to any great extent the duties on foreign productions, have burdened home manufactures and produce with very heavy duties, that effectually putting a finishing stroke to native enterprise or industry.

Other and happier countries are thus able to send their goods in so much cheaper, that there is but little commerce here of any real advantage to the body of the people. In fact their condition, and that of the Pashas, is perfectly illustrated by the beautiful white marble palace and a more wretched hovel than Ireland ever produced. However, one can hardly be sorry to see that the country is so drained that there is but little left to steal; and, come what may, the poor cannot be worse off.

I must not forget to tell you that the Cadi, or magistrate, of every village fixes the price of provisions. He is himself paid, and upon being told his annual stipend, you ask how he lives. The butcher, baker, etc., pay him so many piastres a week to keep the price of meat and bread above what it should be. A man who ought to be bastinadoed, is glad to give his ten, twenty, or thirty piastres, according to his means, to be let off; and a man falsely accused is equally delighted to make his little present and be let off with a whole skin too. If a man is punished here, you may be pretty well sure that he has not been able to give enough to his Cadi. Can you imagine any state of things more dreadful than all this?

Most of the Turks are fine open-countenanced looking fellows. Even when a tradesman tries to get out of you more than double the price of the article in question, your pity for him overcomes any other feeling. He is obliged to get what he can, under the great pressure constantly bearing him down and threatening starvation.

Sometimes he has been fortunate enough to get a little money hidden away, to help him in his business in some particular way: well, a minister of finance, to rake up a few thousands to build a summer-palace, or to buy Georgian slaves and led horses, absolutely alters the value of the paper money or of the poor coins saved up, and so the people lose largely on frequent occasions.

People who have worn out their sympathies upon Hottentots and South-Sea Islanders, and need the excitement of Exeter Hall to keep their benevolence up to the mark—those who must have a foreign country and people to help—had better come here; for here are horrors and difficulties enough.

The barbarities of mere savages do not impress one at all in comparison with the profound melancholy which one feels in this magnificent grave of truth and freedom, where soul looks sorrowfully and dejectedly out of the fine dark eyes of the people, who have nothing to hope for in their wretchedness, but to become as guilty as the men whom they hated and despised in the honest days of their misery and labor. Many, who know them well, believe that they deeply feel the degradation of their country, and would like to rise up among nations if they could. Alas! the poor working-man who says so, believes at the same time that it is hopeless; and when his turn for temptation comes, falls with the rest, or else ends his life in the misery in which it began. Fancy a well-inclined baker or carpenter at home resisting a crime which he sees every day may lead to fortune, and sees every day committed by those above him, as a matter of course. Fancy a man in office being able to refuse a bribe, or to avoid taking what the others take in the next palace. He remembers what he suffered in the days of his poverty, and grasps what he can while the sun shines, which, politically speaking, is uncertain enough here.

Some of the Pashas are of old date of course, many professing to be descended from the Dere-Beys, or "Lords of the Valley;" but they are, generally speaking, men of a day, and risen from the lowest class, as I have told you. It is time indeed that the civilized world should know the state of its unhappy neighbor, so well described by the Emperor Nicholas.

I heard a gentleman say the other day, "the English government (although of course it knows much) has no adequate idea of the disgraceful state of this country and its ministry; or of the extraordinary difficulty which one meets with in doing any thing with the Turks." The fact is that English and French delicacy shrinks from openingly saying to a Turkish minister, "I know you are cheating." Not understanding the delicacy, however, the Turks think that you either do not see through their knavery, or are finessing with them after their own fashion.

Our kiosk is halfway up the hill in Orta-kioy; look-down upon the miserable village in the valley, and just catching a glimpse of glittering palaces on the edge of the Bosphorus. The sun has burst out this morning after the rain, and over such a country! Stranger as I am, my heart could but bound, as many others have done, on looking over the loveliest hills and valleys that fancy ever dreamed of—so beautiful still, in spite of all the evil works of man! trees felled never to be replanted—vineyards rooted up never to clothe the hillside again—thousands and thousands of acres lying uncultivated, where ought to be waving corn. Superstitious veneration for the dead only plants cypresses, to break with their rich clumps the otherwise monotonous ranges of hills on either side the Bosphorus. The cypress-gardens cannot be robbed; fruit-trees and orchards soon would be! Here Byron's poetry is *truth,* splendidly and forcibly told.

> "His ill-got treasure soon replaced:
> Would question whence? Survey the waste,
> And ask the squalid peasant how
> His gains repay his broiling brow!"

One thing surprises me very much, and that is, the

exaggeration pervading most of the books I have seen about Turkey. To read them, you would think that the Turks were idle, but happy—poor, but contented. How different is the real state of things! I cannot help wishing that Admiral Slade's book, which I once mentioned to you, were as well known as some volumes of pretty-sounding unreality. It seems to me a positive sin to give to the civilized world so false a notion of the social and political state of a people, whose only hope now rests, though unconsciously to themselves, upon the genius, patience, and philanthropy of happier nations being exerted in their favor.

I thought the other day, when standing under the plane-trees where tradition says Godfrey de Bouillon once encamped, that a nobler crusade may be fought here by earnest wish and good example of Christian nations now admitted, than ever was fought before against infidels in the olden time by lance and spear. As far as I have yet seen, however, there is but little of this spirit afloat among the French and English. After they have once amused themselves by laughing at the peculiarities and the miseries of the Turks, they are very well inclined either to let them alone, or, with mischievous and unprincipled levity, to tempt them to drink wine, or commit some act of English folly, which cannot give them a very exalted idea of either our kindness or morality.

LETTER XVIII.

OUR GREEK COOK—CALLIOPE'S DESPONDENCY—TROUBLES IN THE KITCHEN—APPROACH OF WINTER—THE SULTAN'S VISIT TO THE MOSQUE—A MALTESE DOG.

Orta-kioy, December 30th, 1855.

My dear Mother:

Our Greek cook has arrived from Scutari, and we already feel like mice in harvest-time, after our lengthened starvation. I was busy in the garden when he came. He is very like our old picture of "The Banished Lord," and lifted his cap with a lofty magnificence of manner, which I humbly admitted to myself was infinitely more dignified than the look of supreme satisfaction of which I felt conscious. He is very tall and very pale, with a long black beard and heavy projecting brows. He looks famished and misanthropic, is evidently silent and sarcastic; and Calliope is broken-hearted. She has been so dull, so disappointed at not finding us in the very heart of Stamboul, or of Pera at least (which the Smyrniotes consider a paradise of flirtation and gayety), so hopeless of a mistress who does not appreciate sitting dressed out at a window, like the Smyrniote ladies, and has no notes or bouquets going backward and forward—no, not even one—and who writes and reads or strolls in the garden all the day long, that she had looked forward to the arrival of the cook with great joy. And now to find him married, misanthropic and surly, dressed in an English coat with sleeves too short for his long thin arms, no gay embroidery, not even a sash—the poor Greek maiden's ill-fortune can no further go. It is carnival time too, the streets of Pera are gay with noisy and wandering crowds, and Calliope's suffering and *tristezza* are almost more than she can bear. She sighs dismally at this last blow, and wipes her immense black eyes with a bright yellow handkerchief after handing my coffee. "Vassili" treats her with haughty distance, and desires her to show him the way to the kitchen, whence he instantly dislodges the Armenian woman with profound expressions of contempt, and sets about arranging the charcoal in the stoves with the air of a master of his art, but looking much more like a conspirator, or a brigand under difficulties, than the domestic being which we are accustomed to consider a cook. His arrival is certainly a great event in our domestic life here. He promised the "signor" should have a well-dressed dinner, and kept his word admirably, the only drawback being Calliope's sighs and tearful looks, as she attended in a most languishing and desponding manner. But, seriously speaking, this is very annoying, especially to me when alone, and I entreated her yesterday to return to Symrna, or to look out for another situation here, as I could not undertake the task of keeping up her spirits or provide her with amusement. As the weather becomes more wintry, it is what she calls duller still; the Bosphorus is very rough and the streets very dirty. When we sat down to breakfast this morning, a distant mountain on the Asiatic side was glittering with snow; the effect of the sunbeams on it was very beautiful, and I wished myself there with a long and free walk before me.

It is Friday, and I have been down to the mosque to see the Sultan go to mid-day prayer. He came from his palace at Tcheran; English, French, and Turkish ships-of-war saluting him with a perfect roar of cannon as his beautiful gilded caiques floated by. The guard surrounded the mosque, and lined the narrow street leading to it. They marched from Tcheran, with their band playing alternately European airs and marches, and wild and barbarous Turkish tunes, in which fifes and drums predominate. I stood on the white terrace surrounding the mosque, but the crowd of guards and pashas prevented my getting a good view of the Sultan, who was besides pretty well hidden beneath a bright-red silk umbrella. I consoled myself by admiring his magnificently gilt and carved caiques floating gracefully on the blue water, or moored with their fine picturesque crews by the white marble steps of the mosque. Some of the men were standing up in the finest possible attitudes, others reclining on their benches. It was a most striking and beautiful picture of Eastern life. There were six or seven caiques, some with golden and velvet-lined canopies, and one or two with the effigy of a white dove, with outspread wings, fluttering on an almost invisible gilt stem in the prow, which had a charming effect, rising and falling on the waves. The Sultan remained about an hour in the mosque, his miserable-looking soldiers keeping guard around, and a few pashas and officers of state lounging and gossiping on the terrace. I was watching for the red silk umbrella, but was again disappointed; for when the fifes and drums announced that the Sultan's prayers were over, instead of approaching the principal entrance of the mosque, the royal caiques were turned toward the palace; and I was told that the Sultan had dismissed his suite, had slipped quietly out of a private door, and, with two or three attendants, had gone to pay a visit to his favorite sister, the wife of Mehemet Ali, at Arnautkoi. So we strolled homeward through a crowd of soldiers mustering for their return to the palace, and the usual motley groups of villagers, caiquejees and fishermen, beggars, sherbet-sellers, and street-dogs.

In our garden we found an Armenian of the village awaiting our return. He had a beautiful little Maltese dog to sell, which, after much bargaining, industriously interpreted by our friend Antonio, became ours for the sum of eighty piastres. It is a merry little creature, and I have named him Fuad. Edith will be delighted with his fun and frolic, his snow-white coat and bright black eyes. The poor Armenian widow Almira, was solacing herself with a cigarette and an ancient friend on her doorstep. She seemed pleased at my delight with the dog, and going indoors, presently returned with a little necklace of blue beads, which she hung round his neck, and begged earnestly that I would allow him to wear it as a charm against the "evil eye;" for she would not have me grieved by his loss, Antonio earnestly wrote, in his pretty *Eastern* Italian. So, with a dog, I now find our little kiosk beginning to feel something more like a home; and in the short twilight before dinner-time, the little fellow sits with me before the open door of our stove, in which the wood burns cheerily. Instead of a pan of water on the stove, I have placed a small kettle, and its song is the sweetest music in the world to me, as I scorch first one foot and then the other in my frantic endeavors to get thoroughly warm, and my obstinate folly in persisting in a dream of an English fireside.

LETTER XIX.

CHRISTMAS-DAY AT CONSTANTINOPLE—BEAUTY OF THE BOSPHORUS—CROWD OF VESSELS—MYSSERI'S HOTEL—TALES OF THE CRIMEA—THE GREEK CHRISTMAS—CHRISTMAS DINNER AT THE EMBASSY—MISS NIGHTINGALE—CHRISTMAS GAMES.

Orta-kioy, January 5th, 1856.

My dear Julia:

Often I look very wistfully over the Sea of Marmora on returning ships, and long for the day when we may be sailing over it again, homeward-bound. Sometimes I am very much depressed, thinking of the distance which separates me from Edith and you all; then I lash up my courage and become cheerful and contented and grateful again. A mail is due to-day, and I *may* have letters to-morrow morning. I know you will be thinking much of us by your Christmas logs. The weather here has been most bright and lovely: soft south winds and uninterrupted sunshine for the last ten days, difficult to understand at Christmas-time.

We went into Pera on Christmas-day, Lord and Lady Stratford kindly taking pity on our loneliness, and asking us to dinner. I wish you could have seen the Bosphorus as it was when we embarked in our caique from the little wooden pier of Orta-kioy, the Sultan's white marble mosque shining in the morning sun. Numbers of Greeks and Turks were basking on the rickety woodwork, idly watching the turbaned fishermen in their gayly-painted boats pulling in nets quite silvery with multitudes of glittering fish; so does the Bosphorus teem with every variety of finny inhabitants. Once on this lovely sea, you forget all about the miseries and calamities of Turkish towns and villages, and can only think it the most beautiful place in the world, as your caique darts along the waves, and you mark palaces and gardens and distant mountains.

The Bosphorus on Christmas-day was particularly beautiful to us, unused now to see outward signs of a Christian people. The almost innumerable European ships were gayly dressed with flags and pennants, which fluttered in the brilliant sunshine. You may imagine the effect in the Sea of Marmora, with Prince's Islands like clouds rising from the sea, and far in dreamy distance, the Asian mountains glittering with ice and snow. It was delightful to feel the warmth of spring in your caique, and to look upon shining avalanches above the clouds themselves.

The beauty of this place on the sea, is so great that, even while looking on it, you do not believe that it is real. I feel this every time I row near "beautiful Stamboul," and by the Maiden's Tower, which stands built on a rock in the Sea of Marmora, where you see stately ships coming in from England and France, for this great war.

Nearer to Constantinople, Pera, and Tophana, is literally a forest of masts, and it is marvelous that more accidents do not happen than one hears of, for caiques and Maltese boats dart by hundreds in and out, under the very jaws of the leviathans, the ships at anchor on each side taking up a very deep border of the Bosphorus. Several English and French men-of-war on Christmas morning were taking in from caiques famous stocks of good things to make merry; oranges, dried fruits, grapes, and Turkish sweetmeats, whose name is Legion. We passed close alongside the "Queen," who always gives the Sultan such a hearty salute, that she almost sends his majesty's gilded caiques flying in the air instead of skimming the water. The English soldiers and sailors often give a passing countrywoman a tremendous cheer, recognizing a bonnet immediately among the crowd of vails. I got a first-rate one, with caps waving a hearty adieu, from the crew of a transport slowly steaming down from the Crimea on her way to England. I so rejoiced with the poor fellows, after all they had gone through in this terrible war, and would have given something to have been going home too with that fine and jolly company on Christmas-day.

It is very pleasant to hear the sound of English now and then from a ship or passer-by. Being in a Turkish village, as we are, is a very different thing to being at Mysseri's Hotel at Pera, which, since the war began, has been crowded with English officers. There, one hardly seems in a strange country. Mrs. Mysseri is extremely fond of flowers, and always has some very beautiful ones on her terrace and in the deep windows of the staircase: they look so pretty and refreshing, on coming in from the hot and dusty streets. On Christmas-day all her orange and lemon trees adorned the salaamlik; the country-people had brought her in immense branches of myrtle, which abounds here; ("Know ye the land of the cypress and myrtle?") and the place wore quite a festive air, except that there was no holly, and that told more than any thing else that one was not in old England, which every one adores when away from, and grumbles at when in it.

I am quite at home at Mysseri's now, and am acquainted with several people staying there. Want of occupation is the principal complaint, and I enjoy Mrs. Mysseri's kind permission to arrange and water her flowers when we are staying there. The poor officers get terribly "bored," having no amusement of any kind but standing at the door, watching the curiously varied stream of human beings perpetually pouring through the narrow street, varied with occasional strings of donkeys, and now and then of stately stepping camels. Many have been "knocking about" since the war began, and are of course more particularly longing to see their families and friends just now. It was useless to wish them a merry Christmas; one could only hope for a happier one next year, if the war is ended. They certainly bear every thing very cheerfully and well, including hardship and danger in the camp before Sebastopol, and illness, *ennui*, and a stab now and then from their gracious allies here. A young officer showed me this morning a tin case, which he said with glee contained a plum pudding, made by his sisters in England. He was going to keep it for the Crimea when his leave at Constantinople should have expired. He told me that hundreds of puddings had arrived, and that last year it was the same, many officers "sporting" slices of it fried, up to the time of the taking of Sebastopol. However, the Crimean ants are sad lovers of good things, and seem determined to exercise their utmost ingenuity to obtain a conqueror's share of what the fortunes of war have sent to their barren coasts. Lieutenant Coote, a brave young man and a great friend of ours, amused me very much with a description of the war which he carried on against them. They certainly troubled him even more than Russian shot and shell, for he said that, however hungry, he could never make up his mind to swallow a dozen or so at a mouthful. His mother sent him out potted meats, marmalade, and other things, which he carefully barricaded in his tent. The moment he returned again from the trenches, he ran with a bosom friend to his stores. No matter how ingeniously he had covered them up, the enemy were certain to be in possession and full regale. At last they got, for a great sum, a large earthenware jar, which was constantly kept in a tub half-full of water, and this soon became the fashionable pantry of the camp, and completely defeated the ants. Although under a deep snow, they are very snug in the Crimea just now, having plenty of excellent provisions, plenty of clothing, and good wooden huts. The Russians still keep up firing from the north side. I saw a traveler the other day who had just returned from Sebastopol. He says that it is impossible to walk about "pleasantly," as shells are frequently thrown in. One day he stopped with a friend to have the treat of a glass of ale, an adventurous Englishman having set up a small tap in one of the deserted houses. They were just paying, when a shot dashed in at the already dilapidated window, shattered what was left of the frame to pieces, split the rickety table into fragments, broke all the glasses, and so frightened mine host, that he declared, with tears in his eyes, when the first fright was over, that he *must* give up the place, "it was so very *worriting* to be fired at like that every now and then."

I have asked Mr. Evelyn to give me an account of how they spend Christmas in the Crimea, and will send you his reply, as no doubt it will be interesting. When we could no longer see the gay flags and pennants flying from the ships on the Bosphorus, Pera gave no signs to English eyes of a holiday. There was of course the same crowd of noisy Greeks, the same strange mixture of many nations. French and English soldiers were strolling about, evidently making a melancholy attempt to enjoy themselves.

The Greek Christmas-day is on our Twelfth Night this year. Mrs. Mysseri was able to give us a comfortable room with a lovely view, and we had plenty of visitors all the morning. The heat and closeness was so great, that every one seemed more or less ill and depressed; many, too, home-sick. Edmund and I congratulate ourselves on being in fresh air, every time we return from Pera to Orta-kioy; the noise and dirt of Pera are so great, and want of exercise so trying to health and spirits. But it is of no use minding mud and bustling crowds and dead rats; so Lady Poulett, who has just returned from the Crimea, and who bears every thing in the same brave and cheerful spirit, Captain Keppel, and I, managed to get to the great cemetery for a walk among the solemn cypress-trees and countless groups of turban-stones. Captain Keppel is just appointed to the command of a squadron of gun-boats, and everybody who knows him says that this a cheerful instance of "the right man in the right place." We looked in at Signor Preziosa's on our way home, and admired his beautiful sketches of this place, groups in the bazaars, and fine old fountains. Captain Keppel bought two vailed ladies to grace his cabin, and I took a fancy to a wild and ferocious-looking dervish.

But I must tell you about the Christmas dinner at the Embassy, for every thing is so different here to any other part of the world. My Greek maid has run away, so Lady Poulett most kindly allows her English one to dress me, which is a great relief to my mind, coming from such savage parts as I do. We go down-stairs together. Two ridiculously painted and gilt sedan-chairs are in the hall, with the Turkish bearers for each. Mrs. Mysseri comes out of her room to "see us dressed," and loving flowers so much herself, has kindly made up for Lady Poulett and myself a lovely bunch of myrtle and roses, which she declares is all that is wanting to strike all beholders. Our gentlemen in waiting, dressed for the dinner-party at the palace likewise, and with Crimean orders on their breasts, (don't envy us too much, young ladies,—we are the only creatures of womankind amongst hundreds of our countrymen), advance to put on our wrappings. We step into our chairs, and feel ourselves picked up as if we were linnets, by the marvelous strength of our bearers. Three Turks, carrying lanterns, each containing two or three candles, escort our party. Once outside the doors of your hotel at night, you begin to feel nervous. The streets are now almost deserted, except by the party going to the Embassy. The houses are closely shut up, and only gleam out in their picturesque irregularity by the fitful glare of the lamps as the Turks pick their way over the great loose stones of the "pavement," and heaps of filth here and there. Every now and then a dark figure steals by, wrapped in a large cloak, and you feel, what is so strange to the English, that murder lurks in every dark place. Once I nearly upset my chair by suddenly trying to look out; for Edmund had disappeared out of the light of the lanterns. He had only joined a party of officers, and they soon came up, laughing and talking. The street dogs eyed us suspiciously from their lairs in the dark corners of the streets. Some of them look like hyenas lurking about at night. A guard of Turkish soldiers was drawn up in the narrow street leading to the palace, and motley groups were assembled by the gates to see the company arrive; Greeks Turks, and groups of mounted officers in full dress look so well by torchlight,—very different, certainly, to the black coats and carriages of a London dinner-party.

The palace looked very beautiful—its spacious white stone corridors, richly and warmly carpeted, and an air of *perfectness* very striking here. Beautiful orange and lemon trees, bearing both flowers and fruit; bright, shining myrtles, and gorgeous scarlet cacti, had a charming effect. There were a few branches of Turkish holly, which is small and stunted, but not a single berry of the cherished scarlet. Misseltoe is found on many of the old oak-trees in the Crimea, but I have never seen any here. The ladies at the Embassy have great taste in the arrangement of flowers and shrubs, and the drawing-rooms seem so beautiful to me after our savage little kiosk, that I feel like an Esquimax suddenly imported into Belgravia, and, seated on a low sofa canopied with orange and myrtle, delight mine eye exceedingly. I never thought to have looked with so much interest at a blazing fire-place as I do now, not having seen one for months.

Lady Stratford was not in the drawing-room when we arrived. We found General and Mrs. Mansfield, Lady Frederick Fitzroy, Sir Houston Stewart, and several officers, naval and military. The embassador most cordially wished everybody a happy Christmas. His lordship always wins my heart by asking the latest news of Edie, and he *can* talk so delightfully on light matters when he has time, which is not very often. Like poor broken-hearted Lord Raglan, he has deeply and painfully felt the attack made on him about Kars. He had a pleasant chat about Orta-kioy, its ancient name, the curious fraternity of dervishes now living there; and about a Russian princess whom Lord Stratford had once vistted in a fine old Armenian house just above our kiosk—a kind of good fairy, of whom the Greeks of the village still speak with reverence, she being of their own Church, and very charitable. But by-and-by the drawing-room doors are thrown open, and the embassadress enters, smiling a kind and gracious welcome. Behind her are her daughters; by her side, a tall, fashionable, haughty beauty. I could not help thinking how beautiful she looked; but the next instant my eyes wandered from her cold unamiable face to a lady modestly standing on the other side of Lady Stratford. At first I thought she was a nun, from her black dress and close cap. She was not introduced, and yet Edmund and I looked at each other at the same moment to whisper, "It is

Miss Nightingale!" Yes, it was Florence Nightingale, greatest of all now in name and honor among women. I assure you that I was glad not to be obliged to speak just then, for I felt quite dumb as I looked at her wasted figure and the short brown hair combed over her forehead like a child's, cut so when her life was despaired of from fever but a short time ago. Her dress, as I have said, was black, made high to the throat, its only ornament being a large enameled brooch, which looked to me like the colors of a regiment surmounted with a wreath of laurel, no doubt some grateful offering from our men. To hide the close white cap a little, she had tied a white crape handkerchief over the back of it, only allowing the border of lace to be seen; and this gave the nunlike appearance which first struck me on her entering the room, otherwise Miss Nightingale is by no means striking in appearance. Only her plain black dress, quiet manner, and great renown, told so powerfully altogether in that assembly of brilliant dress and uniforms. She is very slight, rather above the middle height; her face is long and thin, but this may be from recent illness and great fatigue. She has a very prominent nose, slightly Roman; and small dark eyes, kind, yet penetrating; but her face does not give you at all the idea of great talent. She looks a quiet, persevering, orderly, ladylike women. I have done my best to give you a true pen-and-ink portrait of this celebrated lady. I suppose there is a hum all over the world world of "What is she like?"

Through the beautiful flower-vases on the table, I noticed another pale and care-worn face; but this was a gentleman. I asked my neighbor who he was, and no longer wondered at his haggard looks, when I heard that he was Dr. Sandwith, just escaped from all the horrors of starvation at Kars. I was sorry not to be able to hear what he was saying; but Sir Houston Stewart's rosy, seaman's face, merry chat, and truly Christmas "Ha, ha, ha!" made it impossible to any one near him not to smile and feel very merry too. At Christmas-time mirth is particularly infectious.

But after dinner there was great fun; for all the midshipmen of the different men-of-war lying here were invited; such fine, brave-looking little fellows! My heart always warms to a middy. Lady Stratford received them most kindly as they came marching in, looking so fresh and nice in their little, old-fashioned blue coatees with gilt buttons. I think they thought it rather formidable at first, but Lord Stratford proposed a "round game" for them, and they soon became as jolly as possible, brightening up with the Christmas fun and laughter. We all played like so many children; the admiral, the life and spirit of every game.

Many officers now arrived, and the new ball-room, which is a very beautiful one, was thrown open. Several Christmas games were played, in which almost every one joined. The middies were wild with delight, and afforded the greatest amusement, now that they felt quite at their ease. Their feeling of the *excessive* fun of playing with the admiral was intense. In one of the games Sir Houston ran round the wide circle, ball in hand, and crying, "Earth, air, water!" The game is, you know, that the person, into whose lap the ball is thrown, must name some object, or some animal, from the last-named element, which is sometimes difficult in a second, for the ball comes to you when you least expect it, and the words are very rapidly spoken.

"Earth!" cries the admiral, to a merry-looking, fair-haired middy.

"An ass!" promptly replies the little fellow.

"An ass! So you mean to call me an ass, do you, sir?" said the admiral, pretending to frown. I really thought the little boys would have expired with laughing at the bare idea!

Miss Nightingale was still very weak, and could not join in the games, but she sat on a sofa, and looked on, laughing until the tears came into her eyes. There was afterward a dark room, with a gigantic dish of snap-dragon, and we all looked dreadfully pale in the blue light. The red coats of the officers turned orange-color, their stars and orders of the most unearthly hue; and each wondered at the other's spectral looks, except the middies, who showed a marvelous capacity for eating fiery plums.

I thought as I looked round, what a curious group it was playing children, even the children having acted their part in this fearful war-struggle. Many a scar still remained on the cheek and brows of officers now scrambling for snap-dragon; the poor Doctor from Kars looked like the spirit of a famished man; Miss Nightingale's nunlike head-dress, still more quaint in that strange, blue light. I said to her "How delighted the mothers of these boys would be to see them now!" She replied, "Ah! the poor mothers!" How the middies enjoyed the good things and delicious sweetmeats afterward handed around! Lady Stratford was so kind, and took immense pains that they should pass a happy Christmas evening. Edmund had charge of them all to their hotel, and we were a merry, torch-light party, scrambling through the quaint and narrow streets. It seemed so odd to see such little fellows as these going to an hotel alone in a country like this. A son of Sir Charles Wood particularly struck me, as a handsome, clever boy. Sir Houston Stewart told me that most of them had been under fire, and had behaved gallantly.

So much for our Christmas-day in 1855. Perhaps we may never have so remarkable a one again.

LETTER XX.

GREEK SERVANTS—CALLIOPE'S SCHEME—KNEELING TO THE SAINTS—LYING PROPENSITIES—DOMESTIC LIFE—GREEK AND TURKISH CHARACTER.

Orta-kioy, January 10th, 1856.

My dear Julia:

I am very quiet here now; much more comfortable since Calliope ran away, although her tears and her everlasting yellow pocket-handkerchief haunt me still. She was a thorough Greek, and could not help intriguing over a potato. I believe that the quiet was dreadful to her; even some one to quarrel with would have been a relief. But I must tell you all about her "flitting," and how thoroughly I was taken in. However, the Greeks certainly tell lies with such a grace that I do not feel the least abashed at my want of penetration. It is quite different from the bold and vulgar untruth of the same class in England, it is diplomatic and artistic: as actors, I should think they would make their fortunes.

Well, Fuad and I were lounging on the divan one fine morning. We had been watching Edmund as he rode away, and an Armenian baby at the opposite lattice, and a "row" among the street dogs, and a vailed Armenian lady riding down the hill astride on a milk-white mule, with an attendant on each side of her, and our neighbor's bread going to be baked in the long wooden troughs (we are getting quite Paul Prys, Fuad and I, at our windows), and an old Turk selling sweets to the fat muezzin of our mosque, who carries his little child in his arms, munching a green apple or a cucumber. Every thing here is new to me, you know, and Fuad likes it too—dear, merry little beast!—and as there are only two of us, we can play the fool together without offending any one. So I watch all that is going on, and he looks at the wild cats prowling about our garden, tell Edie, and gets so angry that I have to pull him back by his white curls, for fear he should tumble out, in the intensity of his wrath.

Well, I am a sad rambler! Calliope came rushing up-stairs wringing her hands. I boxed Fuad's ears to make him quiet, and said in Italian, "What's the matter now?" "Oh! my mother, my poor mother is dying, and has sent for us all to say good-by (*prendere l'ultimo addio*); what shall I do?" The girl was *really* pale, and trembled visibly.

"Do?" I said; "go at once, of course."

"But how can I leave *you?* how can I leave the signora?" turning to Vassili, who, looking as grim as usual, was putting wood into the stove. Vassili looked a degree coarser, and made no reply beyond a Greek shrug of the shoulders. I said: "Oh, never mind me; go directly."

So Calliope rushed to the fountain in the little hall and began sluicing her face with water, then again ran up to me, arranging her long hair-plaits, crying and uttering vehement lamentations. One of her speeches was: "Ah, my poor mother, she said when we parted, 'Adieu, my Calliope! I feel growing so weak, that I do not believe we shall ever meet again.'" I said: "Don't cry any more; but eat something before you go, or you will be ill."

I asked several questions about the mother, of Calliope's sailor brother, a dark-bearded, corsair-looking young gentleman, who was waiting in the garden. I remember now that he looked at Calliope for answers as to the old lady's age and ailments. I comforted them both, and gave them some wine, and waved my hand in answer to Calliope's frequent and anxious lookings back at my window, and felt so sorry for the grief which they had to go through, and sat musing a long time over her clasped hands and passionate sorrow, so doubly touching in Italian.

When Edmund came home, I hastened to tell him: "Calliope is gone; her mother is dying." Would you believe it? He had met her in the streets of Pera, the merriest of the mad mob of street-revelers! Her brother turns out to be *not* her brother, and of course we have sent to her relations to tell her that she need not trouble herself to return. Her message in answer was, that she *should* come back, whether we liked it or not; that her mother was better, and that she should now feel happier and more contented at Orta-kioy. However, the grim Vassili promises to keep the garden gate bolted, and I hope to be no more tormented.

The old Armenian woman is reinstated now as a naked-legged housemaid, in which capacity she scrubs the floors, scratching like a hen with a small birch rod in the hollow of her right foot. I thought this, by-the-by, a most awkward and laborious process, and making up a little mat, and tucking up my dress, knelt down and showed her how we do it in England, in dumb-show, of course, for Red-jacket and I possess not the vulgar aid of language in our interesting communications. She looked very indignant, *extremely* so for a calm Eastern charwoman, and I, who thought I had been doing great things, was quite puzzled. At last I clapped my hands for Vassili to interpret. Red-jacket still stood in a magnificent attitude, her arms folded, and her little birch-broom still tightly clasped in her dripping blue toes. "Tell the Cocona," she said, "that we never kneel but to the saints." I of course, made a most humble apology, but always fly the approach of those dreadful red legs and the little birch rod.

But to return to Greek falsehood. It is certainly marvelous, from all that one hears and sees daily and hourly. How dangerous and dreadful, that elegant and clever untruth! The girl, Calliope, for instance, mixed up and *used* truth with such fearful skill, to gain her end. We knew beyond a doubt, from those who were well acquainted with them, that she was devotedly fond of her mother, and was the principal support of both her and her sister. Most probably the mother really said those words at parting, "Ah, my Calliope, we may never meet again!" The very talking of her mother and repeating her words, lashed her wild, excitable, and affectionate, yet lawless nature into real agitation. At least that is how I read her, and how I analyze what I hear of her countrymen and women.

It is a fearful state of things, heart-aching to see a fine people so completely false and demoralized, socially and politically. Even little children can scarcely be called innocent or truthful here. Why should it be permitted? is often a painful thought, as well as, How long can it last? A rotten apple can scarcely hang on the tree forever.

From all I hear and observe, it seems to me that ages of Turkish misrule and corrupt example have had two opposite effects on two peoples of very opposite natures. The Turk, like a slow, phlegmatic lad at school, neglected, sinks into nothing; is quiet, stupid, contented, and unambitious. The clever boy—the Greek—uncontrolled, ill-treated, and with a bad example before him, turns his great talents to wickedness, and, to gain his own unscrupulous ends, uses his invention, his genius, his great eloquence, and his marvelous quickness, for the most degrading, when it might be turned to the highest purposes. But I must not venture into such difficult and perplexing subjects. Captain Burton says that I am in the first stage of English indignation and disgust. He says that in a few months he shall see me quietly seated on a divan, taking every thing as matter of course, and not only reconciled, but thinking it is "Kismet," or Fate, and better as it is. I replied: "May I become a tortoise first!"

LETTER XXI.

NEW-YEAR'S EVE—HOUSEKEEPING—DISCUSSING PRICES—A GREEK LAUNDRESS—NEW-YEAR'S MORNING—SECLUSION OF THE TURKISH WOMEN—THE CEMETERY—THE PERSIAN EMBASSADOR—BALL AT THE EMBASSY.

Orta-kioy, January 17th, 1856.

My dear Mother:

On New-Year's Eve we thought very much of you all in England. It was a lovely evening, as mild as Spring, and Edward Barker came down with a bunch of red and white roses for me, from his terraced garden, which must sound strange to you, frost-bound as I hear you are at home. He also brought a message from his mother and sisters, inviting us to spend the last day of the old year with them; so I put on my cloak and off we started, my little white dog Fuad, who is now petted after the orthodox fashion of lap-dog votaries, washed, combed, and blue-ribboned, strutting on before, and valiantly defying street dogs who could swallow him up, foolish thing! in a minute. Our man Vassili, and Mr. Burckhardt Barker's wild-looking Albanian, carried lanterns before us, after the fashion of the place. Edward and his young brother amused themselves by clinking their sticks on the stones, as the watchmen do, and presently the younger one, full of fun and boyish mischief, cried out the long wailing Turkish cry of "Yangin-var!" which means, there is a fire.

Nothing can be darker and quieter than a Turkish

village at night. So profound is the silence, that you might almost believe the place to be deserted. However, an instant after our lively young friend's cry had sounded through the narrow, cloisterlike streets, we could see the shadows of many forms moving rapidly across the lattices, no doubt to ask news of the watchmen, or to listen to their cry of where the fire was.

"Get on," said Edward, "we shall have some angry Turk out upon us."

I caught up Fuad, and we hastily turned out of the street into another narrower still. The Greek men were in ecstacies, their lanterns rolling about in their laughter, from one heap of stones and mud to another. It was just like half-disturbing a few drowsy owls. Mr. Barker's house is higher up the hill than ours; and, after you have climbed up the steep stony little streets, there are three flights of terraced steps to mount, which is very tiring at first, as indeed all walking is, in this part of the world.

We passed a very pleasant New-Year's Eve. There were no sweet-sounding English bells to listen to, ringing the old year out; but we had music and an agreeable conversation on Eastern matters with Mr. Barker, who both knows a great deal and how to tell it pleasantly. His children are pretty, amiable little creatures, doing the greatest credit to their excellent mother, especially in a country like this. I have already told you how much kindness I have met with from Mrs. Barker and her daughters. Indeed I hardly know how we should have got on without them. Every Saturday morning, rain or shine, saw Miss Clara seated on my divan, with all the wretched

Greek scrawls of my weekly bills before her. Then came a battle of two or three hours with milkman, butcher, and baker, poor savages! trying to take us in, and to charge double the proper price, because we were English.

Now, thanks to my kind friend, I know the proper price of every thing, and my housekeeping grows less and less stormy every day. Washing is at present my greatest difficulty. There is a Greek lady in the village (I can call her nothing else but lady), who has sometimes condescended to return us a few torn, coffee-colored things, which we can just recognize as our own, and to ask in return about their value—perhaps a little more. She is the most dignified little person in the most dignified rags. I often wonder, when I look at her, whether she takes off that green jacket trimmed with fur, even on washing-day, and whether she does not often put down her iron, to wrap it round her, and stand with folded arms, like the queen of a ruined kingdom, as she does now. Sometimes I hear the sound of her loose slippers dragging over the matting of the outer room, as I am reading quietly alone. She strolls into my little drawing-room: "Buon giorno, Signora!" is the extent of her Italian. She then takes a majestic survey, first of myself, and then of the room, pats Fuad encouragingly, and chirps to the Bashia. She has left the "washing" on the divan in the next room. Oh, my poor collars! But it is worse than useless to complain, so I say nothing; only on asking: "Quanti piastri?" I find the sum which the lady asks too ridiculous, compared with what my friend Miss Barker has told me to give. I remonstrate gently, by signs, and in Italian. She folds her arms, with an injured look, arranges the faded embroidered handkerchief round her head, and seats herself on the divan. Then I clap my hands for Vassili, whose very mustachios curl with ire when I tell him what is the matter. Then such a "row" takes place! you would think that nothing but a good sharp Damascene blade could settle the question. At first I used to be rather bored at scenes like these, of almost daily occurrence, but now I know how long the storm will last, and what it means.

In this country there is no fixed price for any thing —it is what can be got. If the debate is with any one who can speak Italian, I give them a volley myself; if only Greek or Turkish is understood, Vassili "goes in," as the school-boys say, and interprets fire and fury for me. You cannot hear your own voice, or get in a single word, while this sharp and deadly skirmish goes on. I sit quietly doing whatever I may be about, or calmly stroking Fuad's pretty white ears, and marveling at the violence and gestures of the combatants, when, as suddenly as a squall drops on the Bosphorus, the storm ceases, your money is taken with the usual Eastern salutation, and your interpreter tells you that your hand is kissed with many thanks. This is a scene of last Monday especially.

I ventured to ask why the things looked worse than usual. The lady tucked her hands into the fur pockets of the green jacket, and asked indignantly what I could expect of things ironed on a chair, for it seems that her wretched hovel contains no table, and this accounts for the marks of rushes on the shirt-fronts. We then tacitly agree to drop the subject, and enter into an amicable conversation about the miseries of the Greeks, and Turkish oppression. She complained bitterly of the want and suffering of the poor, who worked for the Turks, feasting and idling. I was very sorry for her, and gave her a few little things for her children. I asked if she could come and help Red-jacket; "Not the next day;" it was Saint somebody's day. The next? No; it was Saint somebody-else's day; and between feast-days and fast-days, she could do nothing that week. I said I hoped she would not think I wished to say any thing disrespectful of her religion, but it seemed to me that the observance of so many feast-days and fast-days kept her very poor, and her children very thin. She shrugged her shoulders, laughed, and said nothing. I hear from Vassili to-day, that two of her children are very ill. Heaven help them, poor things! for there are no nurses but ignorance and superstition here.

But to turn to a very different subject. I must tell you how we spent New-Year's day. Lady Stratford de Redcliffe gave a ball, for which I took caique into Pera as usual, and wended to Mrs. Mysseri's, my favorrite quarters. It was a lovely day, the ships were dressed with flags, and the Bosphorus as gay and sparkling as it always is in sunshine.

To talk against this place is to talk against a great beauty when she is not by—she is false, she is treacherous, she has a thousand faults:—even her splendid array costs pain and misery to others. Yet only to see her, is quite enough; you are charmed again, and forget every thing but her fascination. This New-Year's morning, these palace-fringed shores and many-tinted hills and cypress-shaded cemeteries, with here and there a distant bit of landscape which you have never seen before, brought out by the sun's rays resting fully upon it, looked even more varied and interesting than usual. The Sultan's snow-white palace, too, rises beautifully out of the dark blue water, which reflects even the purple pigeons upon its roof. As your caique darts by, you can often detect a shadowy form peeping through the close white lattice-work of the Seraglio windows, no doubt longing for liberty. I used to notice, some time ago, one window in which three or four flower-pots were set, and which were evidently taken great care of, by one of the fair prisoners. Then I noticed them faded and scorched by the sun, and now they are gone altogether. I wonder what has happened to their poor mistress. However, the Sultan's ladies proverbially enjoy greater liberty than any other Turkish women of rank here, and their yashmaks are certainly the thinnest. Some time ago they were frequently seen at the palace windows, but this created great scandal, and a guard of blacks now walk up and down the marble terrace beneath.

The higher the rank of the women here, the more closely they are guarded and shut up. Our great beauties are seen everywhere; a great beauty of the old and highest Turkish fashion is often married without ever having passed beyond the walls of the harem garden, and without having beheld the face of any other man than her father. This is the highest Turkish *ton*. Women of the lower class are comparatively free, and can go, even unattended, into the streets and bazaars whenever they like, but of course vailed and feridjeed, so that it would be impossible to recognize them. It being lovely weather on New-Year's day, there were hundreds of Turkish women "taking the air," some in telekis, guarded by blacks, others on foot, shuffling along in their loose yellow slippers.

I was stopped by the crowd for a short time when we got out on the Bridge of Boats. I and my dress were examined with the greatest curiosity, for these shrouded dames never seem to tire of staring at Englishwomen. One very pretty creature in rather a thin vail, was quite charmed with the flounces of my dress, feeling them with her red-stained fingers, and saying, "Ghuzel, ghuzel!" which means pretty. They have very simple, engaging ways, and seem so inclined to love you, taking hold of one or two fingers, as children do, and looking into your face appealingly, which is very touching to me, for they seem to think us so free and happy, so different to themselves. I can say a few words of Turkish now, and hope soon to learn more. It is difficult, but a very fine and harmonious language—charming when spoken by the women. My pretty friends on the Bridge were delighted when I said "Allahá iss marladik!" which means "Good-by, God bless you!" and which, it must be confessed, I had learned to say the evening before, like a parrot.

It was with great difficulty that Vassili forced a way for me through the dense crowds of Galata and Pera. The noise, shouting, dirt, and confusion, seem worse every time you go there. It is really frightful since the war, quite impossible to be conceived unless seen. However, we at last got to Mysseri's, where I had agreed to spend the day with a friend. Edmund was enjoying a holiday, shooting at Kandilli, where he was to dine, and then join us at the ball in the evening.

Mysseri's was all bustle and confusion. Officers

had arrived from Scutari, Kulalee, and other places, to attend the ball. Poor Mrs. Mysseri was half distracted, for English, French, and Sardinians came pouring in with their servants and portmanteaus. The great topic of conversation is the fall of Kars—so gallantly defended, so cruelly allowed to fall. It is very perplexing and painful to listen to all this; and what have I not heard of the conduct of this war! Do not fail to read Mr. Duncan's book, called "A Campaign with the Turks in Asia;" it is very good, and tells you much about Kars, and its thievish pashas, like wasps in a hive.

It was curious to talk over all these things about the war, walking again with a friend in the cemetery, among thousands of clustered turban-stones and gigantic cypress-trees. There is a magnificent view of Stamboul from the ancient well on which we sat, and of the seven ruined arches of the Roman aqueduct, which still speak boldly of old Rome across the clear blue sky, even among the minarets.

Lower down, in a row of melancholy-looking houses, looking on the dark slopes of the burial-ground, I found the house in which my father once lived for a year. It was a *pension*, or boarding-house, in those days (there were no hotels then,) kept by a Madame Josephine somebody, who has long since slept in the Frank burial-ground at Pera. He little thought that I should ever stand on the threshold of that door, and look on the same headless Janissary stones, and on the same mournful, dreary-looking trees! To-day a small flock of sheep and goats were browsing there, tended by a picturesque and ragged shepherd. The reverence with which the Turks are said to regard their cemeteries seems to consist, at least in these days, in merely letting them alone. Hundreds of stones have fallen down in these two great cemeteries, and in many smaller ones which I have visited, and lie moldering on the ground. On the side next to Pera, dogs, geese, and fowls stroll in, and an occasional donkey. Goats browsing, or climbing over the stones, and children swinging, are constantly seen. But in these days the Turks seem to neglect everything, and the same melancholy state of decay is visible everywhere.

On leaving the cemetery in order to regain the streets, we had to walk over a heap of garbage large enough to distemper a whole city. It was so large, that small paths or tracks had been made across it, in which your foot often sank above the ankle. A band of ferocious street dogs were playing, barking, and basking on it. Presently we came to a large puddle of filthy water. One of the largest fallen tombstones had been placed across it, and Turks, Greeks, and Franks were glad enough to avail themselves of it as a temporary bridge. So much for the sacredness and good keeping of Turkish cemeteries!

Well, but for the ball at last, which was really a very beautiful sight; such a splendid gathering of English, French, and Sardinian officers, plenty of stars and orders, and plenty of diamonds. An ordinary ball will seem but a very dull affair after such as this. There were some Armenian ladies literally covered with diamonds; they sat still and glistened (at least their jewels did), but were remarkable, I should think, for nothing else. One of them had, too, a spray of brilliants on each side of her head, made to represent a wide wreath of laurel or bay, and the same kind of branch *en corsage*, with enormous loops of truly Oriental pearls.

Most of the Turkish ministers were present, one or two of them mild, gentlemanly-looking men, but I cannot say much for the rest. I should think that they cannot enjoy a ball much. Most of them sit, quietly talking, on the sofas,—others walk through the rooms and corridors, holding each other by the hand, after the manner of little boys. Rustim Bey is quite of the modern European school, and has positively learned to dance, no doubt to the great disgust of many a true Mussulman. He asked me the usual question of how I liked this country; and of the *country* I was able to speak with enthusiasm, just lightly touching on the things which we English missed, roads, etc., etc. A pasha, who spoke Italian pretty well, hoped I should live long among them; a wish which I devoutly trusted, *sotto voce*, might never be realized.

The Persian embassador came late, with his suite, walked through the rooms with the Oriental attaché, looked at the dancers with quiet amazement, and then seated himself on a low divan: a curious-looking old man, according to our notions of dress, but after all, the most sensible-looking person in the world. He wore a deliciously soft flowered dressing-gown, a long gray beard, through which some very fine diamonds on his breast glistened now and then, and a high conical cap of curly black lamb-skin. Lord Stratford conversed for some time with this remarkable old gentleman, through Mr. Smythe. I heard that his lordship considered the conversation not very satisfactory with regard to the alliance of Persia with England. Persia is too much exposed to the tender mercies of the Russians, who, after all, manage to keep their neighbors in great awe. Even the Turks are beginning to be very doubtful as to the ultimate success of the Allies. England has lost dreadfully in millitary reputation lately, I am sorry to say.

It was three in the morning when we left the ball-room, and they were then dancing "Sir Roger de Coverly." A more splendid and varied assemblage could hardly be imagined, although there was rather a scarcity of ladies. We returned to Mysseri's as usual. Most of the officers had ridden to the ball, to avoid getting splashed with mud, as those on foot must be, and the crowds of horses and orderlies in the court-yard of the palace, amongst a mob of Greeks, and the Turkish guard drawn up around, looked very strange in the glare of torches and lanterns, large and small.

But I must say good-night, being fairly tired out with my long letter, and after all I do not feel sure that it will be an interesting one to you. I have always so much to say, that I begin to write off that which first comes into my head, without thinking enough, perhaps, of what you would like best. When the weather is more settled, I am going to pay a visit to one or two harems, to which I am offered an introduction; then to see the mosque of Santa Sophia, and the Sultan's new palace; in fact, to "do the lions" of Constantinople, which I have not done yet, for various reasons; one of which is, the almost inexplicable aversion I have to run over beaten ground, or to go where I am told "everybody" goes.

LETTER XXII.

EASTERN CIVILIZATION—THE REFORMING SULTAN—THE LEVANTINE POPULATION—THEIR IGNORANCE AND PRETENSION—EARLY FLIRTATIONS—LARGE FAMILIES—A LEVANTINE YOUNG LADY.

Orta-kioy, January 20th, 1856.

My dear Mother:

All well, and a packet in from England, and no doubt we shall have letters from home. We hear that a telegraphic dispatch has arrived, announcing that peace is almost certain, and trust it may be true. What sorrowful stories one hears here! People ought to be very happy who are safe at home, and have not lost those dearest to them by some violent or distressing death. We do not think much of the glory of the war so near the scene of action. One can only hope and believe that much ultimate good may come of it, but it is very disheartening to see the almost hopeless state of things here, and what unsatisfactory races of people we have been helping at such a cost. Civilization seems to have begun the wrong way, and to have introduced its follies and vices before any thing else. The worst people are those most Europeanized, and the prejudiced and intolerant Mussulman, who hates us, is far better than the unprincipled renegade who cheats us. In dress it is just the same. First of all, Sultan Mahmoud, the Reformer, waged war against the turban, which not only admirably suits the Turkish cast of countenance, but protects the head from the burning rays of the sun so much better than its substitute, the fez. Next the Sultan tried to put down beards, the pride and glory of Mussulmans, which not only gave great offense and sorrow, but greatly disfigured men with small and receding jaws. There are a few fine beards left, though; and they still flourish in undisturbed magnificence in the provinces. Prezioza's charming sketches will no doubt be much more valuable as pictures of Eastern life, when all is altered here, and the European stiff, ugly dress, takes the place of flowing robes and rich coloring.

As you know, the Turks, since the days of Osman, have been distinguished as splendid military horsemen. The Sultan has taken away their short stirrups, and, in comparison, they can hardly ride at all. This is certainly an extraordinary country for doing every thing the wrong way (at least the little that is done at all), and for producing incompetent or wicked rulers. Then the waifs and strays of all nations settled here,—what a set they are, and how ashamed their respective mother-countries would be to own them! People living like flies in the sun, with no moral or religious existence, no social life, no love of country; no schools, no means of instruction; they seem to belong to no one, and no one feels any responsibility about them. The Greek and Levantine women are generally, and indeed almost necessarily, ignorant, tattling, and insipid. The Levantines are a thoroughly mongrel race, despising the two dominant races, and yet possessing all their faults without any thing that is good in either. A would-be Periote fine lady figures as a badly over-dressed Frenchwoman in an evening, and lounges on a divan in true Eastern indolence of a morning—only in a faded dressing-gown and shoes down at the heel, instead of the elegant robe and fair naked foot and embroidered slipper of the real Turkish lady. A Turkish lady's ignorance, too, does not matter, in her quiet garden life, for it is almost like that of a child. A Levantine is detestably pretentious, if she has chanced to learn to play a waltz badly of some wandering music-master, or can write a note of five lines so as to be intelligible, or to equal one by an English maid-of-all-work.

They begin their silly, trumpery love-affairs long before our English children are out of their pinafores. How often have I longed to carry off some wretched child, beflowered and bedizened, flirting away in cast-off fashions and with the most ridiculous airs in the world, and first to whip her soundly with a good and true English birch, then put her to bed before midnight (their usual hour), and array her poor wasted and pinched-up figure in good brown-holland, strap shoes, and plain straw hat the next morning, preparatory to the process of making her a child again, if possible.

The Levantines like to be considered English or French, according as their pretensions to either origin are nearest. They worship and imitate both, with a vulgar notion of making themselves "smart" and "genteel" above their neighbors, *a la* Morleena Kennigs. They affect to despise every thing here, and are always speaking of some cousin or friend who has been to England, and are dying to go themselves, confident of making a sensation. They visit you and flatter you, and beg the patterns of your gown and bonnet, and try to find out how many pocket-handkerchiefs you have got, and how you have lived in England, and if you are acquainted with Lady this or Lady that, whose name they may have seen in some stray Album of 1821. They all speak through their noses, with a terrible twang. They chatter or cackle, they do not talk; and chatter a trifle threadbare too. The most ambitious get a few shilling copies of bad novels and consider themselves literary personages. They dress their hair a pefect caricature of some way in which it was worn in Paris and London a year ago, and consider themselves leaders of fashion. They gossip and laugh with the Greek servants, and complain of them. Like them, they intrigue and tell falsehoods by bushels, but not with their happy invention and native grace. They are a terrible tissue of dirt and finery, ignorance and pretension. They can do nothing well, and you feel that nothing is in them, which is worse. Both Greeks and Turks seem to hold them in very light estimation. I said one day to Vassili, "But Madame So-and-so said so." He said, "The English speak the truth" (a piece of Greek flattery to me, I suppose), "but all the Levantines" (with a gesture of disgust) "are liars." I am afraid there is a great deal of truth in this, as well as in many other things that are said of them; and they are certainly not well calculated to give the people of the country a flattering notion of Europeans.

The Levantines almost invariably have families here so large as to be better suited to rabbits and mice, or any animal of gregarious and inexpensive habits, rather than to human beings. I have seen a faded, slovenly mother, with children of all ages, from a daughter looking as old as herself to a baby in arms. Such mothers often tell you that they were married here at fifteen, and delicately hinting that they have been grandmothers for some time, look down with a simper, and evidently expect a compliment on their youthful looks. Poor faded things they generally are! up at midnight from babyhood, as they have been. As years go on, there are successions of babies, more idle, useless, Greek and Albanian servants, more household confusion and complaint. You may imagine what is the fate of the elder children. In a conversation of the most melancholy ignorance, the daughter of a rich Levantine merchant said to me: "Ma never has time to consider what to do with us, the little ones and the servants are such a bother, and the baby is always crying. There have been one or two schools here, but they never lasted [a yawn],—always gave up—I don't know why [another yawn]; perhaps because it didn't pay, or some stupid reason or other. Ma had a governess for us once. Uncle Frank got her out from England. She cost Ma a great deal, and she was very cross to us (we plagued her finely though). These governesses are always doing something disagreeable when they come out here; they either get the cholera, or get married, just as you are beginning to get on. Our creature got married, nasty sly thing; and only fancy, she was actually engaged, it seems, when she came to us, only she couldn't marry because they had nothing to live upon, or some excuse of that kind, I know Ma said." I assure you that this is really pretty Stella's conversation, or rather drawl, as she lay on the sofa after breakfast one morning. A few questions put to me will give you a further idea of what the Levantine or Periote girls are as companions.

"It is horribly dull here, Mrs. Hornby" (with a doleful yawn). "Really I don't know how we shall get through the day." I must tell you that we were visitors at one of the loveliest villages on the Bosphorus, with a most exquisite view from the drawing-room window,—books and music,—a charming garden, our host's pride and delight,—and nothing to do but to amuse ourselves till the gentlemen returned in the evening. I thought how much I should have enjoyed being alone there without this tiresome, insipid girl; but, after looking with feelings of despair at a table covered with new books from England, I felt that I must give every thing up for gossip—she took hold of me in such a despairing manner. "I wish we were at Smyrna: there are plenty of officers there, and it's so nice; I'm afraid you will be very dull here. Mr. Host is very kind, but he's a queer man, who does not care for dancing nor any thing else that's pleasant; he only cares for a lot of dry, rubbishing books, and that nasty dull garden, where I am sure there's nothing to see.

"I suppose you're fond of reading, Mrs. Hornby?" I replied that I was. "Ah, the English have written some very pretty things; I have read a great deal at one time and another. I think one ought to be intellectual in a nasty, dull country like this, with nothing but those stupid Turks to look at. I think I almost know by heart every number of the 'Family Herald.' Don't you read the 'Family Herald'? La, you quite surprise me! It's so pretty! Now you should read 'Rosalie, or the Secret Attachment,' and 'Lady Matilda Wilhelmina,' and 'Sighs and Tears, from Anastasia's Scrap-book.' I suppose you've read Byron? There's a little house, close to Pa's, at Smyrna, where 'he lived once. I don't know what he meant by coming out here, I'm sure. I suppose, being a lord, he had plenty of friends in England. He was a very queer man,—eccentric, don't you call it? The old Turkish gardener has often told Pa how the English lord used to frighten him, walking up and down the little orchard and talking loud to himself and throwing his arms about. I suppose that's the way he wrote his poetry.

"He went to Greece after that, to look after some property that had been left him, they said at Smyrna, but he died in some outlandish place or other. It was very funny of him, when he might have been so comfortable in England. He had a very grand funeral in England, hadn't he?" I replied that I thought not, and that to the best of my recollection his heart was taken to Newstead and buried quietly there.

"Oh, indeed, how funny! I thought he had a very grand funeral in London, for I remember reading a poem, a long time ago, where there was something about a 'funeral note' and 'his martial cloak' around him,' so I thought it was Byron; Ma said so."

Here ended the literary part of our conversation, which I assure you is almost *verbatim*, only I cannot put in all the yawns, and the nasal drawl of this beautiful girl of nineteen, who is, I must add, quite above the average of Levantines. One of these heard an Englishman laughingly say something about the Ides of March the other evening at an Embassy party. I suppose she thought that he alluded to beans, or some other vegetable, for she said very promptly, "The green peas are not up yet." (Whenever we have any beans now, we call them the Ides of March.) There is certainly much to be done in this part of the world.

LETTER XXIII.

NEW-YEAR'S DAY—COSTUMES—GREEK WOMEN—REVELS—VISIT TO AN ARMENIAN FAMILY—VASSILI—INTERVIEW WITH A BASHI-BAZOUK—VILLAGERS—TURKISH CHILDREN.

Orta-kioy, January 24th, 1856.

My dear Mr. Hornby:

I told you, in a former letter, how we spent New-Year's Day at Constantinople. The Greek New-Year's Day falls upon the 13th of our new year. The old watchmen chanted prayers at daybreak, at the doors of all Greek houses. Except the poorest of the poor, every one sported something new and gay on this day. Some of the embroidered Greek and Albanian jackets displayed by the young beaux were really beautiful—scarlet braided with gold, and others green and gold. The Albanian jacket is worn with the sleeves hanging over the shoulder, like those of our Hussars. How strange and dark English dresses will seem to me, after all these brilliant colors! How will my eyes endure a fustian jacket and hideous English hat or an English villager's waistcoat, after having been so charmed with every variety of picturesque form and brilliant color? With the beautifully embroidered scarlet and gold jacket, for instance, you often see full trousers of dark rich green, bound round the waist by a many-colored scarf, into which is stuck a richly-mounted yataghan, or silver-embossed pistol—frequently both. The under-jacket, or waistcoat, is also richly embroidered, and with a double row of dead gold buttons. Three or four rows of silver chain, just like a *châtelaine,* complete the gala dress of a Greek village beau. As it is winter, I must not, however, forget his gayly-embroidered leggings, which are something like the Indian moccasin. His mustache is perfect, pointed, and the pride and delight of his life. A few dark curls peep from under his fez, and he toys with his cigarette with the air of a prince. Alas for our village belles, if he were but to saunter among them some sunny evening! and alas for the honest fustian coat and ugly English hat!

The Greeks seem to be fond of paying visits on New-Year's Day. I was greatly amused, watching from my window different groups of them winding round the hill or crossing the narrow road halfway down the valley. Some of the women still wore the beautiful Greek dress, with fine plaits of hair wreathed round their heads, or handkerchiefs charmingly put on, the colored trimming so arranged as to form a chaplet round the brow. I must bring home some of this pretty trimming, so like leaves and flowers. But I am sorry to say that the national dress of the Greek women is disappearing in these parts much more rapidly than that of the men, and they disfigure themselves sadly by aping English and French fashions. I was grieved to hear last autumn that some caiquejees' wives and daughters had made their appearance at the Sweet Waters of Asia perfect scarecrows, from an absurd attempt to copy the dress of some Frenchwoman whom they had seen and admired. What a pity that civilization should begin the wrong way! In the villages, however, this painful transition state is not so much seen as at Pera, and

Orta-kioy certainly presented a genuine picture of Eastern life on New-Year's Day.

There was plenty of dancing and singing going on in the valley, if a nasal kind of chanting can be called singing. Long after midnight the wind, setting in toward our hill, bore sounds of revelry, and the monotonous roll of a little drum, which seems to be the favorite accompaniment of the Romaika, or Greek dance. The Greeks are a marvelously active, restless race. The night's revels are scarcely over, when, at dawn, the watchman chants to prayer. They shout and gesticulate almost as loudly in the Mass, as they did half an hour before in the rude Romaika. I went to one of their religious services some time ago, and was painfully impressed with the glare and tinsel, and the sensual, dirty appearance of the priests, who looked more like robed brigands than any thing else.

The pictures of saints and martyrs are extremely hideous, nearly black, and barbarously ornamented with silver or tin hands and "glories." Those who are able to make a rich offering will order the entire picture of a saint to be covered with silver, except the face, which peeps darkly through. The people bend and pray with extraordinary reverence and devotion before these pictures, many of which are of great antiquity.

My Armenian neighbors were early at prayers on New-Year's morning. At a later hour Fuad and I were pacing up and down our little trim garden, and I gathered a few violets to remind me of England. It was a lovely morning, and we watched three or four swans flying northward; and long flights of cormorants pursuing their way on the opposite coast, sometimes in straight lines, then in a dense body, then in the form of an arrow, then in a strange and fantastic manner, like a long and undulating serpent. Poor Simione, the mute, came to gather me a few stray flowers which the winter storms had left; roses and verbenas have lasted longest here. His mother looked out from her lattice, smiled, and saluted me sweetly as usual: she has such a mild and placid face. She asked me something by signs, but I could not understand it, and shook my head despondingly, on which she sent Antonio down with a note written in his ever-ready Italian. These little epistles amuse us so much that I preserve them carefully, and send you a translation of this morning's.

"Dearest and illustrious Lodger:

"My widowed mother and my sisters salute you tenderly and with all their hearts on this New-Year's morning, and your General [Antonio will persist in calling Edmund, Signor Generale]. They wish to know if your house pleases you, if you are contented, and if they can do any thing to serve you. They hope that the child you love so much is well, and that God may bless you with great prosperity. They thank you for the good dish with which you have regaled them. Always, dearest lady, your friend and servant, ANTONIO ALMIRA."

I made signs of thanks, and that I would write a further reply. They begged me to walk into their house, which I did, admiring the dim old hall, with an orange-tree on each side of the foot-worn steps, its broken marble fountain, trellised roof, and the quaintly-painted birds and flowers and pomegranates, on its whitewashed walls.

The whole house looked dilapidated and dismantled, and every thing wore the air of an impoverished and decayed family. The divans and even footstools were still covered with black, as mourning for the husband and father; heavy hangings to the doorways of the vast and numerous rooms were of the same sad hue; the only gay thing was a picture of the Virgin and Child, which was decked out with flowers and tiny wax tapers in honor of the New Year. Huge *braseros* stood in the principal room of the first suite of apartments, which is evidently that generally used by the family, and where I always see the sisters sitting at their embroidery, as I walk in my garden; but there was no fire, and my dear old friend looked pale and cold in her thin and faded mourning. I wrote my note of the kindest words I could possibly pen, and we sat on the divan admiring the lovely view. Far and wide, how beautiful every thing looked in the bright morning sun! People here learn to sit quietly, while the eye roams about with the keenest pleasure.

I was now served with sweetmeats; Dhudu and poor Oscu vying with each other affectionately to do me honor. Neither of them would sit before their mother and myself, on so state an occasion as my first visit. Antonio stood by my side, pencil in hand, by the aid of which and of signs we kept up an animated conversation. How little serves to please when there is really the wish on both sides! Simione placed a little inlaid table before his mother and myself, and I saw with alarm that they intended to give me a feast.

First, Dhudu handed sweets, cherries delicately preserved, and a rare old china jar full of preserved rose-leaves from Persia; then Oscu presented two large glass cups of water with her thin pale hands; after which came delicious little cups of fragrant coffee, and a dish of figs from Smyrna, mixed with bitter almonds. The old lady, who seemed to take as much affectionate pride in cramming me as if I had been a darling schoolboy home for the holidays, now tore some of the largest of the figs open with her fingers, and, stuffing them with the almonds, presented them to me one by one. You may fancy the dismay with which I was filled, on seeing the prompt and zealous preparation of these boluses. I felt that I must be ill, and gave myself up for lost; my situation was indeed so ludicrous that I laughed outright, and they thought that I was highly delighted. Poor things! they have few visitors, and but little to amuse their lonely life; so I considered that one fit of indigestion could not do me much harm, and yielded to the fun and amusement of the fête. How delighted the dear old lady was to please me! How fast she peeled the oranges, and popped little pieces on to the pounded sugar on my plate, and helped me to large pink slices of preserved quince, and talked of me to her daughters, and patted my hand affectionately; Antonio and Simione looking on approvingly all the time, as proud as if they were entertaining a princess—such kind and simple people are these! At last I thought the feast was happily ended; but, alas! Dhudu opened a fine rich-colored pomegranate, and, scooping out all its bright and shining seeds, placed them, sprinkled with fine white sugar before me. Oh for the enchanted cock of the Arabian Nights' story, thought I, to pick them all up for me! But my philosophy could go no further; I was obliged politely but firmly to refuse both that last dainty and also a cigarette made by the fair hands of Dhudu. However, the ladies each took one, and, smoking with great complacency, we had a little quiet chat about England and things in general, and then I took my departure, amid much bowing and many adieus. They all came down to the little garden-steps of our door with great ceremony. I must not forget to tell you that Fuad was of the party, kissed and romped with by the ladies, and regaled with almost as many sweets as his mistress, which however, thoroughly Eastern as he is, seemed to afford him unmitigated satisfaction.

Vassili is very kind to my little dog, and sometimes takes him into the village for exercise; Fuad likes the crowded, narrow streets better than I do. Vassili is certainly an oddity; he is generally extremely gloomy, and only condescends to be cheerful upon rare occasions. I believe he seldom speaks to Georgy, our new and handsome sais; but his great friend is Nicola, Mr. Wilkin's man, who has known him for years. Nicola says that Vassili was once very "well off," but was robbed at Cairo, by an Egyptian, of every thing he had in the world, which has soured his temper ever since. So whenever he looks more gloomy than usual, we say that the "robbery in Egypt" is full upon him. He has a wife and four children at Smyrna, and sends off his wages to them the moment he gets them. He always asks if the "Signorina" is well, when he sees me reading letters from England. I thank him, and say "Yes." He then invariably adds, in Italian, "Heaven be praised! the young are always charming." I said one day to him, out of gratitude for his inquiries, "And how are your children, Vassili; have you heard from them lately?" This offended his taciturnity; he had not bargained to be so much more gracious than usual, and returned a snappish reply of, "Poor men's children are always well, and with great appetites." Thinking he would be pleased to hear of the Sultan's firman in favor of the Greeks, I told him of it one day when he was laying the cloth; but he only growled out from under his black mustache, "I dare say our Patriarch has given some pasha a heap of money for it; *we* shall get nothing by it." Vassili takes to heart greatly the oppression and poverty of his countrymen, but we think that the robbery in Egypt is the principal cause of his misanthropy and melancholy. Vassili takes great delight in cooking, and places a favorite dish upon the table with a grim look of satisfaction. He was quite in despair last week when Edmund only took invalid's allowance. The way in which I always show anxiety is by not eating; and the other day, when every thing went away untouched, he exclaimed angrily, "Che ha Vossignoria, che non mangia?" (What is the matter with you, ma'am, that you do not eat?) I took the rebuke meekly, and spoke of want of exercise, etc.

The other night he asked leave of Edmund to bring in a Bashi-Bazouk, a friend of his, who was anxious to join the Turkish Contingent with a thousand men. The Bashi came up,—a fine savage-looking fellow, with a sashful of yataghans and silver-mounted pistols. Mr. Wilkin was here, who speaks Turkish. At first the

Bashi would not say a word. We found this was because of Antonio the Armenian, who was quietly sitting smoking by our stove. When he was gone, the Bashi became eloquent about what his men would do and dare. Edmund and I thought it a pity that we had not made the Bashi's acquaintance before the fall of Kars, as with another thousand such free-lances we might have cut our way to them with a few camel-loads of provisions. As it is, he has written to General Vivian, now in England. Some time ago the Contingent were greatly in want of recruits. Vassili and Georgy are extremely anxious about this affair, and stood on the stairs while the conference lasted in our outer room. Espinu tells me that Vassili is to have a new coat, and Georgy a sword, if the Bashi and his men are accepted by the general.

We have often questions asked of us by the village people. I found a Turk waiting in our outer room the other day, who evidently wished to ask some favor. He could not speak Italian, and Vassili was out; so he went away disappointed. Another day I met him in the garden, and then Vassili told me that he wanted Edmund to write to General Vivian about his brother Omar, a captain in the Contingent, who had left his family in his charge. The wife was ill, and pined to see him. They were also falling into great poverty from her sickness, he having left them only a hundred piastres (about fifteen shillings) a month. Edmund will do what he can to get Omar leave of absence.

The three little Turkish children were brought to see me yesterday, two boys and a girl, the latter a perfect beauty, but dressed in pale lilac and yellow gauze,—on such a cold day,—embroidered slippers, and no stockings. She laughed at the few Turkish words I was able to speak, sat down with gravity on the divan, and gave me the kiss I asked for. We then discussed a few sweetmeats, and I took her down to her uncle, who remained in the garden, no persuasion having the slightest effect in inducing him to enter a lady's room.

With the old-fashioned Turks you must be very careful not to offend their notions of female delicacy. I used to offer my hand, but they evidently think it so indecorous that I have left it off, except to those few who have mixed with Europeans. Dr. Zohrab tells me he has often been sent for to a great man's sick wife or slave, and has been shown a heap of shawls lying upon a sofa, and told to prescribe for it: in extreme cases only was he allowed to see the face or touch the hand. These poor women are almost constantly ailing from want of air or exercise: the higher their rank, the more they are shut up. Bleeding in the arm and foot is a common remedy, even among the Armenians. My friend Dhudu came limping in from this cause the other day: I said to her brother, in Italian, that a good walk would have been better for her.

The minarets of the mosques here, and the opposite ones of Kulalee, were illuminated the night before last in celebration of Mahomet's birthday. It is so pretty to watch the wreaths of lamps glittering in the darkness, high in air.

But I must say adieu. Colonel Ibor has just come down, and dinner will soon be ready. I told you we had a flying visit from Mr. Mansfield, on his way to the Crimea; he stole a pot of Vassili's preserves for his friends there. Captain Giffard could not come, as his ship was to sail that very day.

Mr. Gisborne has brought me a beautiful white cloak (*burnous*) from Cairo. He is delighted with Egypt, at least with the country, antiquities, and climate; the people are as oppressed and as miserable as they are here, although a far livelier race.

Admiral Slade is coming to see us to-morrow, so I shall have plenty of Turkish news. The wind is still bringing snow and frost from the north; I fear Edmund will not lose his severe cold while it lasts. Love to you all.

LETTER XXIV.

WINTER LIFE ON THE BOSPHORUS—ARMENIAN BISHOP—BILL OF FARE—THE PIANO-FORTE—CURES FOR NEURALGIA—WRECKS FROM THE BLACK SEA—POOR JEWS.

Orta-kioy, January 29th, 1856.

My dearest Mother:

You wish to know what sort of a life it is on the Bosphorus in winter time. Mine is certainly a strange one, and of great extremes, for I am either alone for hours here, or in the midst of crowds at Pera, when the embassadress's invitations summon me. Edmund usually leaves home about nine in the morning. Fuad and I generally accompany him to the pretty little stable-yard, where there is an ancient-looking well, and a drooping willow whose branches wave to the ground. Our new Sais, a remarkably handsome Greek, who, in his rich embroidery, looks exactly like the portraits of Conrad, in drawing-room copies of the "Corsair," keeps his stable in the nicest order. On saints' days and holidays, a pretty wreath of flowers is always arched over the door. He sleeps there, on a few raised planks, covered with a quilted Turkish counterpane. On a little bracket by the side of this rude bed is an antique-shaped pretty vase of flowers; and, close by, hangs an instrument something like a small guitar, on which Georgy plays of an evening to a select friend or two. Georgy takes vast pride in his appearance, and loves his horses dearly, next only to his black Maltese dog,—an elfish-looking beast, with a few red beads hung by a stout string round his neck, as a charm against the dreaded "evil eye."

Well, Fuad and I see them off, and admire "Sultan's" arched neck and shining skin. He is what they call here a golden bay. Georgy just bestows one slight glance on some Greek girls who are admiring him from an opposite casement, and then, mounting "Turkish Johnny," gallops after his master, who is slowly winding down the hill. I wave my hand, Vassili snappishly calls Fuad in, shuts to the gates, and we are alone until seven in the evening.

Our great mastiff has arrived from Trebizond. He is a magnificent creature, and we have named him Arslan, or Lion. I am afraid he misses the liberty of his free mountain-life, and think that both he and I feel rather like prisoners, as we pace up and down the tiny paths of our trim shawl-pattern garden. Fuad, full of fun and frolic, affords a striking contrast to his grave demeanor and gigantic proportions. Arslan and Fuad, looking out of my window, would make a most amusing sketch. Dignified as he is, Arslan does not despise a morning lounge on the divan. If Fuad is too frolicsome, Arslan holds him down between his huge paws, where he looks like a little white struggling mouse. Sometimes the two play together in the most absurd manner, Arslan taking Fuad up in his mouth like a snowball.

Nothing can be more perfect than my solitude is at times. You know I have often wished to be quite alone for several months, that I might do what I liked without being disturbed. Now I have certainly got my wish. My day is so long that I can afford to sit on the divan beneath my windows, dreaming for hours, looking out over the blue Bosphorus and the hills beyond, or noting all that takes place in the valley beneath, and watching the passers-by.

The Armenian bishop and his wife in the latticed house opposite have many visitors; they seem to be of the old school, and the lady is always closely vailed and muffled in a feridjee whenever she goes out. I have seen her twice in her garden, and once in the ruined garden-plot beside it, "gathering simples," and she then wears the full trowsers and jacket of Eastern costume. Vailed ladies often call at this ancient house. After knocking at the quaintest-looking old knocker in the world, an old Armenian servitor admits them courteously into the high-walled court-yard; and presently we, from the divan, can see their shadowy forms flit across the lattices of the second floor, evidently the women's apartment. Robed priests are also frequent visitors, and these are admitted to the rooms on the ground floor, whence the bishop himself often emerges to give alms to a wandering pilgrim, or to buy sweetmeats of a great friend of Fuad's and mine, who carries the most delicious condiments about, on a pretty painted stand. There are three beautiful children in this house. Two little boys play about in the courtyard, and sometimes the nurse holds the baby above the lattice for me to smile and wave my hand to it. We are told that the bishop wishes to make our acquaintance, and intends calling on us. I should have thought that our military visitors would have rather puzzled him; for many redcoats find their way here on their way to and from the Crimea, and may be often seen joining the canine party on the divan under the window to talk with delight of old friends, old times, and news from home; all of which must be very shocking to Eastern notions of propriety.

Vassili's reputation has certainly caused an increased amount of affectionate attention from our friends. Our little dinners are pronounced delightful. Only fancy the treat of excellent soup, delicious red mullet, lamb, and pistachio-nuts, ducks stewed with chestnuts, and quails in vine-leaves, to these half-famished men of Asia Minor and the camp in the Crimea! There is some pleasure in being hostess here in these days of war and famine; something more than giving a dinner-party, in feeling that you have been feeding a favorite son or a hungry husband.

But to give you an idea of what an Englishwoman's life is here. After my stroll in the garden, and gossiping lounge on the divan, and feeding the Bashi-Bazouks, and arranging a few flowers, I turn to the poor old piano-forte, which four stout hamals, directed by Vassili, carried up-stairs into the salaamlik for me the other day. We were fortunate enough to find a young German belonging to the Opera at Pera, who by degrees got the poor instrument into something like tune. I was much amused at Dhudu's explanation of its being so much out of order. I said one day, through Miss Clara Barker, who was with me: "How is it that so new and good an instrument is so rusty and shaken?" Dhudu replied, in her quiet, gentle way, that some time ago they were staying at a country-house by the seaside, when a fire broke out, and they were obliged to throw the piano out of the window. "It fell into the sea," said Dhudu, "and has never been quite in tune since." They are delighted to have it restored, and it is the greatest pleasure I have, next to my letters, to sing and play for hours, until poor Fuad, after lying long and patiently at my feet, can bear it no longer, and sits up on his hind legs, entreating with his black bead-eyes that I will leave off. Then I pace up and down for an hour or more by way of exercise, quick march, to circulate my blood; for the stove in the inner room gives but little heat, and the weather is so piercingly cold, that I am obliged, whilst writing or singing, to wear Edmund's tiger-skin. How you would laugh to see me, with the paws crossed over my shoulders, sitting alone so silently that the little bright-eyed mice come out fearlessly to eat bread and milk out of Fuad's saucer by the window!

The kitchen is in the garden, and quite away from the house. On snowy days our hall-door is closed; and when the little Greek maid, whom Mrs. Barker kindly lends me for an hour or two in a morning, is gone, I pace up and down, as lonely as Mariana in the moated grange. Toward evening Vassili comes in with a replenished basket of wood for the stove, which he puts in silently. This quiet life seems to suit him well. He told me the other day that the Armenian lady had asked him how I passed my time, so much alone as I was: he replied, "Scrive e legge, legge e scrive," (She writes and reads, and reads and writes.) This made the dear old lady very uneasy about me; and this morning she paid me a long visit, with Antonio), whose fine dark eyes were full of anxious kindness, as he wrote in Italian, entreaties that I would take more care of myself, and that I would consent to see the Imaum of the mosque here, in order to cure my neuralgia. They consider him, of course, an "idolater," wrote Antonio, but fully believe that he possesses the art of charming away pain by passing his fingers over the part affected. The old lady illustrated his treatment by pressing her fingers down the side of my head and throat, where I have lately suffered acute pain. It certainly relieved me very much, and from the extraordinary cures which she tells me the Imaum has performed, I should think the Turks are good mesmerists. However, I did not promise to try either this remedy, or the usual infallible Mussulman medicine, of a verse of the Koran inscribed on a slip of paper and dissolved in water. My kind neighbor's sympathy did me great good, and I believe that a fireplace, and good stone-walls, instead of thin planks, would do still more.

The weather has been very severe. I often see, in a morning, mere hulls of vessels towed down from the Black Sea—rigging, masts, all swept away. The cold of the East is sharp and pinching—just as if old Winter had caught you between his finger and thumb. How the poor must suffer in this miserable valley! I often look, in a morning, to see if the tents in the ruins are still standing among the pools of mud and water, and think with horror that they are the only shelter of many children, and even babies. A few wretched wooden houses are inhabited only by Jews: the casements are still unfinished, and the famished and dripping wild-dogs prowl in and out at their pleasure. On Friday evenings these poor Jew people light little lamps for their expected Messiah; they flicker faintly over a scene of wretchedness such as only an Eastern village can show.

But I must say adieu. The twilight is short here, and the Muezzin is calling the faithful to evening prayer. My little stove is burning brightly, my kettle singing its usual merry tune, my birds settling to roost, and Fuad wetching for his master's return. So you see how cheerful I am after all.

LETTER XXV.

GOING TO A BALL—THE TELEKI—JOURNEY TO PERA—MONUMENTS—ADMINISTRATION—DOLMA BATCHE—BAD ROADS—CEMETERY AT PERA—CYPRESSES—SOLDIERS—ILLUMINATIONS—BALL AT THE EMBASSY—THE SULTAN—CHIEF OF THE EUNUCHS—A BEAR AT THE BALL—ESPINU'S ENTHUSIASM.

Orta-kioy, February 8th, 1856.

My dearest Mother:

Going to a ball from a village near Constantinople is a very different thing to going to one in England, as you may suppose. Edmund had directed our two caiquejees to be ready by four o'clock, to take me in to Pera, but by noon a tremendous north wind came rushing down from the Black Sea, and the Bosphorus was soon lashed into fury.

Of course a caique was now quite out of the question, even to me, who glory in a good rough sea; so, after a short consultation, Vassili sallied forth into the village in search of an araba, or teleki, and after an immense amount of bargaining and disputing, the dilapidated affair (which we had often seen moldering in a ruined outhouse) was announced as likely to be ready to take me to Pera within half an hour.

After many difficulties, my Spanish dress was finished to perfection. The difficulty, of my little Greek maid being too young and too pretty to be left for many hours alone in a palace, was got over by Mrs. Barker most kindly offering to lend one of her servants. Espinu was delighted, and an object of the greatest envy to Nicoletta and the rest of the servants in the dark-red Turkish house above us.

Espinu speaks only Greek, of which I know but a few words, so, as you may imagine, I should have infinitely preferred Nicoletta, who speaks Italian. However, if not useful to me, Espinu was at least highly ornamental. She is really a very handsome woman; and all her little finery was displayed on this occasion. A dress of bright-green silk and gold bracelets, a fez on her head, with the thick purple tassel combed down all over it, and bound round by two immense plaits of splendid black hair, a gayly-embroidered handkerchief round her neck, very prettily put on—in fact, quite a saint's-day toilet.

How I laughed when the crazy teleki came to the door! Imagine a very dirty, tawdry, diminutive Lord Mayor's coach, or a halfpenny edition of Cinderella's pumpkin, with two most wretched white horses tied to it by a strange entanglement of leather thongs and rope. A "charm," of blue and red beads, against the "evil eye," hung round the neck of each of these poor animals, whose appearance certainly was far more likely to inspire feelings of pity than of envy. "Are we to carry the horses, or are they to carry us?" said I to Vassili, as I stood with the magnificent Espinu at the gate. The Greek driver laughed heartily on this being translated to him, but declared that his cattle would do the journey well. Having got the vehicle, the next difficulty to be overcome was how to get into it. No step, no door! I saw with dismay that Espinu and I (neither of us at all in the fairy style) must inevitably take a flying leap through the window, which was obligingly opened for us. I must say that my heart rather misgave me for a moment, especially as I saw the Armenian bishop's eyes gleaming through the opposite lattice; but presently taking shame to myself that an Englishwoman should quail at any thing, and invoking the spirit of the clown I had seen so cheerfully risk his neck in the last pantomime, I tucked up my petticoats as high as consideration for the Armenian bishop would permit, and one spring from the loose stone at our door settled me comfortably on "all-fours" at the bottom of the teleki, with no other injury than a slight knock on the head. Espinu was still more fortunate, for her husband, Nicola, came down to see her off, and giving several efficient "shoves" in the midst of his adieus, she was soon packed by my side.

Vassili then put the portmanteau and Edmund's cocked-hat case and sword upon the opposite seat, the Greek driver seized the tattered reins, yelled in the most frightful manner at his horses, and off we started.

Jolt No. 1 knocked our two heads together; No. 2 nearly sent us through the glass in front; No. 3, down came the cocked-hat case into my lap; No. 3, down went the portmanteau upon our feet. At first we tried to recover the things and put them into the seat again; but some fearful swayings to and fro and bumpings in going down the hill, soon made us regardless of every thing but holding fast, and saving our heads as much as possible.

The shaking we suffered was really something frightful. Every now and then you think that nothing can possibly prevent the whole concern from toppling over. You say to yourself, "Is it possible that we are going over those enormous stones, or round that frightfully unprotected corner, or through that sea of mud?" You think, "Well, we must be over now!" but crash gees the painted, crazy thing, destitute of springs, over immense holes, then perhaps over half-a-dozen huge, loose paving-stones, again wallows into another hole, feet deep in mud, and then hangs all on one side, like a fly on a precipice; the horses being frequently twisted round, so that you cannot see them or the driver, who is generally on foot and hanging on to the reins somewhere. Our carriage had, however, once been very gorgeous, a deliciously barbarous representation of the Bosphorus being daubed over its roof, and yellow satin curtains festooned round the door-window; this, being intended for the shrouding of Turkish beauty, was so cunningly and jealously contrived, that we had to stoop very low to look out. The guards at the Sultan's palace stared, as they always do, to see an Englishwoman in a teleki.

It was a very fine day, and all Beshicktash seemed abroad. I suppose the Sultan was making some presents for I saw several black slaves coming out of the palace with trays upon their heads, covered with embroidered muslin, just as they were in the days of the Arabian Nights. By the fountain was a great crowd; and among noisy and laughing Greeks and the usual motley groups one sees so constantly in this country, the Turks were even condescending to look interested at a little spring-cart containing three French soldiers, *en route* to the French camp at Mashlack. I really think that I was as delighted to see this triumph of civilization and springs as the admiring crowd who shouted after it. We had a cart here the other day, by-the-by, and the whole village was in a state of commotion. I rushed to the window to see what it was all about, and felt proud of my country when I beheld the vehicle with its perfectly round wheels winding its way with comparative facility over the ruts and stones of our village road.

Notwithstanding, however, our shaking, we reached Beshicktash without any accident of moment. Here I noticed a charming little store of pottery, which I intend to visit some day, and spend no end of piastres in. The vessels of clay in general use are really charming, from the monster and griffin style, which is manufactured at the Dardanelles, to the classical and elegant shapes which still hold oil, wine, and water for the Greeks. I intend to bring home an immense hamper of these: few of them cost more than three or four piastres. I was greatly taken with the huge oil-vases, and thought instantly of Morgiana and the Forty Thieves; they are quite large enough to hold a man. It is a delightful thing here to find that Time has not swept away all the pretty things of the Arabian Nights. Even the large silver basins containing covered dishes and plates, cups, etc., which the Genii bring on their heads to Aladdin, are still to be seen, and bought.

The tomb of Barbarossa exists in an excellent state of preservation in this village. Very near it are two huge Roman sarcophagi. The Turks care not a straw for "remains" or antiquities of any kind, so no care whatever is bestowed on either. I shall endeavor to bring home a good sketch of these interesting tombs, but fear that the inscriptions are too much erased for even the learned in such matters to make any thing out of them. It was most pleasant, on nearing the Sultan's new palace, to find ourselves rolling smoothly over an excellent road, with a causeway for foot-passengers, an avenue planted, and lamp-posts all ready for the gas which is to come: all honor to Abdul Medjid! What a relief it was to leave off clinging like cats or monkeys, and to sit still and look about us like rational beings! The Greek mounted the rickety piece of wood pertaining to the driver, Vassili placed himself complacently by his side, the white horses were got into an almost even trot, and it is difficult for you English people, spoiled with every comfort, to imagine the enjoyment which that small piece of road was to all of us. Espinu kept laughing with delight, and crying out "Buono, buono!" I tried to make her understand that in England all the roads were like this: but although she was very polite about the matter, it was quite evident to see she could not "take it in." When we came to the new palace, "Dolma Batche," as it is called, there were between twenty and thirty caparisoned horses standing by the beautiful white marble gateway, through which you see the waters of the Bosphorus, and a lovely glimpse of the hills beyond. A crowd of vailed women, lame, halt, and blind, were dispersing. These always haunt the Sultan, both when he goes to mosque, and when he pays his almost daily visits to Dolma Batche, to watch the progress of the building. A Turkish officer rides close behind the Sultan, and this "official" carries a bag filled with small silver coin (gold on great occasions), and a portfolio to receive petitions, which can only, and as a matter of precaution, be presented to the Sultan by women. These are frequently seen catching at his stirrup, at least when they can approach near enough. You may suppose what a scramble there is for the silver, when it is thrown. The Sultan has a very kind heart, and always makes one of his retinue see that the blind are cared for first of all. When he receives a petition, he hands it to the officer of the portfolio, whose business it is to read it, and subsequently to place it before the Sultan if worthy of notice, returning a civil answer to those which are not. This office, like all that is theoretically good in Turkey, is sadly abused. It is not very often, however, that such abuses are discovered, or if discovered, punished; but the following instance is worthy of record.

A few months ago a gross act of injustice and oppression had been perpetrated on a Turk, either by a cadi or a pasha, I do not remember which, and it does not much matter, for one is generally about as bad as the other. The poor Turk, on the verge of ruin, with no hope of either law or justice, except such as might spring from a direct appeal to the Sultan, found means to present a petition: it met with no reply. After some time he ventured upon another, but that, and a third also, remained unnoticed. Had the Turk been friendless, no doubt his petitions would have been forgotten as many sad ones had been before, and his cry for mercy would never have been heard in this world; but fortunately he had a friend who was on intimate terms with a pasha. The pasha found an opportunity of mentioning the three petitions to the Sultan, who had never seen one of them, the officer no doubt having been bribed by the offending party not to place them in his hands. It was afterward found that he had done this on many occasions, and had refused a favorable answer from the Sultan to those who could not afford him a "bakshish." The Sultan behaved as well as he always seems to do on those rare occasions when he hears the truth: he saw justice done to the poor Turk, and dismissed his officer. This you may rely on as perfectly true.

After passing Dolma Batche the shaking was more terrible than ever. The road takes a sudden turn up a tremendous hill, and is formed of what we call kerb-stones, thrown down in the middle of a field. Half-way up the ascent, the river is like a scene of enchantment; the Sultan's white marble palace, the glittering Bosphorus, the Asian hills, the cypress-trees, and minarets of different villages lie below you; and when, by great good luck, your teleki has arrived at the summit without toppling over, the Sea of Marmora and the mountains in the distance, and, nearer, the beautiful cliffs of Scutari, charm you completely into forgetfulness of the shaking and bruises which you have received. Below, to the right, a cheerful glimpse of a new road which the Sultan is making from Dolma Batche quite into Pera, may be caught. This approach to the town will be an immense comfort to all, especially to Europeans. The inspection of this road, and of the progress which is being made in his New Palace, seems to be the Sultan's only pleasure and delight. Edmund often meets him riding rapidly back to Beshicktash, to avoid the dusk of the evening, with his poor, ragged, badly-mounted Lancers clattering after him.

But I am afraid that I am a very wandering letter-writer. I was at the top of the hill, with the glittering sea before me, and on it many ships of war, and the usual wild-looking Greek feluccas, and flights of snow-white gulls, when I stopped to tell you about the Sultan's new road from Dolma Batche. A few more jolts over still larger and looser stones, brought our carriage suddenly into the thick shade of the cypress-trees of the "Grand Champ des Morts." What a vast place it is, and how truly magnificent are its funereal trees! You know those large poplars in Weybridge churchyard: fancy the effect of a forest of such as these, with innumerable turbaned stones—some slanting forward, some upright, some fallen on the ground—beneath these huge bare stems. The eye follows with awe many a winding, rugged pathway through this silent forest of the dead, and is sometimes startled by seeing a moving turban gliding slowly away in the distance; for these pathways lead to various parts of Pera, just as the different roads in our parks lead to different parts of London. As I told you in a former letter, the Pera side of this cypress-wood is much frequented, and is untidy, dirty, and noisy; but on this side, all is as silent as, according to our ideas, Eastern sepulchres should be; and a vailed Turkish woman stealing noiselessly along, or telling her beads on an ancient wayside stone, as I saw one, adds to the solemn beauty and impressiveness of the scene. Many of the stones seem to be of great antiquity; the inscriptions, in bas-relief, are rapidly crumbling away, and the carved flowers and leaves are almost obliterated, even under that thick and constant shelter. But every now and then you come upon a fresh and splendid group, which is almost startling in the sombre light, and the hush around you. I saw several painted a brilliant blue, and richly gilt. A family party looks extremely well, with the white-turbaned husband-stone at the top (of a square flagstone); and the lady-stone, shorter, and fashioned into something like an upright leaf, at the bottom; with perhaps three or four demure children-stones, ranged on either side in their little turbans; but I must bring home a sketch of Preziosa's. He has a most exquisite one, of a group of those tombs, in the midst of which a lamp is burning in the deepest cypress gloom; and has, it is said, never been extinguished for more than three centuries. What travelers have said of women having no monuments, you see, is not true. There are quite as many women's stones as men's, both here and at Scutari, and in all the Asian villages where I have been. Sometimes there are two or three of these leaf-shaped women's stones in a family group, generally having a rose or a pomegranate-flower carved upon them, but they never of course have either turban or fez. By-the-by, the modern red fez, with its purple tassel, looks very ugly amid the fine turbans of the olden time.

Suddenly emerging from these ancient cyrpresses and monumental stones, and finding yourself in all the noise, bustle, dirt, and confusion of Pera, gives one the sensation of having overstepped three or four centuries. From thoughts of ancient Byzantium, and of the long rule of the Osmanlies, brought most forcibly before the mind by these solemn acres of turbaned-stones representing them, three lurches of your teleki place before you the whole story of the present war. English, French, Sardinian, and German officers and soldiers are seen at every turn, and loud are the fraternizing songs which burst every now and then from the khans or cafés. It is very amusing to note the look of quiet amazement with which the Turks regard the noisy merriment and enthusiasm of our soldiers and sailors. They calmly puff on, in their cloud of smoke, while Jack is singing or speechifying at the top of his voice, forgetting that not one word of his eloquence is understood by his wondering neighbor. It is curious that Jack can never rid himself of the idea that foreigners could understand what he says to them if they only would. "Come, don't be disagreeable," (in the most persuasive tone); "let's be jolly!" accompanied by an affectionate pat on the back, is a favorite way of "coaxing" some magnificent Turk into mirth and conversation.

There was a stir of quite an unusual kind in Pera, on the afternoon of the ball. People looked more inclined to loiter, and were more curious than usual. The Greeks were conversing in groups; unusual numbers of troops were moving about; trays of bouquets were being rapidly conveyed hither and thither; sedan-chairs were evidently in great request, no doubt for the purpose of paying frantic visits to late milliners or dawdling dressmakers; and mounted pashas, looking graver and more important than ever, forced their way along with their usual train of pipe-bearers and cavasses, only just betraying the slightest possible touch of the "flurry" and excitement in which the whole of Pera was plunged.

When I arrived at the palace, Mr. Doria (one of the attachés) was finishing his inspection of the illuminations, which had been entrusted by Lady Stratford de Redcliffe to his care. The words, or rather names, of

"Abdul Medjid" and "Victoria" were to greet the Sultan's eyes, hanging, as it were, on air across the court. The Turks excel in this mode of illumination at the feasts of Bairam and Ramazan, linking minaret to minaret by wreaths and devices of lights. The whole of the palace was brilliantly illuminated. The court-yard was a blaze of light, and lined with the horse and foot Artillery, and two companies of Grenadiers and Highlanders. I had just finished dressing when the roar of cannon began, announcing that the Sultan had left his palace at Beshicktash. Mistress Espinu was quite frantic as to her chance of seeing the sultan; and being constantly employed in climbing up at the windows to watch for him, and at the same time to admire the illuminations, she was certainly of no very particular use to me. Most fortunately an Italian was in the palace, who dressed my hair beautifully, and, having been in Spain, adjusted my mantilla and damask roses to perfection. This was certainly a most exciting moment; the cannon roared away, and every one was on the tiptoe of expectation. In a few minutes the guns left off firing, and then I knew, by the band playing "God save the Queen," that the sultan had arrived. As to Espinu, she was so excited with the illuminations, and the cannon, and the soldiers, and the music, that I wonder the sultan did not tumble over her prostrate form on his entrance.

The sultan had, with very good taste, left his own guard at the Galata Serai, and was escorted thence to the palace by a company of English Lancers, every other man carrying a torch. Lord Stratford and his staff, of course, met him at the carriage-door, and as he alighted, a communication by means of galvanic wires was made to the fleet, who saluted him with prolonged salvos of cannon. Lady Stratford and her daughters received him at the head of the staircase. Then, after the usual royal fashion, his majesty retired to one of the smaller drawing-rooms, to repose himself a little after his jolting. I never shall forget the splendid scene when we entered the ball-room. Any thing more beautiful it would be difficult even to imagine.

Lady Stratford de Redcliffe, in a costume of the early part of the reign of George III., was standing about the middle of the room, surrounded by and receiving a most brilliant throng. Her crown of diamonds, her powder and pink roses, became her well. Miss Canning was dressed in the flowing white robes and oak-leaf crown of a Druidess; Miss Catherine, as Mary Queen of Scots. Mr. Odo Russel, first attaché, looked his ancestor, the Lord William Russell, to perfection. His dress was black velvet; a white plumed hat, fastened with brilliants; a point-lace collar, and below that a splendid collar of diamonds. Mr. Doria was an Exquisite of Queen Anne's time, in a purple velvet coat, lined with figured satin; diamond shoe-buckles, snuff-box, and every thing perfect, from patch to bow; Captain and Mrs. Mansfield in most tastful dresses of the same date; one longed to pop them under glass-cases, one at each end of the mantle-piece. It would take me a day to enumerate half the costumes. But every one who had been to tha Queen's *bals costumés,* agreed that they did not approach this one in magnificence; for besides the gathering of French, Sardinian, and English officers, the people of the country appeared in their own superb and varied costumes. The Greek Patriarch, the Armenian Archbishop, the Jewish High Priest, were there, in their robes of state. Real Persians; Albanians, Kourds, Servians, Armenians, Greeks, Turks, Austrians, Sardinians, Italians, and Spaniards, were there in their different dresses, and many wore their jeweled arms. Some of the Greek yataghans and pistols were splendid. Two Jewish ladies were almost covered with diamonds. There were Fakirs, and Pilgrims, and Knights in real chain-armor, and Dervishes, and Maltese ladies, and Roman Empresses, English Shepherdesses, and Persian Princesses, and Turkish ladies without their vails. Of course, there were also the usual oddities of a fancy ball; there was a Negro king, dressed in white and red feathers, and two gentlemanly Devils in black velvet, who waltzed with their long forked tails twined gracefully under their arms. Italian Bravos and Princes, Spanish Dons and Brigands, were of course plentiful. In fact, every costume in the known world was to be met with: queens and shepherdesses; emperors and caiquejees; Crimean heroes, embassadors, attachés, and diplomatists. The flash of diamonds was something wonderful, especially among the Armenians and Greeks, who pride themselves, when wealthy, on the splendor of their wives.

We were noticing and admiring all this, and had shaken hands with M. de Thouvenel, and spoken to the few of the crowd whom we knew, when it was whispered that the Sultan was coming. Every one of course made way, and Abdul Medjid quietly walked up the ball-room with Lord and Lady Stratford, their daughters, and a gorgeous array of pashas in the rear He paused with evident delight and pleasure at the really beautiful scene before him, bowing on both sides, and smiling as he went. A velvet and gold chair, raised a few steps, had been placed for him in the middle of one side of the ball-room; but, on being conducted to it, he seemed too much pleased to sit down, and continued standing, looking about him with the undisguised pleasure and simplicity of a child. He was dressed in a plain dark-blue frock-coat, the cuffs and collar crimson, and covered with brilliants. The hilt of his sword was entirely covered also with brilliants. Of course he wore the everlasting fez. There is something extremely interesting in his appearance. He looks languid and careworn; but, when spoken to, his fine dark eyes brighten up and he smiles the most frank and winning of smiles.

I am quite charmed with the Sultan, so different to most of the pashas by whom he is surrounded, so touchingly kind, and simple, and sorrowful! The pashas behaved very badly, forcing themselves violently in a double row on the Sultan's right-hand, and pushing every one right and left, like policemen when the Queen is dining in the city; just as if they thought that the ladies were going to carry off the Sultan at once. We were close to the throne, and got a terrible squeezing. My lace mantilla was caught in a pasha's sword, and I thought that nothing could save its being torn to pieces. However, Lord Dunkellin very kindly rescued me, and, thanks to his strong arm, I was able to keep my place and see Miss Mary Canning and the ministers' wives presented to the Sultan. A quadrille was formed, as well as the crowd would allow, which the Sultan watched with great interest, and then a waltz. After that his Majesty walked through the rooms, took an ice, and then departed, expressing, I must not forget to tell you, the greatest admiration of the Highlanders and Lancers who lined the grand staircase, one on each step, and of the Light Dragoons and Royals, who presented arms to him in the hall: most of the cavalry men wore the Balaklava clasp. He certainly seemed much struck and gratified, as the papers say, at this splendid scene. Colonel Ebor, the "Times" correspondent, was there, and saw everything, but was obliged to keep a little out of the Sultan's sight, being attired in the magnificent dress of a Janissary Aga: this amused us very much. After the Sultan's departure the dancing was continued with great spirit. Mehemet Ali, Aali Pasha, the Grand Vizier, and most of the pashas, remained almost to the last. The groups in the drawing-rooms were most striking; and splendid knots promenaded the galleries. Sometimes the waltzers dashed out of the ball-room, and danced down the galleries, which seemed to please the Grenadiers and Highlanders stationed there excessively.

As I was walking through the rooms with M. and Madame Cretzolesko (Wallachians,) we met the Grand Vizier. He conversed in French for some time with Madame C., and appeared to be very intelligent, and far livelier than the Turks are generally. He has traveled a great deal.

The pashas eat enormously at a ball. They are for ever paying visits to the refreshment-room, and drink vast quantities of champagne, of which they pretend not to know the exact genius, and slily call it "eau gazeuse." The English papers talk of Turkish prejudices; generally speaking they have none, either religious or political, unless it suits them. The word "prejudice" means their dislike of any thing which will prevent their living in splendor on the misery and oppression of the people. They drink champagne and brandy, and defy the laws of the Koran, comfortably enough, in secret. I must except your real Turkish gentleman, a strict Mussulman, who is seldom heard of now, and never mentioned in the same breath with "reform" or European manners. It is curious that among the Turks the rich represent the bad; the poor seem almost invariably to be honest, temperate, patient, hard-working, and religious. A poor man here has a strikingly noble countenance; you may know rich ones only too frequently by the sensuality and ferocity of their expression. Here a man can hardly be rich and virtuous; if he keeps a place it must be by dishonest means, and so he goes on from bad to worse.

But to return to the "Sultan's Ball," as it is called. I must not forget to tell you about the Turkish lady, who created quite a sensation there. When I first saw her, she was walking through the principal drawing-room, leaning on the arm of General Mansfield. She was vailed, and wrapped in a gray feridjee, or Turkish cloak, and appeared to be highly delighted at the scene. Many thought that some pasha, or even the Sultan himself, had permitted some fair prisoner to view for the first time a Giaour festival, especially as all her remarks were made in the veritable Turkish tongue. As the evening, however, wore on, the Turkish lady's timidity wore off, and at last she began to behave with excessive levity, walking up to English officers and examining their stars and orders, and looking up into their faces in the most bold and impudent manner. Then a spirit of mischief and fun seemed to possess her, and she had something cutting and sarcastic to say to every pasha who passed by: "Ah! you see we are coming out now. No more cages for us. We are going to see the world and judge for ourselves, and love whom we like. What fine tall fellows these English officers are! I dare say they would be very fond of us, and not shut us up, and tie this foolish rag over our faces, as you do." You may imagine the tittering and laughing, as the Turkish lady's sayings to the pashas got translated. She followed Mehemet Ali about, saying the most cutting and witty things, until the handsome Lord High Admiral hardly knew what to make of it; nor were the rest of his Turkish majesty's ministers spared. It was certainly most cleverly done; the walk, and every movement and gesture of the Turkish woman, perfect. At last, however, Fuad Pasha discovered in the fair dame the Hon. Percy Smythe, one of the attachés, who speaks Turkish perfectly well, and was thus enabled to beard the pashas so successfully.

A most horrible-looking creature is the Chief of the Eunuchs. He is a black, and hideous to a degree positively revolting; yet he is the second man in the kingdom, and the Sultan dares hardly go anywhere without him. He walked about leaning on the arm of a Negro but little less frightful than himself, their long swords clattering as they went. I am told that this creature walks about the Seraglio with a thong of leather in his hand, ready to strike any rebellious lady who may offend him. They say that the Sultan would be very glad to give up his Seraglio if he dared. He is much attached to the sultana, the mother of his children, and seldom visits the seven hundred women shut up in the great cage near him. He has altogether seven wives; the rest are slaves (principally presents) and attendants.

In the course of the evening it was whispered, "Soyer is coming at twelve o'clock with a bear." Accordingly, at twelve o'clock a door at the upper end of the ball-room opened, and Soyer, in a most effective Eastern costume, appeared, leading a monstrous brown bear by a chain. Two Greek ladies screamed; but curiosity appeared to be the ruling passion, and poor M. Soyer and his friend seemed to run a pretty good chance of being squeezed to death in the splendid mob. By pushing a pasha, and giving an appealing look to a Red-Cross Knight, gently elbowing my Lord Cardinal, and sliding beside a powerful Crimean hero, I managed to get an excellent view of Bruin and his manœuvres. His antics were excessively droll and characteristic of his race, but his nose, with its too bright tint of carmine, betrayed him. That Persian Princess need not stand upon the ottoman; those lovely Circassians need not tremble under their silver vails, the bear being nothing more nor less than a distinguished friend of the distinguished M. Soyer. I suppose there was some remarkable story attached to this skin, or the capture of the real gentleman who wore it. M. Soyer was trying to say something, but the laughing, tittering, and pretty terrors of the ladies rendered inaudible every word, and M. Soyer gained no laurels for his eloquence that night. He and his friend were escorted out of the ball-room by the Negro king, his satanic majesty, and the "familiar spirit" in scarlet and black, who each performed such diabolic dances and jumpings round them, that one began to think it was not very often they mixed with beings of this upper world.

When I left the ball-room, at half-past four, it was as brilliant as ever. One could never be wearied of looking, but I knew that this scene of the Arabian Nights must end, and I liked best to leave it in its glory—the same splendid groups still conversing in Eastern languages, and resting on the sofas under the orange-trees, which, as I told you, Lady Stratford has so exquisitely disposed in the drawing-rooms. Edmund and Herbert Siborne left me at the foot of the staircase. A few steps up was perched Mistress Espinu. She was in the highest state of delight; had seen the Sultan both arrive and depart; thought the English soldiers a thousand times "bono;" never believed that there were such dresses and diamonds in the world as she had seen, or dreamed of such music, or of such a large house. The housekeeper had asked her to go down and eat (one of the housemaids was Greek), but the house was so large that she was possessed with the idea of never finding me again if she once let go the balustrades, or let out of her mind the way to my room. So there she had been all night, but was neither cold nor hungry. She told me that an officer with white hair and a "star on his heart" had come up the stairs about midnight. He spoke in English, and asked who she was, she supposed; so she said, "Inglis Hornby," and he nodded and passed on. This was Lord Stratford, who retired early. I made this out, partly from poor Espinu when I got to my room, shocked at her state of starvation, and partly when Vassili arrived the next morning with the white horses and teleki to take us back to Orta-kioy. She herself was highly delighted. The sight of the Sultan and the English officers seemed to have warmed and fed her even on a cold stone staircase: and she will no doubt talk of the "Sultan's first ball" to the day of her death.

Every thing was most admirably ordered; not a single accident nor the least confusion. The next morning we got home with some difficulty, a heavy fall of snow having taken place in the night.

At twelve o'clock the firing of cannon announced that the Sultan was passing, as usual, to the mosque, even after the unparalleled fatigue of a ball. I was sorry not to have been at Orta-kioy, that I might have noticed whether (as is usual) the muskets were discharged at the palace at daybreak, and whether the drums rolled their summons to the Divan at that primitive hour.

LETTER XXVI.

THE SULTAN'S DINNER—TURKISH HOSPITALITY—THE EMBASSY BALLS—THE SULTAN—ASSASSINATIONS—THE WEATHER.

Constantinople, February 12th, 1856.

My dear Mr. Hornby:

You must not think that I have altogether discontinued my long letters, descriptive of Turkish manners, and of what we see and do. There are several reasons why you have not received such frequent packets. Firstly, I have been suffering severely from neuralgia; secondly, our usually quiet evenings have been much taken up by visitors; and thirdly, I have not been inclined to write at length. My pen however has not been idle, but working rather for duty than pleasure; but now that not a single unanswered friend remains to reproach me, and all the bells are over, and my tiresome neuralgia has taken its departure, you may expect to receive long communications as of old. I was extremely flattered and pleased to hear they amused you all so much.

We greatly enjoy the "Spectator," which generally arrives on Tuesday; so you may always imagine us on that evening, reading news from dear old England, in our little drawing-room at Orta-kioy; only remember we are nearly three hours earlier than you; when it is six o'clock in England, it is nearly nine with us at Constantinople.

The Turks are very primitive and sensible in their

habits. We are near the palace, and at daybreak hear regularly the roll of the drums and the discharge of musketry which one reads of in the Arabian Nights. The Sultan dines in the middle of the day. About two o'clock there is always a crowd at the bottom of our village, as the Sultan's cook sells the remains of his master's dinner to any one who chooses to buy a "tit-bit." I believe that no Turk (except porters and the like) is ever seen out after dusk, unless on urgent affairs. The French embassador dined with Aali Pasha, the Grand Vizier, the other evening, and slept at his palace, in accordance with the old Turkish custom, which never allows a guest to depart in darkness and danger from bad roads, or worse evils still. Lord Stratford always returns to the Embassy, however, not liking to sleep out. Almost all Turks, I am told, are in bed by nine, and always rise to prayers at daybreak.

You have no doubt seen ere this, an account of the two Embassy balls, at both of which the Sultan was present. The English embassadress's *bal costumé* was the most magnificent and picturesque one possible to conceive; it deserves a letter to itself, so I will send you a full account. Lord Stratford asked Edmund very kindly to be one of his staff, who met the Sultan at the entrance. It was a most interesting sight: the grand staircase was lined with Crimean troops, cannon thundered, and the band played "God save the Queen." The court-yard of the palace was brilliantly illuminated. "Abdul Medjid" and "Victoria" were hung in the brightest lamps across the darkness, after the Turkish fashion, which has a magical and beautiful effect. The Sultan has a benevolent and pleasing countenance, one that you like at once—mild and melancholy, and exhibits a great contrast to those of the ferocious-looking pashas about him. Sad to say, his troubles and distractions are making him drink champagne and brandy too freely, even for a Frank. He was much amused at the novel scene presented to him, and looked on with interest while a quadrille was formed before him. Edmund and I were close to his chair of state, and saw him plainly. But I must not anticipate my promised long letter. I was, if you care to know, a Spanish lady in a black mantilla fastened with beautiful damask roses.

Herbert Siborne was there, looking extremely well; he had been in Orta-kioy the day before, and could not find us out in the maze of irregular wooden houses. Edmund has just bought a horse to bring to England. He is an Arab, and called "Sultan," at my express desire. Georgy, the Sais, now rides "Turkish Johnny." Well mounted, I hear to my comfort that a man is pretty safe.

There were twelve cases of stabbing last week at Pera; two of the victims were Englishmen. A merchant whom we know had a dispute with a Greek; that worthy said as he departed: "I'll settle you in the streets!" The Scheschell immediately left his office, and got a couple of French soldiers, who marched the gentleman off to the Greek consul's, where the charge was made against him, and he was locked up. If every one were to behave with the same promptness and decision on being threatened, no doubt the effect would be very salutary in stopping such cowardly attacks.

20

The weather here is lovely: there is a south wind blowing, and "white horses" are rushing up the Bosphorus from the Sea of Marmora. In the middle of the day the sudden heat is oppressive. The evenings are cold and sharp, and it is no doubt these frequent changes of temperature which makes this climate so trying. Should the wind change to-night, we might have snow in a few hours, and be pinched with cold after having been quite faint with heat. I feel the confinement to the house very much, and long for the disappearance of the mud in the village, that I may get down to the Bosphorus in a morning. But every thing with us ends in a deep sigh and "Oh, for home!" We poor mortals do not know what a thing is till we loose it.

It is a great comfort to hear such good accounts of Edie. Her "sayings and doings," as described by my mother, are most amusing. Mrs. Austin is quite pleased with her intelligence and fun, and says that she is extremely well-behaved, which I was delighted to hear above every thing else. I always send her little bouquets of artificial flowers for her doll, taken from sweetmeats at the balls, which afford great delight. The same lady received a Turkish handkerchief, covered with spangles, to serve as a shawl.

I must say adieu; the twilight fades into darkness so soon here, and I can scarcely see. Edmund will be home soon, and Vassili is ready to serve one of his nice little dinners.

LETTER XXVII.

THE FRENCH EMBASSADOR'S BALL—DINNER-PARTY—THE SULTAN'S VISIT—FRENCH AND ENGLISH BELLES—PASHAS AT THE BALL—A FIRE—A RUSSIAN PRISONER.

February 13th, 1856.

My dear Sister:

My last letter was full of the *bal costumé* at the English palace. I must now just give you an idea of the ball which M. de Thouvenel gave to the Sultan last night. We took rooms at the Hôtel Bellevue, which is next door to the French palace, and we arrived there from Orta-kioy just in time for dinner.

It was a tremendous *table-d'hôte* of English, French, and Sardinian officers. Kiâni Pasha took me down from M. Cadrossi's room, to whom we had been paying a visit. M. Cadrossi is, as I dare say you remember, Edmund's French colleague. Kiâni Pasha is the Turkish commissioner. He speaks Italian, and we got on admirably. He is rather nervous at table, seeming in deadly fear of putting his fingers into the dishes, or doing any thing else to shock Europeans. Rustem Bey was also there. He has learned to dance, and was anticipating the ball like a girl of eighteen. Our friend, the Vicomte di Negri, the Sardinian commodore, sat opposite to us, and we were charmed to meet. It is very pleasant going into Pera from these savage parts, and stumbling upon all your martial acquaintance. It is also very odd to be the only creature of "womankind" in such a crowd; and one tries hard not to be proud at being fed and tended like an ibis.

The dining-room of the Hôtel Bellevue overlooks the French Embassy. At dinner I could see the Greeks crawling over roof and front, lighting the lamps for the illumination. It was soon a blaze of light, and the champagne and conversation had not made our immense party the less inclined for the ball; so we soon broke up to dress. M. de Thouvenel had begged a particular few not to be later than half-past eight, as the Sultan was invited at that hour, although it was not generally known. Edmund was delayed a little, and my sedan-chair was nowhere to be found. After waiting for it some time, our patience was exhausted; so I put on a cloak, and mounted my husband's goloshes, and we launched out bravely into the sea of mud. However, it was but a few yards, and from the flambeaux and lanterns as light as day; but there was such a crowd of arabas, horses, and sedans, and cavasses, and Greeks, that we could scarcely make our way through. The alley leading down to the Embassy from the street was lined with Zouaves and troops of the line.

The soldiers from the different French regiments stationed in the Embassy garden looked magnificently picturesque by the light of the illuminations and glare of flambeaux. The hall, staircase, and lobbies were adorned with orange-trees and flowers, and lined with picked men of the finest regiments. We found the ball-room frightfully crowded. Every one knew this time that the Sultan was to be there; so they were not to be cheated, and hundreds arrived even before the appointed hour. However, all were put out by his Majesty's having arrived quietly at half-past seven. Fortunately M. de Thouvenel was ready to receive him; and I was glad that he did go so early, as he had an opportunity of looking at every thing without being hunted. The crowd was really terrible, and when the Sultan left the drawing-room and took his place upon the raised seat, as he did at Lord Stratford's, he was literally hemmed in and stared at as if he had been a wild beast. A quadrille was attempted, but could scarcely be said to be danced, so great was the pressure near the little throne. The Periots behaved very badly; and the embassador, in his anxiety to please everybody, had asked too many of them.

The Grand Vizier, the Seraskier, and all the pashas of note were there; also the Chief of the Eunuchs, strutting about as usual. A splendid military and diplomatic gathering, of course. The Princess Stongia was there: she is said by many to be one of the most lovely women in Europe. I thought her very beautiful, dressed in snowy white, with a queenly tiara of brilliants. There is a great deal of good-natured rivalry among the French and English here, as to the respective beauty of the "Commissariat daughters," each of the commissary-generals having one perfect in her way, and possessing as many admirers as there are days in the year. I pronounce in favor of the English girl, who is as charming in a straw bonnet as in a ball-dress. It is very amusing to see half-a-dozen officers, with orders and stars, waiting anxiously while the beauty looks through her tablets, and then quietly tells them that it is impossible for her to "have the pleasure" that evening. "Is there no chance?" murmurs a disconsolate general. "Not the slightest," is the usual reply, with a merry laugh: for she is not the least conceited or spoiled, although in a fair way to become both. Then you hear an attaché say, "I must go and try my luck;" while a disappointed suitor remarks sulkily, "I tell you you have not the slightest chance." Both the "commissariats" looked very lovely at each of these assemblies. Although not *costumé*, the French ball was very brilliant. The suites of rooms are not nearly so large as those at the English Embassy, consequently the crowding was greater; but still it was a beautiful sight.

It is curious to see the pashas walking from room to room, holding each other's hands just like school-boys: this is a great mark of friendship among them. I was very glad of an opportunity of seeing the Seraskier, or Minister of War. He has a very fine face, and is said to be an honest man. (N. B. He is poor.) It was very interesting to watch the ministerial groups conversing on the different sofas, and to notice the quiet amazement of some of the pashas at the waltzing. I cannot help thinking it a pity that they should have seen so much of this. It is too sudden a jump into the questionable amusements of what is called civilized life. I was particularly struck with one fine old Turk who, late in the evening, was watching the waltzers with any thing but an admiring expression. Presently another pasha came up, and evidently asked him what he thought of all this, for he shrugged his shoulders in an unmistakable manner, as much as to say, "Is it possible that our gentle, vailed women will ever rush round in the arms of officers, like these?"

We left the ball at its height, at about half-past two.

There was a splendid supper, but nothing to be got for the crowd. I was just falling asleep, and gradually getting stars and red coats, and the Sultan's kind face, and the Grand Vizier's sharp one, out of my eyes, when the cannon gave the alarm of fire. We are too much accustomed to count these seven surly guns to mind them, or the watchman's wailing cry afterward. When we first came here, and the fire-guns were heard, I used to scramble out of bed and mount a chair, to see where the fire was. But you soon learn to hear them with indifference.

Tell dear Edie that a very pretty little cat sat upon my lap at breakfast, at the Hôtel Bellevue, on the morning after the French ball. An officer told me that Miss Puss was a Russian prisoner, a French soldier having saved her from the ruins of a house at Sebastopol, in which she was mewing piteously, taken her to his tent, and afterward conveyed her to Constantinople, where she was presented to the fat, good-natured landlady of the Bellevue, who prizes her very highly, and with whom she has forgotten her former sorrows.

LETTER XXVIII.

SHEPHERDS—FLOCKS—THE GREEK LENT—NEWS FROM THE CRIMEA—TURKISH CEMETERY—THE VILLAGE OF ORTA-KIOY—AN ARMENIAN BURIAL—FUNERAL OF A CHILD.

Orta-kioy, March 16th, 1856.

My dear Mother:

It is a frightful day, with a piercing north wind, and snow driving before it so thickly that one can only see the shivering Turks and Armenians cowering along when close to our cottage. The valley and the Bosphorus are quite hidden from our sight.

The shepherds are bringing down the sheep and lambs from the hills. Their goatskin cloaks and caps look white and stiff with snow. The poor sheep look very miserable, but the goats are hardier, and skip along cheerfully enough. This mixture of sheep and goats reminds one forcibly of the Scriptures, as does the tender care which the shepherds take of their little flocks.

Pasturage and food is so scanty here that they lead them about from hill to valley, and when the weather is severe, having no outhouses, they take them to the village. The "guide sheep" is a very pretty creature, tell Edith; it is trained to follow the shepherd, having been brought up by him from a lamb, and it lies in the shepherd's hut like his child; all the other sheep will follow it, and it is really charming to see the motherly care it takes of them. By the side of our cottage is a road which leads to the hills, so I generally see them going from, and returning to, the village, night and morning. There is an open part of the ruins where a great many wild dogs congregate, and it is quite a pretty sight to see the "guide" go on a little in advance, look anxiously round, and then trot briskly on, taking a broad sweep, for fear of a sortie from the enemy.

The shepherd, in his cloak of goatskins, generally follows behind with a little rough bay pony, who carries in the large pockets of his saddle any lambs that may be hurt, or weakly. The shepherd has two large dogs on the hills, but they only seem used here as a defense from the wild dogs and wolves; the pretty guide sheep taking the flocks in and out of the villages. My favorite, whom I watch so often, has got a little lamb, tell Edie; he is black, with a white spot on his forehead, and a white tip to his tail: his mother is wonderfully fond of him. The kind shepherd carries him for her under his goatskin cloak, and every now and then she leaves her flock to jump up at her master, and peep in to see how her little one does. Sometimes the shepherd is eating his dinner of brown bread, and she takes a little bit from his hand, so gently, as the party wind up the hill. The young goats are full of fun, skipping about, and playing all sorts of tricks. They give the anxious, motherly little "guide" a great deal of trouble. Some of them are very large, with curling horns, and long, shaggy coats; but there is a smaller kind, of a golden bronze color, which is remarkably handsome, and reminds one strongly of those on Greek vases and relievos. My favorite shepherd has a black assistant; he wears a dark-blue turban, and a stone-colored robe tied round his waist with a piece of rope: he is exactly like that graceful South-Sea Islander of Captain Cook's, whom Reynolds painted, and on whom Cowper wrote some beautiful lines. I forget the name (Omar, or something like it, I think,) but you will know whom I mean. You may easily conceive what a picturesque party my friends are.

The day before yesterday was the first day of the Greek Lent, their New-Year's day being on the 13th of ours. At about mid-day the old watchman chanted some religious verses for the day, at the door of each Christian house. Every body in the village, rich and poor, took the Sacrament,—caiqueejees, porters, street-sellers of sweets, etc.,—the little road was quite crowded. At day-break every morning you hear the summons of the Greek and Armenian churches. Their masters, the Turks, will not allow them to use bells, so they strike an iron bar with another piece of iron, and make a noise somewhat like them, but very curious to the ear at first.

The Greeks keep Lent very strictly. All the village go to church at day-break every morning, and the fast is exceedingly severe. They tell me that we shall soon see every one look starved and miserable, nothing being allowed but soup, little better than water, and an occasional piece of black bread, just sufficient to sustain life.

The sun, never long absent here, has just burst out. The Asian mountains opposite, glittering with snow, look very beautiful. At first I thought they were white clouds. Adieu!

March 18th.

I am writing my letter to you this evening, as to-morrow I have an invitation to go with Lizzy James's friend, Madame de Fitte de Souci, to visit a Turkish harem. It will be a great treat, and I will write you a full account.

We have just heard that Peace is proclaimed. It will give great joy to those who have husbands, sons, and brothers in the Crimea. I had a long letter from the camp last week. Our troops are in splendid condition, amply provided with every thing, and full of ardor; the French suffering severely from want of food and clothing, and we are now repaying, a hundred-fold, what they gave us at the beginning of the war.

All the snow is gone, and the weather here lovely, although the wind is still in the north. My days are passed pretty much in the way which I described to you in a former letter, and the principal amusement of many solitary hours is noting all that is new and interesting to write home about. This morning the Sultan's eldest son rode past our windows; the caparisoned horses and guard of Lancers following looked very pretty winding up the hill. I dare say they were going to visit the French camp at Mashlak, from which we constantly see both soldiers and officers riding or walking past to the Bosphorus or villages about. Rude carts, drawn by white oxen, are often urged up the hill by savage-looking Croats, who beat the poor animals most cruelly. A rich Armenian is building a house on the top of the hill, and the huge paving stones of his court-yard are fastened by ropes on to these primitive and groaning vehicles. The necks of the poor oxen are fixed in a kind of yoke, which sometimes wounds them severely. I can no longer bear to look at this spectacle of cruelty and barbarity, and turn my head from the window whenever I hear the sound of the creaking wheels, and the savage shouts and blows urging the poor patient creatures along.

There are many sad sights from my window, as well as novel ones. Half-way up the hill above us is a small Turkish cemetery, enclosed in a low stone wall. There are not many tombs in it, and no carved or gilded ones, but the place is shady, and the turf always soft and green—a very rare thing here. Even in this quiet and secluded place,

"Where the wild cypress waves in tender gloom,"

headless Janissary-stones still tell the story of Sultan Mahmoud's vengeance.

There has been no Turkish funeral since we came here. They bear their dead rapidly by in a covered bier, at the head of which the fez is hung. The body is placed in the grave sitting upright. The grave is not filled up, and a stone is laid above it. This is because Mussulmans believe that the good and evil spirits, Moukir and Nekir, visit the grave on the first night, and question the departed as to the good and evil which he has done in life. A lamp is left burning for the solemn party, and the dark cypress-trees wave gloomily above. One can fancy their solemn wail over sins unforgiven, life's duties undone.

The Greek and Armenian burial-ground lies higher up, on a green slope, planted lovingly with planes, and many other light and pretty trees; here people sit in the summer evenings, thinking on those beneath, and gazing quietly on the fair prospect spread ing far and wide before them. I notice here many family groups, graves of fathers, mothers, and little children, with often a raised piece of turf, shaded by a tree evidently constantly watered and tended. The other morning a broken bough, weeping over two tiny heaps of daisied mould, was carefully bandaged up, and the turf around it soaked with water. This care and love is very touching. There is something most pleasing in seeing a villager, on a sunset evening, quietly sitting in cheerful communion, as it were, with dear ones gone.

The village of Orta-kioy lies thickly clustered in a broad valley, with a hill on each side. Opposite to that nearest to Stamboul, on which we live, and where I sometimes sit of a morning, in the Greek burial-ground of which I am writing, lies the bleak and dreary resting-place of the Jews,

"Tribes of the wandering foot and weary breast."

The countless stones have neither form nor inscription, merely masses of rough unhewn granite or marble thrown down on the ground, with here and there some resembling broken columns. Nothing can be more desolate-looking than this gaunt and rugged hill. It looks so typical of the despised and despairing race, and of their ruined kingdoms. Sitting there, I often chant over the Hebrew lament:—

"But we must wander witheringly,
In other lands to die,
And where our fathers' ashes be,
Our own may never lie.
Our Temple hath not left a stone,
And mockery sits on Salem's throne."

All these different peoples pass by my windows to

these their last resting-places. It made me sad at first to see them, but now the pale uncovered faces do not haunt me, as they did, for hours after. Sitting quietly, alone, you hear something like a deep-toned, distant hum, accompanied by a shrill one, just as if myriads of giant humble-bees and myriads of thin-trumpeted gnats were coming up the hill together. The first day I heard this, I could not conceive what it could be. "*Un morto viene*," ("There is a dead man coming,") said Vassili from the garden. Just then the procession wound round the high walls of the Armenian house, chanting as they came. First, six or eight boys, in richly embroidered robes, and carrying small waxen tapers; then priests, in still richer vestments of velvet and gold, bearing lofty gilt crucifixes, and swinging censers; then, on an open bier, looking calm and placid, but just a little, little weary, a fine young man, dressed as for a gala day, the bright fez contrasting strongly with the pallid brow. A rich and soft cushion pillowed his head as tenderly perhaps as it had often done on his own divan; a robe richly trimmed with fur wrapped him to the feet; his hands were folded naturally on his breast; he seemed reposing on a pleasant bed, life's weary journey over.

The bier was spread with shawls, and at each end the little arch of woodwork, wreathed with leaves and flowers. Friends, not walking two and two, but pressing lovingly round, alternately bore the burden slowly up the hill; for it is steep here, and they cannot hurry on, after the fashion of the East, which arises from a belief that the soul is restless and unblessed until the last rites are completed. So I have a full view of the pale and regular features, and at first feel startled and shocked by so unusual a sight. Afterward I feel that to my mind it is better and less barbarous than our former funeral etiquette of black feathers, "mutes," and white handkerchiefs pressed to the eyes, whether there be tears or not. Here it is not incumbent on near and dear relatives to attend; so that those who do go, do not affect a degree of grief which they are not supposed to feel. The women usually take a last adieu within the walls of the house, tearing their hair and garments with loud lamentations, after the fashion of the East.

Passing an Armenian house the other day, a bier was carried out; the women had thrown open the lattices of the windows, and were gazing sorrowfully down on the procession, but were perfectly silent in their grief. The chief of the hamals of our village died one morning when we first came here, and was buried a few hours after. He was an Armenian, and old, so they dressed his bier with ripe fruits instead of flowers; bunches of golden oranges, rich-colored pomegranates, and clusters of pale lemons in their dark green leaves;—for were they not falling in the autumn, and gathered in, as he was, ripe in the harvest-time? He was very much beloved, so no heavy burdens were carried that morning, and crowds of hamals bore him on his last journey up the steep hill, where doubtless he had often toiled and panted in the burning sun. Now he rested right royally in his holiday robes, and with soft shawls tenderly wrapped about him. Hands which will never bear a heavy burden more, are folded gently on his breast, clasping the golden cross of the Armenian church. Tenderly his friends crowd around him, vying with each other to bear him swiftly on to happiness and perfect rest. The sweetest air of repose is on his face, that kingly Eastern calm which is so beautiful among the very poor.

The next that came was a bride, with a wreath on her head, and with long threads of gold floating around her bier from the rich dark masses of her hair. I watched her sorrowfully from my window; for she was so young, the very breath of life seemed to hover on her smiling features still, and the long shadowy fringes of her closed eyelids to quiver in the morning sun, as if gazing on the flowers folded in her hands. It was hardly possible to believe that this was death.

But one morning,—I shall never forget that day,—I heard, at a distance, the droning hum of the priests, and, putting by my work, looked out. I thought that an unusual noise accompanied the chanting, something like the jingling of a child's coral. And so it was; for on a cushion, the rich crimson of the velvet contrasting with the lily-whiteness of the face upon it, lay a beautiful baby of about ten or twelve months. It was exquisitely dressed, in snowy robes, as if for a christening, and freshest flowers in its tiny hands and all around it. In the lace rosette of its cap, a little golden cross was seen, and the cherished coral by its side rang out at every step of the Armenian who carried and hung over the cushion as tenderly as if hushing the little thing to sleep. A vailed woman looked on from a distance, following the procession slowly up the hill; I thought it might be the nurse, sorrowing and lingering about. Oh, that sweet baby-face—that touching requiem of its coral, how it made my heart ache; thinking of the last pale one that I had so grieved over but a few months before! I sat down and thought my heart would break.

LETTER XXIX.

VISIT TO THE HAREM OF RIZA PASHA—NEWS FROM ENGLAND—LADIES OF STAMBOUL—CHIEF OF THE EUNUCHS—INTERIOR OF THE HAREM—DRESSES OF THE LADIES—CIRCASSIAN BEAUTY—DRESSES—HOSPITALITY IN THE HAREM.

Orta-kioy, March 20th.

My dear Lady Easthope:

By ten o'clock on Monday morning, Madame la Vicomtesse de Fitte de Soucy, Mrs. Brown, and I were skimming along the Bosphorus as fast as three splendid Greek rowers could take us, on our way to visit the Harem of Riza Pasha. We landed at Tophana, and, guarded by the wisdom and sagacity of Vassili, reached Mysseri's in safety. Here we met M. Robolli, the Pasha's friend, who was to escort us, my husband being too busy at the Embassy.

The streets of Pera were crowded with loungers, five or six feet deep on each side, which rendered them almost impassable. It was the first day of the *Catholic* Greek Easter, and the Greeks seem to like nothing better than to block up the streets by staring at the English and French. It is really hard work to get along in such a crowd, and over loose and dirty paving-stones.

This morning, in addition to the holiday-making Greeks, a string of camels, led by a Turk in a green turban, and a diminutive donkey in a necklace of blue beads, stalked solemnly through the crowd, heavily laden with bales of wool. I do not think I have told you why the donkeys leading the camels are always so small. It is because in crossing a deep ford, the little fellow has to ride over on the back of one of these "ships of the desert:" his weight is therefore of consequence.

Mysseri's was as full of bustle as usual. Captain Haviland, the Queen's messenger, had just arrived, and all were pressing around him for news from England. He had had a dreadful passage: for two days the ship had been beating about, unable to make the port of Malta.

Almost all were grumbling at the news of "every prospect of peace." Numbers of officers have just arrived fresh from England after leave of absence, and all our people seem in such splendid trim, and to be so much at home in this part of the world now, that they feel indignant at being prevented from startling the whole universe with their "deeds of arms."

Nobody believes in the good faith of Russia; least of all the Turks. Our commissariat here is at last in perfect working order: there are immense stores at Scutari and Kulalee, ready for the Crimea or elsewhere at a few hours' notice. Admiral Slade says that our naval power just now is something wonderful. I don't wonder at many of our fine fellows who have got new commands being disappointed.

However, we said good-bye to our friends at Mysseri's, stepped each into a sedan-chair (painted on the back with two comical-looking British lions shaking hands in the most violent manner), and with M. Robolli, mounted on a gallant gray, as our escort, hurried uphill and downhill in the steep side-streets of Pera. Our stout Armenian chairmen hurried the three sedans through still more crowded streets, over the bridgé of boats, and soon into the silent regions of Stamboul, where vailed women were stealing noiselessly along, and the closely-latticed windows and high walls gave one an idea of a convent. Many of these dark-eyed ladies had a vailed black slave behind them, carrying small baskets of hyacinths, jonquils, and other flowers, from the flower-markets. At last, after interminable windings and turnings, we arrived at the half-open gates of an immense court-yard, surrounded by a wall which would have graced a castle of old. I almost expected to see a horn hanging at the gate, with the challenge of the giant within, written in letters of brass. However, M. Robolli rode in without interruption, and the three sedans followed. Some Turks mending the pavement, stared at us with great curiosity. I dare say they thought the pasha had bought three English wives.

We were set down in a large circular hall, covered with matting, and were immediately surrounded by numbers of the pasha's retainers, principally cavasses (a kind of free-lance footmen) and chibouquejees (pipe-bearers). These gentlemen were entertaining themselves with a most minute inspection of us, when down the vast staircase (with two flights *à la Fontainebleau*) came the Chief of the Eunuchs, as hideous and as angry as a Black could possibly be, He dispersed the mob right and left, evidently claiming us as Harem visitors. M. Robolli was conducted with us as far as the first suite of rooms, and he then retired to the apartments of the pasha, leaving us in the hands of this "bird of night," who was now joined by two others, scarcely less monstrous and frightful than himself. These led us through several immensely large rooms, all covered with a rich gold-colored matting, and with crimson divans at either end. No other furniture, except an occasional cabinet, filled with grotesque china, which I should have liked to stop and look at. The ceilings were all carved and painted barbarously enough, and more or less richly. There were no doors, but heavy hangings of crimson embroidered cloth and tapestry at the entrance of the numerous apartments.

At last our conductor stopped on the third and last floor, which is always the principal in Turkish houses, on account of the view. He lifted up the crimson arras, and, with a hideous grin, invited us to enter. Madame de Souci and Mrs. Brown, who are both very new arrivals at Constantinople, were rather nervous, and begged me to go in first. I had seen how sweetly gentle and kind the Turkish women are, and lifted up the charmed curtain with much more confidence and pleasure than I should have entered an assembly of Englishwomen. I shall not easily forget the sight which presented itself. We were in the midst of a vast apartment, with a lofty, dome-like roof, carved with gigantic wreaths of flowers and pomegranates. An immense stair-case was on the other side, lighted by a window which reached from roof to floor; and in the projecting half-moon of the balusters, was a beautiful white-marble fountain. The whole was covered with the same gold-colored matting. Rich crimson divans under each enormous window at either end, and raised three steps. The window looking toward the streets of Stamboul was latticed, with round peep-holes; but the other was free from even a blind, and the beautiful blue Bosphorus and Sea of Marmora, with many stately ships upon them, the mountains in the distance, still glittering here and there with snow,—and nearer, the dark cypresses, and the minarets of Santa Sophia and numerous other mosques, lay in a grand picture of quite inconceivable beauty below it. Here, evidently in a dreamy kind of revery, sat the principal wife of Riza Pasha, surrounded by her slaves, some sitting on the steps beneath the divan at her feet, others laughing together and strolling about. She rose as we approached, and gave her hand, after the English fashion, to each. The slaves all crowded round to look at us, and I assure you that the variety and brilliancy of their costumes was almost dazzling.

But I must first tell you the dress of the great lady. Her selma, or wide-sleeved under-dress, (trousers, etc.) was of a delicate violet-color, bound round the waist by a richly embroidered scarf; her shirt of silvery Broussa gauze. Over this was a magnificent jacket of amber-colored cashmere, lined with the richest sable. On her head she wore a fez, bound round with a large plait of hair, which was fastened every here and there with immense rose-diamonds. A purple lily-flower was stuck straight down this plait, and shaded her forehead. Her ear-rings were of a single pendent emerald, set in a small spray of brilliants. She must have been of surpassing beauty, and was still strikingly handsome, with perfectly regular features, and skin dark but clear, a brow and upper-lip which would have graced a Roman empress. Indeed, we made up our minds at once that it was a Roman empress she was like.

Rising, she motioned us to follow her, and the principal slaves officiously lifted the hangings of one of the numerous doorways surrounding this immense apartment. We entered a charming room, evidently a Turkish boudoir, with an immense window, divans all round it, and the same enchanting view. Here we three poor Englishwomen sat in a row, distressingly anxious to converse, and make ourselves agreeable, and knowing about a dozen words between us, including the detestable "*bono*" and "*no bono*," which we were heartily sick and ashamed of. I tried Italian; Madame Riza shook her majestic head; Madame de Souci murmured a few graceful words of thanks in French; at which Madame Riza solemnly uttered the word "*Oui;*" and all the slaves, black men included, laughed with joy and pride at their mistress's accomplishments. This was accounted for by Riza Pasha having been Minister at Vienna, and his speaking French,

The hangings of the two doors were constantly being lifted, and more women as constantly trooping in to peep at us. Some giggled and ran away; others advanced boldly up the room, and evidently spoke to their mistress about us. Some sat themselves down cross-legged at the further end of the room, staring at us to their hearts' content, and talking about us in whispers. We, meantime, were talking to each other about them. But presently a splendidly dressed black slave lifted the arras, and behind her appeared a most lovely young Circassian lady, who was, as we afterward found out, the pasha's second wife, and a present from the Sultan. She was very tall: but it is impossible to describe her winning beauty, or the exquisite grace of her movements. We were all three instantly charmed with her, and no longer regretted their not understanding English; it was such a pleasure to exclaim every now and then: "Oh you pretty creature!" "Did you ever see such a figure!" "Do look at the shape of her head and throat!" "What a lovely mouth!—and just listen to her voice!" "There's a plait of glossy hair! quite down to her feet it must be when unbound!" This pretty creature, whom we instantly named "The fair Circassian," seemed to be on excellent terms with her majestic colleague. They saluted each other after their usual fashion, and she bowed to us very gracefully when we rose to do her honor, saying something which seemed to be a welcome. I must now tell you her dress. Her trousers, and the robe which twists round the feet, and trails behind, were of the most brilliant blue, edged with a little embroidery of white. Her cashmere jacket was of pale lilac (like the double primroses), lined with a gold-colored fur. A delicate lilac gauze handkerchief was twined round her head; among the fringe of which, diamond heartseases, of the natural size, glittered on golden stalks, which trembled at the slightest movement. Lilac slippers, embroidered with seed-pearls, completed her toilette. No, I must not forget the shining plaits of black hair which escaped from the handkerchief and hung down behind, and a diamond of enormous size and great beauty, which glittered on one of her white fingers. We decided that this must be a present from the Sultan, and that it must be also one of the stones spoken of in Eastern fairy lore as "lighting the chamber," etc.

The two wives now began a little consultation, and from the word *chibouque* being frequently mentioned, we easily understood the question to be, as to the propriety of offering them to us. Both Madame de Souci and Mrs. Brown declared that they should die in the attempt (they are both very delicate); but I, having been taught by no less a person than the Chief of the Bashi-Bazouks, declared that I could take five or six whiffs, not only with resignation, but with pleasure. However, we were not put to the test, for it was evidently decided in the negative; and on the principal wife clapping her hands, some richly-dressed slaves brought in trays of conserves, and water in crystal cups. On the first tray is a glass vase of the conserve, with a beautiful silver basket on either side of it, one of which is filled with spoons of the same metal. You take a spoonful of sweetmeat, and then place the spoon which you have used, in the empty basket on the other side. Then another slave presents you with a richly-cut cup of water. After that the coffee-bearers enter. One of them holds a tray of semicircular form, from which hangs a magnificently embroidered and fringed cloth of gold. Other slaves then take the coffee and present it to each guest. The outer cup is exactly like an egg-cup; inside this, is one of the finest china, which contains the beverage. We admired their outer cups immensely; they were of richly-chased gold, encircled with diamonds about an inch apart and the size of a large pea.

After drinking coffee with great gravity and decorum, the empty cups being carried away by the other attendants, the principal wife again made an attempt at conversation; but after having thanked her, and said what a beautiful view it was, in pretty decent Turkish, I came to a stand-still, although our gestures expressive of regret, were extraordinarily eloquent, I must think, for Englishwomen and children of the North. "Madame Riza," as I must still call her, wanted to know if Madame de Souci was English (Inglis). She laughed and nodded; but still our hostess was evidently not satisfied, having no doubt heard the Vicomte spoken of as a Frenchman. We were sadly puzzled how to explain to her, but at last I held up two of my fingers, making them look as much like a loving couple as possible. One of them, I showed, was intended to represent Madame de Souci—and touching it I repeated the word "Inglis," they all nodded and laughed. The other larger and more imposing one, I touched with great gravity and respect, uttering at the same time the words "Adam (man), fez, Français," or "Her man, her fez, is French." If I had but known the Turkish word "kòja" (husband) then it would have been all right.

This making of signs was very vexing and tantalizing, and the fair ladies of Stamboul evidently thought so too, for they made signs to us again that it was very grievous to them. Thereupon arose another little murmured consultation; the slaves laughed and clapped their hands, and two or three of the principal ones rushed out of the room. We could not think what they were about, and poor Madame de Souci became very nervous. "I hope to goodness they won't undress us," said she, coloring up, and every ringlet shaking with fright; "I was told that perhaps they would." "Never mind if they do," said I, laughing; "the room is very warm, and it would not hurt us. We must look out though that they do not divide our garments among them, and that they turn out these black men." Just at this moment, unluckily for the fears of poor Madame de Souci, our hostess made a sign to be allowed to look at her dress, which she pronounced to be "*chok ghuzel*"—"very pretty;" the fair Circassian then quietly lifted up Mrs. Brown's dress to look at her petticoats. Poor Madame de Souci certainly thought that the dreaded moment had arrived. "But they are such pretty creatures," said I, jesting; "it will be like being undressed by fairies."

So now the heavy arras was lifted once more, and the slaves who had just left, entered, bearing three magnificent chibouques, and two large shawls. Which of us was to be rolled up in them when stripped of our decent European garments? But to our relief, yet bewilderment, the slaves threw the shawls over their mistresses, over head and all, so that they, holding the thick folds beneath their chins, only showed bright eyes and the least tip of nose.

We were excessively diverted by an old lady (an ugly likeness of Liston, in green trousers and jacket) wrapping her head and shoulders up with extraordinary care and anxiety. "Evidently something in the shape of mankind is coming," said we; "can it be the pasha? That third chibouque is evidently intended for some one of consequence." "I suppose he won't offer to buy us before his wives." "I wonder if he is good-looking?" "I promised my husband to be home at four o'clock," said Mrs. Brown rather nervously.

All the young and pretty slaves had now disappeared, as silently and swiftly as so many mice, behind one of the hangings, and only the old and plain ones remained. Two huge black men entered and stood, like sentinels, mute and upright, by a little white fountain in the recess. "What dangerous person is coming?" said we: "with no cashmeres to protect us, how are we to stand such a blaze of manly beauty?" We could not help laughing in spite of ourselves, when again the curtain was lifted, and, guarded by another Black, entered the meek, white-whiskered little beau of seventy-five, our kind escort M. Robolli. After he had kissed the ladies' hands, held out to him beneath the cashmeres, we said: "O dangerous Giaour, pray don't stay too long, nor attempt to peep under that yellow and green handkerchief!" The old lady however seemed determined not to run any risk of inspiring a hopeless attachment, for nothing but the tip of a rubicund nose was visible.

And now began an animated conversation. The presence of an interpreter was indeed a relief. And he took joyfully to the jeweled chibouque presented him, the ladies breathing out clouds of smoke in concert, and with a most wonderful grace. It was certainly a very striking scene—the women-slaves standing and sitting around, in their bright and varied costumes, the Blacks watching our venerable Adonis and listening with the might of their enormous ears, and innumcrable laughing eyes peeping from behind the arras, which was in a constant state of agitation. M. Robolli seemed quite to enjoy the state of excitement into which his presence had thrown the harem. He sipped coffee out of his jeweled cup, and evidently said many "obliging things" to the ladies, who received them very graciously, and then begged of him to tell us how welcome we were, and what pleasure our presence gave them, they touching their lips and forehead at the same time. We of course expressed ourselves very sensible of their goodness. They then begged we would take off our bonnets and make our selves perfectly at home, which we did. They then asked us which we liked best, Stamboul, or London, or Paris? I replied that Stamboul was most beautiful, but that at Paris and London we had more liberty, and the streets were better to walk about in. Then a little murmur of delight from the slaves ran round the apartment: "She says Stamboul is most beautiful!" They asked how many children we had, and said that Edie's blue eyes and fair hair must be very pretty—why did I leave her? I begged M. Robolli to tell them that I feared the variable climate, and also that she was left with my mother. "Don't let them think that we English are unnatural mothers." We all entreated this.

"Madame Riza" then said how sorry she was not to be able to present her own daughter to us. It seems that she is a lovely girl of sixteen; her health is usually good, but she is subject at times to fits of depression and nervousness, amounting almost to insanity. These attacks usually lasted about three days, and this was one of those distressing visitations. She was lying quite alone; her mind, the poor mother said, strangely wandering, speaking of places which she had never seen as if she were there. Her old nurse was the only person whom she could bear to see near her. The mother seemed deeply afflicted when speaking of her beautiful but unhappy daughter, who, M. Robolli says, is charming when well, full of grace and liveliness. While he was talking of her and condoling with the mother, whose whole countenance changed to an expression of profound sorrow, the slaves sitting at her feet moaned and beat their breasts, and even the black men expressed the greatest sympathy: I assure you I saw tears in their yellow eyes.

It was impossible not to be much touched, in listening to this account of the beauty and gentleness and goodness of the poor young girl, alone in her misfortune, and seemingly beyond cure (at least here at Stamboul.) Her mother looked the image of sorrowful despair, her lips trembled, and she could not utter another word. Wrapping her rich mantle round her, she sat in an attitude of queenly dejection, which Mrs. Siddons might have envied. These Eastern women are wonderful for grace. Of course we felt for, as well as admired her, and begged M. Robolli to say how sorry we were to hear of her sweet young daughter's affliction. She thanked us very earnestly and with a simple grace quite indescribable, a grace which makes you feel at once that you never beheld any thing like it before. I said: "It is a very great sorrow for you, but there are others in the world still more unhappy: many who have lost all their children, and many also have ungrateful ones." She replied: "I often think that, and blame myself for giving way to so much grief. My child is good and lovely when she is well. I still have her with me, and Allah may one day please to restore her health and mind entirely." Here she puffed away vigorously at her chibouque, and, putting her hand on her heart, said that it was the very best of comforters in sorrow. We told her the story of poor Sir Edmund Lyons, losing his brave son just in the moment of victory; and two or three even sadder still of this war. She said: "How much England has suffered!" and several of the slaves cried.

We then changed the conversation, which was becoming so melancholy; and they spoke of their summer palace on the Bosphorus, hoping that when they removed there we should visit them. "It is very lovely," they said; "there are hanging gardens with a stream leaping from rock to rock amongst the orange-trees; and the birds are always singing in the shade. There are also beautiful fountains, and rose-gardens; and we think you will like it." We were just saying what pleasure it would give us to visit them in their little Paradise, when a slave, richly attired, entered. She kissed the hem of "Madame Riza's" garment, touched her forehead with it, and then standing upright, with her arms folded over her breast, evidently delivered a message. "Madame Riza" explained to M. Robolli. "I am sorry to say I must go," he said; "another Turkish lady is coming to pay a visit, and although Madame Riza admits me with her husband's consent, he being accustomed to European manners, any other pasha might object to it; and she would not risk getting her friend into trouble." So off went M. Robolli, and off went the fair ladies' cashmeres, and "Madame Liston's" yellow and green handkerchief, and in ran all the pretty young slaves again, like a troop of fawns. I never saw so many women together in my life before; there seemed to be no end of them.

There was one little girl of extraordinary beauty, about twelve, and another a little older, almost as lovely. I never saw any living being, or any picture, so beautiful as the youngest. They told us that she was a daughter of the pasha, by a slave who died last year, and who was also very lovely. The wives seemed as fond of this little houri as if she had been their own child, and were quite pleased at our great admiration of her. Poor child! I wonder what her fate will be.

While I was holding her little hand in mine, and looking at her lovely dark eyes with their deep fringes (you learn what "eyelashes" mean here), in came the belle, for whose sake M. Robolli was banished from the women's apartments. Although not beautiful, I think she was one of the most striking persons I ever beheld. She had none of the almost invariable softness of the Turkish women, but a face of the most marked talent, and decision, and satire, and with a decisive authoritative manner to correspond, and yet perfectly courtly, and with that exquisite ease and grace which is so enchanting in Turkish women. She had piercing black eyes, of immense size and lustre, with thick eyebrows; and hair of so raven a hue that I instantly thought of the younger and more flattering portraits of Charles II. A large, dark mole on the somewhat sallow cheek, made the picture still more striking, and added to this, she had tied a rich lace handkerchief round her neck, just after the fashion of a beau of the Vandyke school, the ends hanging down. She held a lighted Havana cigar between her fingers, and we admired her rich lace and ruffles as she smoked with the air of a Rochester. Her dress and trousers were of amber-colored silk, her waistcoat blue, embroidered richly in silver; round her slight waist she wore a many-colored cashmere scarf, into which a massive gold chain and Turkish watch was comfortably tucked. Her hair was dressed in what they tell me is the old Turkish fashion, cut in steps, as it were, down the forehead—about an inch long by the parting, below that a little longer, by the ear longer still; which has a very curious effect, and gives a rather masculine look. A light-blue handkerchief was twisted gracefully round her head, fastened on with six or seven splendid stars of brilliants. Between the two centre ones, on the forehead, was a long piece of white muslin, about the breadth of one's hand, which, thrown back over the head, fell nearly to her heels behind. A ruby of enormous size flashed and glistened on the finger.

To us she seemed a striking "picture of the East," as she sat pleasantly chatting with Riza Pasha's wives. She and the chief wife sat, or rather reclined, on the divan. The beautiful Circassian seemed to feel cold, and half sat, half knelt by the enormous *mangale* (a kind of brazen tripod, filled with charcoal) in the centre of the room. I thought I had never seen any thing more lovely and graceful, as she dreamily smoked her chibouque, and her great diamond flashed on her white hand, and she lifted up her head now and then to join in the conversation of the other two, or to laugh in the low, musical tone which had charmed us so much at first.

Our visit seemed very like a tale of the Arabian

Nights, especially when the slaves entered with tambourines, and, sitting down cross-legged at the further end of the apartment, entertained us with a concert of "music." A more dreadful noise it is scarcely possible to imagine; you hardly know whether to laugh or to cry. A slave beats the tambourine, and leads the discord with her harsh and grating voice. The rest take up the howl one after another, and yell louder and louder as the story which they are reciting progresses. The fair Circassian seemed to take especial delight in the performance; and, whilst searching for bright little bits of charcoal in the mangale to relight her chibouque, kept prompting them with verses which they seemed to have forgotten—to our great misery and regret; for ears, teeth, and hair were set on an edge and bristling up the wrong way, at this excruciating "treat."

It was at last put a stop to by two things: first, by Mrs. Brown's sinking back on the divan, pale as death, overcome by the noise and the mingled fumes of charcoal and chibouques; and secondly, by the entrance of a very fine baby with his two nurses. He looked so odd to us in his little trousers and fur jacket, and wearing a tiny fez, ornamented with a loop of diamonds. This young gentleman belonged to the visitor lady, and stretched out his arms to her very prettily. He was not at all shy with the Turkish ladies, or with the slaves, but evidently considered us veritable "Giaours," and would not come near us. The nurse who carried him was a lovely young woman: she was dressed in trousers and jacket of a bright green, and wore on her head a pale-yellow handkerchief, fastened with a large diamond. The other was an immense black woman, dressed entirely in scarlet silk, with a little edging of white, and a snow-white handkerchief bound round her woolly head. These two "nurses" would certainly create a sensation in Hyde Park. They appeared devoted to the baby.

But now our imperial-looking hostess made signs that we were to eat, at which announcement we were not at all sorry, the fresh air of the Bosphorus having given us famous appetites. We followed her accordingly into the lofty apartment, with the domelike painted roof; the fair Circassian leading me affectionately by the hand, and the pasha's lovely little daughter gently conducting Madame de Souci and Mrs. Brown. The principal slaves went before to lift the arras, and a motley group followed behind. We could hardly believe the scene to be real: "It is so like an Arabian Night!" we kept exclaiming, as we crossed with the brilliant group over the golden matting of that vast apartment.

At the entrance of the dining-room stood two Arab slaves, richly attired. To each lady, as she entered, one of these held a beautiful silver bowl, while the other poured rose-water over her hands from a vase of the same richly-chased material. Two little slave-girls presented fine napkins, the ends embroidered in gold, on which we each shook the rose-water from our fingers. The dining-room was a most luxurious apartment, closely latticed, for it looked into the streets of Stamboul, but cheerful, and rich in crimson divans and carved and painted flowers on walls and ceiling. All had been done that was possible to make the cage bearable. Riza Pasha's harem is, I am told one of the most "fashionable," which accounted for our seeing a European dining-table, adorned with a handsome centre-piece, and four beautiful vases of flowers and fruit, after the French fashion.

The dining-service was of rare and beautiful china; the silver knives and forks were extremely handsome; the *servietti* delicately fine; the flowers exquisitely arranged, and mingled with oranges and lemons, in the Eastern fashion; the slaves were standing round, three or four deep, awaiting our slightest sign: we felt still more in the land of dreams.

First of all they placed to each guest a sparkling water-bottle and glass. Then a fine china plate containing a flat roll of a kind of rye-bread, called *semeet*, quite new and warm, and covered with a small seed, which, not being a canary or a linnet, I objected to. Then soup was served—a great novelty in a harem: it was most excellent—chicken and vermicelli. Then came a dish of pilauf, of chicken and rice, done brown. I sat next to the chief wife, on her right hand; as the slave held the dish, she pointed out the nicest pieces, begging of me to take them. The fair Circassian sat opposite to me. I was curious to see if they really seemed to like the modern innovation of knives and forks. For the first few minutes they used them—evidently to do as we did; but the Circassian beauty, failing to secure the particular piece of chicken she coveted with a troublesome fork and spoon, threw those incompetent auxiliaries down, and grubbed successfully, and to her entire satisfaction, with her fingers. She then looked at me and laughed; and showing me how to take a piece of bread between my fingers, begged us to eat *à la Turque*, which they were all doing themselves, fast and furious; and, to please them, we accordingly picked a few chicken-bones with our fingers.

We had all three been enchanted with the fair Circassian, as I have told you; with her beauty, her winning yet lofty manners, and exquisite grace. We had seen her smoke, and admired her still. We had even forgiven her for loving the barbarous noise in the "concert of music;" but to see her lick her fingers up to the last joint after each dish—to see her lick her favorite tortoise-shell spoon bright after successive and never-to-be-believed enormous platefuls of sweet pancakes daubed with honey, and tarts too luscious for the Knave of Hearts!—this was too much for Venus herself to have done with impunity! We were perfectly disenchanted long before the feast was over. The rest were not quite so bad, (excepting "Madame Liston," who might as well have had a trough at once); but we began to feel rather sick after the first few dishes were dispatched, and the animal passions of some of the ladies began to be roused by their favorite sweets and jellies, which they tore to pieces with their fingers, and threw down their throats in large lumps. The jester waited at table, presenting the principal dishes with jokes which caused bursts of laughter from the ladies and the slaves in attendance, who seem perfectly at home, and on very free-and-easy terms with their mistresses, notwithstanding their complete submission to them. The jester was a wild and most extraordinary-looking woman, with an immensity of broad humor and drollery in her face. We thought it quite as well that we could not understand the jokes at which the fair Circassian, between the intervals of licking her fingers and spoon, and popping tit-bits on our plates, laughed so complacently, and which sometimes obliged the Arabs and eunuchs at the door to dive under the arras to conceal their uncontrollable fits of mirth.

It was certainly a most singular dinner-party. The dishes of course were innumerable; the chicken and rice, and the *cabeb* we enjoyed; the rest were very sweet and very fat; and we were delighted when our hostess rose, and again the refreshing rose-water was handed to us.

We then returned to the luxurious divan of the smaller room. Again the slaves handed coffee in jeweled cups; again the fair Circassian looked dreamy and lovely, hanging fondly over her chibouque; again we admired the blue Bosphorus, and the distant mountains, and the dark cypresses of Stamboul; again we asked for M. Robolli, and again the fair ladies were enveloped in their cashmeres; the Blacks standing mute, watchful, and listening. We repeated our thanks and adieus; the slaves lifted the arras. M. Robolli kissed the hands of the kind and vailed ladies. The Blacks conducted us down the broad staircase, crowding boisterously round us, and muttering something about *bakshish*.

Our visit to the Harem was over. M. Robolli mounted his "gallant gray," and rode back with us over the Bridge of Boats. It seemed as if we had had a dream.

LETTER XXX.

THE FRANKS—ARRIVAL OF SPRING—LADIES' DRESSES—CHANGEABLE CLIMATE—OMAR PASHA AND THE RELIEF OF KARS—KNAVERY OF THE PASHAS—THE GREEK EASTER—FESTIVAL DAYS AT CONSTANTINOPLE—CHANGE FOR A SOVEREIGN—A LONELY HOUSE—A STORM.

Orta-kioy, March 28th, 1856.

My dear Mr. Hornby:

I am afraid that, although I forward my usual note, it will not leave Constantinople to-morrow. The weather has been so stormy at sea that much confusion is made in the arrival and departure of the mails. Tuesday's steamer has not yet arrived. We heard yesterday, that she had broken her screw, and put in to the port of Syra, but do not know if it be true or not. The Frank population here amuse themselves by spreading false reports upon every possible subject. Nothing is too serious to escape them. Any one expecting husband, mother, wife, or child, is considered but a fitter subject for their merciful "wit." I do not wonder at the Turks' horror of a Frank. I said the other day to Kani Pasha, that I trusted the Sultan did not class the English people amongst such riffraff, for that we should be ashamed to own them. They are often saying at Pera, that such and such a ship is lost with all on board, merely to frighten those who are expecting friends or relations by it.

I told you in my letter of Sunday that all the snow had disappeared. On Monday the south wind set in, and we had a most delicious day, just like the middle of May in England. We went to the harem of Risa Pasha, and nothing could equal the sunny beauty of the Bosphorus. Yesterday was also a lovely day, the sea blue and sparkling, and the villages glittering in the sunshine. It was so clear that I could plainly see the ruins of an old castle far back on the Asian side. Fuad and I sunned ourselves in the garden with the Armenian girls. I gathered a bunch of violets and primroses, to remind me of England; and Master Fuad, always full of mischief, hunted the cats and butterflies, sunning themselves on the borders. Turkish ladies, in their telekis, passed by, paying visits, I suppose. Three of them alighted by our gate to walk up the hill and escape the shaking of their crazy vehicles. I could not help noticing the brilliancy of their dresses, even here. One of them wore a blue feridjee, bordered with broad, cherry-colored velvet; another, an amber-colored feridjee, shot with white; the third, an exquisite violet, edged with black velvet. The best feridjees are made of the richest shot poplin, so you may fancy how beautiful the splendid colors are on a sunny day. The commoner feridjees are made of a kind of merino. Being such a lovely day, I saw a good many Turkish ladies yesterday passing by our road, with their armed blacks to "guard them."

The Bosphorus looked most lovely, and such a fresh, mild breeze was blowing that I almost wished Edith was here; it seemed impossible for any thing to be more pleasant and healthy. A fine English man-of-war came up, with all her sails set. She was going slowly toward the Black Sea, perhaps to the Crimea. It was a beautiful sight. A brig has also anchored just off our little pier. She has the most musical bell on board. It sounds wonderfully sweet, in the night, to hear an English ship's bell ringing out the half hours, and the "All's well," and to know that they are so near us. I dare say they little think that English are so near *them*.

We are in the Turkish quarter, and from the Bosphorus it looks one cloister of latticed Turkish houses. Yesterday it was so much summer that a party of "âmes damnées" were flying up and down, and the Bosphorus was covered with caiques. Most provokingly the wind changed in the night. The increased cold awoke me, and I put my tiger-coat on the bed, quite shivering. This morning it is winter again, —a bitter wind whistling down from the north, and a blinding sleet terrifying man and beast. My poor friend, the shepherd, has to bring all his shivering lambs down from the mountains, where they were skipping in sunshine yesterday.

This is indeed a trying climate. I am glad to say that Edmund has not to return to-night, as he dines with Lord Stratford, to talk over some matters connected with the Loan Commission, and will sleep there. Lord Stratford is very much depressed about the affair of Kars: all the blame seems to be put on his shoulders, as all the disasters of the war were upon Lord Raglan's. Poor Lord Raglan broke his heart (they all say here), and, after he was dead, the papers made him a hero, and spoke of his "devotion to his army," etc. I dare say he was not faultless; but every thing relating to military matters seems to be in such confusion, that the wonder is that we have not more signally failed than we have.

About Kars I am enabled to tell you, from certain

information, that Omar Pasha's visit to the Crimea, many months ago, was for the express, though undeclared, purpose, of entreating assistance for General Williams of both the English and French commanders-in-chief. It now seems that for two or three months before the taking of Sebastopol, both Pélissier and General Simpson were in a state of more than little anxiety as to the issue of the siege. At one time they really began to think that the English and French army ran a good chance of being driven into the sea. Afterward, the great inferiority, instead of superiority, of the Russians came out. But just at this moment of panic and anxiety, Omar Pasha entreated help for the relief of Kars both of the English and French generals. He told them that his men were dispirited, in deadly fear of the Russians, and that, unaided, he could never get them up to face the enemy. But he said, "Give me only a couple of regiments of English, and as many French, and I will undertake success. Alone, and with my raw recruits, who have never been under fire, I repeat, I can do nothing." However, so dispiriting and anxious was the state of things before Sebastopol, that neither of the generals in command would consent to part with a single regiment, not knowing what might happen from minute to minute. You may depend upon this being true.

French, English, Turks, all seem to have blundered. The other day, coming down in the steamboat, we noticed a pasha's caique. "Ah, these pashas!" said a Turkish soldier, standing by, to Mr. Wilkin. "Why, what's the matter with the pashas?" said Mr. Wilkin (who speaks Turkish perfectly).

"What harm do the pashas do you?" "You would not ask if you had been at Kars, as I have," said the man. "When the English general prevented their stealing our money, they began to steal our rations; and we should soon have been starved, only the general found it out, and saw each division fed, with his own eyes, every day." This poor fellow had been sent home sick, before the capitulation, but described the misery and starvation as very dreadful. What the Turkish soldier will bear without a murmur, is something almost incredible. Even here, at Constantinople, it makes your heart ache to look at such unhappy, dispirited creatures, shivering in canvas coats (cloth ones being paid for), and with swords by their sides so paltry and worthless that, as they know, they would probably bend or break with the first blow. If a poor Turkish soldier gets thirty piastres of his pay (about five shillings) he is wild with joy, when perhaps a whole year is owing to him, of which he is too ignorant to keep an account, and would not get it if he were otherwise.

The very worst of the pashas seem to have been concerned in the affairs of Kars. One of them must have been bad indeed, having been disgraced and sent back to Constantinople, in the outset, for robbing his unfortunate soldiers. The general topic of conversation here is, of course, "Peace or War." Peace, however, from the tenor of the latest telegraphs, seems to be generally expected; although, when looking on the Bosphorus and Sea of Marmora, the great war-ships of England and France, with gunboats here, and formidable frigates there, give much more the idea of giants resting to renew the strife.

Mrs. Mysseri, who, as I told you, is great in politics, is deeply concerned for England's glory. "To think," she exclaimed, in a burst of indignation, "that we should be made to leave off, just as we are prepared to do so much, and when we know every thing, just because those French have got nothing to go on with! And to think, that they've got all the glory, and we've done nothing, but sacrifice thousands of men and millions of money, and made fools of ourselves into the bargain!" This is Mrs. Mysseri's notion of the peace.

Monday was the first day of the Roman Catholic Greek Easter; so they had brought Mrs. Mysseri beautiful branches of hyacinths, jonquils, and other spring flowers. I bought a lovely bunch at Stamboul, in a pretty Turkish shop, where the baskets of fruit and flowers were all trimmed with myrtle and laurel leaves, and tomatoes, after the usual pretty fashion. The streets were crowded with Greeks in gala dress. The general Greek Easter does not commence for some time. It is now the Lent of the Protestant population, and a strict fast. I see crowds going to and from church twice a day, even to the caiquejees and porters. The old watchman chants what the services of the day will be, in the street, opposite the different Greek houses. The different days here are quite perplexing. First comes our Christmas-day, and all the English ships dressed with flags; then the Greek Christmas; then the Armenian Christmas. Then the three different New-Year's days; then the Jewish Passover; then Mahomet's birth-day, and all the minarets glistening with lamps. On Fridays you hear the cannon thundering that the Sultan has gone to mosque: it is the Mohammedan Sunday, and the Turks shut up their shops and walk out, carrying their little children. In the evening the miserable cottages of the Jews here are adorned with lamps, hung out in expectation of their hoped-for Messiah. The valley quite twinkles with them, as there are many Jews at Orta-kioy, and thus you may count the different families on a dark Friday evening. Saturday is their Sabbath, as you know, and as a Jew is our fishmonger, we never get fish on that day.

Then comes our Sunday, but we have no sweet-sounding church bells. There is a service kindly read by the chaplain of the "Queen," in a small room of a house on the other hill of Orta-kioy, but I have never been; people talk of almost fainting from heat and closeness, the room being heated with a stove; and this after a long, muddy walk up-hill, seemed to me hardly safe in such a climate. I remember many of the beautiful chants of our church, and sing them every Sunday morning to the old piano. The poor sick Armenian girl, Oscu, likes to stand in the garden and hear me sing the *Te Deum* when my window is open. She came in, the first morning; but when I made a sign that it was a prayer of our country, she sat down quietly, and did not speak, or rather sing, another word. They are kind, affectionate people, simple and unpretending as little children. But to return to the different days. First the Carnival of the Periotes or Franks, then the Greek Carnival, and then the Armenian; the Roman Catholic Armenians beginning on the day when the Protestants of the Greek Church end, and the Roman Catholic Greeks beginning their Easter before the Protestant brotherhood have half got through Lent. All this, with their different saints'-days, fast-days, and feast-days, is almost as bewildering as counting your change at Constantinople.

For change for a sovereign you may get a quantity of dirty paper of the value of a few pence, German kreutzers innumerable, an English shilling, and a huge Turkish crown, mixed with francs and paras, to one's utter bewilderment. The Turkish gold coin is miserably thin and bad, quite illustrative of the fallen state of the country. Our English sovereigns look fair and beautiful amongst them. I always say that the English gold so charms Vassili when his wages are paid, that for a moment the exquisite "chink," makes him quite forget the "robbery in Egypt." He was paid yesterday, and happy and gracious for the day.

But I must say good-night. It seems strange to be in this lonely house, alone, with only two Greeks sleeping below. I was rather nervous when we first came here, and Edmund had to stay all night at Therapia. I used to practice how to cock the revolver before going to my room. Now I do not mind it in the least, and little Fuad sleeps on my feet, and the revolver reposes quietly on the chair. It would be a stout Greek indeed to brave such a trio. Poor Antonio, the dumb Armenian, has been in to see me, and brought me a pretty chaplet of beads for Edith.

Georgy the Sais has had his discharge to-day for bad conduct, and was greatly enraged; so I am more than usually bolted up. The wind is howling dreadfully. These places on the Bosphorus are more like summer-houses than any thing else, and shake with every gust. Heaven help the poor people in the Black Sea to-night! This morning a steamer was towing in the hull of an unfortunate vessel,—masts, ropes, all swept away. We often see this after a stormy night.

The bell of the English vessel sounds so pleasantly! I often wonder who they are on board, and from what part of England they come.

A great many ships are lying just here, I suppose for safety. Their lights look very pretty, twinkling beyond the profound darkness of the valley. Again, good-night! Fuad is sitting up, begging to go to bed. He begs for every thing. Love to all. Dear Edith's doll will soon be ready charmingly dressed, *à la Sultana.*

LETTER XXXI.

WINTRY WEATHER—NEWS OF THE PEACE—THE REJOICINGS—A VISITOR FROM THE CRIMEA—CRIMEAN AMUSEMENTS—LETTERS FROM HOME.

Orta-kioy, March 30th.

My dear Sister:

It is about as bad a day as it is possible to imagine,—a north wind, and sleet falling fast and thick. I have just started Edmund, who has to brave it all, although not at all strong yet. He still has too much responsible and perplexing work to do, and is too anxious about all. He is now sitting on a Commission with General Mansfield and the Turkish Minister of War (Seraskier). How thankful I shall be when we are quiet at home again!

In the midst of the noise of the wind and rain, the rattling of our numerous windows, and all the dreary sounds of a regular winter's day, the thunder of cannon sounded from the different ships at anchor this morning. At first we thought they were saluting the Sultan on his way to Scutari to review the troops, notwithstanding the badness of the weather; but soon after, while Henry and I were wondering, in came Antonio, the dumb Armenian, who wrote in Italian to me: "The Emperor of Russia is at peace with the Emperor of Turkey." Presently the village watchmen went through the streets, striking their staves on the ground as they do at night, and chanting the news of "Peace." I was sorry not to understand what the funny old fellows said. They finished by asking for a few piastres from each house, as a subscription toward lighting up the Greek churches. In the evening all the ships were illuminated, as well as a short notice would admit, and lamps were hung out at the gates of the palaces by the side of the Bosphorus. Muskets were let off at different times all the evening, and every now and then a few rockets thrown up. We could plainly see the rejoicing lights of Kulalee on the Asian side. It was too piercingly cold to venture out. The Armenian bishop, our opposite neighbor, hung out a fine large lantern, containing three or four candles. I possessed only one pretty little one, which I had bought for Edie, and was not sufficiently patriotic to hang it out. I asked Vassili if he had a paper one in the kitchen, but he grumbled out something about their being "too dear to play the fool with;" so our establishment was not distinguished for the brilliancy of its rejoicings. I heard that Pera was very prettily illuminated last night. The ministers went to congratulate the Sultan yesterday. We heard the Sultan's band playing in the evening. I suppose his Majesty was in good spirits.

1st of April.

We were surprised at breakfast-time by a muddy traveler dashing in. This was our Therapian friend, Richard Coote, of the 46th. You will remember my telling you of him, and his dog "Boxer," who was killed by trying to save his master from a shell, in the trenches before Sebastopol. We used to have very pleasant walks together at Therapia, and parted with regret. He is now on his way to England, in the wildest spirits, and as strong as a giant. He was as glad to see us, and as rough and noisy, as a young Newfoundland dog. We could hardly understand him, for Crimean slang has become almost a language of itself. He says they have had "a jolly time of it, this winter"—steeple-chases, theatres, and all sorts of fun. Pelting the Russians on the North side, he said, was no end of a glorious morning's amusement. The English officers throw snowballs, made as hard as possible, with a shilling, sixpence, or half-crown in them. In return comes from the Russians another, of clay or snow, containing little crosses, old Russian coins, and other curiosities. Coote gave me a little cross, contained in a ball of mud which nearly broke his head. He ran on with all sorts of nonsense and fun, and made me laugh immensely. Such a savage-looking being, coated in mud, I never beheld before.

He dares not show his uniform jacket, having done, as he said, the "slow trick" of saving it, until it was impossible to wear it with the truly Crimean trousers. He had had fine large holes in his boots for weeks, but looked the picture of health and strength and good-humor. At first, he said, he was disappointed at having peace, our army being in such splendid trim; but now, he added, "I feel thankful and jolly enough, at the thoughts of seeing my dear mother and England again; and I dare say a good many do besides." He was off to England by the three o'clock steamer, so I could get nothing ready to send by him.

The review at Scutari is put off, I am happy to say, until finer weather. There is also to be a steeple-chase, at which the Sultan has promised to attend. The wind is so cold that I do not think there is any chance of going to Princes' Islands to-morrow. Henry went to Pera in a caique yesterday, taking Vassili and returned with his luggage, which was fortunately found. The letters and newspapers were quite a prize. As to dear Edie's "picture," we went into fits of laughing about it. I never saw any daguerreotype bad enough to match it before, and that is saying a great deal. Tell her that her papa was delighted with the stone, and is going to have a ring put into it and wear it on his chain. The little basket I keep my thimble in, and the two little dolls I shall give to a pretty little Turkish child of my acquaintance here, who will be delighted with them. The myrtle-leaves I keep in my books: thank dear little Edie for them all; I am so glad she does not forget me. The mail is not yet in, being again two days behind time; a north wind keeps them back. The sun is bright and the days are fine, but the wind still cold. Edmund is much better to-day, and, when the weather is warmer, will, I hope, be quite well again.

LETTER XXXII.

EXCURSION TO PRINCES' ISLANDS—SCENERY OF THE BOSPHORUS—PRINKIPO—VISIT TO A CONVENT—THE ANCIENT CHAPEL—CURIOSITIES—CARVING AND PICTURES—BEAUTY OF THE ISLAND—RETURN IN THE DARK—A NIGHT ON BOARD.

Orta-kioy, April 7th, 1856.

My dear Mother:

I have not heard from you since my cousin Henry's arrival. He is, I think, enjoying himself very much, and charmed with the novelty and beauty of the scenery here. On Thursday we went to Princes' Islands, although, from the weather having been so cold and stormy, I hoped the party would have been put off. However, contrary to all expectation, it turned out a lovely morning, with every prospect of its lasting so. Accordingly, at ten o'clock we walked down to the pier, and there was the "City of Paris" gayly dressed with flags and pennants, come up from Constantinople to fetch us. I wished you were there, you would have enjoyed it so.

At Tophana we lay-to, the harbor being too crowded with shipping to venture very close in-shore. The company arrived in caiques. It was very amusing to watch with our glasses who was coming. At last all were assembled, and off we started, the band playing merrily. The sea sparkled in the brilliant sunshine. Henry was perfectly enchanted with Stamboul, and its cypresses and minarets rising abruptly out of the water.

Steaming down toward the islands, we had a glorious view of the Golden Horn and Scutari. The largest vessel in the world, an American, was dozing quietly in the sun in the Sea of Marmora, all her sails set. It was the most wonderful sight. We agreed that the extraordinary beauty of the scene is even distressing. In the first place you never can, by any possibilty, believe it to be real, that you are not dreaming; and secondly, you are half-miserable because every body you like is not with you. When we came within sight of the mountains, leaving behind us the Golden Horn, with its great Roman wall and turrets still guarding the shore, I assure you it was quite overpowering. The sea heaved, and glittered like silver, beneath mountains, in some places higher than the clouds, dazzling with snow and ice on their summits, and clothed with dark fir-trees and heather below, just like St. George's Hills. Halfway up one of the highest peaks, stand boldly out the ruins of a monastery. On the principal island, cottages, vineyards, and olive-gardens peep out here and there; but several of them are mere masses of rock, uninhabited, except by sea-birds, and looking savage and desolate enough. Our vessel stopped at the rough quay of the principal island, called, I believe, Prinkipo.

A crowd of wild-looking Turks and Greeks, seeing our flags and pennants, came rushing down, and with them about a hundred Russian prisoners, in their long gray coats and fur caps. They looked very well, and happy. We disembarked in this crowd, and all the windows of the little wooden houses on shore were full of curious and laughing faces. Some of the children followed us half-way up the mountain. The valley of the island is beautifully cultivated, principally with vines, olives, and pomegranates. A lovely walk we had, although a very tiring one. After following a winding path sheltered with large fir-trees, for some time, and beginning to feel dreadfully tired, to the delight of the whole of the party we came to a convent, the gates of which were wide open. We entered the court-yard, which was in a most ruinous state, and quite deserted, except by a solitary white hen, who walked up to us in a very confident manner, looking sleek and well fed. All round the court-yard was a kind of open gallery with benches, and beyond that the doors of the monks' apartments, in which the giddy young ladies of our party were running about without ceremony. Presently a middle-aged Greek appeared, and looked surprised at seeing so large a party within those desolate and dilapidated old walls. Mr. Leigh speaks Greek; so we asked leave to rest, which was most kindly granted. The Greek told us that there was but one monk left; the brotherhood had fallen sadly into decay. He was old, he said, and did not like to be disturbed by strangers; he was now working in his garden, but we might see the chapel if we pleased. How delighted Julia would have been with the old chapel, built in the early days of Christianity, with its curious pictures of saints, crucifixes, and moldering priests' vestments, evidently once of extraordinary richness.

Here, in the East, things often are found just as they were a thousand years ago, and it was with great feelings of awe that we touched the old volumes in the quaintly-carved stalls where the priest reads. I put aside dark and heavy hangings, and crept through a little door into the holy recess, as it were, of the chapel. Here hung the antique silver censers, curiously carved crucifixes, and strange pictures of saints and martyrs, with silver hands and "glories." Rich priests' vestments lay in the deep recess of the window, but old and moth-eaten, telling a sad tale of the decay of the Christian church and brotherhood. The light was too dim to see much at a glance, and the old Greek soon came in to tell me, by a grave sign, that I was on forbidden ground, which I did not know; but it was to me the greatest charm to touch lightly those ancient things. I believe an antiquary would have gone wild; and I must say that a charming picture of a saint reading, and a crucifix evidently of extraordinary antiquity, haunt me still. The old Greek gave me a curious little cross, and allowed me to take, from a ruined part of the chapel appropriated to women, a small globe of china, which once hung on one of the ancient lamps, now lying broken on the pavement. It is very curious, and marked with the cross of the Greek Church. I am taking care of it for Mrs. Austin.

We propose going to the islands for a month. I then hope to find a few more of these curious things. One lamp, with all its quaint ornaments, was laying moldering on the ground in a corner, and several smaller votive ones hanging neglected, and covered with dust, in the ruined part of the chapel I mentioned. Some of them were alabaster, with silver chains; some curiously worked in brass. If we go to the islands in May, oh that the monk may take a new crucifix for an old, and "new lamps for old," after the manner of the African magician! I went into several of the deserted cells. Each brother seemed to have had a small room to himself, with part of the floor raised at one end of it for a divan. Such an enchanting view from the little casement, of mountains, fir-trees, arbutus, gray rocks, and vineyards, with the sea glittering on each side! The fishing-rods and water-jars of the monks still remained outside several of the doors. By one of them still hung a walking-staff and large lantern, which had once been a very handsome one. The doors of the little carved oak cupboards were open, and a few primitive earthenware vessels still stood within, just as the poor old men may have left them years and years ago. Rude carvings of saints' heads, and a few broken Greek characters were notched on the old bench of the open gallery where I sat. The scene had an extraordinary effect on one's mind. In these vast solitudes things seem to stand still. How different to the whirl and constant change of civilized life! But I shall write you more of these lovely islands and their various monasteries when we are there in May.

M. Musurus is going to ask the Greek Patriarch to allow us to lodge in another convent higher up the mountain, which is in better repair, and was once the prison of Irene, Empress of the East. In the summer many rich Greeks go there for the benefit of the air; so, in these modern days, there is a steamer to the principal island night and morning. We are going to have a tent put up on the sands, for sea-bathing, and look forward with great pleasure to the change when the hot weather sets in. How you would enjoy it, and dear Edie! There would be no fear for her health here; they say it is the finest climate in the world. The largest island has about a thousand inhabitants.

How delightful to have a farm at Princes' Islands, and rooms at Pera for the three winter months, should we be obliged to remain here! We could buy half the island, with garden and vineyard, for £500, and build a good comfortable house, with a fire-place, and every comfort. You would "go distracted" if you were to see it. Fancy St. George's heathery hills rising out of the sea, with shining snowy mountains all around, Asia in the distance, and vineyards and olive-gardens and ruined monasteries in the centre. We left just before sunset; the mountains were violet-color, and the sea the darkest blue. I felt very happy, because, in case of our ever living here, it seemed as if there was a beautiful and healthy home for Edith. We had a delightful passage homeward, but some officers of the party persuaded the captain to go into the Sea of Marmora; this made us late, and, as it was dark when we arrived at Constantinople, they could not take us up the Bosphorus to Orta-kioy.

Few caiques came up to us, and those were only single-oared ones. What was to be done? Only two small caiques for all. So it was arranged at last that, to avoid the night air, I was to accept Mr. Leigh's offer of sleeping on board his yatch, the "Vesta."

The "Vesta" was lying off Stamboul. Her master went on board first, just to say, "Ladies coming," to his men, and Madame de Souci and I sat quietly on deck, watching the marvelous effect of the illuminated minarets of Santa Sophia, Sultan Achmetie, and other mosques, on the water, and among the clustering cypresses. It was just like a fairy dream, if even fairies can dream any thing so beautiful and unique. I thought at first that it was in honor of "Peace," but Admiral Slade told me that it was a great Mohammedan feast-day, the anniversary of Mahomet's entrance into Heaven on a white camel!

At last all our large party got off, crying out many a "good-night" as they stepped down the ship's side to the dancing caiques below. This is extremely dangerous, as you may suppose, unless you are careful, and especially in the dark, with innumerable lights all round, which dazzle and confuse.

We soon reached the "Vesta," lying off a forest of masts. It was wonderful to me how the boatmen could find her out, the darkness was so profound, and the lights of the minarets, and the illuminated masts of some of the Turkish men-of-war, so bewildering, glittering high in the air. Every now and then a rocket whizzed up, and burst over our heads. I was not sorry to find ourselves safe in the charming little cabin of the "Vesta." The old steward was bustling about, and had already prepared a real English tea, as he called it, which was welcome indeed. A bright fire burned in a tiny English grate, and, like a cat, I settled on the hearth at once, and could have purred with pleasure. The "Vesta" is a charming little vessel. She was once a Trinity-House yacht, the one in which the Queen went to Scotland. She now belongs to Mr. Leigh, who has invited us to go to Salonica in her. We shall touch at Candia and other beautiful islands: it will be a rare treat.

After thoroughly enjoying tea and ham, and a chat with our kind host, Miss Barker and I retired to our comfortable little cabin. We were amused to hear Mr. Leigh consulting with the old steward about going on shore in the morning, and what was to be got for breakfast, etc. The night was calm as possible. Only the watch walking up and down, and the sound of the different ships' bells, told that we were on board ship. I thought, as I was falling asleep, that you little imagined I was out at sea, lying off the Golden Horn in a strange ship. At eight o'clock the good old steward tapped with hot water, but I was already up and dressed. We had a breakfast of delicious red-mullet, raimak (a kind of cream), honey from Mount Hymettus, and all the good things which Constantinople could furnish.

We went on shore at ten, and had another long ramble in the cemetery, where there is a magnificent view of the arches of the Roman aqueduct. But I must say good-night, being very tired.

LETTER XXXIII.

SHORES OF THE BOSPHORUS—TOMB OF BARBAROSSA—ANTIQUITIES—DRESS—"APPLE-BLOSSOM"—SYMPATHY IN MISFORTUNE—SCHOOLING—GREEK NAMES.

Orta-kioy, April 12th, 1856.

My dear Sister:

Yesterday's mail brought me your long letter, and the little packet of violets from Edith. There was just one breath of sweetness left, and they were very welcome. How pleasant England must be now! I often think of its hedgerows, and green lanes, and cottage gardens, after the fresh shower—things unknown here. However, we have lovely weather, although rather too warm. The Asian hills opposite are just tinted with the delicate green of spring; there is a breeze from the south, and "white horses," which I love to watch, are rushing in from the Sea of Marmora. I was in a caique yesterday, crossing from Scutari; vast numbers of ships, many of which were homeward bound, and crowded with troops from the Crimea, stood out, a fine foreground to the distant mountains. It was a beautiful sight. The lower range of mountains was clothed in delicate green and the richest tints of brown; the higher looked like white clouds, but shining with snow and ice, which will soon disappear, except from the loftiest peaks. Even now a gigantic hillock of green bursts out every here and there, like a huge daisy-bud amidst the surrounding snow. It is very tantalizing to be in this part of the world, and not have plenty of both time and money. There are so many places of the greatest interest to visit, that I always look wistfully on the mountains, and lay down my map with a sigh. As it is, I am obliged to content myself with seeing as much of Stamboul as possible, and making little excursions to the different villages, and to the charming nooks and valleys on the Bosphorus. The other day I stumbled over the stones of Beshiktash for two or three hours, wishing much to see the burial-place of the ancient Moslem admiral, Barbarossa. I was told that it was easy to discover the old ivy-covered tomb, not far from the wayside; but I did not find it so, and return, with nothing for my morning's walk but a few pretty pieces of common pottery, which I found in a quaint old shop of the village. Vassili bargained for me, with a grim surprise at my caring for such barbarous things. However, I am bound to say that he shows great interest in my wanderings, and does all he can to help me in every way; even to the collecting of old coins and crosses, and inquiring after curious ancient pavements, one of which he tells me is to be seen, of great beauty and in a perfect state of preservation, in a monastery at Halki. We think of taking a small house at the Islands when the warm weather sets in fully: I shall then be able to explore, which I always do with a feeling of regret that you are not with me, and thinking of the old places which we have visited together in days gone by.

My life here is certainly a strange one for a woman. My camplike house gives me but little concern, beyond seeing that it is scrubbed clean; I can go out in a morning, after having exercised my dogs in the garden and fed my birds, without much caring whether it is burnt down or not. My ornamental wardrobe is at the lowest possible ebb—my laces nibbled by midnight mice, my collars tattered and torn by the dignified kindness of the Greek lady. So I should not think it worth while even to shut the door of my room; for the few things that I have of value I left in England. Every article of dress is frightfully dear here, especially since the war; and I carefully hoard my money for potteries, which cost a few piastres, old coins, incense, embroideries, and the many pretty trifles of the bazaar at Stamboul. So expect to see me return with a seeming predilection for savage costume; but don't abuse my appearance until you behold the amber beads I have bought for you, and the scarf worked in myrtle-leaves and gold by an ancient Greek dame of Therapia. By-the-by, I am trying to learn the embroidery. We have a Greek woman now who knows a little about it, and seems willing to teach me: her name is Media, which, by Vassili's learned translation, appears to signify "Apple-blossom," in the vulgar tongue. I always call her "Apple-blossom," it so takes my fancy. She is a worthy body, but sour-looking, and slow in all her movements. At first we thought that she was unhappily of the crab-apple species, but it seems, poor thing, that she has only been blighted; for the love of her husband, a Greek, much younger and better-looking than herself, disappeared unaccountably with her poor stock of piastres, and he vanished as unaccountably himself some time after—no uncommon thing here, I am told, as in other parts of the round world. So, the "Apple-blossom" and Vassili are two misanthropes together the faithless husband and the robbery in Egypt are great bonds of union, and they work on in silent sympathetic gloom. Yanni, the Sais, is a great contrast, always smiling and gay, in the smartest jacket and sash. They are all three very good in their way, and certainly most attentive and devoted to us. Apple-blossom's "only joy" is a spoiled, perverse, and ugly boy of five, whom we allowed her to have with her as a solace to her woes. He killed butterflies, spoiled flowers, stopped up the fountain, let out my birds, half-strangled little Fuad, and committed so many enormities, that he became the plague of my life. At last he was caught dipping his fingers into some kaimak, and that sealed his fate. He is now consigned by day to the tender mercies of the Greek schoolmaster of the village, who undertakes to reform his morals and instruct him in the mysteries of his primer, for the sum of thirty piastres, or four-and-fourpence a month; this certainly cannot be considered an extravagant charge, considering that the Apple-blossom says it is a "select" school. But Apple-blossom, through the favor of her patron saint, Demetrius, whom she ever gloomily invokes in all her domestic troubles, is ambitious for her "piccolo," who certainly already shows slight symptoms of improvement. He formerly entertained a very wholesome but deadly fear of me, the "Cocona;" but we are now becoming good friends, especially since I sat on the garden-steps with him one morning, and begged to be taught a few letters of the poor torn Greek primer, dogs'-eared and blistered with many a tear; for Johannichino is given to crying under difficulties, and does not take kindly to literature and to its representative, the dirty-visaged, dark-bearded Greek dominie. He sometimes consoles himself by bringing his school-fellows as far as the garden door. How one is startled at hearing the old Greek names applied to such dirty little urchins, squabbling against dusty walls for marbles, or screaming for piastres at strangers passing by! — "Epaminondas," "Aristides," "Aspasia," "Sappho!" "Aristides" is perhaps, to your great horror, tormenting and killing flies, or slinging stones vigorously across the narrow streets at children smaller than himself, or appropriating the whole of a seedy melon; "Sappho," sitting in a ravine before the wretched tumble-down wooden cottages, filthily dirty, busily engaged in the unpoetical manufacture of a "dirt-pie," and utterly regardless of the shrill screams of her slipshod mother. Perhaps Sapphos, in these degenerate days of modern Greece, make dirt-pies even at Lesbos! This was a melancholy thought the other day, when standing at my garden-door, and hearing those names called in the noisy children's gambols.

But it is getting late. Vassili is opening the garden-door for Johannichino, who, returning from school with satchel slung across his shoulder, looks quite a Greek edition of Shakspear's Second Age of Man. There is usually a cord attached to our rude latch, like that to Red Riding-Hood's grandmother's, and Vassili is grumbling at having to go further than the door of his den to answer the tinkle of the rusty bell. Johannichino slips quickly by to his mother, in evident fear of being devoured at least by his amiable colleague.

It is now nearly twilight, and I will conclude my

gossip with you, my dear sister, and practice "Adelaide" on the old piano-forte till dinner-time. A string of camels has just passed by, laden with baskets of charcoal: the tinkle of their bells sounds pleasantly in the distance, as they wind round the steep roads leading to the village. I have been so many hours alone, that I could write the history of the day by its sounds, Christian and Mohammedan. What should I do without my letters to you all, by the way of employment? I might take to sighing and dozing by the wayside, like old Fortunata, a Greek woman here; or create myself a female dervish, and practice necromancy and the black art.

LETTER XXXIV.

TEA-PARTY—VISIT OF A TURKISH GENTLEMAN—MORALS IN TURKEY—PASHAS—THE SULTAN—FASHION OF LEARNING MUSIC—TROUBLES OF A MUSIC-MASTER IN THE HAREM—FLOWERS—JASMINE-STICKS—PIPES—A VILLAGE BURNT.

Constantinople, April 15th, 1856.

My dear Mother:

We had an amusing tea-party last evening. Antonio, the Armenian, came in, and wrote in Italian that, if perfectly agreeable, his mother and eldest brother desired to pay us a visit; and at the same time begged permission to introduce a Turkish gentleman, a friend of theirs, who was anxious to make our acquaintance. We were of course happy to see them; and Johannichino was instantly dispatched with a note to my kind friend Miss Clara Barker, to enable us to have the pleasure of also understanding them.

The good old Armenian lady presented the Turk with her usual dignity and grace. He lives in a large yellow house on the Bosphorus, in the harem part of which he has one wife, and his brother two. So Dhudu whispered to me on the divan; for although of the new school, and affecting European manners, he seemed shy of ladies, and soon crept off to the stove and the gentlemen.

I was going to clap my hands for coffee; but they said that he was ambitious of making himself acquainted with English customs, and had expressed a hope, before coming in, that he should see an English lady make tea. So I gave him that pleasure, although I must say that the taste, at least, seemed to afford him any thing but satisfaction. He was asked to take another cup, and declined with great earnestness. He seemed so wretched without his chibouque, that we agreed to offer him one, even in my little *sanctum.* With very little persuasion, Dhudu skillfully made cigarettes for her mother and self, and bowing, they each took to them kindly. The conversation now became animated, for the Effendi's shyness soon wore off under the friendly shelter of his clouds of smoke.

From questions about England, our army, and government, he was soon led to speak of Turkey and its affairs. He told us, very bitterly, many things relating to the disgraceful immorality of the Turkish ministers, sunk in indolence and vice; how devoid they almost all are of the slightest feeling for their unhappy and despised country, the slightest sympathy for its impoverished, ruined state; how they only seek their own interest and and aggrandizement; in fact, all that doubtless you have heard many times before, although not from the lips of one of their own people. There was a certain eloquence about him, or, it might be, that there is something so startling and tragical in the description of a kingdom and people falling to ruin by rapid strides, so rousing in stories of barbaric cruelty and oppression in these days, that we all listened with the greatest attention to accounts of poor olive-growers and unfortunate farmers of the provinces, taxed, robbed, and ruined by pashas reveling in palaces on the Bosphorus, "at this moment, perhaps, drunken with wine, (as many of them I could name constantly are after sunset), and shut up in their luxurious apartments."

He went on to talk of the Sultan—"sovereign only in name—wishing to do much—able, from the prejudices, quarrels, and corruptness of his ministers, to do so little. When, by a fortunate chance, he succeeds with these, some foreign power steps in and with mortifying interference puts the whole thing aside. He is deeply in debt, even for the clothes and jewels of his wives, in their morning shoppings at the bazaars; still more deeply for his favorite fancy of palace-building; his health is wretched, thanks to the wicked and unnatural conduct of his mother, who led him into every excess when a mere boy, in order to gain more power of intrigue herself during his minority. Sometimes there is quite a scene at the palace with the Minister of Finance, about the frightful amount of royal debt and difficulties; and then it is reported that the poor weak Sultan, in his anger and mortification, drinks deep and desperate draughts of champagne and brandy." It is a sad story of so good and kind a heart! One cannot but feel what he might have been, and how much he has had to battle against with his ministers, and, worse than all, with himself, to do even what he has done for Turkey. Although I listened, I did not at all like our guest's talk, feeling shame for him, that he could so speak of these things, even though true—so publish to strangers the disgrace of his own sovereign, and country, and religion. I am afraid there can be little good in him. He regretted very much not being able to speak English. We taught him to say, "God save the Queen," which seemed to afford him vast satisfaction. He took up and buckled on an English sword, and said what would he not give to be an Englishman, and to wear it in her majesty's service! He took his fez off his head, and throwing it on the ground, shook his fist at it. It was very painful, even if he was sincere; and I was glad when he was gone, and the ladies remained for a quiet chat. However, I have promised to pay a visit to his wife very soon, in the latticed house below. He said: "She still wears that rag, that symbol of slavery, the yashmak, which I long to see torn from the faces of our women."

So much for the conversation of our modern Turk, which I did not at all like or credit. He had a sharp, insincere face, and a restless manner so different from the few I have seen of the fine, dignified Turkish gentlemen of the old school of Eastern manners. I had an amusing chat with Dhudu when he was gone—interpreted, as usual, by my kind and constant friend, so untiring in translating that which I fear was not very interesting to herself. You will remember that I told you how poor the Almiras have become since the death of their father. Dhudu spoke very sadly of him, and of his tenderness to them all, and showed us a beautiful ring he had given her; for, after the fashion of the country, they still possess some fine diamonds, although almost threadbare in their dress, and existing on air, according to our notions of living. Talking still quietly of their fallen fortunes, as we listened with interest, poor Dhudu went on to relate a new trouble. It seems that her younger brother, who is remarkably good-looking, and showed a great talent for music, was sent to Vienna in their prosperous days for his education. His piano-forte playing is thought much of here; and being so poor, and the Sultan having set the fashion of Turkish ladies learning music, he now gives lessons to the wives and daughters of several pashas on the Bosphorus. He is married, greatly attached to his wife, and has two pretty children; added to this, he is a grave, shy young man. Well, Dhudu's trouble for her brother is this. He goes quietly in the morning to give his lessons. Perhaps there are two or three vailed ladies in the room into which he is ushered by the attendants. Sometimes the pasha himself is there, but very seldom; there are always two or three black attendants. "The lesson begins," says Dhudu, in a melancholy voice, "and they are generally rather stupid. The men who guard them soon grow tired of looking on, and stroll away to their pipes. They are hardly outside the door, when down goes the yashmak of one of the ladies. She is very pretty, but very tiresome: my brother is afraid to look at her. What should he do if the pasha were suddenly to return, or one of the slaves to enter and report this to him? So he turns his head away, and tries to induce her to go on with her lesson. Would you believe it," says Dhudu, still more indignantly, "the other day she took hold of his chin, and turned his face to hers, and said, laughing: 'Why don't you look at me, you pig?' What can my brother do? The pasha would never believe that it is not his fault. Sometimes one of them will creep under the piano-forte, and putting her finger into his shoe, tickle his foot. Yesterday they slipped two peaches into his pocket, tied up in muslin with blue ribbons, clapping their hands and laughing when he found it out. You know what those peaches mean? They mean kisses," said Dhudu, coloring; "and it made my brother so nervous, for the men were in the outer room, and might have heard all about it. He would be sorry to have them punished; yet they make his life miserable. That pretty one is the worst of all, she is so daring. I visit at that harem, and went with my brother one morning. Knowing them so well, I took him in at the garden entrance, the way I always go myself. We heard somebody laugh, a loud, merry laugh, and oh, what a fright I was in! There she was, up in a peach tree. My brother turned his head away, and walked on very fast. She pelted peaches at him, then got out of the tree, and would have run after him if I had not stopped her." And here poor Dhudu fairly cried, "What can my brother do?"

I thought this account of a Turkish romp might amuse you as it did me, still sympathizing with the kind and anxious little sister.

I suppose these are wild and original specimens of Turkish ladies: those of rank are usually very peaceful and polite, I believe, although perfectly ignorant of even their letters. The little golden flower which I enclose was given me by a gentle and pretty Turkish lady yesterday; it is the blossom of a sort of mimosa, and is greatly prized here for its scent, which I think much too powerful to be agreeable. Small bunches are sold in the streets of Stamboul and Pera, prettily tied on fine branches of cypress or arbor-vitæ; for the mimosa bears so few leaves itself, that they are too valuable to be plucked. We have some very pretty gardens here, on the hill opposite, especially strawberry-gardens, where I am told that in May vast numbers of people come, and sit on cushions on the grass, and enjoy the ripe fruit. This is the village, too, in which the famous jasmine-sticks for chibouques are principally grown. The gardens look very pretty, the trees being trained as standards, from seven to ten feet high, and crowned with leaves and flowers. Great care is taken of these tall stems, which are bound round with linen. Tell Uncle Albert that I can get him a beautiful jasmine-stick here for a few piastres. An amber mouth-piece may cost from five pounds to fifty or sixty—about the latter, if set with brilliants. I am told that Redshid Pasha has two pipes valued at eight hundred pounds each. He is reported to be the richest man in Turkey, as well as one of the best and most enlightened; and great things are confidently prophesied of him, should he ever come into power again.

I must conclude my long epistle, or the mail will start without it. I missed the grand review at Scutari last Monday. The Sultan was there, and they say that it was a very fine sight; our troops looked magnificent. By the way, I went the other day to Kadikoi, the next village to Scutari, with Mrs. Cumberbatch, to visit Mrs. Sanderson, the wife of the Consul of Broussa. I had heen there some time before with her brother, Dr. Zohrab. They then lived in a pretty cottage close to the sea, which was easy enough to find, for your caique landed you on a rough little platform by the door. Now, to my surprise, all the houses dotting the shore of the Sea of Marmora, and clustering thickly behind, with so lovely a view of mountains and waves, had entirely disappeared, and nothing but a heap of ruins met our eyes. We had heard the fire-guns one dark night a short time ago, and had been told that the fire was at Kadikoi, but never expected to find nearly the whole of the village laid low. We were very much puzzled at first to know what to do; but after wandering about for some time among the charred foundations of houses, and ruins of little streets and byeways, we met a couple of sturdy Greeks strolling along, who, in answer to the cavass's inquiries for the family we were in search of, pointed to a few houses still standing on the hill above. So up we scrambled, in the burning sun, through steep and narrow pathways of stones and mortar, thinking how terribly the poor ladies and every one else must have been frightened by so vast a fire. Here and there we saw a Turk quietly gazing on the spot where perhaps his house once stood, or smoking contentedly at the opening of a tent put up within the scorched foundation-stones, and beside the torn and broken walnut-trees—the poor village trees, under whose shade so many cups of coffee had been drunk, so many chibouques smoked! It was a melancholy sight, for many of these poor people are never able to erect their houses again, or at least have to spend months, and even years, in a thin and leaky tent. At last we reached a kind of narrow street at the top of the hill, between high garden-walls, and every now and then came to a closely-latticed house, surrounded by beautiful gardens. We heard the buzz of soft voices, and saw shadows flitting across the close bars, as you often do when passing these poor prisoners on a sunny day.

We now soon found our kind friends, and rested pleasantly. Ramazan, the great Turkish fast, begins in a few days, the ladies told us. Every night the city and mosques will be illuminated; they say that it is a most beautiful sight. But I must conclude, or I shall certainly, in my fatigue, writing so much of matters Eastern, conjure up some frightful Genii of the "Arabian Nights," which, to say the least, would frighten poor little Fuad, sitting so faithfully beside me.

LETTER XXXV.

EXCURSION TO THE CRIMEA—WILD DOGS—FLEAS—INVASION OF RATS AND MICE—ENCOUNTER WITH A SPIDER—GARDENING.

Orta-kioy, April 22, 1856.

My dear Mother:

Before this reaches you I shall have been to Sebastopol and returned. Mrs. Brett, my cousin Henry, Mr. Rumball and myself, with two maids and an orderly of Major Brett's, start from Tophana to-morrow morning. It is lovely weather, and we hope to get there in thirty hours. To our great disappointment, neither Major Brett nor Edmund can accompany us; but they do not wish us to lose this opportunity of seeing the breaking-up of the camp before Sebastopol, or rather its ruins. We have pressing and hospitable invitations from all our Crimean acquaintance, to spare tents, clean straw, ruined outhouses, and capital horses and mules. Russian officers and their ladies come down to the camp almost every day, and we are looking forward with the greatest pleasure to our expedition. Hundreds of troops are daily embarking from Balaklava. We shall be only just in time to have a good idea of the grand encampment.

I shall not have returned to Constantinople in time for the next mail, so do not be uneasy at any unusual silence. Every time the wind waves the fir-trees at Weybridge, do not imagine a tempest on the Black Sea, or fancy you see me clinging to a broken mast, or hencoop, on the wildest breaker there. I will write immediately on my return. Meanwhile I am hardly sorry to leave Orta-kioy, for our lives are literally made miserable by the fleas, which, as I told you, began to appear in alarming numbers immediately on the approach of warm Spring weather. We have passed whole nights without sleeping one moment. Morning after morning I see the sunrise from the divan in the outer room, where I have either sat quietly for hours, or wandered about despondingly in utter despair of sleep.

Sometimes I light a lamp, and attempt to read; but a large party of wild dogs have taken up their abode in the ruined garden of one of the burnt-down houses opposite my window. Whether other dogs intrude on their beat, or what it can be, I know not; but about every ten minutes one or two sharp voices give an alarm, and then the whole pack sweeps desperately down, yelling and barking in the most hideous manner you can conceive. About midnight out creep the mice, which, however, do not much trouble me, if even they carry on their gambols close to me. Rats run between the rafters over the ceiling like so many cart-horses, and, by the time I beat a retreat, may be heard pattering briskly on the keys of the piano-forte. Last week two of them jumped out of it; and on some of the notes of this unfortunate instrument seeming rather more out of temper than usual, we investigated the matter, and Apple-blossom fled precipitately from a huge old rat, who bounced out in her face, leaving a comfortable nest lined with bones and other delicacies behind him, which no doubt he had been preparing for a very happy family. The numerous wild-cats sit upon the housetop, and howl, scream, and quarrel, but do not seem to think of interfering with either rats or mice, after the fashion of respectable Western felines, they only unite with all the other creatures in making night terrible. It is quite tragi-comic to see us all meet in the morning, worn, feverish, and dispirited. At first we lamented and bemoaned with each other loudly, but have now become less lachrymose on the subject, merely bestowing a glance of pity on the last languid arrival at the breakfast-table, or an inquiry as to the particular species of enemy from which the patient may have suffered most.

"Fleas?"—"No, worse." "Dreadful! Another cup of tea? What is to be done!"—"Dogs?" (to my cousin Henry, who is really ill). "No, mice; and a rat, who *would* sit on my bed dressing his whiskers." —"Was that you, walking the garden like a ghost in a white sheet?" "Were you sitting on the doorsteps at sunrise this morning?" "The mosquito season is coming on soon,"—with a deep sigh; "we seem about as unequal to it as they say France is to a continuance of the war." However, we have hopes of getting rid of our worst enemies, the fleas; for while I am away, Edmund goes on a visit, and Vassili promises to have all the matting taken up and every room well washed. The matting is very old, and it is no longer of any use merely to wash its surface; no doubt the habitation of the multitude is underneath. I have often been puzzled at the contradictory accounts of travelers on this subject; many speak of torments they have endured, and yet all agree about the perfect cleanliness of Turkish houses. The explanation is, that in Turkey no really good houses are ever let furnished, or accessible to strangers. There are no Turkish hotels, no refuge for travelers but the caravanserais of the "Arabian Nights" and the peasant's hut.

Lodgings are only let by Greeks, and mixed races of the lower and dirty order, and fleas multiply wonderfully in a dry and warm climate like this, unless a house is kept clean and frequently washed, as the large Turkish houses are. The kiosk in which we live has been uninhabited for some time, the mattings are never scrubbed, and the divans never beaten; so we have suffered, as I say, beyond conception. Greeks and Armenians of the lower class think nothing of fleas here, and those who have not many servants, get used to them. Besides all these pleasant creatures, we are sometimes enlivened by the visit of a centipede or two. I believe that all my movements are now rather grave and sedate, but I flew round the salaamlik faster than ever young lady whirled in a polka, one quiet evening, on seeing one beneath the folds of my muslin dress. Apple-blossom rushed in with the charcoal pincers in answer to my call, and skillfully seized the creature, to my great satisfaction. Mr. Frank Buckland ought to be here—he could carry on his favorite studies so pleasantly, finding interesting subjects and specimens on his very table, without losing valuable time in search of them; in fact, I think they would walk fearlessly into his microscope.

The other evening I happened to be quite alone, writing industriously for the morrow's mail. It was one of those ghostly nights, when the wind howls a little, and white clouds hurry over the moon, and curtains by open windows sway to and fro, rustling drearily, and strange footsteps seem to fall about the house. It was late, and I was very tired, having written several long letters. Vassili had placed a cake—one of his best "dolces"—with some sherry and water on the table before me. Presently I heard a noise, something like the pattering of a kid's foot, on some papers scattered about, and looking up, beheld an enormous spider making toward the cake. Any thing so huge of the genus I never beheld; his long, hairy legs threw a fearful shadow on the white paper. Although accustomed to watching spiders, I could not help shuddering at this gaunt midnight visitor, who made a dash toward me when I moved my hand, and was evidently disposed to fight for the cake. To that he was quite welcome, but I so thoroughly objected to the risk of his running over my hand, that I resolved on capturing him if possible. For an instant we menaced each other; then, as quick as lightning, I popped my glass over him. He gave one rapid run round it, and finding no possible escape, sat a surly prisoner until Edmund came home, and we contrived to put him out of the window unhurt. Certainly this would have been a splendid specimen for our talented and earnest friend. Oscu would charm him too, by knowing where to look for scorpions about the gravel-paths and old woodwork here, and by fearlessly watching their little forceps seize upon flies, as she suns herself under the verandah of their worm-eaten house. In the garden I sometimes find enormous green locusts, and on the hills grasshoppers, with wings and legs of every color, from the brightest blue to the deepest red. Hundreds of these fly before your feet in summer-time, and the effect is very curious; when the wings are opened for a leap, the bright colors gleam in the sunshine, and when they alight on the ground, all vanishes into the light brown of their backs and of the scorched turf, until the next rose-colored leap forward.

I must conclude: my time for writing is shortened to-day, for I have been very busy in the garden. Simione has brought out all his fine orange and lemon trees, acacias, and tree-geraniums from the conservatory, and we have been placing them up the door-steps, and bordering the quaint little garden with them, after the favorite way here. Spring has come on very rapidly. The fig-tree by my window is putting forth its green leaves, and the large passion-flower over the trellis-work begins to revive after the winter storms; it has never lost its leaves, and the verbenas in the open borders have not been killed by the frosts, which, although sharp, do not last so long as in England.

Again adieu, my dear mother! I will write from Balaklava, but do not be anxious if one mail arrives without any news, as I may not have a letter ready on our arrival there.

LETTER XXXVI.

RETURN FROM THE CRIMEA—COMMENCEMENT OF THE FAST OF RAMAZAN—PROTESTANT CHURCH—RETURN OF THE ARMY—THE PEACE.

Balaklava, April 29th, 1856.

My dear Mother:

I hope you received my letter announcing our safe arrival here. A mail is just starting for England, and I send these few lines, to let you know that we return to Constantinople to-day, after a delightful week in the Crimea, which ought to have been three, to enable us to see all we wished. On Thursday we spent a long day at Sebastopol; yesterday Colonel Hardinge most kindly made a party for us to the Valley of Baidar; but I must defer all accounts for a long letter when I have more time. I can hardly believe that we have watched the sunset from the Redan, listened to linnets singing on the banks of the Tchernaya, and gathered you some wild flowers from its stony banks; all seems so peaceful now! General Windham was here yesterday. We have seen Crimean heroes to our heart's content, and talk in our sleep of the Mamelon and Malakoff.

Orta-kioy, May 7th.

Here I am quietly settled in our little kiosk again, after all the pleasure as well as fatigue of our excursion to the Crimea. Every room has been thoroughly cleaned, the mattings taken up, and we can now sleep in peace. My dear little Fuad was so delighted to see me home again. How I wish you could see the Bosphorus in its spring dress; it is really like paradise; and the nightingales are singing the whole day long. Close to the cypress-trees on the shores are shrubs covered with a rich pink blossom; the contrast is beautiful.

Ramazan began yesterday, and the minarets were illuminated in the evening with wreaths of light. The thirty-seventh day is the grand one, when the Sultan goes to mosque at night, in his beautiful state caiques.

Mr. Mansfield has been staying with us here, footsore from his tremendous walks in the Crimea, but greatly enjoying this little garden, which is extremely pretty now, with the passion-flower in full beauty over the arbor, orange-trees and tree-geraniums all put out round the borders, and the old wooden balcony completely covered with clusters of pale pink roses.

The little Protestant church here, on the other hill, was opened last Sunday. It is a very simple and pretty Gothic building, all of wood. The altar was wreathed with wild flowers, and a very impressive service was read by the chaplain of the "Queen." The bells sounded so sweetly, ringing for the first Protestant service on the shores of the Bosphorus.

The weather is warm, but with occasional showers, and every thing looks as gay as possible. Ship-loads of troops are constantly passing down from the Black Sea. Early in the morning we hear the notes of a bugle, followed by a hearty English cheer from the men on their way home. Sometimes a drum beats three times, as the transport steams slowly down, and then as many rounds of cheers are given. The redcoats are clustered, thick as bees, upon deck. I like to see them returning home, much better than to watch them going up to the Crimea, as I used to do before Sebastopol was taken. However, no one approves of this "French Peace," as it is called; and I do not like the idea of our countrymen all going away, and leaving us behind in this strange land. I long for home, and to see a green lane, and a cottage, and a bit of fern again, after all this fine panoramic scenery, which never touches one's heart.

LETTER XXXVII.

START FOR THE CRIMEA—THE BOSPHORUS—A SWELL ON THE BLACK SEA—PLEASURES OF THE VOYAGE—HARBOR OF BALAKLAVA—CHANGES ACCOMPLISHED.

Constantinople, May, 1856.

My dear Mrs. Austin

I am much flattered and pleased to find that my letters from this part of the world afford you any entertainment, and now send you a short account of our trip to the Crimea. I have not had time to do this before, having been out a great deal. I was unwilling too to miss writing you something about the illuminations of Ramazan and the three days' Feast of Bairam, at the moment it was all passing before me.

It was a lovely morning when we started from among the forest of masts at Tophana, and wound our way among French and English men-of-war, transports, and gunboats, into the more open part of the Bosphorus. The broad blue stream seemed to flow on more gloriously beautiful than ever, between the hills and valleys of the two great continents, already dressed in the delicate green of spring. Even those who had lived here for years, stood on deck, glass in hand and thoroughly enchanted, marking the bright pink blossoms of the Judas-tree, contrasted with the rich, dark green of the cypress, slopes of white strawberry-blossoms glistening on the hillsides, with orange-trees and the gayest flowers peeping through the trellised walls of many a harem-garden. On we swept through the sparkling waters, passing many a gay caique, many a light Greek barque, with its sails set and pennants fluttering merrily in the breeze. The white tents of the German Legion, encamped on the heights of Kulalee, shone in the morning sun. On we swept, past the hanging woods of Kandelij, past Therapia and its arbutus-covered hills, past Beicos Bay and the numerous men-of-war lying at anchor there, past the Giant's Mountain and its traditionary grave of Joshua, past the ancient ivy-covered Castle of Roumelia. Then we soon came to the sharp and rugged rocks, so famed in classic story, defending the wild and barren-looking shores of the Black Sea. Breakers were raging furiously against the sides of the watch-tower, and the sea looked dark and threatening before us—so sudden a change, from the bright and sunny waters of the Bosphorus! How many, we thought, have looked on these gloomy shores since the war began, passing by them never to return!

At last we were fairly on the Black Sea. There was little wind, but what is called a heavy swell made our small steamer roll and pitch in a distressing manner. One by one the smiling and enthusiastic voyagers of the Bosphorus disappeared; no laughs were longer heard on the deck, people returned books and glasses to each other, folded their wrappings round them, and assumed a quiet and distant demeanor. Our poor maids became dreadfully ill and desponding, and at last lay helplessly in their berths. Mrs. Brett and myself held out bravely to the last, when I saw her grow pale, looking on those terrible waves. I was just able to place a pillow under her head, and then I, who have always boasted my good seamanship, lay deadly faint on the deck beside her, the ship pitching more and more every moment in that remorseless sea, cruel as in ancient days!

"Poor ladies!" said a kind old gentleman, who was not ill, laying another warm cloak over us. "Just like the Babes in the Wood!" lisped a traveling exquisite, of any thing but gigantic proportions, in a pitying tone; "it is certainly true that we are the stronger sex!" I was just well enough to feel conscious of what a capital sketch this would make for our English friend "Punch."

"Dinner, ladies!" screamed the cabin-boy. We had thought him such a pretty boy in the morning; now he appeared to us something worse than demon, and the voices of those able to eat below seemed like the horrid chattering of evil spirits. Somebody said something about Sir Walter Scott, and that "drunken as the Baltic" was nothing to this mad tossing about; but we were surly, and turned our heads away, lying cold and miserable under our cloaks, until a heavy night mist sent us staggering down to all the horrors of the ladies' cabin below. I will not dwell on our sufferings; we could but bear them well, thinking constantly of our poor soldiers, tossed about in that dreadful sea, and lost in last November's tempest!—we, with every comfort and bent on our amusement—they crowded, comparatively uncared for, and bound to all the sufferings of war.

After another rough day and night, another morning dawned, cold and chilly. Ill and depressed, we felt as glad to hear the anchor drop as we could feel about any thing, and made an effort to look out of a

27

port-hole. Such barren, cheerless rocks, after the sunny hills we had left behind! I remember the thought, or rather the hope, which crossed my mind: "Life's weary journey over, may we arrive at a fairer shore!" It was too rough to land; so, when dressed, we paced the deck, gazing on the grand but inhospitable coast, and full of sad thoughts of all that had been suffered there. Only three or four vessels were anchored near us; and in the profound silence we heard birds piping amongst the gray rocks, over which some huge snow-piled clouds were majestically rolling. The steward, coming on deck, told us that the captain had gone on shore to get permission for his vessel to enter the harbor; but that this was very difficult, crowded as it was now. He had been in the fearful storm when so many of our transports were lost, and gave us some obliging (but, in our depressed state, not particularly cheering) information as to the almost impossibility of keeping a vessel off the rocks in the event of a gale blowing strong upon them; how we were anchored in the very spot where the ill-fated "Prince" went down; how unlikely it was that the captain would obtain permission from the admiral to enter the harbor; and lastly, that, if the breeze kept on blowing steadily as it did now, we should have an excellent opportunity of seeing what the sea could do here. However, nothing was to be done but to wait patiently, and a fellow-passenger kindly pointed out to us General Marmora's white tomb high on the cliff above, the ancient Genoese tower, and Miss Nightingale's wooden hospital huts.

The captain returned, and we met him anxiously To our dismay, he said that the admiral's orders were imperative: not another merchant-vessel was to be admitted into the harbor, already too much crowded. However, Mrs. Brett had long before sent her orderly on shore with our letters; some were to be dispatched up in front, but one of hers was fortunately addressed to Colonel Hardinge, Commandant of Balaklava, an old friend of Major Brett's. How glad we were when the colonel came on board, and kindly offered to take us on shore. From the sea, nothing is seen of the harbor but clusters of tall masts, at some distance, apparently inland, and surrounded by cliffs. As you row on, a small opening in the rocks appears, and, corkscrew-like, you wind gradually into the creek, overhung on both sides by grim and gigantic cliffs, and commanded by the still formidable old tower. It was certainly a wonderful sight, the vast crowds of shipping, the heights thickly studded with huts and soldiers, officers riding down, men, mules, and horses, thick as bees, busily cutting a steep and winding road. Sardinians strolling here, sailors wandering there, red-coats everywhere; high above, and far down below, the same ever-shifting, crowded panorama of one scene of the great Russian War. We walked along the quay. What a sight it was, to look on the vast preparations for the return home of a great army! Some of the countless ships were taking in crowds of hurrying soldiers; others, loads of shot and shell, brought down from the camp by fine sleek mules; commissariat stores of all kinds, Russian cannon, vast quantities of iron, soldiers' clothing and accoutrements. The railway-cars were busily at work, transporting huge bales and packages. Officers, naval and military, were walking or riding up and down, inspecting, directing, and commanding.

All was activity, energy of head and hand, so doubly striking to us, having but just left Constantinople. Every appliance of industry and invention was here; there, all falling into decay and corruption, from a seemingly charmed and fatal lethargy. It was curious to see, at a single glance around, the greatness of the nation, whose sons showed so strangely among those remote and frowning heights, and the vast and dreary steppes beyond. Even the wretched mudbanks of the harbor were metamorphosed into a broad and excellent quay, the railway coming down close upon it. The Russians will surely never recognize the place on their return, Colonel Hardinge and others have worked so untiringly and so well. The foundation of this long quay was made by throwing old hampers, filled with stones and pieces of rock, into the broad border of the morass. But perhaps I may be telling what you know already.

After hearing all the horrors of this place when our army landed—men and horses sticking in mud and mire—it seems now, with its railway and fine roads, a marvelous picture of skill and industry. People in England can hardly form an idea of what our officers and men have accomplished, of the gigantic difficulties overcome at a fearful cost. We were sorry to quit the busy shore, crowded with our countrymen, to return to the ship. After having been so much among Turks and Eastern people, the sound of many English voices was very pleasant.

But I must conclude, my dear Mrs. Austin, or I shall lose the mail, or tire you. My letter has grown so much longer than I intended it to be, that I must send the rest of it in my next huge envelope for Weybridge.

LETTER XXXVIII.

LANDING AT BALAKLAVA—COLONEL HARDINGE—RUSSIAN GOVERNOR'S HOUSE—A PRISONER OF WAR—HEIGHTS OF BALAKLAVA—MISS NIGHTINGALE'S HOSPITAL—"THE SISTERS"—FLOWERS—SOUVENIR OF THE GOVERNOR.

Constantinople, May, 1856.

My dear Mrs. Austin:

We passed a rather rough night outside the harbor of Balaklava, on our return to the ship, and in the morning the sea was so high, that we began to fear it would be impossible to land. Unaccountably we had received no reply from any of the letters sent up to the front, and it seemed that we were to be prisoners on a stormy coast, and to see nothing more of the Crimea, thanks to the admiral, against whom I vented my displeasure as we paced the deck. "Patience!" said my pretty, good-tempered friend; "there is a boat coming to us;" and, dancing up and down on the great waves, came Colonel Hardinge again, and his stout rowers. We looked upon him as our good genius, especially when he offered us a room at head-quarters, that we might not risk being kept out at sea. I don't think invitations are often more cordially given, and am certain that none was ever more delightfully received. Leaving our maids to pack up and come on shore in the ship's boat with the orderly, we stepped into the dancing boat below.

We were soon on the crowded quay. The square, low-roofed, white house, with a sort of balcony in front, which shows so conspicuously in the prints and photographs of Balaklava, is now head-quarters, and was formerly the house of the Russian governor. It is built much after the fashion of Greek houses here at Constantinople, with one large room, from which several others open on both sides. It was very cold, with the sharp and penetrating east wind so much felt in the Crimea. The colonel had ingeniously invented a fire-place, in a hole in the white-washed wall formerly appropriated to a stove; his handsome English terrier was warming his nose before it; a real kettle was singing merrily; a few books were strewn about. We settled down joyfully upon the hearth, and thought ourselves the most fortunate women in the world.

Strange it seemed, to be in a place the name of which had thrilled the world with interest but a few months before, and which we had so little expected to see—we two, strangers to each other then, like sisters now. First, we gladdened our hearts with a cup of tea; then we wrote letters to Constantinople, announcing our safe arrival, and afterward looked over the curious old house, which seems to have been much knocked about when the place was taken by the English.

There were only a few old and worm-eaten chairs and tables in the outer room; ugly brass candelabra, which the colonel had polished up from their ancient dirt, were fixed against the bare and white-washed walls. The large double windows opened on to the wooden balcony. In one of them stood an equestrian statuette of Napoleon, with both arms and part of his cocked hat knocked off: he had suffered severely in the war. One of the opposite rooms was rather better furnished, and the walls covered with paintings after the manner of the Greek church. This was doubtless, we thought, the apartment of the governor's lady. Colonel Hardinge had given strict orders that nothing should be disturbed; and even himself watered a large and beautifully trained hay-plant in the window, which had evidently been a great favorite with the owner. In another recess of the window lay a touching evidence of hasty flight; it was a little doll's cap, with the gay ribbons not yet quite sewn on, and a small toy of seed-beads of many colors, containing tiny rings and necklaces—threaded perhaps with childish delight just as our great ships of war were coming up. Colonel Hardinge had one prisoner in the place, a pretty pigeon, which had been caught and given to him at the taking of Sebastopol. A soldier had made him a strange little pigeon-house out of some rough wood, and after the quaint model of the Greek church at Balaklava. This was placed on a tall beer-barrel in the sitting-room, for fear of rats, which abounded in the governor's house. The captive surveyed us all very complacently from his high place, cooing occasionally; and although his wing was only clipped, he never attempted to leave it. Outside the windows, on the rough old balcony, was the colonel's garden, in which he took great interest during his few moments of leisure. He used to hang over his mignonette, sown in deal boxes, and water his Irises and other roots, with a solicitude enviably philosophic, when one considered that the poor flowers would be left to die in a few weeks, after all his care. This soldier's *ménage* interested us very much, although, on seeing more of it, we felt humiliated to find what delightful little dinners, and cheerful, chatty fire-places, our masters can contrive to produce under great difficulties, without the aid of a single creature of womankind.

The first day of our arrival we took a long ramble on the heights of Balaklava, by the old Genoese castle. On one side is a solitary and magnificent view of sea and cliffs; but pass a sharp and lofty turning, and the crowded port beneath, and all the active military movements, are instantly before your eyes. We then walked among the scattered wooden huts a little lower down—beautifully neat and clean, with broad and well-swept roads between.

Many of the occupants evidently took great pleasure in the names so carefully painted on some of them—perhaps the same as those in which their wives and children lived in England. "Albert Terrace," "Prospect Cottage," amused us much, and especially one tiny wooden hut, looking not much bigger than a toy on those great hills, dignified with the appellation of "Marine Villa." Many of these had pretty little flower-borders, about two feet wide, with not a weed to be seen, and carefully watered. Higher up, we came to Miss Nightingale's hospital huts, built of the same long planks, and adorned with the same neatly bordering flowers. The sea was glistening before us, and as we lingered to admire the fine view, and to look with interest about us, one of the nurses, a kind motherly-looking woman, came into the little porch, and invited us to enter and rest after our steep walk, which we were very glad to do. A deal stool was kindly offered to us by another and younger sister, a bright, fresh-looking, and intelligent woman. On the large deal table was a simple pot of wild flowers, so beautifully arranged that they instantly struck my eye. The good sisters were enthusiastic in their praises of the beauty and rarity of the flowers about the heights and valleys of Balaklava, of which they always gathered a fresh bouquet, they said, in the early morning walk which each took in turn. They were most agreeable women, their eyes sparkling with interest in speaking of simple things and fine views. The first whom we saw, "Sister Margaret," showed us a basket of three beautiful kittens, which she had named Alma, Balaklava, and Inkerman. The little creatures were found and saved at the taking of Sebastopol; they were fat and playful, and seemed to delight as much in Sister Margaret, as she did in them. How charming the little deal-house appeared to me, with its perfect cleanliness, its glorious view, and the health, contentment, and usefulness of its inmates! How respectable their few wants seemed; how suited their simple dress to the stern realities, as well as to the charities of life; how fearlessly they reposed on the care and love of God in that lonely place, far away from all their friends; how earnestly they admired and tended the few spring flowers of a strange land; these brave, quiet women, who had witnessed and helped to relieve so much suffering!

This was the pleasantest visit I ever made. Miss Nightingale had been there but a few days before, and this deal room and stool were hers. There were but two convalescent patients lying in the little ward; but the "Sisters" said that there was a great deal of fever still among the Sardinian troops, and that they knew it by the frequent applications for ice from their camp. At last we said adieu, and parted with regret. Walking homeward by another and less frequented pathway over the heights, we found many of the wild flowers of which the "Sisters" had spoken. It seemed a pity to see horses tethered in the poor ruined vineyards, and vines trampled down, once so carefully tended. It was a curious scene. Far and wide, on the hills and slopes, many a group and many a horseman was returning to camp. The evening light fell brightly on the white crosses of the distant Sardinian cemetery, and on the tomb of their ill-fated General on the cliff; bugles were ringing here and there, and lights were beginning to appear in the valley below.

We had almost regained our quarters, when we heard a voice calling to us; and looking back, we saw a soldier, with a bundle of flowers in his hand. They were specimens of a beautiful blue and yellow Iris, which I had admired at the hut. The kind "Sisters" had hastened to get us some roots, and had sent the old soldier after us with them. We have planted them in a little box, and hope to see them flourish one day in England, a remembrance of our friends and of this pleasant walk. We made the colonel a fresh bouquet for his table on our return, and, while the pleasant after-dinner chat was going on, prepared the different specimens of plants which we had found, to form the first chapter of a Crimean herbarium. Mr. Walker, a friend of Colonel Hardinge's, has arranged some beautiful ones, from every battle-field and all places of interest here, and was most kind and patient in helping us.

We repaired to our room early, anxious to be fresh

for the morrow. The maids were snugly ensconced on a large sofa at the further end of the apartment—our "things" neatly arranged on the large and dreary toilette-table of the fugitive governor's lady. A dilapidated work-box stood on a side-table, the needles just beginning to rust in knitting suddenly left off. A bouquet of hay-flowers stood in a glass case beside it, and a few well-thumbed books were scattered about. On a chest of drawers lay a broken toy; we hoped that the little owner was still safe and well. Opening a crazy wardrobe, to hang up my dress, the governor's uniform quite startled me. There were two rents on the breast of the coat; I suppose the poor man had cut off his two Orders in the hurry of flight. On how many gala and happy home days he may have worn them here! We began to grow nervous, looking over these ghostly things in the deep silence of night; and were glad to remind each other that the governor and his wife were both alive and well. Presently the challenge of the sentinel, and the cheerful "All's well!" reassured us; and it was pleasant to sink to sleep, feeling that we were guarded by English soldiers.

LETTER XXXIX.

BALAKLAVA—THE CAMP—THE BATTLE-FIELD—VISIT TO THE MALAKOFF AND THE REDAN—BOTANIZING—BAIDAR—RETURN FROM THE CRIMEA.

Constantinople, May, 1856.

My dear Mrs. Austin:

Very early in the morning, as you may suppose, every one was stirring at Balaklava, and the tramp of soldiers, the clattering of horses and mules and the thousand other sounds of the great embarkation, began again for the day. Colonel Hardinge had most kindly made arrangements for us to go to Sebastopol, but could not spare time to go himself; it was no joke being commandant of Balaklava just then.

Mrs. Brett, fortunately for her, is a perfect horsewoman; so the colonel mounted her upon a favorite but fiery horse of his own, and her orderly found one somewhere in the camp. I should have been grateful for a humbler steed; but my saddle had been unfortunately left by mistake at Constantinople, and no other was to be got. So Colonel Macmurdo was good enough to lend me an ambulance, drawn by four stout mules, for myself and the rest of our party.

Off we started at a brisk pace through the narrow street of Balaklava, if street could be called merely a few old white-washed Russian houses, scattered here and there among the hundreds of long wooden huts and store-houses of our army. We could but wonder at the fine road which, after crossing the railway, we soon came to—the perfect order in which every thing seemed to be, the prodigious commissariat depots, the fine teams of mules coming down from the front, laden with all sorts of stores to be returned to England; Tartars, in their fur caps, driving quietly along in rough little wooden carts; and crowds of nondescript, half Eastern, half European-looking people, mixed up with soldiers and sailors—English, French, and Sardinians.

The "hotels" were very curious too. All constructed of deal, like every other building, but gayly decorated with little flags, fluttering all round, after the manner of the Crystal Palace, and bearing the high-sounding names of "Hotel de l'Europe," "Hotel de la Paix," painted in large letters on their sides. A passing glance showed the single apartment of these hotels, neatly papered with the "Illustrated London News," with here and there a few gayer scraps of art. Then we came to the different townlike encampments of our army, scattered over the vast steppes and plains of which one has so often read. Every moment something ingenious met the eye by the wayside,—nicely contrived and sheltered little gardens,—tub sentry-boxes, prettily roofed with turf, a fir-tree planted on each side by way of ornament,—neat little fowls' houses, and flourishing-looking cocks and hens sunning themselves at the doors,—a goat tethered here and there,—a cosy turf dog-kennel, the faithful friend in excellent condition dozing in the cleanest straw. In fact, it would have taken us days to see half of the great and small things of interest in this wonderful camp.

The white tents of the French army in the distance, with a glimpse of the sea before them, formed a beautiful picture, in the bright beams of the morning sun. A more touching one, was the wayside cemetery of the 33d Regiment, in which monuments were being erected to the memory of those buried there. The graves were very thick, and the rows of white stone, inscribed with many a gallant name, stood out in sad array against the clear blue sky. Soldiers were busy laying turf around them, planting arbor-vitæ and juniper trees, and placing shot and shell at the head and foot of each. The little paths were also bordered with fresh green turf; and it seems to have been a labor of love to leave these graves as fair as possible.

The whole was surrounded by a strong wall of turf and stone. Far away in the distance, on a vast slope of land, lay the Zouave burial-place,—merely fragments of rock and stone thrown down, with here and there a rough wooden cross,—looking so bare and desolate, compared to our much-cared-for one. How sad it was, to see the thousands left far behind in these dreary plains.

Further on is the ravine called "The Valley of the Shadow of Death," where our poor soldiers were shot off the rugged cliffs on each side, by hundreds, when fighting their way on to Sebastopol. There we met a large party of Russian officers, driving handsome droshkeys, with four horses abreast. They bowed to us with the greatest politeness, and each party regarded the other with interest. We stopped for some time at the foot of the ravine, and collected as relics a few pieces of the vast quantities of shot and shell scattered about. The ground was torn up in every direction, the banks of the little mountain stream broken down here and there, and its clear waters bubbling over more shot and fragments of shell than pebbles. A ruined farm-house and vineyard lay in the hollow; we crossed over to look at the crumbling foundations, and gathered a few sprigs of a poor rose-tree, and some pretty bunches of apple-blossom which had sprung from torn and broken branches, yet marking "where once the garden smiled."

A little further on we caught sight of the sea. Its blue waters, glittering in the sunshine, interlaced, as it were, vast piles of white stone ruins, rising abruptly out of them. And this was once the fair yet dreadful Sebastopol! We looked long with wonder at its utter destruction. Walking up the hill, we met a party of "Sisters of Charity," quietly looking about, and pointing out to each other the ruined garden of the slope beneath. It was indeed a sad sight; noble poplar-trees shattered in the middle of their lofty trunks, their tops hanging down, and broken branches swaying drearily in the wind; masses of gravel and earth hurled upon what were once, perhaps, cheerful gravel paths for the townspeople to stroll about on; fine shrubs torn up and dying; turf plowed up, scorched, and blackened. Ruin on the most gigantic scale, everywhere! And the remembrance of the grief, and horror, and suffering which the struggle had cost to thousands of human beings, made an acute impression of pain on my mind which I shall never forget. The fine barracks, which we next came to, were powdered almost to dust; but as to the magnificent docks, blown to pieces, the huge blocks of beautiful pink granite with which they were entirely lined, toppling one over the other, as if they, and the great oaken gates, had been dashed and tossed up together by an earthquake or some hideous convulsion of nature,—even remembering what war is, it was difficult to believe this to be the work of man.

Then we went by masses of ruined store-houses toward the Malakoff, looking frowning and formidable still, though conquered. We toiled up with difficulty in a burning sun, our feet sinking deep in the loose earth and sand at every step. You may well imagine the almost breathless interest with which we looked at every thing here; at all the signs of the deadly and terrific struggle which had so lately taken place. It seemed almost startling *not* to hear the cries and the din of war, which we had so often heard described. Torn and empty cartridge-boxes lay thick on the ground—shot and shell, as hail after a storm,—here a torn shoulder-knot, there a broken scabbard. We crept beneath eight or nine feet of sand and earth, supported by enormous rafters, into one of the cavities where the Russian gunners lived during the siege. One of the poor fellows' rope shoes lay near the entrance; and I carried off a heavy iron hammer and a small crow-bar, to take to England.

Marvelous defenses these were; their foundations formed of hundreds of baskets, filled with sand, which even women and children toiled night and day to bring up. It was sunset when we gained the summit, and the tower of the Malakoff; and oh, what a magnificent spectacle it was, to look upon the distant range of mountains, the ruined city, and the sunken ships,—on the Mamelon, the Redan, the Garden Battery,—all the grand plan of the attack and defense, bathed in the glorious purple and violet light of the sun's parting rays! The blue sea glittered to our right, and the tall masts of many a stately ship at Kamiesch rose clear in the distance.

It was time, but so difficult, for us to depart; for we felt chained to the place, as if to stamp every thing, and forever, on our minds. Even now I seem to see it all before me, and to hear plainly the air of a little Norman song which one of the few French soldiers left in the tower was singing, as he roasted his coffee in a huge fragment of shell. Nature seemed to remember that it was spring-time, even in this scene of desolation, for a nightingale was singing in the distance, and a few wild flowers springing up in companionship with some bright tufts of turf beyond the line of earthworks. A starling sat whistling on a piece of broken wall to the left, and frogs were croaking contentedly in a grass-grown pool, probably once belonging to the poor farm-house of which only those few scorched bricks remained.

When we reached the Redan, it was still the same sunset picture—grand beyond expression—of the fearful struggle; but there we saw the sun sink beneath the waves, bathing the whole scene and every object, from the broken cannon to the little purple Iris flowers springing up on the trampled earth and amidst shot and shell, in the same unclouded blaze of golden light. Then, in the profound silence, when the gray twilight came falling sadly over all, it seemed to us that the splendor which had entranced us was like the glory our brave men had gained, and the darkness, like the pain and sorrow for their loss. We paced the fearful path up which our soldiers trod, and gathered, from around the huge holes made in it by bursting shells, many of the same wild Irises which we had noticed by the Mamelon; their lovely violet color, mixed with a brilliant yellow, gleaming like jewels among the stones, and looking strangely beautiful amidst those signs of war. These are carefully dried in my book, and prized beyond every thing I possess, as memorials of that sunset. Passing over the vast camp in profound darkness, excepting the light afforded by the large, bright stars, which gleamed suddenly forth,—encampment after encampment,—each marked out by its numerous twinkling lights stretching far and wide over the vast hills and plains and valleys, was another memorable sight to us. Every thing was profoundly tranquil, only now and then we passed a soldier wrapped in his long cloak, and returning to quarters. It was bitterly cold, and we were glad to hear the challenge of the sentinel, on arriving at last at Balaklava, and still more so, to be welcomed back by our kind host, who had begun to think some accident must have happened to us.

But I must write no more of our delightful trip, for my pen lingers with so much pleasure on the recital of many happy days, that it would willingly write much more than I fear you would care to read. However, I must tell you, my dear Mrs. Austin, you who love flowers so much, that we passed a whole day botanizing in Leander Bay, among the rocks, for beautiful orchidaceous plants, and in the green valleys and ruined orchards and mountain slopes about, found an endless variety. We took our luncheon on the steep sides of a ravine, filling our cup from the mountain-stream, leaping its way down to the wide sea beneath, watching the many-colored lizards playing about in the sun, listening to distant bugles, and talking quietly of pleasant things long to be remembered. The day after that, our whole party rode to Inkerman, but, to my great regret, I could not accompany them, having no saddle. So I walked about Balaklava, seeing the admirable hospital arrangements, and other things of interest; and altogether was consoled for not going, by finding Mr. Mansfield and Colonel Campbell at Colonel Hardinge's on my return, having a long chat about Weybridge, and afterward receiving a visit from my husband's old friend Major Loundes, who, as well as other friends, had not been able to find us out before, in consequence of our ship being outside the harbor.

Admiral Freemantle dined with Colonel Hardinge in the evening, and was much amused at having been called a cruel potentate by us both, in our difficulties, and with the inspection of our collection of relics from Sebastopol.

Another pleasant day at Baidar was our last. We passed through the beautiful Sardinian camp, famed for order, ingenuity, and music, and planted with pretty clumps and avenues of fir-trees, to the camp of the Highlanders on the heights of Kamara, and then walked through the valley beyond, gathering specimens of wild flowers for our collection. The thorn, called here "Christ's thorn," was in blossom; linnets were singing, and bugles ringing on the hills; every sound so sweet and cheerful, and we, so thoroughly enjoying a ramble through this fine scenery, that the whole story of the war seemed like a dreadful dream, put by on a bright morning.

How I wish you could have seen the fine Woronzoff road, along which our four sleek mules, with their soldier drivers, stepped out so finely after the party on horseback. It is quite a mountain road, with precipitous fir-clad hills above, and valleys of oak, and woods, and rocky streams, and green meadows below. Spring was just budding in the valley of Allucca; soldiers strolling about in small parties here and there in the sunshine; a few Tartar peasants jogging along in their wooden carts, all quietly enjoying the greenwood. At Baidar we stopped to dine; and by the time Colonel Hardinge's soldier-cook and Tartar servants had spread the feast under a noble oak-tree, the rest of our party came galloping back from the Phorus Pass—one of the most magnificent sea and mountain views, they said, in the world. However, I had had my stroll about the beautiful slopes of the valley, and could regret nothing.

Many a day, we said, even then, we shall talk over that delightful party assembled under the old tree at Baidar. Every thing was so different from the worn-out amusements of ordinary life—all that we had seen so full of interest—the party so well chosen for pleasant conversatiou and sparkling good-humor. Is it not well to have a few days in one's life like this?

I think I see now the party of riders gallantly mounted, and galloping far before my jingling mule-team, on our return home, in another of the glorious sunsets of the Crimea, which light up even its vast plains and huge and dreary cliffs into perfect brilliancy. Now and then each party stopped to admire any particularly fine point together, and then merrily sped on again, across the camp, to Balaklava. But for the last evening! The next morning we said adieu to our kind and courteous host, and to the good old house which had been to us the head-quarters of so many golden days in our memory, and to the many who had shown us every possible kindness and attention. Mr. Arthur Walker gave me a little book, containing dried specimens of flowers from each battle-field, and from every place of interest in the Crimea, including a beautiful white Immortelle, which, curiously enough, he found growing wild on the grave of poor General Cathcart. Mrs. Brett had a square wooden box of flowers in full blossom, which she was taking down to cheer her drawing-room at Pera, and which we called her Crimean garden: the Iris roots of the good "Sisters" were there, snowdrops from the Heights of Balaklava, and many bright things from Baidar and Leander Bay.

On reaching our ship, we found the lower deck covered with a savage and motley crew. Never had I conceived any creatures so fearful in the shape of humanity. They were the harpies of the camp and the battle-fields, returning to Constantinople, now that the war was ended. I often used to watch them, and think of the frightful things they had done. Many of them had the richest cushions and carpets spread upon the deck, and sat huddled up together, frequently opening their dirty bundles, and taking out snuff-boxes, pistols, and things of all kinds to polish, by way of passing the time. One mere boy among them had no less than three watches and chains. Almost all had two or three signet and other rings on their fingers; one dreadful-looking old woman many Orders, especially two of the Russian Order of St. George, which she wanted us to buy. Several of the men had on handsome but stained and dirty boots, spurs, and other things evidently once belonging to English officers, which it made one shudder to look upon. We longed to get to the end of our voyage; but it seemed that we were doomed to mishaps by sea, for a slight accident happened to the machinery one night, which detained us, with fires out and steam let off, for some hours, beating about on the rough waves. Then the captain missed the mouth of the Bosphorus, and we were a whole day steaming down the wild coast of Anatolia, where we saw the wrecks of four small vessels, which had been driven on shore—no cheerful sight, with a strong wind blowing, the ship's officers quite out of their reckoning, and no water on board; for they had shipped bad and brackish water at Balaklava, which even the savage party on deck could not drink, and we were almost famishing with thirst, only wetting our lips now and then with a little claret. I never thought to have been so glad to see again the castles at the mouth of the Bosphorus, as when we at last came to it, and the challenging gun was fired, and we anchored for the night in the well-known place.

Nothing could be more delightful, after the dreary shores and dull waves of the Black Sea; nothing more striking and surprising than the change, in half an hour, to the softest air, the scent of a thousand flowers, the ceaseless trill of the nightingale, and the fantastic streaks of phosphoric light on the musical ripples of the water. It told at once the whole story of the languor and dreaminess of Eastern life. One would think that Tennyson must have witnessed a night like this, to have written his "Lotus-Eaters," for it was like many pages of Eastern poetry, and read and understood at a glance.

LETTER XL.

VISIT TO A TURKISH HAREM—THE GARDEN—THE CHILDREN—SCENES IN THE GARDEN.

Orta-kioy, May 20th, 1856.

My dear Mother:

Yesterday morning, while walking in the garden, the Armenian girls came to ask me to pay a visit, with them, to the Turkish ladies in the yellow house below. I was very glad to go, and off we started; the good old lady, who had put on her sabled jacket for the occasion, leading me by the hand, after the simple and kindly fashion of the country. Rich and fashionable Armenians of the present day attempt the French style of dress; those of the old school still retain the vail and feridjee; my friends adopt a middle course, and wear only a handkerchief bound round their plaits of hair in the street—neither the French bonnet nor the Eastern vail. It was lovely weather yesterday, with a light and refreshing north breeze, bringing down many white-sailed vessels; caiques rapidly threading their way over the swift and silver stream; sea-birds flitting about; while the many-shaded green hills above looked more bright and varied than usual. Transports slowly steaming down from the Crimea, the decks covered with hardy, weather-beaten troops, tell so cheerfully that the war is over. The merry notes of a bugle, or the sound of a hearty cheer, frequently reach the shore these pleasant spring mornings, and make one rejoice for the brave fellows returning home.

We soon reached the garden-door of the harem, and found ourselves in a pretty but formal garden—formal, perhaps, on account of the shade which long trellised paths, bordered with tall orange and lemon-trees, afford in the sultry heat of summer. There was a beautiful yew-tree in the very heart of the garden, and underneath, as far as its rich dark branches extended, a pretty pavement of pebbles had been laid, in small black and white stones. The design was charming, and something like the disc of a huge sunflower. Cushions were arranged all round, and pretty little lamps were suspended from the branches; I suppose, to light up for a supper or concert of music, and the usual night-feasting of Ramazan. None of the ladies were there now; but cross-legged, under a tree close by, sat a hideous negress, with a fair, sickly-looking child in her arms, which she was trying to rock to sleep. She seemed savagely fond of it, and would hardly permit us to look at the poor little thing, but roughly said to Miss Barker that it was ill, and afraid of strangers. No doubt the faithful nurse feared the "evil eye;" and if the poor baby had been worse that night, she would have laid it to our charge. She did not offer to guide us to the house; but, calling out in a harsh, grating voice, some other slaves appeared, and leading the way up a wooden flight of steps, covered with luxuriant creepers, ushered us into a large cool hall, floored with the usual matting. We were then conducted through several rooms, to a shady one, with a painted ceiling and latticed window, looking on to the Bosphorus. Besides the divan, there was nothing in this apartment but a kind of cabinet, filled with some old china, and a table, upon which two gaudy clocks, several flower-vases, and other ornaments, were heaped up, just as if intended for inspection and sale —in fact, as you would see them at a broker's shop. As we were noting these things, and the comfortless look of the room, the door opened quickly, and a young Turkish lady, dressed in a light-colored muslin jacket and trousers, ran up to the Armenian ladies, kissed them rather boisterously, laughed like a school-girl, with a stray shy look at us, and seated herself on the divan. She laughed again in my face when I was introduced to her, and said something, which, on inquiry, I found was, that she thought a bonnet must be a very uncomfortable thing. Notwithstanding this attack on our national costume, I offered my hand in a friendly way, which she took with another giggle, and then clapped her hands for the eternal sweetmeats and coffee, which she afterward declared she had almost forgotten to call for, it being Ramazan. She was not at all handsome: her eyes were rather fine, but the face fat, heavy, and uninteresting, although certainly good-tempered looking. She had several slaves about her, but none of them at all pretty, except one charming little girl of eight, beautiful as an angel, the child of a former wife who was dead, and evidently the pet of the harem.

The lady of whom I am speaking is wife of the Effendi who drank tea with us the other evening. The brother's wife seems to be the chief, and she sent a message to me, begging to be excused, as she was unwell, and about to go to the bath. Of course we begged that she would not disturb herself. The younger lady offered to show us the rest of the harem; and she seemed as much amused as a child, leading us from one latticed room to another, and laughing all the while. An old lady now joined us, in such an odd flannel jacket and trousers, that, looking at her vast ill-concealed dimensions, it was difficult to preserve a grave countenance. I suppose she was some ancient relative, and could not help thinking very favorably, at the time, of the flowing gray or black silks, and the snow-white caps of our grandmothers. Each lady had her separate suite of apartments, and each her separate slaves. One young lady, also a relative of the Effendi's, we were told, was anxious to show us hers, and they all pressed forward, with the utmost kindness, to display anything which they thought might please us, just like children when they have other children to amuse. Our moon-faced friend, (a great compliment, by-the-by, to her face in Turkey), produced with great glee a musical-box, and set it playing. The old lady, seeing that we liked it, immediately touched the spring of a clock, and set it off to another merry tune; a third lady, not to be outdone in hospitality, ran off for hers; and the three, playing vigorously different tunes at the same time, formed, as you may suppose, an exhibition extremely pleasant and novel, and we laughed outright, which convinced the ladies how much we were entertained. We escaped from this infliction at last, by the chief wife of the elder brother sending to say that, if we liked to see her apartments, we were quite welcome. At first we hardly liked to go, but our merry hostess pressed us to do so, adding: "It will do her good to see you; she is dull about her sick child, whom you saw in the garden." So we went. These rooms were prettiest of all, and looking on to the garden. They were hung with pale blue silk, instead of flowered chintz, like the others; for the lady inhabitant had been a present from the Sultan, and etiquette demands that her apartments be better furnished and adorned than all the rest. Her bedroom was charmingly fitted up: a deep alcove covered with rich Persian carpets, filled with luxurious cushions and embroidered coverlets, taking up one side of it. On the other side was a light green and gold bedstead, covered with gauze curtains. The toilette-table was extremely pretty, dressed with muslin and lace, after our fashion; a Persian looking-glass, shaped like a sunflower, in mother-of-pearl, hanging above it. The ceiling was painted with a trellis-work of birds, leaves, and flowers. Three steps led into the cool and shady garden, and to the wide-spreading household tree I told you of. Opposite the alcove were doors; one led into a sitting-room, hung with the same blue silk, and furnished with richly-cushioned divans; the other opened into a beautiful white-marble bath, the air still heavy with steam and perfume. The poor lady had just taken her bath. Oh! how pale and sickly she looked, and how very pretty she was—so touchingly gentle and graceful in her manners. I was much charmed. She talked some time to us in her pretty room, but merely asking a few questions, as to how long I had been here, and how I liked the country. Presently the black nurse came in with the little child. It was still moaning in her arms; and as the poor mother hung over it, it was difficult to say which looked the fastest fading away. My old Armenian friend took it kindly in her arms, and, speaking Turkish, talked over its ailments, while I walked with the other ladies to the end of the apartment: then, seeing their conversation over, I returned to say adieu. A sweeter or a sadder face I never saw: it quite haunted me. Our merry friend did not show much sympathy for the invalid, and insisted upon our returning to her apartments, to show me her clothes and jewels. Robe after robe, carefully pinned up in muslin, was produced, of every color and shade, for all the ladies ran to fetch their whole stock of finery. Dresses of light green edged with gold, and violet trimmed with silver, flowered dresses, embroidered dresses, shawls, scarfs, and jackets, were produced in endless array, and with an immense amount of chattering. Then I must be dressed up in them, they said, laughing with delight as the masquerade progressed. You would certainly never have known me in the gorgeousness of Eastern array, which, however, they pronounced became me very well. Two large sprays of brilliants, set as a kind of convolvulus, with turquoise centres, were fastened in each side of my hair.

All on a sudden, the beautiful little child I told you of, burst into a violent passion of tears, and I was concerned to know what ailed her. "She weeps because she does not also possess jewels and rich clothes," said the black nurse, soothing her. "Never mind," said my merry, round-faced friend, who was trying on a rose-colored feridjee with great satisfaction; "one day or another you will marry, and then you will have plenty."

While we were thus playing children, the poor sick lady entered with her nurse and baby, sitting on the divan at the further end of the room, and languidly looking on. Never have I seen any one look so utterly hopeless and miserable as she did, turning every now and then to her evidently dying child. I said to the brother's wife how much I pitied her anxiety about the poor little thing. Her reply was translated: "Oh, she did not think the child was so very bad; it only had an abscess behind the ear, which the holy Imaum at the mosque was going to lance. The fact was," (and here she giggled heartily again,) "that the mother was suffering more from jealousy than from any thing else." The idea seemed too ridiculous to her sister-in-law. "Her husband had just taken a new wife, and they had gone to Stamboul that morning. He used to be very fond of those two," pointing to the faded mother and child; "but now, of course, he is pleased with Ayesha, who is young, pretty, and sprightly. However, she will soon get used to it; she was stupidly fond of him, and has a jealous temper." I was glad to be able to say to Miss Barker: "Let us go," without being understood.

The very atmosphere of the harem seemed to stifle me; and I could hardly help throwing the jewels and finery away from me with disgust. What Mrs. Longworth told me some time ago is quite right. "If a Turkish woman possesses an atom of refinement, one particle of affection for either husband or children, one thought of the future, she *must* be wretched! Her only chance of contentment is, in being degraded to a mere animal state, eating, drinking, and basking in the sun."

We rose to go; the ladies crowding round, and pressing us not to leave so soon. Poor things! they are so greedy after a little amusement in their utter idleness. I felt more angry and impatient than you can well conceive, and kept exclaiming to Miss Barker, "Say we *must* go; let us get away directly; if we meet the Effendi returning, I shall certainly be taking off my slipper and beating him upon the face in a most savage manner, or breaking his chibouque, or making him 'eat dirt' in some dreadful way or other, to my utter disgrace in Turkey and elsewhere." So, with many civil speeches, they at last consented to allow us to depart.

Going up to the poor sorrowful lady, I said that I hoped to hear a good account of her. She was soon about to become again a mother. She smiled sadly, and shook her head. The Armenian ladies kissed her hand, and would have kissed the hem of her garment, but this she would not allow, and turned again to her child as we left the room. The rest of the ladies walked through the garden with us, plucking flowers, oranges, and lemons for every one, until we were all laden. When we came to the hall belonging to the garden of the gentlemen's apartments, the rest would have turned back; but the chief lady, peeping out first to see if the gardener or any other men were there, caught up the long trailing ends of her dress, and scampered at full speed along the gravel-path after us, throwing at me a beautiful bunch of laburnum, which she pulled from a tree close by, then, laughing heartily, scampered as swiftly back again to the harem garden-gate, and carefully closing the door we entered the narrow streets of Orta-kioy.

LETTER XLI.

FAST OF RAMAZAN—TURKISH NATIONALITY—THE SHEIK-ZADI—END OF THE FAST—PREPARATIONS—ILLUMINATION OF THE MOSQUES—KARAGOS, THE TURKISH "PUNCH"—FIREMEN.

Constantinople, May 29th, 1856.

My dear Mr. Hornby:

I greatly regretted not being well enough to go to Stamboul, and see a night of the great Fast of Ramazan. During this Fast the poor Turks seem to suffer dreadfully, touching no food from sunrise to sunset. The other day, coming from Scutari with Mrs. Cumberbatch, our caiquejees were in an almost fainting state, and could hardly make way against the stream. They kept looking at the sun; and the moment the evening gun was fired, they seized a cucumber, and eagerly bit off two or three pieces of it. Of course the rich do not feel the fast so much, if at all; they merely turn night into day—sleeping all day, and feasting all night. Every mosque is illuminated two hours after sunset, and you hear nothing but sounds of music and feasting from every Turkish house. We hear the Sultan's band begin about nine in the evening. The poor are in a dreadfully exhausted state, especially caiquejees and porters. Poor fellows! you see them turn their heads away from the fountains, as they pass by in the burning sun; for not even a drop of water must pass the lips of a good Mussulman from sunrise to sunset, and the working-classes here are wonderfully good and conscientious in doing that which they think right. The minarets were beautifully illuminated last night, with wreaths and sprays of lamps. An old Turk told us that they ought to be as brilliant every night of Ramazan and Bairam, but the priests (Imaums) steal the oil! They are allowed by government four hundred "okes" of oil for each mosque, and an "oke" is three pounds and a half English weight.

Colonel Ebor has written a graphic and charming account of the Ramazan, which I believe has appeared in print, but which I send, in case you have not seen it.

"The more the intercourse between the different nations exerts its assimilating influence, the more interesting become the remaining traces of a distinct national and social life. In Europe this assimilating tendency has spread so far that very little indeed remains; and railways and steamers efface more and more even the few traces which have been left hitherto, so that a man will soon be able to go from one end of Europe to the other without finding any difference in the appearance of the different countries.

"In Turkey this cosmopolitan tendency has not yet succeeded so completely. There is, indeed, a rage in Stamboul for every thing which is *alla Franca.* The picturesque Oriental costume is more and more giving way to ugly straight-collared coats and broad-strapped trousers, the best specimens of which would disgrace even the shops of the Temple at Paris. The beautiful ceilings carved in wood are disappearing, in favor of wretchedly daubed flowers and trees; the comfortable divans running all round the walls, are replaced by straight-backed, uneasy chairs. But these innovations are scarcely known out of Stamboul, and even in the capital there is a time when a kind of reaction takes place against this tendency, and Oriental life seems to revive for a time. This time is that of the Ramazan, with its days of fasts and its nights of feasts. Then everybody returns to the old style of living; knives and forks, tables and chairs, plates and napkins are discarded, and all eat in the old patriarchal way, out of one dish, with their fingers. There are even people who abandon the raki bottle during that time, and go back again to the pure element. The mosques begin again to exert their attractions; and many a man you may see there, bowing down, who during eleven months of the year is making philosophical comments about the Koran.

"This is, therefore, the most interesting time for a European, who can get, by a stroll through the streets, more insight into the character of Mohammedan life than by the study of volumes. Although the external appearance of the people has been changed, from what it was when Turkish dignitaries rode about in colossal turbans and richly embroidered kaftans—when the only carriage seen was the gaudily-painted araba with milk-white oxen—when swaggering Janissaries and Spahis made themselves conspicuous—and when the old ruins through which you now walk were in their prime—enough still remains to give the whole picture that strange mysterious coloring which we connect in our minds with the idea of the East.

"The day begins for the Moslem, in Ramazan, two or three hours before sunset. There are, indeed, toiling wretches, such as hamals and caiquejees, for whom the day begins as usual, at daybreak, and grows only so much harder by the privations it imposes; but most people do not get up before noon, and bazaars and shops kept by Mohammedans seldom open before the afternoon; even the office hours at the Porte do not begin before that time.

"Two hours before sunset all the town turns out into the streets. It is the time for making purchases of provisions, and for promenading. There is a long, and in most parts tolerably wide street, leading from the place in which the mosque of Sultan Bajazid stands, to the mosque of Sultan Mehmed. This is the centre of all life. Originally a market, flanked on both sides with shops of every kind, it has in a great measure lost its original distinction. The shops have ceded their place to a nearly uninterrupted series of cafés, and the market is converted into a promenade. This is principally the case in the part of the street called Sheik-Zadi, from the beautiful mosque along which it leads. A double and often treble row of carriages, with dark-eyed and thickly-vailed beauties, occupies the centre of the street, while the raised arcades in front of the shops are filled with women in gay feridjees (cloaks) and admiring "swells." It is the Rotten-row of Stamboul, quite as characteristic, and even more picturesque, with its quaint balconies, graceful minarets, cypress-trees, and the shady little burial-grounds stuck among the houses, all illuminated by a gorgeous setting sun. This movement in the Sheik-Zadi lasts till near sunset; as the shadows grow longer, one carriage after the other loses itself, the yashmaks and their wearers disappear, and only the smoke-thirsty people remain sitting on the little stools in front of the cafés, looking every minute at their watches, hating the sun and preparing every thing for the moment of the signal-gun. The water is boiling on the brazier, ready for the coffee, the tumblers are filled with lemonade or any other decoction, but the greatest care is given to the preparations for smoking. It is a work of love, and helps to idle away the last half-hour in pleasant anticipation of the coming pleasures. Every fibre is unraveled and put in with judgment; steel, stone, and timber are taken out; and the most impatient amuse themselves with lighting the tinder and putting it out again half-a-dozen times.

"At length the last rays of the sun have disappeared, and the gun in the court of the Seraskeriate announces it; a faint cry of satisfaction rises, drowned nearly as soon as it rises in a cloud of smoke or in a tumbler of water. As soon as their first cravings are satisfied, every one hastens to the 'iftar,' the first meal of the day. It is the only time when you can see the usual abstemious Oriental gorging himself. Sweets follow meat and meat follows sweets alternately in endless succession. All the innumerable resources of the Turkish cuisine, nearly superior in inventiveness to the French, are put into requisition, so that thirty to forty dishes are no uncommon occurrence at a fashionable house.

"There is scarcely time to swallow all these dainties, wash the hands, and smoke a pipe, when the sharp cry of the Muezzin calls the Faithful to night prayers. By this time the galleries on the mosques have been tastefully illuminated by lamps; the rows of windows under the cupola shine with the lights of the thousand lamps inside. All the cafés, grocers' shops, and eating-houses, all the numerous stands, with ices, lemonade, and sweetmeats, and the thousands of paper lanterns of the thousands of the crowd, with their numberless lights, lend to the whole scene a fantastic glare which surpasses the last and most exciting moment of the Roman Carnival.

"This is the hour when one ought to go and see the mosques. The simple grandeur of some of these masterpieces of Eastern architecture is only to be felt, not to be described. That solemn abstraction from all surrounding earthly objects which characterizes the prayer of the Moslem, rises to a kind of stern enthusiasm, which strikes even the most sceptical with awe.

"By the time prayer is over, the scene outside has even increased in animation. Everybody is visiting everybody; the crowd is so dense that you can scarcely pass through the main thoroughfares; all the seats in front of the cafés and shops are occupied, everywhere you hear chanting, singing, and music. The mosques have increased in light. On a rope stretched from one minaret to another, figures formed of ingeniously hung lamps, representing flowers, animals, birds, ships, and other objects, swing about high in the air. A thousand 'Buyouroun,' ('Please') invite the passers-by to the shops, and mix with the hum of the busy crowd. And all this host, without anybody to direct its movements, is orderly and quiet; no pressing or jostling, no acute noise or excess. This is, perhaps, the most wonderful part of the whole, and gives to the scene an air of mystery, which impresses you almost with the belief that you are witnessing the thousand and second of the 'Arabian Nights.'

"If you have no acquaintance to go to, and if you are tired of the crowd, you may go and see the Kara-goz, the Turkish 'Punch.' He haunts mostly out-of-the-way lanes, and chooses invariably for his exhibition one of the numerous gardens with which the town abounds. You enter the little door, and are received, as in exhibitions all over the world, by the proprietor, who acts at the same time as the cashier, with the polite demand for a few piastres. If you have thus acquired the right to enter, you must look out for a seat; and, according to the confidence in your generosity which your appearance inspires, you will be accommodated with a wooden sofa, a chair, or stool, or you will be banished among the crowd in the background, where you are at liberty to squat down. Most of the gardens where Kara-goz exhibits are covered in by trellises, on which the vines creep along, letting their untrained branches hang down, through which you can see the stars. A solitary lamp, or at most two, form the illumination, except where Kara-goz, the wag, appears. Here a dark curtain is drawn across, except in the centre, where a thin transparent vail shows the scene.

"The performance is acted by marionettes of wood, some of them rather cleverly jointed, so as to enjoy the liberty of all their members. Here, as in Italy, there are stereotype figures—Kara-goz, his friend and rival in wit, Hadji-Vatt, a 'swell,' *the* woman, a Jew, an idiot, a Persian, and the police. The subjects are most varied, but all representing tricks played by Kara-goz on all the *dramatis personæ*, who all rise at last against the wag. The most interesting part, for any one who understands the language, is the dialogue, especially between Hadji-Vatt and Kara-goz, who try to surpass each other in the skirmish of words. Some of them are exceedingly witty, and, what is more, the wit is fully appreciated by the spectators.

"Scarcely less interesting than the performance, are the faces of the spectators. The first row are all children, and never did I hear childish delight and ringing laughter so joyous and free. One could scarcely imagine that those grave persons behind had been likewise once sitting in front. But even these latter did not resist a well-turned *jeu de mots,* in which the whole performance abounds. In general, one would scarcely believe what a fund of fun there is in the grave Osmanli, and how sensible he is of the ludicrous.

"By the time the performance is over, the crowd begins to disperse in the streets, and is wandering home, to wait for the drum which beats two hours before the morning-gun, for the second meal. Now the by-streets, which have had hitherto a deserted appearance, dark and solitary, begin to get their part of the movement, although the want of illumination and the absence of open shops always make a great difference. Indeed, a lover of contrasts could not do better than to take a stroll in the by-streets after having walked about for some time in the thoroughfares; it is like life and death; here and there a solitary wayfarer, or a mysterious lady with a servant carrying a lantern before her, or a sleepy dog, who will rather be trodden upon than move out of the way, is all he will meet. Yet it may happen to him, as it did last time to me, that, as if by a magic stroke, the whole street becomes alive. We have first a dull trampling sound from afar, as if a body of troops were moving in a run. It becomes more and more distinct. The sound of the steps is intermingled with shouting and yelling; at last a lantern appears, and behind it fifty or sixty men, running along at a wonderfully measured but quiet step, and going over every thing which comes into their way. In the midst of them you perceive a dark object, with brass mountings glittering in the dim light of the Fanar. They are the firemen, with their portable engine, the only one applicable in the narrow streets. All the houses begin to get animated, doors are unlocked, windows opened, and everybody inquires where the fire is. When the host of firemen have passed like a wild chase, and inquiry shows that the fire is far off, every thing sinks again into silence and solitude.

"An hour before sunrise the morning-gun puts an end to the feasting, and everybody turns in. Not less interesting than at night, is Stamboul early in the morning, in Ramazan—a city of the dead by daylight. If you lose yourself in the interim, you may go about for half-an-hour without meeting a soul—a strange sight for any one who knows Stamboul in the morning at other times, for its population are generally very early risers."

LETTER XLII.

CELEBRATION OF THE QUEEN'S BIRTHDAY—THE FETE-DIEU—ILLUMINATIONS—"THE NIGHT OF DESTINY"—THE SULTAN'S VISIT TO THE MOSQUE OF TOPHANA—NIGHT OF PRAYER—PRINCE MURAD.

Constantinople, May 30th, 1856.

My dear Mr. Hornby:

The weather here continues most lovely, very hot in the sun, but always with a fresh breeze, so that in-doors it is quite cool. The Queen's birthday was splendidly celebrated on Thursday. I took caique to see the shipping dressed with innumerable flags. The French and English men-of-war looked magnificent, and while the salvos of artillery were firing, one might almost imagine an action was being fought. Lord Stratford held a levée at noon, attended by the French embassador, the whole *corps diplomatique,* and a great number of English officers. The court-yard of the palace was lined with a detachment of Guards and Highlanders, and the fine band of the German Jagers played a choice selection of airs. At the grand dinner in the evening, the only toast was, "Her Majesty!" when the discharge of three rockets from the illuminated palace was answered by a tremendous salute from the "Queen."

In the evening hundreds of ships were illuminated. At nine o'clock, I heard the guns plainly down here; and the tremendous cheers of the sailors were carried from ship to ship, it is said, quite up to the Black Sea. I thought how pleased her majesty would have been, could she have witnessed such demonstrations of hearty affection. I plainly heard the band of the German Legion encamped at Kulalee, opposite, playing the anthem; and Herbert Siborne's men had an immense bonfire, which lighted up the hills far and wide. It was a beautiful sight from our windows, for the minarets and principal Turkish palaces on the shore were also illuminated for Ramazan. Edmund was at the embassador's dinner, and I amused myself at my old seat on the divan, watching all that was going on. They say that Pera had never before seen so gay and splendid a day. The French celebrated the *Fête-Dieu* in the Embassy Church of St. Louis; the palace-yard was tastefully decorated with the flags of the Allies, and a guard of French soldiers was at the door, and lined the walls of the church. Later in the day, all the world was struggling to see the Sultan distribute the medals for the campaign of Roumelia, which took place in the court-yard of the Seraskeriate, or War-office. It is said that there is to be a special decoration for the defense of Silistria—of course one for the Crimea.

Friday was a grand night on the Bosphorus, after the numerous fêtes on shore. It was the twenty-seventh of the fast of Ramazan, or Night of Destiny to all true Believers; and, according to ancient custom, the Sultan went in his state caique to the Mosque of Tophana, to offer up the prayer of night. On account of the Peace, the illuminations and fireworks were more splendid than usual. We were on board Mr. Whittle's steam-yacht, and had a perfect view of the "seven" glistening hills of light, rising out of the most fantastic-looking sea you can conceive; here was a huge, phantom-looking ship, marked out in living fire;

there, the dark-flowing stream; then a man-of-war, one blaze of lamps, and throwing up rockets every now and then, which were beautifully reflected on the waves. Bordering the shore, were moored countless caiques, awaiting the Sultan's approach in profound silence, some filled with vailed Turkish women of the poorer class—all with varied and attentive groups, looking still more picturesque by that strange and dreamy light. This deep silence lasted for a long time, and people seemed to sit in a kind of delighted reverie, gazing far down to the illuminated masts in the Golden Horn; then back to the glittering port; high above, to Santa Sophia, appearing still more like enchantment among the dark cypresses; and then on the Mosque of Tophana, on the shore, where the Sultan was to pray, and where, between the two fire-wreathed minarets, his cipher hung suspended high in air, in lamps of pale and gleaming gold.

Beneath this, in the Court of Tophana, were piled heaps of cannon-balls—trophies from the Crimea—which were converted into pyramids of light, by lamps skillfully placed amongst them. The guard-house was covered with warlike designs, every mosque with mystic ones. It was a beautiful sight. The Sultan came down about nine o'clock. The moment he left his palace, a signal was given, and every one in the row of boats lighted up flambeaux, in the glare of which came, swiftly gliding on, the white-doved, and the rest of the graceful royal caiques. Every English and French man-of-war burned blue and red lights; every public building burst out into a blaze; and every person in the splendid procession could be seen with perfect distinctness, the Sultan's magnificent boatmen being certainly the most conspicuous. After the Sultan has passed to prayer, all is silent and dark again, except for the illuminations; the torches are extinguished, or burnt out. It was as if the city and the sea lay under some spell of enchantment. All the Turks no doubt were engaged in earnest prayer, for this is the night in which their destinies are determined for the whole year to come. Captain Hamilton kindly took myself and some other ladies on shore. We stepped quietly into a man-of-war's boat, and soon landed, among countless crowds of caiques, at the stairs of Tophana. The court was filled with the most extraordinary illuminations—large trees bearing fruit and flowers, in colored lamps—exactly like the garden of Aladdin. Beyond, among the trees, were telekis filled with vailed Turkish ladies, attended by their slaves, all silent as the crowds around; even among the dense masses of soldiers, through which we passed in this enchanted garden, not the slightest sound was heard; all were sunk in deep and dreamlike prayer of Kader Gnedessi, beneath millions of twinkling lamps. About midnight the vast crowd stirred: the Sultan's prayer was over, which was announced by some huge rockets sent high into the air, and scattering about thousands of many-colored stars. The "Melampus," and all the ships of war, burst into a sea of light, as the Sultan stepped into his caique on his return to the palace—each tiny caique, and even Greek and stranger barques, burning their dazzling torches. The fine figures of the caique-jees standing up in the glare, and holding them out to illuminate the royal way—the vailed boat-loads of women and sailor groups behind, thrown into deep shadow—had the finest effect in the dark and shining water. After the Sultan had passed by, the crowds sank down again, and the grand display of fireworks commenced, which is his yearly treat to his people.

The yacht in which we were was fancifully and brilliantly illuminated, and the Sultan's eldest son, Prince Murad, came on board, with his tutor, to see it. He is a tall, pale youth, of about seventeen, with a broad, expressionless face, and large wandering eyes. He asked, through his tutor, that we might be presented to him, and looked very shy and uncomfortable when we were. I said, pitying his nervousness, "Pray say to his Highness that I am happy to have the honor of seeing him." His Highness replied: "Tell her that I am very happy to see *her*." Then I begged the Effendi to say how charmed I had been with the beautiful scene on the Bosphorus that night. "Tell her that I am very glad she liked it," finished our conversation. I retreated on deck, and the Prince looked with an air of relief at the embroidered sofa-cushions, evidently thinking Europeans and European manners very formidable, and congratulating himself on having safely got over an introduction to an unvailed woman. I think I have now almost exhausted my stock of Turkish news, my dear Mr. Hornby; except that there is a report of Omar Pasha's being made chief of a military police at Constantinople, which most people think would be a dangerous appointment for the Sultan—in fact, a second edition of the Janissaries—as he has immense influence over the wild soldiers he commands. The Bashi-Bazouks and the Sultan's Cossacks are said to be in almost open rebellion against the Turkish Government. Since they have been paid regularly, and fed and commanded by English officers, they have been so happy, that they now refuse to return to their former miserable state; no one knows what is to be done with them. Very much I pity the poor Sultan. On Friday he was to have read the Hatti Sheriff to several regiments of his soldiers, but did not do so, and it was said he was advised that it was not safe. However, this is but an *on dit* of a place famous for very absurd ones, and I should think such a thing as reading a proclamation very un-Sultanlike. Stories of approaching rebellion everywhere—risings of the Greeks, and afterward the massacre of all Christians by the Turks, the moment our army is gone—are all the fashion here just now, but they do not trouble us much.

LETTER XLIII.

A SAIL ON THE BOSPHORUS—THE "BELLE POULE"—STRAWBERRY-GARDENS—LAST DAY OF RAMAZAN.

Orta-kioy, June 3d, 1856.

My dear Mother:

I enjoyed my visit to Therapia extremely; the sea was rough, and the cool breeze very refreshing. All the gentlemen whom the admiral chooses to invite, go up to Pera in the morning in his steamer, which has a curious look, waiting almost close to the door of the hotel: the ladies amuse themselves as well as they can. Mrs. Brett and I had a sail on the Bosphorus yesterday with a pleasant party. We all landed on the other shore, taking a long ramble in the Sultan's Valley, and then to the deserted kiosk beyond, where the view is very beautiful, and pretty tortoises are to be found.

The "Belle Poule" is lying off Beicos Bay, among many other ships. She is painted black still, and has been since the time when she brought the body of Napoleon home from St. Helena. After our sail, we walked in the garden of the French Embassy, the hills and the blue sea peeping in through waving boughs; and then, in the pleasant winding shrubbery paths, we talked over a visit to the Forest of Belgrade, and to the old fountain, and Lady Mary Wortley Montague's house near it. However, the weather is too warm inland to make any expedition now, so I must come up from the islands early some morning. We are just off to a cottage there, belonging to a Greek named Giacomo, and Giacomo's cavass is come with a large island caique, to remove our goods and chattels; and the hamals are come, stalking up the stairs; and the Apple-blossom, and Vassili, and our Sais are chattering in Greek and Turkish, as if the tongues of Babel were let loose; so I think it is time for me to say good-by.

June 5th.

How I wish you were here, among other pleasant outdoor wanderings, to regale yourself with the delicious strawberries of our village, which are now in perfection. Parties of Greeks and Turks are constantly visiting the cool strawberry-gardens, spreading their shawls and cushions in the shade, and enjoying the fruit and the view at the same time. With very little cultivation, the plants produce wonderfully. Hundreds of baskets are sent in to Constantinople, besides those which are discussed here *al fresco.* The baskets are of a very pretty shape, round and deep, with a good stout handle, and holding five or six of what we call "pottles" in England. We get a magnificent dish for three piastres (sixpence), and no doubt they are cheaper to the natives. It is a pretty sight to see the baskets going into Constantinople, strung on a long pole, with a Greek in picturesque costume at each end. Every thing is a picture here.

Yesterday was the last of Ramazan, and the Sultan went in procession to the old palace at Seraglio Point, to take the yearly Ottoman oaths of empire. Cannon thundered, drums rolled, and streets and windows were crowded, to see the procession. The minarets were beautifully illuminated last night, with wreaths of pale gold lamps, and words strung from one minaret to another, on this and the opposite shore; last night it was "Marshalla"—*i. e.* "God bless you," in Turkish. The effect is wonderful, and the golden words appear to hang suspended in the air; in fact this place is more like a dream than reality just now. All night the roll of little drums is heard on the hills and in the villages, for it is also a Greek festival. The streets are crowded, and gay parties constantly moving about on the water. The poor here seem to have as greatly too much outdoor amusement as the English have too little.

LETTER XLIV.

END OF RAMAZAN—ILLUMINATIONS—NIGHT—PALACES OF THE BOSPHORUS—FEAST OF BAIRAM—TORCHLIGHT PROCESSION OF THE SULTAN—CEREMONY IN THE MOSQUE OF TOPHANA.

Constantinople, June 7th, 1856.

My dear Mrs. Austin:

Tuesday the 4th was the last day of the Ramazan, and as the rays of the setting sun disappeared from valley and mountain, the roar of cannon from "Ramis-Tchiflik" announced that all true Believers might eat again in daylight. It is said that an Imaum is stationed on Mount Olympus to catch the first glimpse of the new moon of the month *Chevale*, from which dates the Mussulman's new year; and at his signal from afar, carried from minaret to minaret, the spell of this long and weary Fast is broken, as it were by enchantment, by the sound of the announcing cannon; and coffee-bearers and sherbet-bearers and pipe-bearers minister to the longing and famished multitudes of Constantinople—to the rich man who has been dozing or wearily counting his beads all day, and to the poor hamal and caiquejee half-fainting with hunger and fatigue. Before eating, a good Osmanli washes, prays, gravely smokes a chibouque, and sips a cup of coffee: after these ceremonies, he feasts in right earnest.

Two hours after sunset the cannons fire again, for joy that the Fast is ended. Drums roll, fifes are heard on the hills and in the valleys, muskets are let off every now and then, and splendid rockets are thrown high up in the air, which have a beautiful effect, bursting over the dark water or above darker cypress-trees. By the time that the summer's night has fairly set in, the Imaums have finished their work, and

> "Millions of lamps proclaim the feast
> Of Bairam through the boundless East."

As every one says, it is impossible to give an idea of the marvelous beauty of these illuminations. Hour after hour I have sat at the window spell-bound, and with the idea of enchantment constantly creeping over me. The lamps are of a pale gold-color, clustered, thick as bees, round each balcony of the high white minarets; and fantastic devices are hung from one minaret to another, which, in the soft gray light of the summer night,

> "Glitter like a swarm of fire-flies tangled in silver braid."

I have often thought of those lines of Tennyson's during the lovely nights of Ramazan.

The opposite mosque of Begler Bay, on the Asian side, was an exquisite object from hence. Far over the dark waters beneath was reflected a golden cascade of light, with shades of purple waves amid its sprays, ever shifting and moving in the stream: it was just like the Fountain of Golden Water of the Arabian Nights, only I saw it while quietly resting on a soft divan, and without taking the journey up the enchanted mountain in search of the charmed phial. But these Asian hills looked enchanted on the last night of Ramazan: far as the eye could reach glittered bright lights, some moving, some stationary, some by darkest cypress-woods some where I knew stood solitary and latticed houses. The water's edge was fringed with pale and glistening gold; for at the gateways of all these silent, dreamy palaces of the Bosphorus, shone stars, and trees, and often the Sultan's name, wreathed on shore, but sparkling as brightly on the waves. The Imaum chanted to prayer about an hour before midnight, and the deep, full, prolonged notes quite filled the valley. Every sound in this lovely scene seemed as strange to me as its sights.

At last, half bewildered and half as if in a dream, I looked up at the moon, and the sight of her was pleasant enough; for she is always the same in every land, fair, serene, and kind, and always looks like home. The nightingales were singing in every cypress near. It is quite true what Byron says, and here, in summer time,

"The voice of the nightingale never is mute."

Her sweet notes, and the moon's soft and tranquil beauty, were very composing after the fantastic and bewildering sights of this Eastern night's *fête*. The Turkish drums were rolling long after midnight, but I did not wait to see the lamps die out.

So closed to me the last night of the Mussulman Old Year. Before day-break next morning, cannon announced the Feast of Bairam, or the New Year; and presently we heard the heavy tramp of a large body of troops marching into Constantinople. It was a strange scene, the glare of their torches mingling with the gray light of morning, and shining on their arms and accoutrements. They were going to line the streets through which the Sultan was to pass on his way to mosque, as first Imaum, or priest of Islamism, which ceremony he always performs, as head of Church and State, on the first day of the New Year, at day-break. I was very sorry not to have gone, but seeing the fireworks on the 27th day of Ramazan, when the Sultan goes to mosque by torchlight, had so exhausted me, that I did not think it prudent to take a row in the mist at three o'clock in the morning so soon afterward. The Sultan's ladies all went in telekis, and by torchlight; by whom, I was told that the motley crowd of soldiers, fakirs, Armenians, Turks, Arabs, and black slaves, looked most picturesque and striking. All the pashas attended in gorgeous array; the Sultan was of course splendidly mounted; and they went to the Mosque of Tophana, where, it is said, the Sultan reads aloud the laws of the Prophet, and swears to govern by them. We knew when this ceremony was over, because our poor little kiosk trembled visibly at the roar of cannon which follows it. The Sultan afterward held a levee, in the open air, at Seraglio Point, when the pashas swear homage, and are permitted to kiss the hem of his garment, or rather two embroidered strips of cloth, several yards long, which are attached to either side of his chair of state. This is an old ceremony of their camp-life, which I should much like to have seen; but another is performed at the "Courbam Bairam," at the end of the month, and of this I hope to give you an account. These customs, it is affirmed, have been observed by the Osmanlis since the time of Abraham.

We are going to the Sweet Waters of Europe. It is a great day there—the Turkish Sunday, and the last day of Bairam. All the Faithful are in the high est spirits; drums and fifes resound in every valley; the Bosphorus is covered with gay caiques; every Turk sports his best garments, and forgives his enemies, and makes presents to his wives, children, and slaves; for these three days of his New Year are feast-days; all his sins have been forgiven him for the Fast of Ramazan, and he is on excellent terms with the Prophet, and with himself, and with his beautiful Bosphorus. So the Sweet Waters will be gay indeed to-day, for it is also a Greek holiday

LETTER XLV.

A STROLL—THE BOSPHORUS—TURKISH ARSENAL—SUBURBS OF CONSTANTINOPLE—POVERTY IN THE EAST—KIOSKS—STORKS—TURKISH AND GREEK DRESSES—SCENES ON THE RIVER—THE SWEET WATERS—SCENES ON SHORE—THE SULTAN'S KIOSK—THE SULTANA AND HER DAUGHTER—EVENING SCENE—RETURN FROM THE SWEET WATERS.

Orta-kioy, June 8th, 1856.

My dear Mrs. Austin:

It was very sultry yesterday, so I put on my coolest muslin dress and my wide straw hat, and, with the Armenian girl Dhudu and my cousin Henry, strolled slowly through the village in search of a caique to take us to the Sweet Waters of Europe, whither all the world had gone hours before. We scarcely met a soul in the usually crowded narrow streets. All were holiday-making in the shade, whither the noisy street-commerce had also followed. Only a few Greek beggars, and the surly scavenger-dogs, dozed, or quarreled in groups here and there, on the loose pavement-stones of the wayside. Even the little *café*, usually crammed with noisy, laughing Greeks, was almost deserted to-day, and many a bright nargileh stoood neglected on the clean and polished table. We found our two favorite caiquejees fast asleep in their boat, which was moored in the shade beside the mosque. Vassili soon roused them up. They took the handsome boat-cushions from under the linen covering, made the caique comfortable, greased the leather thong of their oars, and out we dashed, through ships unloading cattle from Varna, on to the middle of the Bosphorus. Our white umbrellas sheltered us effectually from the sun, and we had the usual delicious breeze. It was delightful sitting still; but large, round drops soon fell in showers down the bronzed faces of the rowers, who merely shook them off, like a Newfoundland dog when he gets out of the water, and dashed on in splendid style under this burning sun, with nothing but a thin white jacket and a light fez to protect them from its scorching rays. We met but few caiques; all were gone to the Sweet Waters, either on the Asian or European side. The flags of the English and French men-of-war at Stamboul scarcely stirred; all was quiet, sultry heat. The very tar seemed blistering on the sides of the vessels, and not a soul was to be seen, even on board the French frigates, where all is generally stir, and music, and life.

The Bosphorus was of the loveliest blue, and the sky only just a little paler with the lightest "fleck" of white cloud every here and there, borne by the south wind from Mount Olympus. It was very lovely; for, in the midst of this gorgeous Eastern-summer's scene—from trees and flowering shrubs in their freshest, fullest beauty, rising out of the waters at Stamboul—you had but to turn your eyes to the left, past the Maiden's Tower and the shadowy Prince's Islands in the Sea of Marmora, to behold distant mountains glittering in snow, reposing in their cold and solitary grandeur, as if disdaining the gay summer and leaves and flowers of the lower world. This place is like a beautiful dream; but we were soon gone from it, and had passed under the Bridge of Boats, and arrived at another, so like the Chinese representation on plates, that I almost expected to see "Sing-sing's" parasol peeping over it. Presently we came to a Turkish arsenal, and noticed an immense ship with its huge skeleton just completed. Before the arsenal lay four or five Turkish men-of-war (three-deckers,) in one of which we counted a hundred and thirty guns. They were dressed with flags, from the top-mast down to the very water's edge, in honor of the Bairam, and made a splendid appearance: except for the huge gilt lion at their prows, I should not have known but that they were English ships, though perhaps a sailor might. Mehemet Ali, the Sultan's brother-in-law and Capitan Pasha, was going on board one of them; his boats were also gayly dressed with flags and awnings, and the Turkish frigates had bands of music on board. I could not help shuddering, as I looked on the standard of the Crescent and Star, now waving quietly over the water, and wondered if any of these ships had been at the massacre of Scio, when the Turks so mercilessly put all those unfortunate Greeks to the sword: one hears such frightful accounts of that barbarous affair still, from the Greeks, who have never forgotten or forgiven it.

After passing the last bridge, we had an excellent view of the suburbs, and the poorest part of Constantinople, with here and there a ruined square tower, or piece of ivied brickwork of the old Roman wall, peeping out from tumble-down wooden houses, which could only be inhabited by the very poorest of the poor, and look as if the first rough wave would wash the wretched tenement away. Many of the supports and rafters have really crumbled and broken away, leaving only a few rotten boards between the happy "ténant" and the Bosphorus. A few miserable donkeys were standing patiently on the shore, laden with stones, just brought in by a large Greek boat, whose bowsprit was knocking in a friendly way at a frail little casement, and playfully threatening to demolish it altogether. I wish Prezioza would take some sketches of the Turkish poor and their habitations. Though miserable enough, I must say there is nothing so frightful in their poverty as in ours. Street vice of every kind is a thing almost unknown here, except at Pera, and that which is caused by Europeans.

Poverty here is respectable, in every sense of the word. A hamal's bride is like Cæsar's wife, free from all reproach, though dining upon an artichoke and a piece of brown bread; she is stately and vailed, could not be noisy, and never hangs out clothes; but half-starves magnificently on a little old divan, with a fox-skin to represent costly furs, and a dearly-cherished chibouque as a consoler for every sorrow, at which she puffs away with the air of a princess. Poverty does not seem to degrade or vulgarize in the East; its very rags are worn so royally, that one no longer wonders at King Cophetus, who says,

"This beggar-girl shall be my bride."

She would ascend the throne with the same native grace, as that with which she a moment before accepted a para, or asked for a piece of brown bread in the name of the Prophet. But I shall never get to the Sweet Waters if I linger so by the way.

We are now rowing up a narrow creek of the

Bosphorus with the environs of Pera on the right, and of Stamboul on the left. What a vast city is Constantinople! It is wonderful to think how people manage to find their way among the distant and secluded parts of it, lying in dense masses as it does, without positive streets, and without any name or direction shown on any part of it. The Stamboul suburbs seem very pretty, the dark-red masses of houses relieved here and there by green trees, which have sprung up in large spaces made by fires long ago, and by ruined walls covered with creepers of the most luxuriant kinds, especially the Virginian. We passed the great fez manufactory, which belongs to the Sultan, and brings him in a large revenue, being a royal monopoly. His majesty has a beautiful kiosk, or summer-palace, close to it, with a mosque and shady garden adjoining; making about the hundredth he has on the Bosphorus. The windows of the harem part were not latticed, but a high white railing, built far out in the water, pre vents all prying caiques from going near enough to tell a yashmak from a feridjee. In the shallow water, near the railings, grew a large tuft of tall water-flags, and near it was a magnificent pair of storks, the first I have seen here. One of them was standing perfectly still, as if admiring her snowy plumage and bright-red legs in the water; the other was fishing at a little distance very adroitly, wading about, and every now and then swallowing a glittering fish with evident satisfaction. Our caiquejees treated them with great respect, and told me they were very good birds —"Chok izi kush." We were much amused all the way, learning Turkish words of our caiquejees: they told us the Turkish names of different things which we passed, and we returned the compliment by instructing them in the English, each party repeating the word or sentence over and over again. Nothing can equal the good-humor and good-breeding of these fine fellows.

But now the creek has become much narrower—about the breadth of the Thames at Weybridge—and we are far from palaces and minarets and Roman walls, and far from tumble-down houses and arsenal stores. We have left the seven-hilled city behind, and are rowing up a valley surrounded with green slopes and mountainous hills. Our caiquejees tell us that this valley and these fine hills belong to the Sultan, who has a kiosk higher up; but this we had divined, for magnificent trees begin to appear, which only adorn the land about Constantinople when it belongs to the Sultan or some great pasha—to make their paradise perfect. But now, borne on the soft breeze over the scented water-flags, come distant sounds of revelry.

This delicious shade from overhanging trees, and the pleasant sound of our oars in the dark-green water, with the glimpse here and there of a gay caique moored against the sedgy banks, bring pleasant thoughts of the "lotus-eaters," and many a dreamy Eastern fancy, as we lean back in the caique, and wish every one we love was with us. But as we speed on, the crowd of caiques becomes thick, and our dreams are chased away as we look about and admire the various occupants, and by the more prudential care of minding that wild young Greeks do not dart the sharp prow of their boat right through your new straw bonnet or the back of your head.

Another turn in the river, and the most beautiful, the most brilliantly colored and varied scene was before us. Fancy an Italian villa in a richly ornamented style, mingling its shadows in the water with the high trees surrounding it, the blue sky peeping in above, and a distracting glance of rose and orange gardens on either side, in which Turkish ladies, vailed and splendidly attired, are walking slowly about, or reclining on cushions in the shade. Fancy knowing that one of these, and the fairest, is the Sultan's daughter, and the rest her ladies, enjoying the Bairam, in this happy valley, for the day. Fancy opposite the windows of the palace, floating idly, her oars at rest, a huge caique, gilt and flowered at prow and stern, and filled with picturesque Greeks in bright holiday attire. The women have stuck roses and lilies into the embroidered handkerchiefs wreathed round their heads. The men's jackets are resplendent with gold and scarlet and green. Three boys in the stern play on a kind of guitar, and a rude drum made out of an earthenware water-vase. They are all laughing in the wildest mirth, taking up the song one after another.

Fancy, in contrast to this, a Turkish boat, stealing noiselessly along, filled with vailed and silent women, and carefully guarded by hideous and ferocious blacks. In the middle of this boat stands up a lovely Turkish child, about five years old. She must be a pasha's daughter, for down the front of her velvet and embroidered cap is a badge of brilliants, with a large emerald in the centre. Her dress is a jacket and trousers, of that soft green satin of which the feridjees are made; and round her waist the dear little beauty wears a belt of gold embroidery with a jeweled clasp. She is pointing to a most singular group. About twenty huge musk-oxen have waded into the water, and their hideous, black, fat heads, and crooked horns, look so strange among the sparkling waves, and in the midst of this brilliant scene. It must be very sultry, for they will not move, even for the raps which they get from the numerous oars in passing by, but their large black eyes glitter with pleasure and enjoyment. No doubt they have brought to the Sweet Waters many a weighty load of Turkish beauty, in their crimson and gold-canopied wagons, and are now reposing, in luxurious Asiatic abandonment, after the heat and labor of the day.

I was thinking what a gorgeous picture of Eastern life this group before the kiosk would be, when the rapid approach of a splendid Tunisian boat obliged our caique to dart rapidly on, in order to make way. Seated under a richly-fringed white and scarlet canopy were two Tunisian officers, in full costume, and with military orders on their breasts. Noble, swarthy-looking men they were, and would have made excellent "fancy portraits" of Saladin or Osman, or any other famed Eastern warrior of olden times. Their boat, painted in stripes of white and green, was rowed by sixteen men in flowing white robes, with an under-vest of scarlet showing down the breast. Two soldiers, bristling with splendid arms *à la* Bashi-Bazouk, sat in the stern. Of course all wore the scarlet fez, with its rich purple tassel. Their gay standard flutters proudly in the breeze: they make a dazzling appearance, and you fancy that they must be going to pay a visit to the Caliph Haroun Alraschid.

But now the river has become so crowded, that it is with the greatest difficulty we can get on. The caiques are so thick that it is only possible for our men to pull a few strokes every now and then. There is an immense amount of shouting in Greek and Turkish, especially at antique-looking Greek boats with fringed and beaded prows; for the revelers in them are singing, and drumming, and shouting, in the wildest manner, allowing themselves to float as chance may direct, and not troubling themselves to get out of anybody's way—much to the disgust of the majestic Turks, who float by, with their calm and dignified aspect, looking neither to the right nor to the left.

The banks meanwhile are most lovely to look on. Your eye is charmed, delighted, and contented, for there is nothing to wish for, nothing to imagine: it is a full, complete, and harmonious picture. Here and there guitars hang on the trees. Group after group, in the most splendid and varied costumes, are seated under the dark plane trees, from their deepest shade down to the gay and sparkling water's edge, where a beauty in snow-white vail, and shining lilac feridjee trimmed with silver, is laughing with a lovely child and her black attendants, who are carrying embroidered cushions from the quietly moored caique. Every turn on the river brings you upon different groups on either side, the last appearing more striking than the first.

By the landing-place the banks were literally lined with Turkish women in white vails, and feridjees of every possible brilliant or delicate color, from blue, trimmed with rose-color, and cherry trimmed with silver, to delicate apple-green and the palest straw-color, The dark-brown and dark-green feridjees of the slaves, or the poorer women, prevent one's eye from being wearied with too much brilliancy. It is perfect, and you are delighted even with the rude Greek songs and their wiry-sounding guitars.

The Greeks keep mostly on the left bank of the river—of course men and women together; but no Turk of any rank is ever seen with his womankind; the women sit or walk in groups with their children and slaves, and laugh and eat, and enjoy a summer's day like a bird or a fish. They have little to prize but the hour, poor things! so they may as well be happy while they can, until their beauty is gone, and they are less esteemed than the ox which carries them.

At last we are on shore, and mark well the spot by an old willow-tree and a few rough planks where our caique is safely moored. One of our caiquejees, mounting a pair of coarse-knitted socks and an old pair of red canoelike shoes, follows us with camp-chairs and white umbrellas. We are on the edge of a wide plain, over which English officers are galloping, with every here and there a Turkish lancer, and a couple of wild Greeks dashing recklessly along, determined to win the race for the honor of the new scarlet and gold jacket, and because a splendidly-mounted French officer is looking quietly on. The sun is excessively sultry on the plain, and the arabas make a great dust; so we dart under the shade of the trees by the water's edge, and admire the nice contrivance of a Turk for the distribution of really cool sherbet and lemonade to the multitude. His emporium is in the shape of a gigantic canvas umbrella. You look at it with respect, for it might have belonged to Jack's vastest giant. It is covered with fresh green boughs, which cast a pleasant shadow over the little table underneath, delicately adorned with a white cloth, and graced with three enormous decanters of sherbet, each stopped with an immense lemon. There is a great crowd here, and our Turk, in his blue and white turban, looks contentedly on his heap of piastres. .

His next-door neighbor is a Greek, who has very cleverly made a rude kind of altar out of clay. On this some charcoal is burning. Little white and gold cups are in a basket by his side. There are a few rough stools around him, just in the shade. This is a *café;* and the Greeks, Armenians, English, French, Circassians, Arabs, Blacks, Croats, and Persians of this motley throng stop, as they stroll by, to take a fragrant cup, or to rest awhile on the little wooden stools under the tree. The gayly-dressed Greek strawberry sellers look very picturesque, carrying the pretty baskets of fruit on long poles from shoulder to shoulder, stopping at the doors of arabas by the wayside, and then darting off to distant parties of revelers, whence still come sounds of laughter, and of guitars, and of little drums.

We still press on through the crowd, past sellers of many-colored sweetmeats, of *yahoort,* (a kind of sour milk, white as snow,) and of *sémeet,* bread sprinkled with small seed, and hanging in tempting brown wreaths round the basket. A magnificent old Turk is selling kabobs, (small pieces of meat strung and roasted on sticks), which are kept hot by a little iron machine turning round a charcoal fire. A large wild dog, with a strong infusion of wolf about him, sits at a little distance sniffing the savory smell; but that is all the poor wanderer seems likely to get for his pains.

We amused ourselves by watching the crowds for some time, and then walked on to get a peep at the Sultan's kiosk. It seemed in bad repair, for I believe he seldom goes there, but the trees around it were magnificent, and we heard nightingales singing in the deepest shade. The very luxury of neglect seemed delicious on this sultry day, and peeps of distant grass-grown walks and sedgy fountains were charming. At the gate of the kiosk stood, or rather lolled, a depressed-looking Turkish soldier, holding his musket all on one side, (as they always do), and when bored, tossing it about as a school-girl does her parasol.

The gateway looked down a fine avenue of trees on to a canal, very like those at Hampton Court, but neglected of course, and only suggesting what the place might be in other hands. We walked down the banks of this canal, under the shade of the huge waving boughs. On the opposite side were rich meadows belonging to the kiosk; and grazing here and there were all the Sultan's favorite horses, turned out to grass for the summer months. It was a very pretty sight, for there were at least two hundred of these fine creatures; and the attendant Arabs and Turks, quietly smoking at the doors of their tents, looked the very picture of turbaned happiness and content, as they gazed on some beautiful white, or brown, or chestnut favorite, pawing in the distance, and rejoicing in its strength and liberty.

These rich pastures are on the left side of the canal; on the right is a broad road, and up and down this drove arabas and ox-carriages with crimson and gold awnings, filled with vailed women, and rude wooden carts filled with Greeks in holiday attire. How astonished Rotten Row would be! I thought this, as a fine Turk of the old school rode majestically by on a snow-white mule with scarlet trappings. He was evidently a descendant of the Prophet, by his green turban: his flowing robes were of spotless white; his bare legs of a fine bronze color, and his shoes red. He was quite a picture, though moving along under the old plane-trees by the wayside; but so was an English officer, dashing by with two Crimean clasps on his breast, and a little bunch of golden acacia-flowers in his hand, (sold in all the streets here, and having a delicious scent), I suppose to give to "somebody;" and so were two stately Circassians, in their flowing robes and splendid arms; and so, in fact, was every thing in the Valley of the Sweet Waters, including two wild Negro boys mounted on the same horse, and stopping by the fountain to dispute merrily which should alight for water. On the bank by the fountain sat a poor old Dervish and three or four vailed Turkish women, enjoying the shade, for the fountain tree is a very fine one. But I shall never get to the end of my journey if I attempt to describe half the groups which delighted me so much.

We sat down to rest a little further on, in a small thicket of trees very like some of those in Bushy Park, and we rested right royally. First we sipped some delicious sherbet; then we ate a few crisp almond-cakes, dotted with pistachio-nuts; then we clapped our hands, and the "musicians" came and entertained us with "a concert of music," sitting cross-legged at our feet. I must confess that it would have been intolerable, but that we were possessed with the notion of doing all as in an Arabian Nights' story. Then we drank delicious coffee, handed by a graceful young Greek, who spoiled the effect of his classical countenance by looking too sharply after piastres. Then we laughed immoderately at the coaxings and nonsense of three beautiful wild Arab girls, wanting to tell our fortunes in real Arabic, and regretted deeply that we were not artists and geniuses, to paint their splendid features, raven hair and eyes, and most royal rags. Then we looked admiringly at our neighbors, seated on cushions on the grass--four beautiful Turkish women, like tulips for bright raiment, and with shy smiles for all, behind their thin vails. Their ox-car was close by, caned, and with large gilt wings carved on its sides. The white oxen, with their cheeks and foreheads painted red, and with necklaces, of blue beads, worn as charms against the "evil eye," lay contentedly resting by the slaves, who chatted and laughed, and were as merry as the rest. This was a beautiful group. Golden sunlight, stealing through the boughs, illumined the soft vailed faces, the richly embroidered cushions, and the antique-shaped water-vases, the rude but magnificent car, the gentle white oxen, and the richly-attired black slaves.

It was one of those splendid pictures so difficult to leave; but the Sultana's carriage was crossing the little white bridge from the Sultan's kiosk, and we hastened (as much as it is possible to hasten in this charmed land) to get a look. The Sultana, or chief wife of the present Sultan, is the mother of his sons, and it is said he is greatly attached to her. Her daughter, lately married to Ali-ghalib Pasha, the son of Redshid Pasha, is considered the prettiest woman in Turkey. Over the picturesque white bridge came their carriage, drawn by four superb black horses. A Turkish officer, mounted on a white horse gayly caparisoned, rode before, and about twenty Lancers brought up the rear. The carriage was peach-colored, and completely covered with barbarous silver ornaments; the spokes of the wheels were gilt, and the axletrees silver; the ends of the reins were peach-colored ribbons; the coachman, a mixture of mountebank, Turk, and dressed-up monkey.

But the ladies inside, how beautiful and gentle and delicate they seemed to me! The Sultana occupied the princial seat in the carriage, and her daughter sat opposite. The Sultana is very small and very pretty, but melancholy-looking, and with an air of exquisite refinement about her which is difficult to express. I had just time to notice this, when my eyes fell and rested on the Princess. Fortunate that I was not Abulhassan the Prince of Persia! It is quite true that a Turkish beauty—really a beauty—"strikes you all of a heap," as the sailors say. The Princess sat, bending slightly forward in the carriage, her "gazelle eyes" resting thoughtfully on a Turkish fan of snow-white feathers, which she held in her hand, the centre of which was entirely of emeralds and diamonds—slight as a fairy—the exquisite tint of her skin, seen through the misty white vail, just the hue of a shell where it approaches pink. The delicate robe of palest sea-green, and the wreath of diamonds trembling round her head like splendid drops of water in a charmed crown, instantly reminded me of Undine in her softest mood, traveling in this rich but fantastic equipage to visit some great River Queen on shore for the day.

About fifteen arabas, more or less gilt and flowered, followed the royal carriage. In the first four all the ladies of the Harem were dressed alike. First pale-blue feridjees with diamond stars shining under their white vails: then a magnificent amber-color shot with white, green trimmed with gold, purple, pink, and violet, gems shining on every head and breast. It is something to see the ladies of the Harem, on the fête-days of Bairam, in all their splendor. We saw them well, as the carriages stood still for some time on the plain, until, I am sorry to say, the disgraceful conduct of the English and French officers obliged them to move on. After driving slowly once round the plain, the train of arabas disappeared down the winding road which leads through the valley to Beshiktash.

The shadows were by this time beginning to lengthen, and we agreed to look for our caique. It was very pleasant to sink down on its cushions again, after all the walking we had had through the valley and avenues. The river-scene was beautiful beyond description, in the purple light of the setting sun, falling upon departing caique-loads, upon the fine trees and distant mountainous slopes, where here and there a scarlet feridjee moved slowly along or rested by the way, and on a few splendid groups of Greeks, still remaining on the banks. Almost all the Turkish women and their attendants had left, but the Greeks seem to be the most insatiable people in the world for pleasure. They were now singing, laughing, and dancing, as if they had that moment commenced. The children, and many of the young men, had made crowns of rushes, which they wore with evident delight. Others had twisted chaplets of wild-flowers round their heads. The little liquid-sounding drums were beating time to the songs as industriously as ever, which, although rude enough, mingled pleasantly with the sound of oars and the splashing of water, as countless caiques dashed down the stream. Presently we came to a secluded creek, and under some large trees was a singular group preparing to depart.

Some French officers had "fraternized" with a party of Arabs, and were taking an impressive adieu, before stepping into a man-of-war's boat with the tri-color fluttering gayly in the evening breeze. Some of the Arab women, with their loose vails flowing round their dark faces, came tripping with bare feet among the thick water-plants which shrouded the prow of the boat; and a little child, with its single ragged garment fluttering in the air, was scampering down with them to see the last of the companions of evidently a very merry repast. Some French sailors were bringing down baskets and other evidences of their good cheer under the plane-trees that day.

How we enjoyed our row back in the purple light of the evening, and the cool, pleasant smell of the water-plants, which we touched with our oars now and then in avoiding the crowds of caiques! I looked for the storks again, and saw one of them still fishing and wading about in the water.

When we got as far as the arsenal, the crowd of returning caiques was really a wonderful sight; carriages returning from "the Derby" in England were nothing to it, and I could not help comparing the two almost national fête-days. Here was the wildest mirth, but neither drunkenness nor vulgar mischief. The Turks were floating by as calmly and composedly as they went—the Greeks, wild among themselves, but offending no one. I shall long think of that return from the Sweet Waters at sunset, with the minarets of beautiful Stamboul shining before us, and the picturesque groups on the purple water. Here the sun sets, as has been so truly said,

> "Not, as in Northern climes, obscurely bright,
> But one unclouded blaze of living light."

Now the distant domes of Achmetie and Santa Sophia, the lofty cypresses, the masses of dark-red houses, the flag-embellished men-of-war, with their huge gilt lions, the turrets of the Roman Wall, and the windows of many palaces were illumined in a clear haze (if I may use the expression) of purple and gold, which must be seen to be believed, but which we watch with delight every evening stealing over the Asian hills.

Two antique caiques, lashed together, made a magnificent picture in this gorgeous light. Several of the men in them were remarkably handsome, and one was standing up, reciting a story with great emphasis and gesture, to which all listened with attention while another, with a wreath of wild-flowers and rushes round his head, reclined at the stern of the caique, with one foot dangling in the green waves as they floated slowly on. In another of these bound-together caiques some rude dancing was going on, as well as circumstances would permit, the dancer singing and reciting loudly all the time. These fine figures of Greeks looked wonderfully well, standing up, in their gold-embroidered holiday jackets and rich sashes, in the sunlight. But just before coming to the first bridge of Constantinople we were delighted indeed; for on two enormous piles of timber, in a kind of arsenal-yard, close to the sea, were crowded, in every shade of bright and sombre-colored feridjee, hundreds of Turkish women; they were sitting by the wayside to see the rich and gay return from the Sweet Waters, just as those who are unable to go, watch the crowds return from races and fêtes by the wayside near London. But this was a splendid sight, the purple and gold light of the setting sun falling upon two vast piles of groups of richest dye, and on the soft white vails, and upon little children playing with the ripples at their feet. What would a painter not have given to have seen it, and what would the world say could he paint it!

But my description of our day at the Valley of the Sweet Waters must come to an end, or you will be as tired as our poor caiquejees were, pulling up the rapid stream of the Bosphorus.

We left all the revelers far behind long before reaching Orta-kioy, and enjoyed a rest in our cool, quiet little arbor, before relating our adventures at dinner-time. We had certainly spent a very delightful day, and our quiet friend Dhudu thought so too. In the evening we sipped coffee on our divan under the window, listening to nightingales singing far and near, and watching the fire-flies flitting among the orange-trees and passion-flowers, and the illuminated minarets of the last night of Bairam.

LETTER XLVI.

THUNDER-STORM—RETURN OF TROOPS—THE COMMISSION.

Orta-kioy, June 9th, 1856.

My dearest Mother:

I am writing to you in the midst of a tremendous thunder-storm. About seven o'clock huge black clouds came frowning down from the north. The Bosphorus was quite darkened over, and we could not see halfway down the valley. Presently down came large, heavy drops of rain, pattering upon the dusty fig-leaves; then such floods as I have only seen *here*, tearing the very roads to pieces. In about a quarter of an hour an angry stream of turbid yellow water (almost a river) dashed down from the hills, over the road by the side of our house; and loud was the conflict of wind and water, where only an hour before weary cattle had panted up the hot and dusty hill! Down the noisy stream tumbled and rolled, first a dead dog, then a cat, and lastly the skeleton of a wretched ox, which had died on the road of hunger and thirst a few days before, been skinned where it lay, and its miserable carcass left for the dogs, after the horrid fashion of this place.

We soon turned to our other windows, overlooking the garden. The poor roses, all in their fullest beauty, are sadly spoiled, and many bunches of orange-flowers lie strewn on the ground. The passion-flower over the arbor and wall (a few hours ago covered with fine buds and flowers) is a little torn, but the great aloes look very fine and fresh, after such a gigantic shower-bath. Poor little Simione, the Armenian, will be busy in his garden to-morrow!

What a night it must be in the Black Sea! the storm has evidently come down from thence. It is now nearly dark, but violet-colored lightning illumines the whole of the valley and the hills beyond. Then comes the thunder, crashing and echoing from hill to hill, far away on the Asian side. Our little wooden house quite shakes and trembles beneath the storm, but they say that lightning is not so dangerous here as it is in England. Another prolonged flash! and the houses in the valley beneath, the minarets, the dark Bosphorus with shipping here and there, the villages and mosques on the opposite banks, are lighted up with a stream of colored light. The effect is most beautiful. The large fig-tree by my window rustles in the heavy gusts of wind. Our muslin curtains wave ghostily to and fro. The mice shriek, and run frantically round (or between) our wooden roof. My poor canaries wake up, and flutter about their cage with fright. The wild dogs howl in the most dismal manner. There is not a light to be seen in the Turkish camp opposite, nor further on at Kulalee, where the music of the German Legion usually enlivens the banks in an evening. I wonder how their thin tents have borne the tremendous gusts of wind and torrents of rain.

This is the first summer storm I have seen on the Bosphorus, but we had many as violent in the autumn last year. The huge black clouds are now sailing slowly down toward Stamboul, and the worst of the storm has broken just over our heads. We can count several seconds between the blaze of violet-colored lightning and the crash of thunder, which shows that the storm-fiend is passing on to the tall minarets of Constantinople. The rain still pours down in torrents, and the large cypress-trees on the hillside sway to and fro in the hurricane of wind which comes with a shrieking sound down from the north. We are all looking anxiously at each other, hoping that our ships in the Black Sea may ride out the storm in safety.

June 11th, Wednesday evening.

It has rained with little intermission all day. Several large ships have passed by from the Black Sea, crowded with troops. Poor fellows, what a time they must have had! I noticed that only one ship had an awning, and that just at the stern of the vessel. All on deck looked drenched, cold, and miserable, clustering at the sides of the ship, and no doubt longing for the shelter of a roof. However, they are going home, to forget all the sufferings of war.

I was sadly disappointed yesterday, on hearing that the mail had arrived, but no courier, who, owing to one of the railways in France being out of order, had missed the ship at Marseilles. Edmund is quite well again. Vassili and I had contrived a shower-bath, which has done him great good? Every day I hope to hear something about the Commission being finished, but Edmund has some cases to settle for the commissariat, which takes up much of his time; for many weeks he has never had a moment to himself, and sits up terribly late. But I must say good-night, with dearest love to Ediebelle!

LETTER XLVII.

EDUCATION OF TURKISH WOMEN—REARING OF CHILDREN—WANT OF INSTRUCTION—BOOKS—THOUGHTS OF HOME—THE CLIMATE—RELICS FROM THE CRIMEA.

Constantinople, June 26th, 1856.

My dear Mrs. Austin:

We have a most valuable and agreeable acquaintance here in Admiral Slade; he is an Englishman, in the Turkish service, has done much for their Navy, and has resided at Constantinople for several years. He has also traveled in the provinces, speaks both Turkish and Greek perfectly well, and has written a very clever and pleasant book about Turkey. His name among the Turks is "Muschaver Pasha."

I believe he is considered rather an eccentric man by the English, since he infinitely prefers the ease and freedom of an Eastern life, to the rigid conventionalisms of London and Paris. Spite of all that he laments in their executive and government, he thoroughly loves the Turks as a people, and, I should think, thoroughly understands them. We had a long chat about the women the other day, and agreed that, pretty, gentle, and intelligent as they generally are, their ignorance would be in the highest degree ludicrous, were it not so lamentable.

Then the question comes, "What can be done?" and what I want to ask your advice about is this, my dear Mrs. Austin. Admiral Slade promises that, if I can get a few little books, of the simplest instruction, from England, for these poor women, he will undertake to get them translated into the Turkish language, and given to such of them as can read. He assures me that there will not be the smallest difficulty in their being allowed to accept them, and suggests, as the most important subject to begin with, a few words on the rearing of fine, healthy children, for thousands are annually laid in their little graves from the ignorance and folly of the mothers. The whole race may be improved by the women being told that there are such things as digestive organs, muscles, and nerves, which perhaps not one in five thousand have ever heard of. I assure you that I have myself seen a baby at the breast stuffed with raw chestnuts; and it is quite a common thing to see a child with not a single tooth through, gnawing a large lump of cucumber. The other day, as I was passing near the mosque here, the Imaum was standing by a fruit-stall, with a most miserable-looking child of about eighteen months in his arms, which he was feeding with green apricots.

But these things you may see all day long, in every street in Constantinople, besides many a poor baby borne by on its little bier—killed by an over-dose of opium, given to keep it quiet if fractious from teething. I am afraid, however, the English of the lower classes may blush at this accusation.

From the immense quantity of sweetmeats given here, mere babies have black and decayed teeth; and it is by no means uncommon to find boys and girls, from seven to ten and twelve, with not a single sound one in their heads, nothing but a mass of black and broken stumps, most melancholy and sickening to see. The boys are brought up in the harems, lounging with the women on divans, until fourteen or fifteen; it is easy, therefore, to see the vast importance of teaching the mothers how to rear fine and healthy boys, to take the place of the present miserably emaciated, listless race of Constantinopolitans.

I am assured that the women of this country are far before the men in intelligence, far less prejudiced, and far more willing to know and to adopt wiser and better ways.

The fresh mountain girls from Circassia and Georgia, who are always coming in, are very different in mind and body to the poor slave bred and born in a harem at Stamboul. Their admiration of the strength and beauty of the English race knows no bounds, and I have no doubt that almost every mother would be thankful to be taught how to rear such beings herself.

I am really in great spirits about this cheerful little ray of light for the poor Turkish women, my dear Mrs. Austin, at least if you will lend your head; your heart I am sure of, as every body is, in a good cause. Great caution will be important, that our books may "creep and gang," without rousing the prejudices or fears of jealous masters. Tract-giving people would stop the whole thing at once. What is wanted is all-powerful common-sense and general information. I think we should soon get to pretty moral and instructive stories.

What a different idea would a Turkish boy have of his mother, if he saw her gently occupied in reading and teaching instead of sitting on a divan, slapping and quarreling with her slaves for want of something to do, and sunk in the most degrading ignorance!

The Sultan's ladies have lately had a translation of the Arabian Nights given them, and a book of love-songs. Other books there are none, but Admiral Slade assures me that they would be eagerly caught up by the few who can read. As I said before, he undertakes himself to get them printed in Turkish here; and he is no visionary, but a kind-hearted and clever man, who thoroughly understands and knows the people, and what will answer with them. Here then is really something useful and interesting to do, which is frequently so great a want in many easy lives.

Mrs. Campbell once lent me a very useful book, called, I think, "Hints to Mothers." It was by a physician, but I believe there are many such, from which the most important directions might be extracted and simplified. In fact, the language must be as if written for children of seven years old. Of course any works prepared with this view need not be printed, as I could easily get them put into Turkish writing here, with the aid of my friend the admiral, who is greatly interested in the affair.

How profoundly you would pity these poor degraded women, when young, so pretty and soft and gentle and intelligent—but mere animals, though they be gazelles or fawns—and when their first bloom and vivacity is past, indolent to disease, gluttonous, spiteful and hopeless! Such they are made by the tyranny of their masters, when Nature has given them every thing.

I would help them with all my heart, and only wait

for you to show me how, my dear Mrs. Austin. I hope to hear that you are tolerably well, and enjoying your garden and the green lanes and fresh heaths of Weybridge. After all this grand panoramic scenery, one longs for the charming detail of England. A hill looks lovely here at a distance, but when you get to it there is no fern, "or old thorn;" nothing small, or pretty and refreshing; no roadsides, no cottages, no little gardens. But in this world one must be away from a thing to prize it at its full value. I always loved my home, but now it seems a little paradise, which it were too much happiness to hope to see again.

The Loan Commission is rapidly coming to an end, and, I am happy to say, satisfactorily; only I sometimes fear for my husband's health, with such anxious and responsible work, in this exciting climate, and with the excessive fatigue of riding and walking over these crowded and sultry streets. However, I hope that all will go well, and that we shall return to Weybridge early in September. This variable climate is so very trying, that I could hardly wish to see my dear Edith here. It is beginning to tell very much upon us both; for, unless one leads the life of a tortoise, one always has a certain amount of fever and sleeplessness as soon as summer fairly sets in. The heat now, in the middle of the day, is frightful. Yet it is such a strange climate, that, immediately after sunset, or even in the shade during the day, if you were to sit in the shady garden for an hour, you would most probably feel a cold chill creeping over you.

The languor and laziness brought on by the climate

have prevented my writing you an account of my rambles in the Crimea; but, besides that it is fresh in my memory, I made notes in my pocket-book of all I saw, and, if you think the letter would be worth having, I will write it soon with very great pleasure. When we meet, I will illustrate it by my collection of dried flowers, from the different battle-fields and other places of interest. I have also brought snow-drop and Iris roots from Balaklava and the beautiful valley of Baidar, shot and shell from the Malakoff and Redan, a Russian gunner's shoe and hammer, which I picked up in one of those subterranean holes in the Malakoff in which the besieged ate and slept. Those defenses were indeed marvelous. We saw the sun set from them,—the ruined city and the sunken ships all bathed in the purple and gold tints of these regions. A nightingale was singing close by the Mamelon, on our right. Every thing was peaceful, and all that one had heard of the dreadful strife and slaughter seemed like a dream. We then went to the Redan, and counted silently and with great emotion those frightful four hundred feet of slope up which our poor soldiers had to fight: in fact, it was not fighting, but entering a fiery pass of shot and shell. An officer who was there told me that he saw several of our poor fellows dodge right and left once or twice before they could resolve on dashing in.

But I must not attempt to tell you more now. The ground is literally plowed up with shot and shell. I picked up a torn epaulette, the broken scabbard of a sword, and several other sad remembrances of that dreadful day. A Russian soldier was there, who insisted on shaking hands with me, and gave me a little cross.

LETTER XLVIII.

THE PRINCES' ISLANDS—THE "EDITH BELINA"—SIGNOR GIACOMO—CHURCH ON THE ISLAND.

Prinkipo, July 6th, 1856.

My dear Mr. Hornby:

Here we are in a cottage at Prinkipo, which is the largest of the Princes' Islands, or the "Islands of the Blest." It is just like the Surry hills, rising out of the sea, only with rocks and mountains all around; and among fir-trees are mixed fig and olive-trees, with every here and there a patch of sloping vineyard, the bright scarlet flower of the pomegranate, and picturesque Greek shepherds lying in the shade, with goats and sheep browsing about them. The view of the coast and mountains opposite is very fine; Constantinople in the distance, rising as it were out of the blue sea, just like Venice out of one of Turner's pictures. It is beyond all things beautiful. We have just returned from our evening walk, winding through heather, cistus, and arbutus, down to the seashore. The fir-trees overhang the cliffs, which are green almost to the water's edge. I picked up several pretty shells for Edith.

Yesterday we saw a cloud of heat hanging over Constantinople, where the thermometer was a hundred and two degrees. Here, in the evening, it was but eighty-four in my room. To-day a delightful breeze has sprung up, and the noise of waves dashing against the shore is most pleasant. We already feel quite refreshed, and have been watching the "white horses" hurrying over the sea. Numerous island caiques, with their white sails set, are bounding along. I must tell you that we have got a very nice caique of our own; it is called the "Edith Belina." I wish you could see her riding so gallantly over the waves, her Union-jack fluttering merrily in the breeze. Our house faces the sea, of course, and a door at the back opens on to a rough path just cut on the mountain. We are up very early in the morning, for the steamer leaves before seven, and there is no other for the rest of the day. Sometimes the Greek milkman has not yet come up from the village, and then it is most amusing to see the zealous Apple-blossom, with her long plaits of hair unpinned, running after the goats on the mountain, with a tin basin in her hand; she looks so comically cross when the tiresome things skip about as if to plague her. They are Signor Giacomo's goats, but every thing which belongs to Signor Giacomo—or "Jackeymo," as he is almost universally called—is at the "disposizione" of his tenants.

Signor Giacomo is a Maltese—was a little ragged sailor-boy, with bare feet, when he first entered Constantinople, as he delights in telling every one. The store at Galata, which he arrived at by many patient steps, has been a mine of wealth to him, and he now owns all the best land in the island, and has built quite a little nest of white terraced houses. His own is a large and pleasant one, above a garden of three terraces, adorned with a multitude of white roses, which strike the beholder at least three miles off at sea.

This we always call "Giacomo's delight," for here in the evening doth the cheerful and flourishing Maltese delight to sit, smoking a chibouque with an amber mouthpiece, which a pasha might not disdain. Giacomo, when in his garden, arrayed in white, and with a broad-brimmed straw hat, is not unlike a small and smiling Napoleon, engaged in agricultural pursuits at St. Helena,—at least, such representations as I remember to have seen in children's books. Signor Giacomo hath chubby sun-burnt children, too, almost innumerable, generally playing in the sand, but very gayly arrayed on Sundays and fête-days. Madame Giacomo is a kind, unpretending little body, who enjoys life merrily enough, and wears plenty of diamonds on occasions quite easily. She said so unaffectedly the other day, that, being extremely fond of music, she had begged Giacomo to buy her an excellent barrel-organ, which she thought better than attempting any accomplishment at her age; so, frequently of an evening, pleasant airs are wafted to my window from Madame Giacomo's little drawing-room, and I know that she is cheerfully turning the handle of her organ, to amuse herself or friends. Signor Giacomo's hall is adorned with several statues, and with pretty plants and shrubs in vases. All the family ironing is unpretendingly done here, and it is by no means an uncommon thing to see the master's broad-brimmed hat hung upon the head of a Flora, plaster though it be, or his gun (for Giacomo is given to quails, among other good things), resting securely against one of the Graces.

Signor Giacomo is much liked and respected in the island. The French soldiers quartered here for some time have given him their little wooden church, in which they held two Masses daily. Signor Giacomo announces his intention of giving a piece of land, fronting the sea, on which to more firmly erect the church, and offers to be at all the expense of workmen, and to help to keep a "Padre" when the building is finished. I asked what it was to be: he said, "A Christian church," but seemed to be perfectly indifferent as to whether a Roman Catholic or Protestant minister should volunteer the cure. I liked his look of wonder at any one wishing to know more, than that it was to be a "Christian church, and free to all."

LETTER XLIX.

THE SULTAN'S BANQUET—TURKISH ARTIFICERS—THUNDER-STORM—LONG DAYS—VASSILI'S MISBEHAVIOR—DOMESTIC CHANGES.

Prinkipo, July 23d, 1856.

My dear Mother:

Yesterday the Sultan's dinner-party came off. It has been the talk of Constantinople for the last three weeks. Famous cooks and waiters, it is said, have been engaged from Paris, and the Sultan seemed determined to have every thing quite perfect, after the European fashion. I heard, last week, that the royal mind was greatly troubled as to the number of chairs of the same pattern in the hall of the palace of Dolma Batche. There were not enough, by ten, for the guests invited (one hundred and thirty), and no artificer was to be found in Constantinople, "cunning" enough to make some more to match. However, I dare say every thing was very splendid, and am anxiously expecting Edmund's return, that he may tell me all about it.

I can see the steamer coming in. The sky is so blue and clear, and the sea so calm, that one can distinguish it, the size of a bee, just as it leaves Stamboul. I am anxious to know how the guests reached the palace yesterday; for, about seven o'clock, a large thunder-cloud, which had been hanging over Constantinople some time, burst with tremendous violence. Forked lightning darted round the minarets, and every now and then a splendid flash lighted up the whole city. Then I saw floods of rain fall, the great black cloud stretching from sky to earth. It was a very grand but awful sight. Then the storm moved slowly over the hills of Scutari, opposite our windows, and flash after flash of beautiful violet-colored lightning illumined the dreary coast and bare mountains.

The island caiques, with their sails bent, made fast for the shore. The sea here soon rose, and a heavy shower splashed into the angry white waves; but we had no thunder, which I was not sorry for, as it shakes these wooden houses in a way that is not pleasant. Mr. Hall came down very kindly by the steamer, knowing that Edmund was dining at the palace.

It was Tuesday, and I grieved over not getting my letters from home. It is a long day to pass here alone: the steamer does not get in till seven. I have been walking on the beach, collecting shells for Edie, and drying a few flowers, and working a little, but one's days are fourteen hours long, and I have no books.

Vassili, you will be surprised to hear, is gone away: he had unfortunately taken to drink *raki* at the "Magyar," which did not do, and I so much alone. He was dreadfully sorry for being insolent one evening, and hung about the house for a week, hoping to be taken back again, as he said to Apple-blossom; but Edmund would not hear of it, and Apple-blossom's faithless husband is to take the place as soon as the Sultan's grand dinner is over, which I suppose is to-day. He, Eugenio, has been helping at the palace. Melia, with the exception of half-a-dozen Itàlian words, only speaks Greek, which is not particularly cheerful for me; but her husband speaks Italian, French, German, Turkish, and Greek perfectly well. Our present "footman" is a wild Greek of the Islands, in blue trousers to the knee, bare brown legs, scarlet jacket and fez.

The steamer is in, and the "Edith Belina" off to meet her; so I shall stroll down to the shore for letters and news.

To my disappointment Edmund is not come back. There is a grand dinner-party at the Embassy to-day to all those invited by the Sultan yesterday. I have not heard much about the royal banquet as yet, except that it was magnificent.

There was a great fire at Pera last night, closing a most eventful day.

LETTER L.

ORDER OF THE MEDJIDI—THE SULTAN'S DINNER-PARTY—THE PALACE—THUNDER-STORM—"COMMISSARY JOE"—VISITORS FROM THE CRIMEA.

Prinkipo, July 23d, 1856.

My dear Mrs. Hornby:

You will all be pleased to hear that Edmund has received his Order of the Medjidi. It is a handsome silver star, with an enameled and circular Turkish inscription in the centre, surmounted with a small enameled star and crescent. The ribbon is a rich green and crimson; and the Sultan's creation as a Companion of the Order is written in extraordinary characters, and enclosed in a white satin bag, with a silver tassel. It is a great pleasure to know that the Sultan is satisfied with the course which the Commissioners have pursued with regard to the English Loan.

Last Thursday the Sultan's grand dinner-party "came off" at the new Palace of Dolma Batche. A tremendous thunder-storm burst over Constantinople about seven o'clock. I sat at the window alone, watching the angry clouds and zigzag lightning over the sea, and wondering how the unhappy guests would escape the torrents of rain which made one dense purple mass from sky to earth. I should have been very glad at that moment to know that they were all seated in the magnificent dining-hall of the palace when the storm-fiend arrived from the Black Sea—all but the principal guest, Sir E.

Codrington, who found it impossible to land, and, after battling with the storm for some time, was obliged to drop anchor almost within sight of the palace. He and his brilliant staff were seen for a moment, full-dressed, from the shore. It must have been particularly provoking, as the Sultan had already put off his dinner more than once, that the English Commander-in-chief might be present. Edmund was among the fortunate people who rowed to the beautiful white-marble steps and gate of Dolma Batche with Lord Stratford and staff, in the magnificent state caique. He was charmed with the palace, which they say is like a dream of the Arabian Nights. Some people assert—critics do—that in detail it is imperfect; but the effect produced on the mind is wonderful, and a guest has neither time nor opportunity to examine the perfectness of the gilding, or the framework of the windows, or the polish of the marble columns and fountains. Ordinary mortals come home, as I say, enchanted—nothing more nor less—and can scarcely believe afterward that they have not visited such a palace of Haroun-al-Raschid as Tennyson so splendidly describes; only the "serene and argent-lidded" Persian girl is not to be seen. However, critics, unhappy mortals! say that it is not "well-finished," go prying about in search of faults, and lose the beautiful idea and dreamlike effect altogether. Nothing can be more lovely than the shadow of this snow-white palace reflected in the dark blue waters of the Bosphorus.

But to return to the dinner. The company were received by the Minister of Foreign Affairs, Fuad Pasha, and by Aali Pasha, the Grand Vizier. They were conducted through a white-marble hall to a simple but elegant apartment, the roof of which was supported by plain white marble columns. There, on a divan, sat the Sultan, in his usual military frockcoat and fez, his collar, cuffs, and sword covered with brilliants, and his majesty himself looking particularly shy and uncomfortable, as he generally does before strangers. He rose; Lord Stratford presented the English guests, and M. de Thouvenel the French. The Sultan had a few kind words to say for most, and plenty of smiles and bows, when he began to feel more at his ease. The dragoman, Count Stefano Piasani, translated courtly speeches in the most courtly manner, with many a pretty turn about "alliances," etc., between England, France, and Turkey. All this over, more bows and smiles from the Sultan, and the company were led out, in the most gentle and courtly manner, by the Grand Vizier and Fuad Pasha, and conducted to the great white marble hall, where a magnificent banquet was spread, with vases of flowers, centrepieces, and gold and silver plate, after the English and French fashion of a grand dinner. The chandelier in the middle of the hall is of great size and beauty, and cost an immense sum of money. The Sultan is very proud of it; it burns four hundred jets of gas. About two hundred wax candles illuminated the lovely Eastern flowers and other ornaments of the table.

The hall, which has a lofty and glittering dome of glass, was lined with a guard of Turkish soldiers in their picturesque costume of the old Sultan's Guard, now never seen. I heard that the effect of their dress and plumes was quite spoiled by their slouching and dejected appearance, and unsoldierly bearing.

The dinner was profuse in number and variety of the dishes, but cold and ill-served, the European waiters evidently not well understanding their work. It was tediously long, for, interspersed with the French dishes, came Turkish ones of all sorts, to please the pashas (including pilauf); and the pashas did eat of every thing, to the wonder and amazement of all around. The Sultan's band was posted at one end of the hall; but, after playing one or two airs, the musicians grew frightened at the storm, which now crashed with great fury just over the palace, and ran away. These valiant men left a large door open in their flight, which, producing a tremendous draught, half the lights were blown out, so that the end of this splendid entertainment was not as well lighted as could be wished; indeed, the rare dessert was demolished almost in the dark by Turk and Christian.

Many were greatly struck and impressed with the grandeur and solemnity of the scene, as peal after peal of thunder crashed over the dome of the palace, "so lightly, beautifully built," and vivid flashes of lightning played on the glittering array of Christian guests—the first whom the world ever saw assembled in the palace of a Sultan. Some of the Turkish dignitaries looked gloomy and terrified, no doubt thinking that the wrath of Heaven had fallen on them as a punishment for eating with "infidels." To Christian fancy, it only wanted "the writing on the wall," to be read as a warning to the corrupt and fallen Moslem Empire.

I had almost forgotten to tell you that it is not etiquette for the Sultan to dine with any one, so I suppose his majesty moped on a corner of his sofa, or condescended to peep through the lattice-work of the women's gallery, while the feast went on. The latter proceeding I should think most probable, considering the interest which he had taken for some weeks in watching even the smallest minutiæ of the preparations. The French, English, Sardinian, Prussian, and Austrian uniforms, and various Stars and Orders, made a goodly show, as you may suppose. Omar Pasha was among the Turkish generals. The dinner was over by half-past nine. The next day Lord Stratford gave a grand military dinner at Pera. Lord Lyons, Sir Edward Codrington, and the principal Sardinian and French officers were there.

Edmund returned to the Islands on Saturday evening, glad to get a quiet walk after much hard work, and the glitter and fatigue. The heat at Pera has been frightful, and almost every resident there is ill, so I cannot help congratulating ourselves on being here in sweet and fresh air. Every now and then "the commissioner" gets a holiday, when, after two or three hours' writing, we go out fishing among the rocks, or sail in the "Edith Belina" to the coast of Asia, land, and take a long ramble in some ancient and solitary village at the foot of the mountains.

Herbert Siborne left us this day week, having spent a couple of days with us here. He looks pale and thin from hard work and anxiety about his men and horses. I do not think this climate agreed with him. Scutari is frightfully hot, and he seems delighted at the idea of getting back to England. He has with him Edmund's horse and dog, Sultan and Arslan, and all my valued relics and remembrances of the Crimea.

About ten days ago, who should find us out one evening but the celebrated hero of Kertch, named by an admiring army "Commissary Joe." He had had a severe attack of illness; we have nursed him, and he is now in a most jovial and flourishing condition, just the man to have with one in a strange land. He makes bargains for me in true military style, knocks refractory Greeks on the head, calls us up at five in the morning for our health's sake, making noise enough to wake the dead, goes into the sea, and splashes about with the enjoyment of a dolphin, does all sorts of housekeeping commissions for me at Pera, and copies Reports on a most gigantic scale of handwriting when "the commissioner" is hard pressed. He goes down to the village every evening to look at the Greek and Armenian ladies, who sit at the "Magyar" in rows, to chat, drink coffee, flirt, and smoke cigarettes. There was a great show of beauty the other evening, and he begged me to "take up a strong position," where we could see them all to advantage. Presently he gave some ponderous sighs, declared that he "couldn't kill a fly," and that he was quite overcome by pretty hats and dark-eyed beauties, not having been accustomed to such dazzling things at Kertch. However, bitter ale consoles him for every thing, and he is now fast asleep in the vineyard, with an immense cigar nodding and jerking about in the corner of his mouth, and looking very much like an overgrown cherub in a jacket and foraging-cap. His arithmetical, commissariat, and mercantile knowledge is so useful to Edmund just now, that

Commissary-general Smith agrees to let him stay with us on full pay as long as the Commission lasts, which I am very glad of, both for the usefulness to his country, enjoyment to himself, and for his kind and cheerful company. He is greatly liked and highly spoken of, both by his colleagues and by the commissariat powers here, although that is generally no great praise.

How glad I shall be to get home I cannot say. Edmund almost wished me to return by the "Himalaya" last week; but I could not make up my mind to leave him. In no country, it seems to me, is a comfortable home so necessary as in this, and constant care too, about good and fresh food, clean linen, and a clean house. As it is, I think we have every possible comfort in the way of cleanliness—for Cristo "scratches" the floors most industriously—wholesome food, excellent dinners, and delicious tea. Many a wandering officer drops in at seven o'clock, and we have often more visitors than chairs and plates. I hear that we are loudly lamented at Orta-kioy, and many have found us out here. Edmund seldom comes home without somebody, and company from the Crimea give no trouble, a sheet and pillow thrown down upon the hard divan being considered a luxury; so they are certain of a warm welcome from "Apple-blossom." We have often two or three such encampments, especially on a Saturday night; and many a tale of the war is told, and we talk of what we hope to do some day in old England. But I must bring this epistle to an end, with my best love to all. From day to day we hope to know the time of our return from these Moslem lands.

LETTER LI.

CONVENT OF JESU CHRISTO — FISHING EXCURSION — BATHING-HOUSES — EARLY RISING—ISLAND OF HALKI.

Prinkipo, Sunday, July 27th.

My dear Sister:

I sit down to write you a few lines after a rather tiring day. We have had a long walk over the mountain-path by the sea, returning by the old convent of Jesu Christo, and its gray rocks and fir-trees. The monk was at home, and as Mr. Sanderson, the Consul of Broussa, who speaks Greek, was with us, we had a long chat with the gray-bearded recluse—such a pleasant, kind old man, a singularly good specimen of a Greek priest. He told us that he had made the acquaintance of two English officers who have been staying here, and seemed to regret being left to his usual dreary and uneventful life, now that the war is over and all are taking their departure. He said that the conversation of his military acquaintance, and their descriptions of that world which he had never seen, was so instructive and pleasant. One of his friends was a Colonel Dickson of the Artillery, and we promised to give his love and greeting if we ever met the Colonel in England on our return. We went into the chapel—built, they say, by the Emperor Theodosius. It looked quaint and dim and ancient as usual. Several Greek ladies were offering lighted tapers before the picture of a "gloried" saint.

We afterward turned over the illuminated parchment leaves of Scriptures six or eight hundred years old, and the chapel possesses some even older, which I hope one day to see. The monk gave us a glass of delicious spring-water and some preserved cherries. He seems to have nothing to do in his garden just now: he was very busy in it in the spring, but now the weather is hot, and he seems to give himself up to gayety; smoking, with great enjoyment of the glorious view before him, receiving visitors in the little ruined court-yard, and hearing news of the great world whenever he meets with any one who speaks Greek. Miss Barker is coming to see me on Friday, and then having an interpreter, I propose paying many a visit to "Jesu Christo" and its solitary graybeard, and finding out all about the ancient chapel and old paintings and crosses and tombs.

There is another monastery on the island, St. Giorgio, and there lies buried the Empress Irene (of Byzantium, opposite), who was banished to Prinkipo, where, in the days of her greatness, she had built the convent.

We went out fishing the other day in the "Edith Belina," Colonel Hinde sailing along in his caique close to us. Yanko and Pandelij are so proud of our Union Jack, which flutters gayly in the breeze. We sailed nearly round this island, and soon came to another, with only one house upon it, where dwell the poor family who tend the olive-garden and vineyard. By the side of their hut is a huge white marble sarcophagus, with two Greek crosses carved on it; it is said to be that of one of the Byzantine princes, who was banished here in the time of the Greek Empire. The good old Turk keeps his onions in it; and, as he munched his brown bread, seemed to wonder why we thought it curious.

We then went to fish on a magnificent group of rocks. Our caiques were moored close by, the cushions brought out, and a curious group soon made, which we said we should like to have photographed for you all in England—Edmund with a large beard and mustache and Arab white cloak, gun in hand, perched upon a rock; I sitting leaning back on one, with my feet dangling over the waves, and Colonel Hinde, in picturesque costume, pointing out to me the swarms of fish and many-tinted sea-weed in the clear water below; the caiques, with their white sails furled, at a little distance, and the Greek boatmen in their bright dresses, some sleeping, and others waiting upon us, and climbing backward and forward over the rocks; Mount Olympus, crowned with snow, in the distance; opposite, the grand coast of Asia; islands here and there rising out of the blue water. "Commissary Joe," dozing on cushions in the "Edith Belina," called out, "It's Paradise, only a little hotter." However, whether like Paradise or not, wherever we go, that worthy never moves without a good stock of Bass's pale ale in the caique. Colonel Hinde's men dredged for oysters, and with the contents of Apple-blossom's basket we made an excellent luncheon.

I am quite well and strong again; the sea-bathing has set me up. No doubt the great heat made me feel so low and weak. There is much illness at Pera, but, though hot in the middle of the day, the air is always fresh and lovely here. Signor Giacomo has built me a bathing-house in our little bay, nailed to the few rough boards which make the tiny pier.

Here lies the "Edith Belina" at anchor, and it is such a quiet place that seldom any other caique enters it, except a fishing-boat now and then on a rough day. The bathing-house is roofed over with branches of fir with beautiful cones, and the water looks so pretty with their reflection waving over the golden sands and seaweed underneath. All round is a place to stand and dress on, and I have had nails put up for my clothes, a cushion to sit on, and a shelf for my book. It is such a pretty Robinson-Crusoelike house! and I often wish Edith could see it. I had such a laugh, tell her, the other day. I happened to say to the Greek who made it, that I was sorry there was no door seaward, so that I could swim out on the sands on quiet mornings. I suppose that he mentioned this to Giacomo, for the next day there was a little dog's hole, or beaver's hole, cut for me to get out of, and you cannot think how funny my house looks now. I used to dive underneath before. You would be amused to see me sitting at my door, with only my head out of water, and a great piece of seaweed fastened on the top of my comb to keep off the sun, hanging becomingly down my face. I believe that any English sailor passing by would try to catch me as a fine specimen of mermaid, so pray look at any such creature attentively whom you may be invited to see "for sixpence."

This island life is really delightful, especially since some rather stormy weather has set in. It is very hot, but about eleven in the morning a strong wind has begun to blow every day from the north, which soon makes a rough sea, the very sound of which is refreshing, after the still, quiet sultriness of Constantinople. Rising as early as we do here, too, is another way of making the best of the climate. I am often dressed, having bathed in the sea, by five in the morning, but at any rate am almost always up by that time, when it is cool and most pleasant. It is a beautiful sight to watch the snow-white mist, tipped here and there with rose-color, roll slowly over the mountains of the Asian coast opposite; and then, turning your eyes seaward, in the far distance to track huge ships, dimly seen in the morning mist, slowly moving down the Sea of Marmora. Then, as the sun gleams out brighter, it gradually reveals to you, bit by bit, in a gold and violet light, the cliffs of Scutari, and the minarets and cypresses and cupolas of Stamboul, far away, like a dream, rising out of the blue water. To the left, in the foreground, is the lovely island of Halki; it is three-hilled, and forms a beautifully undulating line, the valley dipping down so low that you can see the sea on the other side. On the highest hill, and overhanging the sea, is a fine old monastery; the bell ringing for morning prayer floats sweetly over the sea, to where I sit at my window. In the valley below is a magnificent avenue of cypress-trees. The houses lie principally in the hollow, clustering thickly down to the water's edge, where countless caiques and large Greek sailing-boats are moored, and where the islanders are sipping and smoking in the little water-palace cafanées all the day long.

Olive-gardens and vineyards are dotted about here and there over the hillside. But I must write one of my long letters soon to give you a good idea of these islands, and of the summer gala-days of the Greeks.

LETTER LII.

ERECTION OF A CHURCH IN PRINKIPO—MONASTERY OF HALKI—GREEK CHURCHES—A GREEK WEDDING—BISHOPS—THE PATRIARCH—AVENUE OF CYPRESSES ILLUMINATED—RETURN HOME.

Prinkipo, August 10th, 1856.

My dearest Mother:

Sunday was a proud and happy day for Signor Giacomo, who, as I told you, laid the first stone of the little wooden church left as a parting present to him by the French troops. He invited a large party of friends and neighbors, his children were dressed in their best, and Madame Giacomo's organ was grinding away at merry tunes all day long. At five o'clock Giacomo came in to say that they waited for us to assist at the ceremony. On the terraced walls of the garden before the spot where the church is to stand, waved the flags of England, France, Sardinia, and Turkey. It was a proud moment for Signor Giacomo, when he handed the venerable old Catholic priest off his donkey, and led him through the vineyard to a round wooden cross, stuck among the wild heath and cistus, which marked the proposed altar-site of the church. Here the reverend gentleman read the Latin service of the Church of Rome, assisted by a lay brother and several wild-looking Croats, no doubt recent converts, who stood with their fezzes off and their wild locks waving in the wind.

Mr. and Mrs. Cumberbatch were there, an English officer, and more than a hundred Greeks, including visitors and the islanders themselves. It was a beautiful and impressive scene. Here, among thousands of Mohammedans and wild sects innumerable, the name of Christian alone is a tie very different to that which one feels it to be in England. Delighted to see the cross raised, and simple words of peace and love spoken within sight of the mountains of Asia and the minarets of Stamboul, I should have been quite startled at that moment to remember the bitter feeling existing in England between Roman Catholic and Protestant, High Church and Low Church.

The cross was marked with the name of the regiment to which it had belonged: no doubt it had comforted many a sick and wounded soldier. I thought, what a picture it would make, backed by the arbutus-covered mountain, the venerable old priest reading beside it, and the wild-looking Croats regarding him with a kind of savage worship.

At the conclusion of the service, Signor Giacomo spoke a few impressive and eloquent words in Italian. So simple was this little oration, that I much regret not remembering every word of it. I confess that I had expected a speech of a somewhat different character, not giving the little man credit for so much good taste, and thinking that the temptation to seize such an opportunity for self-laudation would be too strong to be resisted. Nothing however could have been better. All was said that ought to be said, and in an excellent spirit. All praise to Signor Giacomo for the good feeling which prompted him!

And now every body was invited into Mr. Giacomo's terraced garden, to rest in the shade of his waving acacias, and partake of coffee and sweetmeats. We were however obliged to forego this hospitality, for our caique was waiting to take us to a Greek wedding at the monastery at Halki, which I was anxious to see. So down our party rushed to the shore, for, as it was, Dr. Baretta (the bride's friend) feared we were late. The sun had just dipped into the Sea of Marmora behind Halki, as Madame Baretta, her pretty daughter, and myself, took our seats in the "Edith Belina." There was a fresh breeze, so the caiquejees hoisted her sails, and we dashed swiftly on through the sparkling waters to the wedding. The dear little "Edith Belina" carries her Union Jack gallantly. A strange sail passing by saluted her most deferentially, and I felt for her a sort of pride while teaching Yanco, our first caiquejee, how to return the compliment.

We soon reached Halki, landed at its tiny wooden pier, passed through groups of sleepers and smokers on the benches of the little sea *café*, through the silent and narrow streets of the village, to the magnificent avenue of cypress-trees which leads up to the monastery. It was impossible to help pausing a moment before the ancient gateway of the court-yard to admire the lovely view. The cicalas were still singing about the heat, and the distant snows of Mount Olympus were delicious to the eye after a rapid walk up the cliff. Inside the walls of the monastery is an old fountain, shaded by a tree, and here numbers of the Greek peasantry had assembled. Two sides of the square court are the monks' apartments, with the church at one end, and a suit of apartments belonging to the patriarch at the other. The latter are often given up to the use of rich wedding-parties during the summer months.

After ascending two flights of rickety wooden stairs, with old and curiously-carved balustrades, we found ourselves in an open room or salaamlik, crowded with Greek gentlemen, friends of the bride and bride groom. Coffee and sweetmeats were being handed round. Beyond, and leading from this, were two other apartments; the door of one was open, and revealed a crowd of ladies in gala costume. A graceful Greek lady came from amongst them to welcome us, and this, Madame Baretta whispered to me, was the mother of the bride, which was surprising,—she looked so young. Madame Baretta is a Greek, but speaks Italian very well; she immediately conducted us to the apartment of the bride, a pretty, quiet room overlooking the cliff, and furnished with monastic simplicity. Here, on a divan, pale and thoughtful, sat a young lady in the simplest white dress, made after the English fashion, a light white vail falling from the Greek chaplet of flowers on her head, to the ground. She rose gracefully to receive us, and sat down languidly again amongst her cushions. She seemed wearied with the heat, and no doubt also with the agitation of the day.

I did not think her pretty at first, for her features were not perfectly regular, and she had a dark olive complexion; but when she raised her long black eyelashes and spoke, her face brightened, and we thought her charming. The shape of her head was exquisite, and, as Mr. Hall afterward said, "put on in the most distracting manner." Ladies, young and old, were constantly coming in to shake hands, kiss, and congratulate.

The heat of the room was most oppressive, and I

was glad when Madame Baretta said that it was time to go to the church. There was a pleasant breeze in the old court-yard, and the vaulted archway through which we had to walk. Passing through crowds of Greeks, men, women, and children, lining the usually quiet walls and empty benches, we at last, with some difficulty, reached the church. It was lighted up with innumerable tapers in the centre, the aisles were left in deep shadow, and the effect was really beautiful.

By day, although interesting from its antiquity, this church, like all other Greek churches, is tawdry in the extreme; but by night the dark carving looks well, the pink and white glass chandeliers appear less trumpery, and the pictures of the saints, with their silver hands and "glories," less barbarous. The silent nooks, where the antique votive-lamp burns dimly before the shrine of some favorite saint from age to age, make a great impression on the mind. At first there is just light enough to reveal the silver chains of the lamp; the flame is scarcely more than the light of a glow-worm, which it seems as if a breath would flutter away. Then you dimly discern the face of a saint, or Madonna and Child. You touch a wreath of faded flowers, suspended by the picture, and it falls to dust at your feet. On a little ledge you see a crucifix, evidently of extraordinary antiquity; on another lies a book of Greek manuscript, the leaves falling to pieces with the breath of centuries. Here lies a silver heart curiously worked and embossed,—some offering of love, gratitude, or repentance, from a human one, silent long ago; there, some ancient robes of the church, the once gorgeous embroidery glistening here and there, as it may have done centuries ago, in processions before kings and emperors.

The feeling of antiquity, in the dim aisles and corners of these old Greek churches, produces a sensation difficult to describe, and to me singularly delightful. I feel a kind of thrill, a mysterious joy, at quietly touching these silent evidences of ages long past away. There is a great charm in the reverence and care of old things, and the deep affection which, in the midst of much superstition, the Greeks show in their religion. A wild Greek woman, beating her breast in an agony of supplication, with the tears raining down her sunburnt face, in that part of the Litany when the people chant after the priest, "Lord have mercy upon us!" would startle the refined, indifferent, and well-dressed religionists of some of our fashionable churches; or a ferocious-looking creature in sheepskins, with wild eyes, and wilder wandering locks, bending before a Madonna, with the love and tenderness of a repentant child, and perfectly unconscious of all around.

But I am wandering as usual, and forgetting the bride and the wedding altogether. As I told you, the centre of the church was illuminated with an immense number of tapers; the arrangement of the pulpit and old carved stalls on either side was much after the manner of our cathedrals, only pictures of saints, and martyrs, and apostles, covered the arched walls of the aisles on either side. A small table, with a richly-embroidered velvet cover, was placed in the centre of the beautiful mosaic pavement; on it lay an ancient-looking volume, with large silver clasps, and round it were three or four rich Persian prayer-mats for the bride to walk on. The smell of myrtle in the church was delicious, the pavement being thickly strewn with fresh branches of it, from the door to the table. The crowd was already great, and it was with difficulty that Dr. Baretta got us even standing-room near the table, the stalls being filled with Greek ladies, and the aisles behind crowded by the peasantry, work-people of the convent, boys, babies, caiquejees, and nondescripts of all sorts. However, close to the pulpit, in a stall by herself, sat a Greek girl of the island, evidently quite comfortable and happy. Unfortunately for her, a robed Greek priest motioned her to give me her seat. I made a gesture expressive of "Pray don't disturb yourself!" and she hesitated, until a thundering reproof from his Reverence, sent her flying into the crowd. I was sorry for her, but nevertheless glad of her place, like a new minister here when his friend had been banished or bowstrung. I had now an excellent view, and could leisurely survey the curious and novel scene before me. Two figures interested me greatly: one was an old Greek woman leaning on a staff, her white hair bound round the scarlet fez upon her head; the other a sweet, fair child of five, who had seated herself unceremoniously in the old pulpit, and kept looking, with a quiet air of amusement and pleasure, from the pictured saints and martyrs to the blazing lights and robed priests and crowd of eager spectators.

And now we heard the curious, droning kind of chant used in all ceremonies of the Greek Church. It was evident that the bride and bridegroom were coming. A man who would have been a beadle in England (he was a swarthy, thin, robed, and bearded potentate here), knocked a number of impatient boys on the back, or pulled frantically at their ragged locks and jackets, to keep them quiet, and cast a peculiarly ferocious look at the "singing boys," to keep their wreathed rushlights straight—gave a woman a push, whose baby was engaged in an earnest attempt to pinch the little silver finger of St. Demetrius—separated two fiery, brigand-looking youths, greatly inclined to stab each other upon the pulpit-steps—hushed a couple making love too desperately under the very blackest and primmest Madonna, and gently insinuated a large and particularly threatening-looking island dog out of the crowd. O English beadle! what would you have said?

But here come the "footmen" of the bride, most respectable-looking men; for the bride's family are, I am told, rich, and boast "highly respectable" connections. These fine specimens of stalwart Greeks carried lighted tapers about five feet high, each composed of three candles, bound together after the fashion of the fasces of Roman lictors, but affectionately, in this case, with white satin ribbons; while as near the united flame as may be prudent, smile orange and jasmine blossoms in bonds of the same gentle, promising, and fair white satin, with long shining ends, expressive of the fullest measure of happiness. Well, the Greeks, with these gigantic wreathed tapers, stand aside, and in sweep, chanting solemnly, the long-bearded and magnificently robed priests. This is a very grand wedding, for the Patriarch himself is here, and no less than eight bishops. Hand-in-hand in the midst of them walk the bride and bridegroom. The bishops range themselves at the further end of the table, the young couple standing before them, and then begins a solemn Litany, to which every one makes responses, bending low and reverently. Now the Patriarch himself advances toward the bride, gives her his hand to kiss, and swings a beautiful silver censer, breathing delicious incense, over her bowed head several times; he is a most amiable-looking old gentleman, but small, and sadly muffled up in an immense white beard, with gorgeous robes and a scarf much too large for him. According to our notions, I cannot say that I discovered any thing earnest or impressive, either in the Patriarch or in the service. The Patriarch hurried over it as fast as possible, stopping now and then to reprove, in a snappish way, any priest who made a mistake in the responses, which, by-the-by, they often seemed to do, and the old gentleman had sharp ears. The chanting certainly is the most horrible nasal noise possible to conceive. I have thought over many words by which to express its effect upon my senses;—*brutal* is the only term, strange and harsh as it may sound. The first time I heard this chanting was at a grand thanksgiving: I first laughed and then cried, and was never more shocked or distressed in my life.

Most of the bishops look like a mixture of Friar Tuck and a brigand; their huge beards shake with their stentorian voices, as they bawl one against another, and haul their heavy mantle over their burly shoulders as if it were a coat-of-mail. One of the robed boys, holding a taper, was letting a stream of fat fall on the floor; a bishop gave him a hard slap, accompanied with a ferocious look, and then went on with his Litany.

I was glad when the chanting was over: the heat was frightful, and we felt ready to faint. The poor bride, closely hemmed in with friends, bishops, and crowds of spectators, looked very pale; not a breath of air stirred, the smell of incense was overpowering, and it was sickening to see the tallow streaming from the tapers on to the flowers, and large drops falling from the faces of the priests. How I longed for the ceremony to be over! But now began the most interesting and important part. The bride and bridegroom slowly and distinctly repeat a vow word by word after the Patriarch, who then joins their hands. Each gives the other a ring, which is exchanged several times from one to the other, with a prayer from the Patriarch, and at last placed on the finger of each. Then comes another chant, to which there is a solemn response of "Ameen" from priests and people. The Patriarch then takes the bride's ring again from her finger, and touches with it her brow, the top of her head, her temples, each side of her head, her eyebrows, between her eyes—in fact all her phrenological bumps. This ring he now puts on the bridegroom's finger, and again taking his lately given one, touches his bumps with it in the same manner as he has just done those of the bride, and with the same prayers and exhortations he places it once more on her finger.

The couple are now married, and I see the bridegroom press the lady's hand with a look of great satisfaction; he is a fine and tolerably good-looking young man. Now his "friend" brings forward two beautiful wreaths of artificial orange-blossom and jasmine, over which fall a profusion of long glittering gold threads; they are fastened together with rather wide white ribbon, two or three yards being allowed for the "tether." The patriarch places one on the head of the bride, and another on that of the bridegroom, who looks remarkably uncomfortable and somewhat ridiculous in it; the gold threads tickle his face, and ramble in confusion amidst the luxuriance of his black mustachios; these wreaths are changed three times from head to head, and are then allowed to remain.

After this the Patriarch takes the hand of the bride (who kisses his with great devotion), and leads her round the table, her husband following like a lamb, and by this time perfectly subdued by the gold thread, and by terror of his wreaths falling off. Three times they scamper hurriedly round, the bishops and priests following in splendid confusion as best they may. Then the wretched couple kneel, and kiss the grand old missal, and receive the benediction of the Patriarch. But the heat now became so frightful, and the crowd had increased so greatly, that it was impossible for me to see every thing that passed. I only know it was a great relief to hear that it was over.

The mother of the bride now entered the church, walked up to the velvet-covered table, knelt, and kissed the book. Then she rose and kissed the hand of the Patriarch, and then turned, with evidently great emotion, to her daughter, who instantly knelt on the pavement at her mother's feet: the latter raised her, and kissed first her marriage wreath and then her face many times. Then she kissed her son-in-law's wreath and face; he seemed very fond of his mother-in-law, kissed her half-a-dozen times, and then wiped a good shower of tears hastily from his eyes. Then began the general kissing of both. First the bride's sister, a verp pretty girl, with golden hair, gave a long embrace, with a few tears,—then the brothers,—then the friends. First they kissed the wreaths, then each cheek, and lastly the lips. I was very much amused at the heartiness with which young ladies on tiptoe gave kiss after kiss to this wreathed, flushed, and happy-looking bridegroom, who returned them all, with interest, in the most obliging manner. But the Patriarch and bishops feeling, I dare say, tired and thirsty from the heat, soon put a stop to this, and the procession was again formed. First went the torch-bearers; then the Patriarch and four robed priests, their gold embroidery glittering in the uncertain light; then the bride and bridegroom, hand-in-hand, still wearing their wreaths, and looking of course supremely happy although rather fatigued; then the rest of the priests and bishops, chanting as they went in a confused mass of guests, island Greeks, monks, and women.

Oh, the delicious breeze, when at last we reached the portal and gained the court-yard! Here we stood to mark the fine effect of light and shadow, as the procession crossed the cloisters and entered the Patriarch's house. The dark faces and picturesque costumes grouped around and under the old fountain-tree looked splendid, illumined fitfully by the flaming torches held by the Greek servants, and by the garlanded tapers of the procession.

A splendid German band, which has been some time in Constantinople, now struck up some graceful music, to which we listened for a few minutes, and then followed the procession into the monastery. The salaamlik was fearfully hot and crowded. The principal room beyond was lighted up with wax candles placed in old-fashioned chandeliers round the wall. On a table in the middle of the room was a splendid bouquet of Eastern flowers. The bride and bridegroom, wreathed, sat on the divan at the top of the room, still accepting and dispensing kisses and shakes of the hand. Presently the wreaths were given by the Patriarch to the bride's mother; they are preserved with the greatest care, and buried in the grave of which ever of the two who wore them dies first.

I have little more to tell you. I wished the bride all happiness, and she thanked me very sweetly and gracefully. Beautiful trays of sweetmeats were now handed round by the bride's sister and mother, and each person had a lapfull; I tied mine up in my handkerchief, and have kept the prettiest for Edith. The Patriarch and bishops, now in their old black gowns, and tucked up comfortably on the divan, were very sociable, and chatted to every one who could chat to them.

We took each a glass of pink liqueur together, and then made our adieu, for all the ladies were ranged around the room waiting for the dancing to begin. They much wished us to stay, but a fresh breeze had sprung up, and I did not think it prudent to delay crossing, as a tremendous current into the Sea of Marmora runs between our island and the one where we had been witnesses of the ceremony of which I have been giving you a sketch. We had a charming walk to our caique. Nothing could be finer than the magnificent old avenue of cypresses, lighted up by the monks with flaming torches of pine-wood, to guide coming and returning guests. We found the sea very angry, and huge waves dashing violently against the shore. It was moonlight, and the "Edith Belina" was soon in a flow of wild silver waves,—leaving the dark island of Halki, with the blazing lights of the monastery on the heights, and the twinkling lights of its cottages beneath, far behind her.

The bride will receive visitors for three days; and for three days coffee and sweetmeats and liqueurs will be handed round to all comers. After this patient long-suffering, things settle down to their ordinary routine. A very tedious, fatiguing affair a Greek wedding must be altogether! But I must say good-night. The heat has been fearful to-day. It is now ten o'clock: the cicalas are still chirping, but every thing else is languid and quiet. Best love to all!

LETTER LIII.

EXCURSION TO ISMID—MOUNTAIN SCENERY—ISLANDS—FISHING-VILLAGES—RAMBLES ON SHORE—VEGETATION—ISLAND SCENERY—INSECTS AND FISHES—RETURN TO PRINKIPO.

Prinkipo, August 18th, 1856.

My dearest Mother:

On Tuesday last Signor Vitalis, a rich and hospitable Greek merchant here, invited us to join a party of friends going to Ismid, the ancient Nicomedia. I had often wished, in our caique excursions, to get further, within view of the misty mountains to our right, and was delighted at the prospect of steaming along the coast of Asia to the very end of the Gulf of Nicomedia. It was arranged that we islanders were all to assemble on the pier at Prinkipo, at eight o'clock in the morning. Nothing could be more lovely than the weather—sea and sky one unclouded blue. The white walls and minarets of Stamboul shone in the bright sunlight far over the waves, and on the wild Asian coast the solitary fishing-villages, scattered few and far between, and the white-sailed caiques moving slowly about, were plainly visible.

Like a little speck, a white bird on the waters, we first saw the "Sylph," miles away—the air is so clear here. When she came nearer, she looked very pretty, with her white awning and gay flags. We were soon off, every one being punctual, (except a little island donkey, who had to bring a supply of spring-water on board, and kept us a few minutes waiting), and were soon steaming as close in to the Asiatic shore as possible. The view opposite these islands gives you a great idea of vast space and solitariness: hill upon hill, mountain upon mountain, immense slopes, broad plains, low marshes, long vistas of sandy beach, and not a sign of a human being, not a human habitation or wreath of smoke, to be seen. Sometimes, after noting all this solitariness for awhile, you feel quite startled by making out a far-off field or olive-garden, and then, screened by a few cypresses, some ancient-looking wooden houses, desolate as the burnt-up fields around them.

Nearly opposite the Convent of St. George here, the Asiatic coast becomes more and more mountainous. I often watch with great interest two magnificent peaks, where snow-white vapors, tinged with rose-color, rise majestically from the valleys on the other side, and flow slowly over them, throwing beautiful shadows over the dark-green slopes of the mountain. Near the summit of the lowest of these peaks is a small group of cypress-trees; and tradition says that this is the burial-place of Hannibal. Irene, the imprisoned Queen of Byzantium, must have often thought of this when standing on the heights of her convent here. This part of the world is marvelously full of historical and legendary interest.

Some cool morning (if ever there will be one) I intend trying to reach those cypress-trees. They say it can be done in five or six hours, and at least one would have a magnificent view of Mount Olympus, and of these lovely islands, the Sea of Marmora, and the Golden Horn, far, far away, besides the curious delight of thinking that one *may* be sitting by the grave of Hannibal.

I am writing very lazily, for the heat is great, and I am afraid of giving you but a faint idea of the marvelous loveliness of the islands, sea, and coast, through which we passed. But fancy one of the sweetest bits of the Surry Hills rising abruptly out of the water, only with gray rocks, covered with dark arbutus, heather, and all sorts of wild plants, reaching to white sands and dark-blue waves. Fancy misty mountains, with snow glittering on their tops, on one side, a wild and magnificent coast on the other; wild sea-birds and wilder-looking Greek feluccas occasionally darting by; a convent or ruin standing out here and there in the bold outline of some noble cliff, and you may have some notion of what I think would be quite Paradise, *if* the trees were larger.

We passed several small islands, which seemed uninhabited. Stone-pines grew so close to the cliffs as to hang quite over them. The rocks were of wonderful beauty and variety of color, and the contrast of the brilliant green of the luxurious arbutus and heath growing on them, with the dark-gray and red-and-brown of the different strata, was the most beautiful thing to the eye that can be conceived. Every now and then a dark eagle soared calmly round his possessions, scarcely ever deigning to flap a wing; or large black-and-white sea-hawks flew round and about the huge masses of rock that had toppled far out into the waves, which were surging up them with a pleasant murmur. It was very lovely, and I often thought how you would have enjoyed moving along in these dreamlike seas. The last island was the most charming, having an uninterrupted view of Mount Olympus and the coasts on either side. On it, embowered in the fir and arbutus trees, we detected three or four small, heather-thatched huts, and in a little creek covered with white sand, lay several fishing caiques idle, and their sails furled. A small scarlet pennant floated from each tiny mast, in honor of the Courbam Bairam. It seemed almost surprising to see any note of holidays in so remote and silent a place.

Soon after passing these green island-gems we were fairly in the Gulf of Nicomedia. It is much wider than the Bosphorus: the mountains are three times the height, and, instead of white palaces and lovely terraced gardens, the shores are marvelous in rocks and cliffs and the wildest caves imaginable. I do not know why I should compare them, only a thought crossed my mind of the wonderful beauty, in its way, of each Strait—the Bosphorus, soft and flowing, dreamy and luxurious—Nicomedia, wild and grand, and savage and solitary, to me so much more beautiful.

I often think that, once past the island of Antigone, you are at home, that you can love the country as well as admire it. It is our own dear mother Nature here, and all her sounds are alike sweet and pleasant. On the Bosphorus you constantly hear the Muezzin's call from the minaret—the thunder of guns announcing that the Sultan has gone to mosque, or that it is Ramazan, or Bairam, or some other Mohammedan feast, or the day when the Prophet went to heaven on a white camel, or when he rode among the faithful on a brown one; you can never forget, or lose sight of the unhappy, degraded state of the women—you are always longing to do something signally dreadful to the pashas, and secretly grieving for the people—you are constantly vexed to see dirty streets, dilapidated mosques and fountains, and every thing going wrong. In fact, one grieves and mourns and rails at Constantinople till one is tired; but this sea might be the Lake of Como, and the land the Surry hills, only with rocks and cliffs and caiques and figs and olives and old convents and pomegranates and eagles and centipedes and monks; and it is really extraordinary what variety of scenery and objects a sail of two hours along these coasts offers. You may imagine then how delightful it was to leave island after island, village after village, far behind—to come within sight of lofty mountains crowned with vast forests, range after range, one beautifully undulating line after another, until terminating at the shore in vast cliffs and towering rocks covered with plane-trees and pine-trees and superb laurels, heath, and juniper. Every now and then this grand landscape—the profound silence, and the absence of every sign of humanity—the huge rocks, rising like islands abruptly out of the sea—the mountains shining with snow far above the dark woods, Mount Olympus hemmed in like a giant in his holdfast, and crowned with his white helmet, which even this fierce sun has no power to pierce—the hazy, dreamy light above the highest points, uniting them in a soft violet bloom to the masses of snowy cloud—all this wild and silent magnificence impressed us much with a feeling, or rather sensation, that it was antediluvian. Enormous dolphins were sporting about, sometimes rising completely out of the water, just like those in ancient prints. It must be a grand place for fossils: I dare say we might have found the bones of some leviathan on the shore. However, there are plenty of jackals and wolves, wild boars, and some bears too, who might possibly feel inclined to add ours to the collection; so it might be as well not to venture without a good guard. Signor Vitalis talks of going in the winter with a hunting party and well armed.

At last we turned the corner of a noble gray rock crowned with superb tufts of heath and arbutus (the richest and brightest green conceivable), and here were signs of life. Eighteen fishing caiques of the antique form, their lofty beaks and prows adorned with a rude embroidery of large blue beads, lay at anchor in a little bay formed by the jutting rocks. It was the prettiest and most picturesque little fleet one could well imagine, and covered with Turkish flags and streamers in honor of Bairam.

A small fishing-village lay half-way up the cliff, approached by a winding path through an olive-plantation. On each side were vineyards; beyond them, the wild mountainous, arbutus-covered land; the minaret of a tiny mosque showed from behind a small clump of cypresses, but not a soul was visible; all I suppose were reposing, as it was Bairam and mid-day. We were now making but slow progress, for a strong breeze had sprung up against us, which soon lashed up a stormy sea. Some of the waves dashed up so high that two or three of us sitting in the prow of the vessel got a good ducking. The full rolling tide of dark-blue water, with the "white horses" rushing furiously along, looked singularly beautiful, contrasted with the many-shaded green of the woods, and olive-gardens and vineyards. Our eyes followed with delight Greek barks bounding along, every snow-white sail set, and tacking for some distant mountain-village, just to be made out high, high above, nestled in dark oaks and cypresses. Immense dolphins kept darting after our ship with singular rapidity, sometimes leaping quite out of the water, and then suddenly disappearing in its sparkling depths. It certainly was a most lovely journey.

Presently we came to a Greek fishing-village again, but of considerable size. By its side were the ruins of a large fortress, the walls of which were covered with the same bright-green shrubs of the most luxuriant beauty. Here also the caiques lay in the same holiday idleness on the beach. The vineyards seemed to be very fine, and large golden-colored melons were basking by hundreds in the sultry fields near the houses. Every here and there we perceived, nested among the rocks, the little huts of shepherds, but neither sheep nor goats were to be seen. Nothing seemed stirring on shore, and on the sea only ourselves, and the restless sea-birds, and one or two wandering feluccas. The rocks beyond this were surpassingly fine, picturesque, and varied. We often thought, "Here are the walls and battlements of a ruined castle, with huge masses fallen down and heaped upon the shore;" but, on looking closer, we found that no mortal hands had ever piled or hewn them, that the lords of these giant keeps had never been other than the eagle or sea-hawk—as good masters perhaps as the ferocious chiefs of olden time.

The breeze had now increased to a gale; some of the ladies were ill, others frightened, and we made but little way against the rush of wind and water rolling down the gulf. To my great regret, Signor Vitalis told me there was no hope of reaching Ismid (Nicomedia) in time to return that night; it is seventy miles from Constantinople. I was greatly disappointed at first, wishing so much to see the remains of an old castle and wall built when Nicomeds, the King of Bithynia, lived there. However, there was nothing to be done but wonder why people who are ill with a breeze ever go to sea for pleasure. Signor Vitalis was most kind, and anxious to please everybody.

Another pretty wild-looking village soon came in sight. We looked out anxiously for trees, and seeing some of considerable size in a little valley near the shore, agreed that it would be very pleasant to land there, Ismid being now out of the question; and so our anchor was quickly cast in the quiet bay. Here, with the usual fun and laughter and chat and flirtation of a picnic, we dined; at least, a most tempting repast was served; but it was too hot for any one but cheerful "Commissary Joe" to eat, and to drink we were afraid. Somehow or other I think it would take a great deal to make that remarkable man and Crimean hero afraid of iced champagne—an earthquake, or comet at least, some one suggested!

A number of large caiques, rowed by fine, hardy-looking Greeks, now glided up to the "Sylph," and all bent on pleasure and with the spirit of adventure, started in them for a ramble on shore. There was a little wooden pier stretching some distance out into the sea. The village seemed to be inhabited also by Turks, for in a remote corner rose a small minaret, with the usual dark cypresses, gently bending their heads to the wind. Once on shore, people separated and went their several ways: some walked straight to the trees to sit down; others proposed a stroll through a magnificent ravine, leading inland; many wished to see the village, which seemed primitive and picturesque. One mentioned ripe grapes in the vineyards, and hinted at green figs; another pointed to a glorious gray cliff covered with arbutus and myrtle, and commanding a view of marvelous beauty. "Bother your fine scenery!" growls Commissary Joe; "I shall do like a sensible man, go and drink a cup of coffee with that jolly old Turk there." He disappeared in a little wooden kiosk built over the sea, at the door of which several villagers quietly smoked and regarded us. I do not know who followed him, for a few of us resolved to stroll along the shore, and see what was to be seen beyond a fine cliff, which stretched its rugged green sides far out into the sea. But it was easier to *talk* of walking than to *walk* to-day, the heat was so oppressive. The ground was so hot that it quite burnt our feet, and the sun struck from the rocks with the scorching fierceness of an oven. Without the wind it would have been impossible to move; as it was, we did not meet a single living thing—not a sound but the dashing of the waves below, and above, on the olive and fir-trees, the constant "trill, trill," of countless cicalas. We found ourselves toiling up a rough, chalky road, cut in the most picturesque manner out of the cliff. Below us lay the sea, then came rocks, and then a thick border of olive-trees skirting the pathway. High above us, on the other side, were luxuriant vineyards, studded every here and there with a dark fig or pomegranate. This side of the road was fenced also with olive and wild Daphne, and many (to me) unknown shrubs. I noticed one in particular, which I saw last year growing on rocks by the Black Sea. It is like the ash, only smaller and much more delicate-looking, and bears the loveliest bunches imaginable of berries just like coral, its stems charmingly shaded in delicate pink and brown. On this and many other of the trees hung a very pretty parasitical plant; long threads of pale, delicate green, with an exquisite little bunch of tiny golden flowers, at about four inches apart, on it. I was so concerned at having neither my boards nor even a book with me to preserve a specimen. Here also grew in profusion on the rocks the kind of juniper, bearing clusters of bright yellow berries, of which they tell me henna is made, which dyes the Turkish ladies' hands and feet. There were wild artichokes, their heads hoary with soft white wool, wild asparagus, and, what I was charmed to see, the real, wild, original hollyhock, single but brilliant, and not nearly as large as the favorite of our English shrubberies. Then I came upan large masses of a plant of which I was determined at least to try and get a specimen. It grows seven or eight feet high, and is covered with long spikes of lavender-colored blossom, having a most pleasant smell, something, to my fancy, like eau-de-Cologne: the leaf just resembles that of the lupine. Round these bushes fluttered a marvelous display of insect life; superb butterflies, large and small; immense purple humble-bees, looking at first more like beetles; and richly-feathered moths, with mouselike faces, beautifully streaked with cream-color and pink down the back. A collector would have been wild with delight and perplexity which to catch first, the lovely yellow butterfly with purple eyes, or the black-and-white velvet one, or the one studded with jewels and "eyes" quite shaming our "peacock," or the tiny white-and-scarlet thing, or the gleaming blue, or the exquisite green. I have long resisted making a collection, not having the means of depriving the poor happy things of life quickly and effectively. However, I have succeeded in getting two excellent specimens of the sweet-smelling plant and insect paradise to add to my Eastern "Flora." They laugh at me very much for scrambling about in the heat, but it is impossible to see so many pretty things unmoved.

Here I found two snail-shells of gigantic proportions, richly streaked and ringed with brown. Some goats had evidently been clambering up the cliff, and had dislodged them from the loose broken-up chalk and iron strata. I shall show them to Dr. Hassell, believing them to be very curious and rare.*

We now came to a truly magnificent fig-tree; its wide-spreading branches and massive leaves quite overshadowed the little mountain-road, and made a pleasant shade. Sloping upward from it was a vineyard, and many pomegranates covered with yet unripe fruit. "Here we will rest!" we all exclaimed. So we rested, and talked about the sultry heat, and listened to the cicalas, and wished for the cool, soft song of a bird, and marveled at the huge piles of rock fallen near us (among even the figs and vine,) and at

* Mr. Buckland tells me that these snails were highly esteemed by the Romans, and that even in these days they are evidence of a Roman settlement having existed on the spot where they are found.

the splendid beauty of the forest-covered mountains opposite and the fir-clad shore. We regretted a little too not getting on to Ismid, as the coasts were becoming finer at every turn. But that was useless, and as the rest of the party were too tired and too much exhausted by the heat to move just yet, I resolved upon seeing if possible what was beyond the next projecting cliff. So off I started, promising to return in ten minutes.

I gained the top of the hill, and the view was indeed glorious. Then who could resist winding down again into the valley, it was so beautiful! I sat down on a piece of rock shaded by some olive-trees, thoroughly enchanted. Before me lay a vast fallen cliff, almost coverd with bright plants and shrubs; but what pleased and charmed me most was to see a silvery shower of "Travelers'-joy" streaming down its rugged sides. How it reminded me of English woods and lanes! I had not seen it before in Turkey, and it seemed like an old and dear friend.

This was a delicious place to rest in. I watched the bright lizards creeping in and out of the crevices in the rocks, and fancied that sometimes their quick bright glance rested on me. Opposite was a dark-brown cave; heavy creeping-plants hung in thick masses over its entrance, and laughing, fluttering vine-leaves peeped in from above. Pretty rock-doves were cooing, and constantly flying in and out—the only sound that broke the profound silence. "Now," I thought, "I must go, although I shall never see this lovely place again." So I arose, with a lingering look at the deep shade, but still could not turn back, and resolved quite desperately to see round the next cliff. I kept my face turned as much to the wind as I could, and ah, what a delight it was to see a new reach or vista of this magnificent gulf! Never shall I forget it! The path now wound downward, and I found myself within a few feet of the shore: it was impossible to resist, so I scrambled over burning rocks and stones, and soon stood by the waves—the same mighty rush of dark-blue water—a nearer view of Olympus! Plunging my little white umbrella into a pool amongst the rocks, in order to defy the sun's ray, I rushed on from stone to stone, forgetting the heat, the distance from my party, my promise, every thing. Never had I conceived any thing so beautiful and so grand! The sea and the mountains, and the solitary shore garlanded with vineyards and pomegranates and all sorts of bright and shining plants. At last I sat down in a beautiful little bay.

So great was the impression this scene made upon my mind, so keen the delight with which I almost desperately endeavored to impress upon it even the smallest details, that even now I have the greatest pleasure in recalling it, only with a deep regret at the feebleness of all description in comparison to the reality. I kept saying to myself, "In this life I never shall behold it again," and literally could not tear myself away. On many of the smooth stones lay beautiful pieces of sea-weed, and several corallines of great beauty. I tried to gather some of these, but the heat of the sun had made them brittle, and to my great regret I only preserved a few fragments. Here one might think that some of the large stones had lain undisturbed since the Deluge. I saw many petrifactions —in fact enough to make one's heart ache, having no means of transporting them. However, I am partly consoled while writing now, by two pieces of stone on my table before me, one white and the other red, completely incrusted with fossil-shells, which I managed to carry off, together with two small ones. I could not have come away without some token from this lovely shore.

I do not know how long I sat there, and it seems now a vivid and pleasant dream of the old world, unchanged since the imperial galleys of Diocletian floated by. I remember tracing out the tracks of snow on a far-off mountain, and thinking that shining in the rays of the evening sun, they looked like silver streams broken loose from some enchanted fountain—and watching the lights and shadows on the distant valleys, and suddenly discovering a tiny village, built of dark wood, nestling under a hanging pine-forest, and its little pathway winding—winding through the brushwood, and thinking I should like to know all about the solitary lives of the peasants in this wild home, and many other things. A little pool of the clearest water lay at my feet. How delighted Edie would have been to watch the small, many-colored fish darting about in it, and the "soldier-crab" (his small crimson body hanging out of the long spiral shell to which he has fitted himself,) fishing industriously for his supper! I noticed one remarkably pretty crab, of a delicate salmon-color, spotted richly with brown. He seemed a most intelligent little fellow, and was fishing dexterously for a tiny sand-colored fish, not much larger than a shrimp. When he succeeded in catching one, he buried his little back in the sand to keep himself steady, and ate his prey with great gusto: then tidily and briskly cleaning his feelers, he bustled off sideways in search of another in the bright and shifting sand. Shining at my feet, amongst the sea-weed, lay a lovely purple-lined shell, which I had never seen before, and was delighted to add to my collection. I thought of Tennyson's exquisite inquiry as to the inmate of a shell found on the sand, "void of the little living Will, that made it stir on the shore:"

"Did he stand at the diamond door
Of his house in a rainbow frill?
Did he push, when he was uncurl'd,
A golden foot or a fairy horn
Through his dim water-world?"

But every pleasant hour must come to an end, so I took another wide, long look, put my stones under my arm, and my tender corallines, protected by sea-weed, as safely as I could in my pocket, and bent my steps toward the little valley of the fig-tree. Now I began to think that it was a long weary way off, that they would be frightened about me, and that there were Greek pirates all along the coast, they said, in the shape of the fishermen and others. Man Friday's footprint on the sand could not have startled Robinson Crusoe more than a fine bunch of grapes lying on a stone did me, for I knew that some wild Greek or Croat must be near. However, on the next hill I saw Edmund, who had come to meet me, and to scold, and I was taken down to the village at a rapid pace, hugging my treasures, and feeling very much like a naughty child taken in the act of straying and birds'-nesting.

We found a detachment of our party in the little cafanée, sipping coffee and lemonade. They were all delighted with their several strolls. Some had been into the vineyards, others up the deep ravine into the valley beyond—in winter, a mountain-stream. There were a few fine Turks of the old school, with magnificent turbans, smoking their nargilehs calmly on the benches. They seemed to wonder what we were about—indeed to wonder exceedingly, when they beheld my stones, and fossils, and my tired looks. The coffee and lemonade were both excellently fragrant and good, and after such a tiring excursion doubly enjoyed. The wind had now dropped, and we rested pleasantly in the little cafanée, listening to the calm ripple of the waves on the shore, and to the deep whispered conversation of our majestic neighbors, sitting cross-legged on the benches. Then we bade adieu to these picturesque and kingly villagers, and stepping into the caiques were once more on board the "Sylph."

We steamed rapidly and pleasantly back, and reached Prinkipo just as the moon was rising, and the monotonous evening songs of the Greeks, and the twang of their guitars, were sounding from the "Magyar." I hope my account of a long summer's day on the shores of Asia will not have tired you. My chief pleasure when alone is in writing down all that has delighted me.

LETTER LIV.

THERAPIA—GREEK VILLAGE—ROMAN RESERVOIRS—SERVICE ON BOARD SHIP.

Therapia, August 25th, 1856.

My dear Sister:

We came here on Thursday, and found the cool breezes from the Black Sea very delightful. The next morning Mrs. Brett, Captain Murray, and myself started for the Forest of Belgrade. We took caique to Buyukdere, where a teleki awaited us, drawn by two wretched horses, meant to be white, but their natural brilliancy rather obscured by patches of dried mud. Our driver was a Greek; and a wild-looking Tartar boy sat by his side, and assisted in torturing the animals into what is commonly called a "jog-trot." How we envied Captain Murray, galloping on a bright bay at our side, especially when one terrific jolt dashed Mrs. Brett's head through one of the crazy windows, and I received a mild reproof from the driver for permitting mine to do the same at the next. We might well enjoy a ramble on the forest, when we got there, after such a shaking!

We stoppped near the village, for I was enchanted at the sight of a fine old fountain, overshadowed with ancient trees, and in a good state of preservation. Two Greek women stood there, in graceful attitudes, and with water-vases on their heads, just as they must have done in Lady Mary Wortley Montague's time. Do you not remember she describes this fountain, and the villagers assembling around it in the evening? We searched about the forest for the old Embassy-house in which she lived, and which still exists in tolerable repair, but unaccountably missed it, although we were afterward told that we had been close by. The villagers had not even a legend of either house or lady. However, we must go another day; for I would not miss seeing it on any account. We had such a pleasant day, walking about in the fine forest glades, richly tinted with many bright shades of autumn, and spreading far and wide. We made charming bouquets of wild flowers, finding a very curious one—a bright scarlet bell, closed at the bottom, and containing a single large red berry.

We took luncheon under a noble horse-chestnut tree, by one of the great Roman Bends, or reservoirs, and pleased ourselves with thinking that Lady Mary must often have sat on those very stones, beneath its shade, and listened to the roar of the waters, as we did. We lingered, unwilling to depart, till very late; and positively, by bribing our ragged drivers, we returned through the woods at a gallop, although how we escaped an overturn in the dark glades and roughly cut paths, I cannot imagine.

Yesterday we heard service on board the "Royal Albert," Lord Lyons kindly sending his own boat for us. We had the great pleasure of a short chat with his lordship; and when Lord and Lady Stratford arrived, all went on the upper deck. It is a magnificent ship, and the sight was a most grand and impressive one. About eight hundred men were ranged on the lower deck, sailors on one side and marines on the other, immense Union-jacks forming a screen behind them. The service began with the Morning Hymn, sung by all on board, and led by the trained band of sailors and a few wind instruments. It was almost too much to bear, so profoundly affecting was the deep and powerful burst of voices on the quiet sea, and so far away from home, of men returning safe to England after all the dangers they had gone through in this terrible war. Many still bore traces of severe wounds; almost all wore two or three medals. Adieu!

LETTER LV.

CLIMATE AND SCENERY—PARADISE OF THE GREEKS—BOATING EXCURSIONS—THE MONASTERY OF ST. GEORGE—THE OLD GARDENER—HIS SUMMER RESIDENCE—"THE MAGYAR"—ARMENIAN AND GREEK LADIES—GREEK HOMAGE TO BEAUTY—BURNING A CAIQUE—FISHING BY NIGHT.

Princes' Island, September 6th, 1856.

My dear Mr. Hornby:

I find life in the islands very pleasant in summer-time, even with nothing more to occupy me than the birds and crickets, and holiday-making Greeks. Not having wings, and not having learned to smoke cigarettes on a donkey, I idle about in the "Edith Belina" from one shady creek to another, or make excursions to the monasteries, or to the opposite shore. The days are very long, for the early mornings are so deliciously cool and fresh, and the Greeks so noisy and restless, that sleep after five or six would be difficult even for a dormouse. I have been up several times by daybreak. It is such a beautiful sight to see the huge volumes of mist roll upward, the outlines of the opposite mountains gradually revealing themselves, and the first rosy tints of sunrise stealing over the dark gray of sea and land. When the sun bursts forth in all his splendor, it is a picture indeed, or rather a series of most beautiful ones, from the distant minaretted city to the green islands near. Presently, by the glittering of window-panes, you can mark tiny villages nestled far up the wild mountain-side opposite, and here and there fishing-villages clustering along the shore. Caiques, with their white sails set, are soon out and busy on the blue waves; the monotonous chant of the fishermen sounds pleasantly in the fresh morning air. Then a picturesque-looking Greek sportsman steals by our cottage, his gun on his arm, and accompanied by two or three dogs of irregular breed, and almost as wild-looking as himself. Then slowly come the shepherds, their mixed flocks of goats and sheep frisking merrily to the sound of the tinkling bells of the "guides," who snatch fragrant branches of the arbutus and cistus as they go by. The scent of the wild shrubs here is very pleasant, and they grow in the greatest luxuriance on the stony, uneven ground. I have found several varieties of heath in great beauty. There being no large trees on these islands, they always look most beautiful morning and evening, when the sun is low, just touching the sloping vineyards, and the short, dim, olive-trees; and then, of course, the fine gray rocks and the ruined monasteries above seem to rise higher out of the dark blue water.

The Greeks of Constantinople consider Prinkipo as their paradise on earth, and begin a regular course of monotonous amusement from the first moment of their arrival; which is scarcely varied for a single day, up to the last instant of their stay. About seven in the morning all the visitors who have not departed for Pera by the early steamer, are to be seen (if you take caique toward the village) wending to the little wooden bathing-houses on the shore. Some of these people have returned from an early donkey-ride up the mountain—most from the divan and cup of coffee. Through all the sultry hours, until about four or five o'clock, everybody lies *perdu;* not even Signor Giacomo's Croat gardeners are to be seen, not even his sun-burnt children—scarcely a single caique moving about on the water; only under a large fir-tree opposite our windows a red-capped shepherd, fast asleep, with three or four drowsy goats about him, and a large, dark eagle or two soaring majestically about. The only sound is the ceaseless chirp of the cicala, a deep-toned grasshopper, which here dwells principally in the fir-trees. A dark cloud of heat hangs over distant Constantinople. I fancy that, if even we were nearer, we should hear no "city's hum" at mid-day. My caique is the only busy thing about.

I do not care the least for the hottest day here. With my straw hat filled with vine-leaves, the best defense against the sun, and my small and dripping white umbrella, immediately after bathing, I start on some pleasant little excursion. The Apple-blossom, who is really an institution, as Mr. Smythe says, packs up my luncheon, which Johannachi carries in a little basket. It usually consists of part of a chicken, hidden away in cool lime-tree leaves, bread, and a fine melon or bunch of grapes. There is almost always a pleasant breeze, even in the middle of the day; the sea sparkles so brightly—the waves dash round the rocks with such a pleasant sound—the "Edith Belina" bounds so delightfully from point to point—the mountains look so enchanting in the distance—that, lying on a comfortable cushion, with a book by my side, and no present care at my heart, I feel as gay and as inclined to wander on as the water and air about me. Sometimes I make the boatmen row as close in to the rocks as possible. These are wonderful in variety of shape and color, and what beautiful tints they throw on the water! Sometimes from the deepest recesses, wild doves and pigeons fly, startled by the sound of our oars, and then stop to coo in the next place where cool water gurgles in the shade. Wild festoons of sea-weed shade these pretty clefts above; below, sea-anemones and sea-weeds of most vivid and beautiful green, harbor swarms of many-tinted fish, which fly, startled, as you pass. Now and then you find a creek abounding with several kinds of pretty shells, and here and there a charming spot where heath and cistus and arbutus grow down to the very edge of the rocks. I should not dislike much to be a Byzantine banished princess, provided they left me in peace here with a good caique, and with liberty to do as I liked, and allowed Mr. Frank Buckland to pass a day or two with me occasionally. How startled the civilized world would be with tales of the lizards, rats, tortoises, crickets, sea-weeds, butterflies, ants, and frogs of this peculiarly favored spot!

But I must hasten to tell you what you wished to know—how one passes a long summer's day in the "Islands of the Blest." Well, sometimes I point to a small bay, about half-way round the island. My sturdy rowers pull rapidly in. The Monastery of St. George, perched on the very highest peak of mountain above, looks no bigger than a doll's house, left there by some spiteful fairy, to be shaken by winter tempests and scorched by summer glare. Walking a few paces over the white sand of the creek, you cross a low hedge-bank into the deep shade of some ancient fig-trees. This is the garden of the Monastery. The lay brother must be an active person I should think, if he descends the mountain every morning for the ascetic salads. The gardener is a remarkably fine, picturesque old Greek; he always comes to meet me, attended by his two wild, shaggy dogs, helps the boatmen to bring the cushions from the caique, and carefully picks out the coolest bit of shade under the wide-spreading fig-tree. He keeps a nice piece of matting, and some antique-shaped earthen water-jars of spring-water, always ready for the use of occasional visitors to his creek. The garden does not seem to be very productive, tomatoes being the principal crop, with here and there a patch of Indian corn, or a pomegranate-tree, and wild-looking vines trailing about, more remarkable for beauty than promise. The fig-trees are evidently the glory and richness of the place, and beautiful trees they are; their massive and deep green leaves just letting in enough golden sunlight to make pleasant shadows beneath. Johannachi spreads the luncheon with great glee, Janko and Pandalij search with the old gardener for the finest figs, while I stroll away to the hedgerow on the beach, in search of specimens for my collection of island plants. Hundreds of butterflies and beetles, and strange-looking purple bees are humming over a large scented plant with a lilac blossom, of which I know nothing, except that the leaf very much resembles that of a lupine. I must send a piece to my old friend and teacher of botany in pleasant days "lang syne," Dr. Arthur Hassall. After luncheon I sit and read. What thorough enjoyment it is, and how often I wish it were possible you could spend a morning with me! Having risen so early, by eleven o'clock I begin to feel tired, and generally enjoy a sound sleep on the cushions under the fig-tree; the caiquejees slumbering profoundly meanwhile in the "Edith Belina," and my tiny guard Johannachi either discussing melons and figs, or playing in the garden with the old man's dogs. By-the-by, the gardener's summer dwelling-place particularly struck me the first time of seeing it. Two or three planks were placed across some stout benches in the middle of an ancient fig-tree, opposite to those under which I am sitting. A Turkish quilt is neatly folded up upon them. Above this primitive bed, a piece of thick matting is hung, as a screen in case of a shower. Two or three brackets of rough wood are nailed up within reach. On one is a water-jar, on another a horn spoon. The poor old man's slippers are neatly placed on a small piece of matting at the foot of the tree, and two or three ancient garments hang on a broken branch close by. This fig-tree completely tells the story of his simple life and few wants—pleasant enough, I should think, in that lovely spot, with his faithful dogs and cheerful garden-work, had he books and a knowledge of them. If I ever turn recluse, it shall be in the Princes' Isles. In fact, the East must be a most perfect refuge for any one tired of "the world," or not having enough to exist on in it. How much bettter a garden and cave, or fig-tree here, with a knowledge of "simples," a reputation of being "uncanny," and the tender regard of the country-people in consequence (who would provide melons, and figs, and rice, in consideration and out of respect for your necromancy and your star-gazings toward Olympus), than the paltry battle of life in a great city! I think I shall set about founding a sect of female Dervishes composed of ill-used, distressed governesses, companions, and portionless daughters—kind, pitying young Dervishesses, who would put by their musings and missals, and cross a mountain now and then, to help the poor, ignorant, helpless people who believe in them. The Superiors should be elected from the sensible girls who preferred this sort of life to a *marriage de convenance*, or to an undignified dependence. What do you think of my plan? I know one or two young ladies to whom I should very much like to propose it. Fancy Louisa or Stella, attired in serge, in my fig-tree! One has plenty of time to dream away here—different from the constant movement and occupation of life in England. With a few dear friends within reach, this calm and freedom would be perfect. But I must continue my account of a day in the Islands.

By the time the sun begins to dip a little, we gather up cushions and books, and rouse the boatmen. Johannachi and I ramble on shore while the "Edith Belina" is made ready. Sometimes we find shells for Edith's collection, sometimes small pieces of malachite. Oh, if Danby could see the glow of purple and gold over the sands and rocks, and over our pretty caique and her Greeks!

We run away in that gorgeous light, waving an adieu to the kind old man, and his dogs who stand with friendly waggings at his side. He little knows what a picture he makes there, standing on the shore until we are almost out of sight. We soon land in our own creek, almost as lonely as Robinson Crusoe's; but by the time I reach the top of the hill, I see that all the beauty and fashion of Prinkipo is astir again.

The steamer is seen coming in from Pera, and Greek and Armenian ladies, with bright parasols over their heads, are hastening down to the "Magyar," at the pier, to meet their husbands and brothers, to smoke cigarettes, drink lemonade and sherbet, and eat walnuts ready cracked and pealed, which are handed about in glass water-jars by dirty Greek boys, at about twenty a piastre.

The "Magyar" is a kind of open-air coffee-house, which from morning till night is seldom quite deserted, but which is crowded with men, women, and children of an evening, when there is generally some kind of barbarous music as an accompaniment to the smoking. I never notice much conversation going on. The men are drinking *raki* among themselves—the women bedizened with all their little stock of finery, Eastern and European, staring at the men, but particularly at passing strangers. They really do not seem as if they had *esprit* enough to plague each other, or even to talk scandal! It is an amusing scene for once; but once is enough, for there is much that is painful. There is a Greek girl of seventeen, who ought to be extremely beautiful, and naturally as pale as marble. She has heard of English ball-dresses, and perhaps heard the English complexion admired, so she has thrown off the beautiful Greek dress in which I am told she looked lovely a year ago, put on an ill-made low dress, and painted her cheeks a light brick-dust color. Then came long rows of Armenian and Greek ladies, stars of fashion and caricatures of the worst style of French dress; then ancient dames, who, discarding the trowsers of old, have adopted half measures, and content themselves with flounced dresses

—retaining the fery or handkerchief on the head, and indulging occasionally in a cigarette; then, children, poor little things, dressed up in the most ridiculous manner in the world, so bedizened that you can scarcely see them, and the dirt beneath the finery—then a grave Turk or two walking quietly apart—Greek nurses—sherbet and fruit-sellers—noisy boys, dogs, waiters and caiques—all huddled up in a close atmosphere of tobacco and *raki*. There are three or four Magyars at Prinkipo. The largest is close to the pier—merely a covered way, but this is the most fashionable, as the ladies vie with one another for the foremost places on the benches, and little wooden stools, so that they may be well seen by those who arrive by the steamer. But there is one very pretty Magyar in the heart of the village; it is held under the wide-spreading branches of a magnificent plane-tree; a wooden seat is fixed all round the "giant bole," and dozens of little wooden stools are scattered about within the shade. At night the lower boughs are lighted up with lamps, and the picturesque groups of smokers and coffee-drinkers are really very striking in the broad light and shadow. Quaint, tumble-down rows of wooden houses lie in the shade on either side; here and there is a cafanée, filled with noisy drinkers, and lighted with the fitful glare of torches. Rows of silent Greek and Armenian ladies may be made out, sitting under the old trellised vines outside—perhaps listening to the most horrid scraping and groaning of the "Band" opposite; perhaps enjoying themselves, but they do not give any evidence of it. There are two or three beauties here this season; but, except to Greek eyes, it is difficult to discover them by the glaring and irregular light of the tree lamps at the Magyar, even when dozens of *madahs* are burning in their honor. The *madahs* are torches, which burn with a blue light not very favorable to any style of beauty but a spectral one.

When an admirer wishes to please the object of his particular devotion for the evening, he whispers to the master of the cafanée to burn so many piastres' worth of *madahs* opposite such and such a bench. The motley crowds strolling up and down the houses, the smokers, the rows of ladies, and above all *the* Beauty, are instantly lighted up in a glare of the most unearthly hue. The dark eyes of all the other ladies turn with envy to the object of this homage; the adorer makes a profound Eastern bow toward the bench on which she is seated. It is almost dark again, but the fiddlers scrape on. The next morning you people say: "So-and-so had two hundred *madahs* burned for her last night by So-and-So." I have heard that twenty or thirty pounds have on particular occasions been spent by a rich and enthusiastic young Greek for a very great Beauty; but an ordinary amount of gallantry is expressed in a few piastres' worth of blue light. When kind Lord Lyons brought all his midshipmen down here for a treat the other day, he burned so many *madahs,* in honor of the ladies generally, that half the heads in the Islands were turned by this homage from the great English admiral. His lordship left about ten o'clock, in a beautifully illuminated steamer, which we watched far on its way back to Constantinople. The boys were delighted with the trip, and their loud huzzas were heard on shore when the vessel was some distance out at sea. The word *madah* means "moonlight," but I am afraid Endymion would be disgusted at the very idea of a Magyar. In hot weather it is kept up all night. I do not know how late the ladies stay, but the men gamble and drink raki and smoke hour after hour. Often when the fresh dawn is breaking, I still hear the discordant notes of the droning music, borne over the water from Halki. I suppose this is a Greek form of pleasure.

We have been down to the village in an evening three or four times, just to see what was going on. The first night of our arrival, it was a kind of annual festival, when a caique is burned on the shore, as a peace-offering to malignant sea-spirits. The blaze of the burning boat spread far and wide, and groups of fishermen and caiquejees in their picturesque dress were very striking. They afterward joined hands, and forming a wide ring danced round, to a rude and measured kind of chanting. Their movements were extremely awkward and clownish, and the shouting any thing but harmonious—but this, I was told, was ancient Romaika. The whole scene would have been very fine on a vase.

I came home at about mid-day from Maltapè a village on the opposite shore, and have not stirred from my desk since. The steamer is very near the island, and I see the caique with its little red flag going out to meet her at Halki, which saves Edmund the steep walk up hither from the village.

Our caiquejees make it a point of honor for our boat to be first, and woe betide any caique which attempts to pass the "Edith Belina!" What a strain she gets for nothing! Mr. W. Tyrone Power is coming down again to-day, to stay a day or two—at least if the mosquitos will allow him. We find him an extremely agreeable companion. He has just come from Circassia, and has charmed me with his account of its shepherd warriors. There the mountaineer defends his own family—makes not only his own powder, but his own gun—shoes and dresses his own horse—shoots his own particular Russian enemy—is remarkable for beauty, hardihood, and intelligence! I shall ask more about them, and about the renowned chief, Schamyl, when we stroll by the sea-side in the quiet part of the island this evening, for so'will end our day. We always stay to watch the beautiful tints on the mountains and waves while they last, and then return home to tea. As soon as it is dark, fishing caiques appear with lights on board, which are used to decoy a particular kind of fish. They look so pretty, rising and falling on the sea in the soft gray of night.

LETTER LVI.

EXCURSION TO MALTAPE—GREEK WOMEN AND TURKISH CAFANEE—MARBLE FOUNTAIN—ANCIENT TREE—THE MOSQUE—THE IMAUM—VILLAGE SCHOOL—TURKISH WOMEN—CURIOUS LAMP.

The Islands, August 28th, 1856

My dear Mr. Hornby:

My last excursion was with Mr. Gisborne to Maltapè, a fishing-village on the Asiatic coast opposite. There are several larger ones further inland, nestling in the sides of the mountain, but it would not be safe to go so far without a strong escort. Some brigands robbed and murdered a poor man from Halki there but a few days ago. They supposed that he had a large sum of money about him, and said they were very sorry he was shot, as he lay dying upon the ground! His companion was allowed to depart in peace, with many polite expressions of regret. Since hearing this, I take Eugenio with me well-armed whenever I go to Maltapè. It is a pleasant sail across when we get a fair wind. The fishermen's children playing on the shore run down to the crazy little wooden pier of Maltapè to see us come in; some of them are pretty little creatures, but sadly neglected and dirty. Numbers of the youngest were mere babes, sleeping in the sand by the wooden walls of the Cafanée, beside the street dogs, who had scraped themselves comfortable nests there. Squalid, wretched-looking Greek women peeped out of the broken casements of their tumble-down wooden houses at us.

Some of them might have been extremely handsome, but hard work, poor food, and utter neglect had only left a harsh outline of the fine features which nature had given them. Such women at twenty have lost all trace of youth. Don't talk of witches, until you have seen some of the old ones! Many of the girls of ten or twelve here are beautiful—at least *would be*, if they were washed, and their long plaits of rough black hair combed. Lower down on the shore, numbers of the womankind of Maltapè were gathering fish in baskets from some large caiques; others were washing coarse garments in the waves, which came rippling gently round their bare feet. A few idle young girls, with gay handkerchiefs on their heads, were lolling in the sun at their doos, before which some brigand-looking Greeks were smoking on benches, under the usual trellis and vine-tree.

Further on was a Turkish cafanée, and three or four Turks were calmly enjoying their narghilies. They were of the old school, and looked majestic in their beards and turbans. We sat down at a little distance, and Eugenio brought us coffee from the curious old China fireplace within. We bowed, and they bowed; they seemed to enjoy our society, and we enjoyed theirs; we enjoyed the view of sea and land, so did they; language did not seem to be of the least consequence to such dignified, thoughtful people. The only sound was the ripple of the waves on the shore, the gurgle of the narghilies at their feet, and the twitter of swallows, so tame that they sat on a little wooden ledge just above the heads of the men, and on the rails of the bench beside them. It was quite touching to see the confidence which they showed in these kind and simple people. We paid the quaint master of the cafanée for the coffee, (I believe Eugenio had solaced himself with a chibouque in some mysterious corner,) and then went to explore the centre of the village, leaving the boatmen to enjoy themselves after their own hearts in a rough wooden cafanée overhanging the sea, where they could meditate amid clouds of smoke on the superior merits of the "Edith Belina" dancing below, over those of all other caiques, fishing or otherwise.

In the very heart of the village, shaded by a fine old tree, stands a large fountain of white marble, with inscriptions all around. It must once have been a very fine one, but is fallen sadly to decay; weeds and rank grass grow on the top, overhang the once illuminated letters, and stop the course of the water, which streams over the ground, instead of flowing into the little open tanks designed for the use of the thirsty traveler by the Hadji (pilgrim) who built it. Some Greek girls were filling their pitchers there, and a sturdy villager looking on. We begged Eugenio to say to him what a pity we thought it that they did not repair such a magnificent fountain—it might be so easily done. It now flooded the principal path, and gave the women who came to draw water so much difficulty in wading through the mud, especially the poor girls with bare feet. He answered all we could say to rouse his pride, or humanity, or common sense, with a shrug of the shoulders; which I suppose the whole village of them would do.

Opposite the fountain, on the other side of the square which forms the centre of the place, is one of the most magnificent old trees I have ever seen, evidently of great antiquity. Its branches are prodigious. Round the trunk is the usual rude wooden bench; and two or three rows of benches placed further out have no doubt received the principal part of the villagers of an evening, through many generations of smokers and coffee-drinkers, long since passed away. Close by is a raised fire-place for making coffee, and supplying charcoal to light the pipes: it is made of clay and stones, and lined with blue tiles of a curious pattern.

This is a most primitive and interesting old place, poor and ruinous as it is; and, as if to complete the picture formed by the ancient trees, and fountain, and hearth, a rude wagon crossed the square as we sat there, drawn by two snow-white oxen, strangely yoked and adorned, and led by a gem of an old Turk, white beard, rich turban and all. How I wish that some great artist would come here, that the eyes of generations to come might be charmed with these Old World nooks, and with the harmony and richness of coloring, and the dignity of bearing among a few of the people still remaining, which is rapidly diappearing before Western progress, and its hideous "civilized" attire! But the crazy ox-car rumbled and groaned on toward the fields, out of sight, and the picture of a thousand years ago is gone, with many regrets on my part that I can only give you this faint idea of it with my pen. As for myself, if I never see the East again, I have but to shut my eyes to possess a picture gallery. But I ought to tell you that, even knowing your tastes as I do, my heart has sometimes failed me a little in writing these long letters, when I think of the people who have visited the same places, and made the same excursions as myself, who have seen nothing in them, and whose account would only agree with mine as to the wretched appearance of the villages and the people. However, I can only write as my own eyes see things, and according to the impression which the country has produced on my own mind; and as it amuses you all, there will be no great harm done.

The mosque of the village is a very small one, for the population consists principally of Greeks. There was a kind of open porch before it, and we sat down to rest. The door of the mosque was open, so presently I put off my shoes and walked in, very much to the surprise of a poor Turk, who was doing something to the lamps in a very desponding way. The mosque looked very shabby and very poor. Over the pulpit is suspended the usual piece of carved wood, shaped like a minaret. Hoop-shaped lamps, and numbers of large painted ostrich eggs, hang from the ceiling. On my return to the porch, the Imaum himself came, saluted us, and making us a sign to be seated, sat down himself on the opposite bench, filled his chibouque, and evidently prepared for a chat. Eugenia, who speaks Turkish, interpreted the conversation, which amounted to—We were welcome—Where did we come from?—and a desire to hear all about the English troops,—Was it really true that war with Russia had ended? We told him all the military intelligence we knew, and then in our turn asked who built the fine marble fountain close by, and who left it to decay? Hadji somebody, a very famous pilgrim, built it, he said, only about a hundred years ago. He, the Hadji, was a great benefactor to the village altogether; but now it was very poor, and there were but few of his religion in it, to keep up the mosque and fountain. I was glad to find that he was concerned at a stranger seeing it in such neglect and decay. It is one of the saddest things here to find how little the people care generally either for the past or the future. "If I were the Sultan, I would repair the old mosques and fountains, instead of building new ones," I said to our new friend, who only shook his head and smiled a placid Eastern smile, as he caressed his chibouque. It seems like talking against destiny to wish any thing saved from ruin here!

As we sat quietly talking, I heard a kind of chanting in children's voices, not very far off, and asked what it was. The Imaum replied that it was the little ones of his school, learning their lessons. I said I should very much like to see a Turkish school. He said kindly that it was but a poor one, but that I was most welcome. Accordingly we crossed a small ruined court, and entered the walls of a building which had evidently been burnt, all but the stones and mortar, years before. Up a crazy stair-case, made of rough deal, we crept to a sort of loft, the planks of which were so wide apart that you could plainly see through to the ruin beneath. The stairs were so shaky, I fully expected that Mr. Gisborne, myself, the Imaum, the Muezzin who followed, Eugenio and all, would fall through together. However we got into the school-room in safety, and the sight of it was well worth the trouble. It was neatness itself, though the only window was unglazed, and the deal walls only adorned here and there with pieces of rough pasteboard, on which were inscribed texts from the Koran. Two planks were placed about a foot from the ground, down the centre of the room, and some very charming little girls sat at either side of one of them, and seven or eight boys at the other. They all sat cross-legged on white sheepskins: each had a book before him, and the Imaum explained that each was chanting the same verse of the Koran, until they all knew it by heart. I should think that none of them were more than seven or eight years of age. Nothing could be more charming than the behavior of the little girls. The one at the end of the row, and nearest to me, motioned me to take a seat on her sheepskin, upon my asking what they were learning, and my question being translated to her. Pointing out the verse, she chanted it softly over. Seeing that it pleased us, the dear little things all took it up, and repeated it over and over, until the Imaum, smiling at the door, evidently said "Enough!" The girls all pressed round my sheepskin, to show their neat books, and the boys soon joined the little crowd. The Imaum tried to call them off, but Mr. Gisborne, as well as myself, was delighted, and they soon laughed freely and seemed much amused with strangers—about as rare to them as white camels, I suppose. I asked the name of my partner in the sheepskin; "Ayesha," she said, raising her shy dark eyes to mine. I assure you this child was perfectly beautiful,—her eyes and lashes wonderful, her simple manners and grace more enchanting than those of the sweetest fabled princess you ever dreamed of. I held her hand, as we sat on the little mat; poor child, I could not take my eyes off her, thinking of her probable fate in that miserable village. I could not make up my mind to leave her, and said to Eugenio, "Ask her if she will come to England with me." Her rich, soft Turkish sounded so musically as she uttered the simple and touching words; "I am the only child of my mother, or I would." One or two of the little girls were extremely pretty, with long plaits of dark hair nearly reaching to the ground, but not to be compared with Ayesha. The boys were sturdy little fellows; I asked all their names,—one was called Hamed, another Mohammed. They were coarsely dressed, but very tidy and clean, and one or two were adorned with bright scarlet fezzes. Altogether the school did the poor Imaum great credit, and the children seemed very happy and good under his gentle rule. He made them chant some favorite verse for me, which I was sorry not to understand. But at last we were obliged to say good-by, even to Ayesha, and left them all looking very happy at the little fistful of piastres which Mr. Gisborne asked leave of the good Imaum to give to each.

We then walked far along the shore, sending the "Edith Belina" round to meet us at a large garden there. The men brought out the cushions and the luncheon, which Eugenio spread under the shade of a plane-tree. It was a very pretty spot: for a large vine had festooned itself round the tree, and its long tendrils waved in the cool sea-breeze. Close by was an enormous well, with an old Egyptian water-wheel, like those which are used on the Nile. Two or three poor Turkish women were gathering a few tomatoes in the garden, which seemed to belong to the village. I gave them some grapes, and some white bread, and they seemed inclined to be very sociable with me, but, although vailed, would come near nothing masculine; so, as I could get no interpreting from Eugenio, our mutual friendliness was limited to smiles, signs of regret, and a waive of adieu. How glad I should be to speak Turkish well! I think Mr. Gisborne enjoyed his ramble very much. We sailed home in a magnificent sunset; the water blue; the sky and mountains, every shade of rose-color.

I had almost forgotten to tell you that the kind Imaum gave me a curious little lamp, such as they use in the mosques at Ramazan and other festivals; it is of a coarse kind of porcelain, something in the shape of a pine-apple, with little holes for small wax candles all round it. He tells me that in rich mosques they are made of gold or silver. I assured him that I should prize this one very much, which seemed to please him. What do you think of this conquest of a Giaour over a true Believer—on the Asiatic coast too!

LETTER LVII.

OLD CHURCHES AND MONASTERIES—ANCIENT MANUSCRIPT—TOMB OF ST. GEORGE—PICTURE OF ST. GEORGE AND THE DRAGON—DONKEY PROCESSIONS—A GREEK BEAUTY—THE SUPERIOR OF THE MONASTERY—CURIOUS PAINTINGS—LEGEND—LUNATICS—TREE-FROGS.

Prinkipo, September 2d, 1856.

My dear Sister:

I send you this account of another day of my idle life here, because I know you like any thing appertaining to old churches and monasteries, and because whenever I visit them, the only drawback is that you are not with me. Of course you know that there is nothing in an architectural point of view, as Mr. Pecksniff would say, to admire in either; but they are so beautifully situated, contain so many relics of the earliest days of Christianity, and old in themselves, have so risen out of the ashes of the very earliest persecuted Christian churches; and, with all their poor tinsel, and false carving, and daubed pictures of Saints, they carry the mind so vividly back to past centuries, that one cannot but feel a very deep and peculiar interest in them. I felt this most strongly at Jesu Cristo, when my good friend the monk there unlocked from an ancient chest, and allowed me to look over a copy of the Scriptures, written on a kind of parchment, and, according to the tradition, dating even from the days of the Apostles themselves. The Brotherhood has had some difficulty in keeping this manuscript; but, though very poor, never yielded to the temptation of selling it. Its value is however lessened by the shameful conduct of a Russian traveler, who upon being shown it some years ago, contrived unseen to cut away a leaf here and there. The other monasteries here possess no manuscripts of any antiquity. They were all destroyed when Byzantium fell into the hands of the Moslems, the monks tell me; but at St. Nicholas at Prinkipo, and St. George at Halki, are some very old and curious crosses of silver and carved wood, although the jewels with which they were once adorned have been taken out ages ago.

I have been three times to the Monastery of St. George here, founded by the celebrated Empress Irene. The first day I asked if they could show me her tomb. One of the three monks pointed out an ancient-looking sarcophagus of white stone, evidently of considerable antiquity, above which a silvered picture of St. George had been placed. One half of this massive tomb was outside the wall of the church, so that it was evidently of older date than the church itself; and why the wall was built so, one cannot conceive. There is a mutilated inscription running round the base of the tomb, which unfortunately I could make nothing of, and had no means of copying. Eugenio emphatically declared the characters to be old *Turkish!* Since my better acquaintance with the Superior, or Papa, he assures me that the present church does *not* stand on the site of the original one; and one day, conducting me about two minutes' walk over the rocks looking toward the Olympian range, discovered among the huge masses, what now seemed a small cavern, almost entirely filled up with ponderous fragments. It was difficult to judge whether these had been hewn by the hand of man or not. On a smoother slab of granite lay a ragged quilt, and this he told me belonged to a poor pilgrim just arrived, who was sleeping there, and who believed, with many others, in the legend, that *this* was the true altar of St. George of Irene. So I am afraid it is very doubtful whether the tomb which they show in the church is that of the Empress, which is said to have been *within the walls of her church.* The inscription may clear up the mystery, and the monk has promised to copy it for me. He gave me the other day an exact copy in outline of the ancient picture of St. George and the Dragon, which is preserved in a case over the gateway. It is a very curious production: St. Peter stands by, in a kind of tower in the sky, watching the contest between the knight and the dragon. He lolls his head on one side in a most comical manner, and holds his keys in his hand, which hangs over the side of the tower; he is evidently anxious to let the conqueror in, as soon as the fight is ended. I will send you the drawing; pray take care of it.

Miss Barker and I spent yesterday at the Monastery, riding up the mountain on donkeys. We walked through the pretty French camp, and admired the neat wooden houses which the soldiers have built for their sick officers in the most lovely situations among fir-trees overhanging the sea. At a little distance in the valley below is their cemetery, which is carefully walled round, and planted with rows of simple wooden crosses, like those in the Crimea. The East has gathered many dead from distant places since the war began. The few French troops remaining here are soon to embark on their return home; so they have been busy planting and adorning the graves of those they leave behind forever. The view of the sea and distant mountains and islands is most beautiful here.

Miss Barker and I sat down on a bench under some old fir-trees, near the convent of San Nicoa; and, while we rested our dapples, listened to a gay French air, whistled from a tent close by, where two wounded or rather convalescent soldiers were amusing themselves by persuading a starling to imitate them. It is quite curious to see the pains which soldiers take with their pets. We sat a long time here; for several donkey processions appeared, winding down the ravine before us, and we did not wish our little beasts to carry us amongst them, as they infallibly would have done if they could, being accustomed to scamper along, helter-skelter, in large bodies. These donkeys processions are really most amusing to watch, as they wind about all parts of the island, some rapidly, some slowly, according as the expedition may be one of pleasure or sanctity. Here comes a pretty little girl, in a Greek jacket and straw hat, foremost of a party. She is mounted astride of a large black donkey, which is adorned with scarlet trappings, and a gay charm of blue beads against the Evil Eye, for he is sleek and comely: two little brothers in fezzes scamper after, trying to pass her at a narrow turn of the rock. Jolting along, also astride, and calling to them to stop, comes the mamma, her gay and wide-flounced dress so completely covering the animal on which she is seated, that only its tiny hoofs are visible, ambling along.

Next comes a fat, joyous-looking Greek girl, who

is evidently the nurse. Her donkey is rushing down the steepest part of the ravine, and her saddle has slipped all on one side; but she tucks a mild, passive-looking baby fearlessly under one arm, while she grasps the reins, a formidable stick, and a colored handkerchief full of pomegranates, with the other. This young lady shows more of her legs than I well could describe, and rides after the same safe and independent fashion as the rest.

Far behind, comes the *Paterfamilias*, pale and grave, and looking steadily on the ground, which his long legs nearly touch. A wild-looking Greek servant-boy brings up the rear, evidently carrying the provisions. I daresay they are going to spend the day at San Giorgio, and we shall meet them jogging back to the village by sunset.

But presently came by a most devout-looking old lady, of large dimensions, with a very rich handkerchief and heavy plaits of hair bound round her head. She rode astride with a dignified air; but her stirrups were so short, that her knees were rather too high for perfect ease and grace; and I thought she looked rather disconcerted, when her beast willfully chose the steepest places. She was evidently making a pilgrimage to the picture of a favorite saint; for the bare-legged youth in a scarlet jacket, running by her side, carried in his hand a huge waxen taper.

One thing that puzzles me in these donkey processions is, that the riders never seem to look either right or left, but press on, down ravines, and up mountains by the seashore, and over the heath hills, looking straight between the ears of their wretched animals.

Sometimes you hear the clink of hoofs behind a rock, and round come perhaps half-a-dozen handsomely-dressed Greek ladies, riding astride as solemnly as mutes, attended by as solemn-looking a gentleman or two; all perfectly silent, and utterly regardless of the glorious sunset spreading over the sea and mountains around them. The only variety in the pursuit of island donkey-riding is, when two parties of the animals meet, and take it into their heads to rush together *pêle-mêle* and fight, which they do desperately, making the most unearthly noises all the time. Some of the ladies scream—some of the men dismount; the owners of the donkeys belabor them violently with abundance of invectives; a terrible cloud of dust is raised; when at least one family-cavalcade being collected winds one way, and the other another. I met a large party the other day, who had experienced a *contretemps* of this kind, and were just gravely riding out of it; but they were some time before they got quite arranged again, for it was a party of pleasure, and they had mounted a band to play before them, which had got scattered in the *mêlée;* the different instruments, perhaps excited by mountain air or raki, perseveringly continuing to play among the braying of the delinquent asses, and at the most irregular distances from one another. I was particularly struck with the disgusted expression of the largest donkey of the musical party, who seemed to have headed the rebellion. His rider was playing the trombone, frightfully out of tune, close against the ears of the unfortunate animal, who showed what he thought of the infliction by laying them down flat on his neck and by making hideous grimaces.

There is now a Greek beauty in the island, who has dozens of *madahs* burnt for her every night at the Magyar. I often meet her donkey party. She generally leads the way, being a dashing beauty; and as she is mouuted on the largest and most adventurous donkey in Prinkipo, she is often far in advance of her mother, a ponderous old lady in green, with a yellow handkerchief on her head, who covers all but the ears and tail of the animal she bestrides. Several of the Beauty's retinue of admirers follow as best they may. Some of them manage to keep pretty close to her; but, curiously enough, we always afterward pass her intended, a pale, desponding-looking man, mounted on the most wretched donkey in the island, and so far behind as to be quite out of sight both of his bride and of his rivals.

But to return to our morning at St. George's monastery. Having kind Miss Barker to interpret, made the visit so much pleasanter. We found the Superior standing before the old gateway of the court-yard of the monastery, throwing a few dried leaves to the flock of goats which came bounding over the vast piles of rock which lie heaped around. He is a fine, stern-looking man, his active energetic movements and long beard contrasting strangely with the old dark-blue satin petticoat peeping out from beneath his black outer robe. A few rough tools were lying on a bench beside him; he had been patching up a little, he said apologetically, against the winter-storms, for the place had not been repaired for years, and the brotherhood here was too poor to spend any money on workmen. Their goats, he said, were almost all they had to depend upon in winter, besides the produce of the garden at the foot of the mountain, of which an immense heap of tomatoes were drying in the sun: it must be a hard and lonely life. I asked if he had copied me the inscription on the old tomb. He has not yet found time, but promises to do so. We went into the church, and he showed us a very curious cross, of great antiquity. It is about seven inches in length, and the frame is of light and delicate filagree-work, exquisitely wrought and designed. The hollow centre is composed of minute figures in carved cedar, of our Saviour, the Virgin Mary, and the Apostles on one side, and of several saints and martyrs on the other. There are holes for jewels all round, and a few small ones still remain. On particular days this cross is placed on the altar of St. George, above the old tomb, where a lamp is always burning. We were particularly amused with an old picture in honor of St. George, which hangs in a remote part of the church. Crowned kings, pilgrims, queens in gorgeous array, children and beggars, are seated stiffly round a tank of water, supposed to have sprung from the favorite well of the saint. Some of the ladies certainly look rather tipsy, especially one seated near a very jolly-looking and roysterous king, whose crown is too big for him. All are lifting up their heads and eyes, as in some way or other expressing a comical kind of surprise in the miraculously healing effect of the draughts they are quaffing.

This picture, offered to St. George after a cure performed at his shrine here, cost a great deal of money, and was considered a very fine one, the monk said. There is one at Halki, by-the-by, still more famed, which I saw the other day; it represents the temptations of this life, heaven and purgatory, and is hung up in a covered court in front of the church, before the benches on which the brothers sit to meditate—or smoke. The immense number of figures on the canvas, and the glaring colors, make the homily difficult to read by unpracticed eyes; but I know that there is a bright blue river of life, winding like a snake between a land of imps and demons on one side, and a company of saints and angels on the other. The devils are urging the travelers to step their way; the saints do not interfere much, but sit in stiff rows in a garden of orange and myrtle trees, not nearly so tall as themselves. Their paradise looks very formal, and extremely uninviting. Down below, is a kind of cave, and a select party of demons of all colors are busily employed in tormenting their unhappy captives in the most jocular manner possible. One of them, in a burst of merriment, is grilling half-a-dozen over the bars of a huge gridiron; another, stirring up a seething cauldron. A small party of brilliant wits are pouring melted brimstone and streams of flame down the throats of their agonized victims; while others, looking on, rest on their forks in ecstacies of delight, or cut the most ridiculous capers.

Though you will have had enough by this time of Greek pictures, I must tell you about the St. George in this place. The whole of the picture, except the swarthy face of the saint, is covered with silver, barbarously enough laid on. It is said to be the original picture belonging to Irene's church: and the legend adds, said one monk, that it was buried by one of the ancient brotherhood, when Constantinople was taken and its Christian churches razed. Many sac. ɛd treasures were so preserved in those days. A young shepherd of Prinkipo, two or three centuries later, sleeping on the mountain, dreamed that St. George appeared to him, and, directing him to dig on the exact spot where he lay, assured him that he would there find the long-lost picture of his shrine. Of course the shepherd dug, and of course he discovered the picture, which he restored to the present church, since which time it has been famous for miraculous cures, especially in all kinds of madness. The shepherd left his flock, turned monk, and ultimately died Superior of this monastery, and in great odor of sanctity. The well of St. George is close by the church. A small stone cell has been built over it, with seats hewn in the rock for the use of pilgrims. We drank some of the water which the monk drew up for us, and presented in the iron cups. It was very cold, but our friend assured us gravely that it would do us good.

Tied to a nail in the wall of the cell, was a large bunch of hair of all colors, from roughest black to the lightest gold. These are offerings shown from the heads of pilgrims, who have been cured by the healing waters of the saint. They look so dreary, waving to and fro in the wind, so unlikely to please the spirit of *our* cheerful Knight, St. George! Afterward, when I went to the church again, to look at a stone belonging, they said, to the old convent, I asked the monk what the large iron rings were for in the pavement before the shrine. At first he did not seem to like to answer, but at length said that they were used to *chain the lunatics* to, who were sent up the mountain to be cured! Can you imagine any thing more horrible? By an iron collar fixed round the neck, they are sometimes chained to these rings for three days and three nights, until, from struggling and exhaustion, or cold, perhaps all these together, they sink down on the stones before the picture of the saint, who is then supposed to have cured the paroxysm. Can you conceive any thing more barbarous?

We sat down to have our luncheon under the old walnut-tree in the court-yard. The poor starved cats and dogs about the place looked wistfully at us, and we gave them a right good meal. The Papa would not sit down with us; he said he was fasting, though he did not certainly look so; but an old woman belonging to the monastery, who milked the goats and made the cheese, and who looked as black and dried-up as the picture of any Greek saint of old, waited upon us, croaking out all sorts of questions about England and the war, and ending by being quite friendly; directing Eugenio where he could find some fine figs to add to our repast. He brought back with him a small tortoise, which he had caught under the tree. It has a beautifully marked shell, and is evidently very old; it *may* even have raised its tiny eyes to the great banished Queen, standing on these lonely rocks before the glorious view of sea and mountain, and thinking on "the various turns of fate below." I shall call it "Irene."

While we were looking at the tortoise, a young Greek, who had been wandering listlessly about the gallery, came up to us. He looked ill and wan, and we offered him a pear. I thought he snatched it in rather an odd way, and on looking at him more attentively, saw that he had an iron collar round his neck, and a gash on one of his cheeks, which it sickened one to think of. He seemed perfectly quiet and harmless then, but the priest came angrily up, and speaking roughly to him in Greek, drove him away across the court, opened the door of a shed, and shut him in. I noticed that he did not turn the key, and, watching an opportunity, I ran across the court, opened the door, and went in. There the poor creature lay on a heap of rubbish, with a ragged coverlid beside him. When the door was shut, the place must have been perfectly dark, for there was neither window nor opening of any kind, and it seemed to have been formed out of some ruined stone building or cell. Fancy his solitary, hopeless days there, when quite sane, as they say he often is! He looked up surprised when I spoke, but did not stir. I think he understood Italian. I offered him a pear, which he did not take until I said: "Do eat another," and then he stretched out his thin hand and smiled. He seemed to watch the sunlight very wistfully, which streamed in at the open door as I stood there; and I shall never forget the pain it cost me to shut it out from him. I have since made many inquiries about these poor unfortunates, and find that their treatment is the fault of their superstition, and not that of any particular priest. Mothers, fully believing in miraculous cures before the shrine, send up their sons to receive this treatment, paying a trifling sum for board; and the patients themselves, when they feel an attack of their malady coming on, will endeavor to return of their own accord. However, I am happy to say that St. George has now but two patients; and we saw several empty rooms within the gallery, which the old woman told us were once full of the richer class of patients and pilgrims too, but which were now seldom used. This last summer some grand English officers were lodging there, who had evidently quite won her ancient heart. We finished our day by quietly drinking coffee, seated on the moldy divan of one of these apartments. I should have gone to sleep, as indeed we both tried to do; but my tortoise, which I had tied to my wrist in a handkerchief, kept trying to escape, and Miss Barker was too much afraid of the countless pilgrim fleas to close her eyes. So we looked again at the glorious view of the Sea of Marmora far below, and at the old walls and distant minarets of Constantinople glittering in the evening sun, and then prepared to depart.

It was a perfect calm, the sea like glass, and caiques threading their way about, looking no bigger than mosquitos, from the great height at which we were. The mountains, and hills, and vineyards looked so beautiful, that it made us grieve to think of the miserable degradation of every thing else here. I brought my tortoise home in safety, and Johannachi has undertaken the charge of it—an occupation just about suited to his intellect, poor little fellow! He also helps me to catch flies, for the beautiful little tree-frogs which I brought from a piece of marshy ground on the coast near Maltapé, and which have become tame enough to spring off the branch we have fixed in a box for them, and snatch their prey out of our fingers. Edmund takes great interest in these pretty little green fellows, and has stolen my best lace vail to hang before their door. But I am afraid we shall never be able to bring them home; so we intend to let them out before we leave, which I suppose will be soon now. I told you that my dear little dog Fuad was lost. We have heard no tidings of him. Herbert Siborne has taken Arslan to England, and we have no pets now except a tame fly-catcher, which follows me everywhere, even into the vineyard, without wishing to stray. It had hurt one of its wings when I found it some weeks ago. Adieu! I have sent home by Herbert, who has kindly taken charge of a box for me, a motley little collection of curiosities. You will find three small antique vases from Tarsus, most kindly given to me by Mr. Hughes, who has just returned from thence—a piece of fine carving, given me by a monk here, representing the Empress Irene, and a robed priest holding a book—a rosary of black beads from Jerusalem—otto of roses fresh from Persia—some Russian medals and crosses taken after the battles in the Crimea—a piece of pink granite, and a piece of oak from the dockyard at Sebastopol—a Russian gunner's shoe, and several other things picked up in the Malakoff and Redan—a pipe, made of the stone of Sebastopol by an English soldier—a collection of dried plants— an Arab bride's ring—three or four ancient silver coins—some wood of aloes, the famous incense—a little Damascus dagger—a tin bottle of water from the Jordan—a rose of Jericho—and, above all, a cross made of olive-wood, cut from an old tree in the Garden of Gethsemane. The acorns are to be carefully raised in a pit: they are from the Forest of Belgrade, close to Lady Mary's house. I am very anxious about the safe arrival of my box.

LETTER LVIII.

THE LUNATIC AND THE PRIEST'S DONKEY—APPEAL TO ST. DEMETRIUS—THE LUNATIC SENT HOME.

Prinkipo, September 8th, 1856.

My dear Julia:

As I was sitting alone about mid-day yesterday, busily writing, I heard a knocking at the door of the Salaamlik, which opens on to a rough path just cut on the mountain. A young Greek about seventeen was standing there, holding a donkey by the bridle. Both looked tired, and I understood that the boy asked for water; so I called Eugenio, and told him to let them rest, and see what they wanted. The donkey was laden with large branches of pomegranates and quinces, and had a colored handkerchief-ful of them tied round his neck. His master gave me the finest of the branches, and then sat down on the bench in the shade. Presently I heard an exclamation of surprise from the Apple-blossom. "What is the matter?"—"Oh, Signora! he is a madman, and is asking for St. George." Poor fellow, we then saw the iron collar beneath his vest, and noticed his cut and bleeding feet and haggard looks. On a close inspection, too, it turned out to be the priest's sleek donkey, which looked so unusually hot and tired, from being dragged about in the burning sun. The poor boy kept asking for St. George, and seemed to have some indistinct idea of having lost his way. Kind-hearted Melia was deeply moved at his calling so imploringly on the Saint, and rushing to her room for her much-prized, dirty little picture of St. Demetrius, brought it to him, fully believing that the sight of it would comfort or restore his wandering mind. But she pronounced him very bad indeed when he turned away, and asked me again for St. George. At last he suddenly seized the donkey's bridle, and starting off, tried to climb the steepest part of the mountain, dragging the poor little beast through bushes and rocks after him. The donkey seemed dreadfully distressed, and at last positively refused to go any further. I got Eugenio, and Signor Giacomo's strong Croat gardener, to get them both down, and then directed Eugenio to see them safely back to the Monastery by the right path. They started quietly enough, and Eugenio returned some time after, saying that he had guided them as far as the foot of the mountain, and that the poor young man was riding quietly on. I was vexed that he had not gone the whole way, and lo! presently back came the unfortunate creature, still asking for St. George, and almost fainting from fatigue and exhausation. Melia and myself now kept him quietly on the bench, while Eugenio went for the Priest, who we heard was in the village, searching for his patient. The poor boy had escaped with the donkey since the morning before, had passed one night on the mountain, and all this time had been without food, unless he had eaten the unripe pomegranates and quinces with which he had laden his companion. He went back quietly enough with the Superior, who promised me that he should not be punished, which promise I sincerely trust he has kept. I shall go up to St. Giorgio in a day or two and ask after him. The bunch of pomegranates hanging up in my room makes my heart ache.

LETTER LIX.

VISIT FROM A TURKISH LADY—HER TASTE FOR MUSIC—HER NUBIAN SLAVE—EXHIBITION OF AN ENGLISH GENTLEMAN—GRATIFICATION AFFORDED BY THE SPECTACLE.

Constantinople, September 20th, 1856.

My dear Mother:

I had a visit yesterday from the Turkish lady whom I went to see some time ago with our Armenian neighbors. About ten in the morning Melia came running to say that a Harem was coming, and I quickly recognized my merry acquaintance through her thin yashmak, as she came up the garden-steps. She was attended by two pretty slaves, and by a hideous black woman, who led by the hand the lovely little girl whom I mentioned to you as crying after the jewels, the day of my visit to the Harem. They all put off their shoes at the foot of the stairs, and came up in the pointed-toed embroidered slippers beneath. As I knew the lady spoke Greek, Johannachi was instantly dispatched with a note to my constant friend Miss Barker, who came down immediately. Melia hastened to serve coffee and sweetmeats.

I led the Cocona into my room to take off her yashmak and apple-green feridjee; she ran about like a pleased child come to have a holiday, looking at every thing there; and the slaves followed her example. When we returned to the drawing-room, she sat down to the piano, as if to surprise me, and strummed in the most ludicrous manner for about half an hour, the slaves standing by with evident pride and satisfaction. She then rose, and begged to hear me play or sing. I never felt more puzzled in my life what to choose, but at last fixed on Blangini's "Cara Elisa," as simple and pretty, and began to sing. My guest was seated cross-legged on the divan behind me, so I could not see the effect of my favorite canzonetta upon her; but at the end of the first verse, the Nubian crossed the room, placed her black elbows on the piano, leaned her hideous face on them, and stared at me with such an intense expression of astonishment and disgust, that it was with the greatest difficulty I could keep my countenance. At last she uttered a dismal groan, and made such a frightful grimace, that I could resist no longer, and fairly burst out laughing. The Turkish lady seemed greatly relieved to be able to laugh too, and asked her favorite if she did not like English singing. "Horrible!" said the Black, showing her white jackal-like teeth from ear to ear. "That is the way they sing at the Opera at Pera," said the lady. We asked how she knew. She said that her husband had been there one evening, and had described the singing to her. Pity my vanity, wounded in its tenderest point!

She then turned round quickly and asked where the gentlemen were. I replied that Mr. Hornby was gone to Stamboul, and Mr. Mansfield (who she knew was staying with us), to visit a friend at Pera. She said she was very sorry to hear this, as she had set her heart on seeing an English gentleman near, as she had only seen them passing in the street. Just at this moment she looked into the garden, and there, in an arbor, sat Mr. Rumball quietly reading. I did not know he was there. "*There* is an English gentleman," cried out my willful guest; "pray ask him to come up, that I may see him." I replied as civilly as I could, that it was quite out of the question—that the Effendi had trusted tacitly to my honor in allowing her to visit me, and that I could do nothing of which I knew he would disapprove so highly as the admitting any gentleman into the room while she was there. When Miss Barker translated this, she was as angry as any spoiled child, turned her back upon me, and kept striking notes on the piano with one finger, as she sat pouting on the stool. Presently she said something very spitefully, and I asked what it was; "Tell her she is jealous—say that she is afraid of letting me see any of the men." I verily believe that she thought I had locked them all up. I tried to bring her to reason, and begged Miss Barker to call her attention quietly to the black slave, who was looking furiously angry at hearing her mistress's request. We took her into the next room, and asked her how, even if it were right to deceive her husband, she could trust the discretion or the fidelity of her slaves; she *must* see how the black one was glaring at her! For all we could say, she replied that she did not care, and that it was very spiteful of me to disappoint her so. At last a compromise was agreed on, provided that the Nubian gave her consent; and a little coaxing, and no doubt a promise of a bakshish, soon gained that.

It was agreed that the lady and her slaves were to put on their yashmaks and feridjees, to sit in the little room with the door ajar, and that Mr. Rumball should be brought upstairs and placed near enough to them to be distinctly visible. I could not see any harm in this, and therefore gave my consent, provided they kept their promise of remaining vailed. I then went down to Mr. Rumball, and solemnly adjuring him to behave with the utmost discretion and gravity, brought him before the door of the room, where the lady was seated as if in the best box of an Opera, with her attendants behind her. He was very much amused, and made them all giggle vastly by throwing a handkerchief over his face, and pretending to be shy. However, they would not endure this long, and called out to me to pull it off, which I did. I stood by his side, like a showman exhibiting some rare beast; and when I would have led him away, the audience within murmured like children who beg to have another look. But at last I was suffered to let him say adieu, and I drove him away into the garden again, laughing and kissing his hand.

When he was gone, they all said, throwing off their vails, that he was very good-looking, and that they had been very much pleased with the sight of him; they thanked me very much, and hoped I would show them Mr. Mansfield and Mr. Hornby another time—which of course I promised to do. Then the Cocona sat down to the piano again, and again strummed until my head fairly ached. You may fancy how tired I was, when I tell you that they stayed from ten till four. At last, to my great relief, they put on their vails and feridjees and hurried away, seemingly delighted with their visit, and promising to come again soon!

LETTER LX

BOATMEN'S SONGS—GREEK SINGING—SPECIMENS.

Constantinople, September 12th, 1856.

My dear Julia:

Last year I promised to send you, if possible, some of the boatmen's songs of the Bosphorus. Through the kindness of a friend, who speaks and understands Greek perfectly well, I have at last procured a few of the most popular,—such as are constantly heard in the villages, and before the trellised doors of the cafanées after sunset. In Constantinople the caiquejee is almost invariably mute and dignified, keeping time with his oars with splendid strength and regularity, neither looking to the right nor the left, except casting a rapid glance now and then to see that the way is clear.

A grand Turk would be horrified at his boatmen speaking unless spoken to, except it was necessary in the navigation of the boat. I do not know what he would do if his majestic silence were disturbed by a song, after the manner of Venetian boatmen. However, the silent beauty of the Bosphorus, only broken by the deep and measured plunge of oars in the water, is something peculiarly delightful and dreamy, and you never wish the charm disturbed. Besides which, the Greek notion of singing is peculiarly harsh, inharmonious, and monotonous; it only sounds well, mellowed by great distance; when one becomes more accustomed to it, it is not unpleasant to be awakened by the chant of the fishermen as they draw in their nets, or by a love-song from some caique darting rapidly down the stream, or moored idly in the shade of a palace wall. But it is in the evening that you hear this monotonous sound rising from every valley,—from cafanées overhanging the waters of the Bosphorus, to the shady fountain-trees of the villages, under which, in fine weather, the poor almost pass their lives. Sometimes it is accompanied by a little liquid-sounding drum or by a small guitar, and this goes on all the night long, often until after sunrise. There is little or no melody,—in fact, the word *song* scarcely applies to a monotonous and somewhat melancholy chant, which is always in the Minor mode, and frequently approaches recitative.

Remember that I do not send you these scraps as curious specimens; they are merely rough translations of the ordinary every-day songs of the Greeks here; and I fear that "the heroic lay is tuneless now," for they are but trifles. However, in the original Greek they really sound very sweet and melodious, and, although understanding but little, their smoothness particularly charmed my ear. Of course this is completely lost in the literal translation, as well as their great tenderness.

But here is a village swain, in despair at the departure of his love. He is supposed to be addressing a sympathizing friend, or fellow-sufferer. She is evidently a great beauty and breaker of hearts.

"Didst thou not see the fair one?
Alas! I too beheld her yesterday,
When she stepped into a little boat,
And departed for foreign parts.

"The wind blew, and the sea was rough;
The sails filled,
Like the plumes of a little pigeon
When it spreads its wings.

"Her friends stood on the shore,
With mingled grief and joy;
And she with a handkerchief
Returned their adieux.

"And a sad adieu
I also would have said;
But the cruel one
Denied me even this.

'I weep not for the boat,
I weep not for the sails,
But I weep for the fair one
Who is gone to foreign parts."

Here is one illustrative of Eastern life:—

"'Good-evening to thee, my lady,
On this high terrace
What art thou planting and watering,
That thou turnest not round to behold me?'

"'What is it to thee, young man,
What I am watering and planting?
Sweet flowers I plant
For the youth I love.'

"'Plant not these flowers, my soul;
Lady, plant not these flowers;
But plant basilica,
That their seed the nightingales may see
And eat, and make sweet melody.'"*

Now comes a lovers' quarrel, in which the gentleman shows a considerable amount of Greek ingenuity.

* I cannot find out what is meant by the nightingales eating the seeds of basilica, which no doubt means basil, held sacred by the Greeks, the true Cross having been found shrouded in its leaves.

"If any wicked person, or liar,
Hath spoken ill of me,
Yet thou must not forget
So soon our tender vows.

"My love! I see thou art grieved,
Very much grieved for me;
Yet I know of no other fault
Than of too much love for thee.

"My fair one! after so many vows,
And cherishing many fond hopes,
How canst thou grieve me, my life?
Ah! it must be *another* you love!"

Is not this little scrap of pretended jealousy and "turning of tables" a masterpiece? This song amused me excessively; it is so smooth and plausible and persuasive in the original. One can so easily imagine the beauty relenting, and raising her large dark eyes, to say—

"And was it really true?" etc.

Songs of this length do not seem to be so popular as those of two, or even one verse. Over and over again, to the same monotonous chant, an idle boatman or a gardener, resting in the sultry heat of the day, seems to take a quiet sort of delight in repeating such lines as these:—

"Three months elapsed before I saw thee,
Ma-ri-a-me-ne! Ma-ri-a-me-ne!
I thought they were three years.
Three sharp knives into my heart did enter,
Ma-ri-a-me-ne! Ma-ri-a-me-ne!

I can just fancy the splendid young caiquejee in snowy garments and crimson sash and cap, singing this as he rows gayly along,—

"As many stars as in the skies,
As many windows in Stamboul,*
As many damsels I have kissed
On the eyebrows, on the eyes."

Or this—

"I send thee my love,
With a rosy apple;
And in the rosy part
A tender kiss is hidden.

"Let us make our vows
Under sixty-two columns;
And if I do not love thee,
Let them all fall and crush me!"

This is to a shrinking, sensitive young lady, and is very musical and pretty in the original Greek:—

"My little white rose!
My queen of flowers!
Hast thou discarded love,
That I may despise it too?

"An old man may discard it
A hundred summers old,
But can I live without it,
Who but eighteen have told?

"Maiden mine! fairest girl!
Thou art trying to cause my death.
But I will not die, I will not die
My love is so great
That thou *must* be mine,
Thou must be mine!"

This is a curious verse:—

"Pale hands which the sun has never seen,
Which the doctors touch,
And say to one another,
'There is no hope of life.'"

*Mr. Smythe speaks of the many windows of Stamboul at sunset charming the bewildered fancy of a provincial on his first arrival.

The following description of the garden, in the evening, set in order, and fair at the same time, with both fruit and flowers, is really very pretty in the original:—

"One Saturday night
I went out to walk
In a beautiful garden,
Of which all are envious.
It was in blossom,
And decked out fair,
And bright with many fruits."

To the lady walking there:—

"Oh, thou bright sun! thou golden light!
With thy brilliant rays
Thou hast taken away my sight!
Beside thine mine eyes have grown dim;
So then let my lips say
That I love you;
That the leaves of my heart*
May be cured."

But I think you will have had enough of Greek love-songs, and must conclude. Edward Barker has promised me some of a different kind, real Romaic war-songs, about liberty, and all that the Greeks talk of,—independence, love of Greece, etc. Adieu!

* The Greeks liken the heart to a rose with five leaves or petals.

[Two or three of the Letters belonging to the foregoing series not having come to hand, the following, which has been received since Mrs. Hornby's second departure to Constantinople, is inserted.]

LETTER LXI.

SEVERITY OF WINTER—LIFE IN A KIOSK—THE GOLDEN HORN FROZEN OVER—WOLVES AND FOXES—THEIR MURDEROUS INCURSIONS—SCARCITY OF FOOD AND FUEL—HIGH PRICES—ENGLISH AND GREEK SERVANTS—DEATH OF REDSHID PASHA.

Orta-kioy, February 5th, 1858.

My dear Mrs. Austin:

A thousand thanks for your kind letter, and for the pretty book. Edith was very much pleased with it, and I often read to her with great pleasure those of the poems which she can most easily understand, about heath-flowers and all that reminds us of dear old Weybridge.

I hear that the weather is mild and pleasant in England. Here we have undergone all the horrors of a most severe winter, in a thin wooden house, perched on the top of a range of ills, perfectly exposed to the north. For the last six weeks the storms have been almost uninterrupted, and the country has been covered with one vast sheet of snow, driven down with great violence from the Black Sea. Night after night I have lain awake, expecting every moment that the whole side of my room, consisting of *nine* rattling windows, must inevitably be blown in. The stove I had put up was of little use against the piercing draughts of air which poured in from all parts of the room. A candle was often blown out, and the Persian rug literally danced and flapped about on the floor. Snow was often forced into a little drift on my table, in the middle of the room. Now we have nailed up skins and pieces of carpet, which protect us from the blasts on the north side.

Water stood in solid masses of ice in all our rooms last week. This will not surprise you, when I tell you that part of the Golden Horn is frozen over, and that many hundred persons crossed over on foot. Wolves and foxes have come down from the mountains in great numbers, and several persons, including a poor charcoal burner belonging to a village near us, have been killed by the ferocious attacks of the former. Their tracks have been seen in the snow in the vineyard close to our house, and in the wood opposite; so that even when the weather clears up, I shall be afraid to venture beyond the garden with the children.

Last week, after a snow-storm of three days, the front of our kiosk was entirely walled up in a snow-drift. Every window of our little drawing-room was completely darkened, and the effect of fire and candle-light inside was most curious, reflected on the white flakes and on the icicles. Our men had to cut their way out of the street-door, and sally forth in quest of a whole sheep; for I was afraid that all supplies might be cut off for some time. The only white bread to be got is made at Bebee, a village on the European side; and, as all communication was cut off, I had to put everybody on rations. My mother and I were so afraid of eating any of the white loaves, that, after the storm was over and the steamer able to get up the Bosphorus with provisions, we had three left.

My husband went to his Court at Pera on Monday morning, and was unable either to come, send, or even hear of us until the Friday following, as neither caique nor steamer could venture to move in the blinding sheet of snow on so dangerous and rapid a stream, with much shipping lying about. I had a most anxious and trying time, with about as wretchedly helpless a set of servants as it is possible for a poor mortal to be plagued with. I got Edmund's tool-box, fastened up refractory doors, put pegs into rattling windows, shamed them into clearing snow away by beginning to do it myself, and, besides taking care of the children day and night, had to be constantly thinking and doing for these ladies and gentlemen.

If we could have got to Pera, we should have done so; but of course this was impossible, and nothing remained but to weather the storm.

Wood and charcoal have been at a frightful price all the winter. In the autumn, the powers that be ordered all the boat-loads of wood, arriving here from all parts of the country, to sell their freights at so much a *cheki, filling their own stores with it at that price.* The poor people lost by it, and of course would bring no more; so that this pretended law for the good of the people has caused much suffering.

I keep one good wood fire all day in the dining-room, for the children, and one in the drawing-room, only lighted about four o'clock. During the storm we had come to our last basket, and were already burning our packing-cases—a dreadful state of suspense to be in! Our boatmen, who sleep in a bath-room a short distance from the house, were shut up and obliged to be dug out. They then pushed their way to a neighbor, and borrowed a small quantity of wood. That night all the sheep of this and many other villages

42*

and hundreds of oxen, were frozen to death, to the utter ruin of many poor families.

In the midst of the howling of the wind, and the constant beating of sharp snow against our windows, the fire-guns on the hill near us often thundered their alarm—three or four fires glaring on the snow in one week! This has indeed been a gloomy winter; every thing is of course at famine price.

I tell you all this, my dear Mrs. Austin, as you asked to know all about us. I have but little news to tell you, beyond what, no doubt, Julia has recounted of our domestic misfortunes, in not being able to get a house, and in being, so far as I am concerned, tormented, beyond all that you have heard, or could have conceived, by the airs and graces and helplessness of the English servants of "high character" whom we brought here with us. The poor Greeks, so happy with us before, have left in despair and disgust; so that when we go to our new house, we have to get others. At last I think I have conquered the English ones, and that we shall have peace; even without giving Edmund's groom cold woodcocks for his breakfast, and an unlimited supply of the finest loaf-sugar for his green tea.

My dear children are quite well; my mother is a most cheerful and faithful companion to them. She has thoroughly enjoyed all the difficulties of this terrible winter. I do not believe any thing could have pleased her so much; for she has felt how necessary she has been to us all, and how dreary I should have been without her. My husband is very happy in the satisfactory progress of his new Court: I see but little of him, except at dinner-time. His only holiday has been a shooting-party to a village in Asia Minor—a most primitive place, where he stayed three or four days, bringing back plenty of game, and part of a deer, for our Christmns dinner.

The death of Redshid Pasha has caused much real regret here. His friends strongly suspect that bronchitis had but little to do with it; but no inquiries were made, and he was buried before we, living in front of his house, had heard of his death.

But I must conclude, dear Mrs. Austin. My letter will, I fear, be but an untidy affair. My drawing-room is filled with smoke from the green wood, and I am obliged to write in the children's room, where they are making a great noise with their father's two spaniels, driven indoors out of their snow-covered houses.

THE END.

www.ingramcontent.com/pod-product-compliance
Lightning Source LLC
LaVergne TN
LVHW021320110826
845150LV00003B/629

* 9 7 8 1 4 2 5 5 5 6 1 4 3 *